Management and

D0306615

1 WEEK LOAN

Return to Learning of ssue
Fines are charged at £2 per **day**
No renewal

Management and Organisation Development

Beyond Arrows, Boxes and Circles

KEITH PATCHING

First published 1999 by
MACMILLAN PRESS LTD
Houndmills, Basingstoke, Hampshire RG21 6XS
and London
Companies and representatives
throughout the world

ISBN 0–333–75413–1 hardcover
ISBN 0–333–75414–X paperback

A catalogue record for this book is available
from the British Library.

This book is printed on paper suitable for recycling and
made from fully managed and sustained forest sources.

10   9   8   7   6   5   4   3   2   1
08 07 06 05 04 03 02 01 00 99

Copy-edited and typeset by Povey–Edmondson
Tavistock and Rochdale, England

Printed and bound in Great Britain by
Creative Print & Design (Wales)
Ebbw Vale

Contents

List of Figures and Tables

Figures

Table

Acknowledgements

In the long history of my own personal learning and development I have gathered valuable insights from people too numerous to mention individually. However, in recent times, I have had special help in forming my ideas from one or two very close friends. I should like to thank these personal mentors for both their encouragement and ideas. Over many years my wife and children have put up with long periods of absence as I buried myself in the writing, and I thank them for their patience. Most recently, my enthusiasm and drive for understanding has been given new dimensions by my colleague at Cranfield, Robina Chatham, with whom I am working on several new initiatives. I should also like to thank other colleagues who have worked closely with me, especially Martin Clarke, Liz Bridge, Don Skilling, Pam McCarthy, Terry Lockhart, Andrew Kakabadse, Iris Sampson and Graham Abbey. Extra thanks go to Gerry Dehkes, now of Lucent Technologies who, as a client and friend continues to remind me why I am in this business.

However, the book is not a statement of the philosophy of Cranfield School of Management. It is a set of personal perceptions with which many of my colleagues would wish to differ. For that reason, any errors within it are mine alone.

KEITH PATCHING

Preface

One evening recently I was parking my car outside our new Management Development Centre at Cranfield. It was becoming dark outside. I could see through the windows of the lecture rooms three concurrent events taking place. In each case, a group of managers were seated in a U-shape, facing a screen. Beside each screen stood a lecturer, each an expert in his or her own area. On each screen was projected some words, which were too far away for me to read. But as well as the words, each screen showed a series of boxes and circles, connected by arrows. These are the arrows, boxes and circles of my title.

In earlier days I studied social anthropology; now I frequently attempt to refocus my eyes to recapture that naive wonderment with which ethnographers first confront a society or culture new to them. It was in this state of mind that I looked through those windows. The cultural icons were extraordinarily consistent. People sitting, listening and looking, all seated in the same shaped arena. The lecturer was standing, and the screen illuminated. But most fascinating to my ethnographic mind was the arcane symbolic significance of those arrows, boxes and circles.

I began to ask myself anthropologist's questions. Most of them touched upon the same issue: how has it come about that managers and organisations which seek to better themselves in some way accept that this ritual of gazing up at boxes and circles connected by arrows will achieve that improvement? Of the almost infinite number of ways in which we can help managers, surely, to the uninitiated, this kind of ritual is not what would first come to mind as part of an effective learning process for managers.

Clearly, among the portfolio of management and organisation development activities there exist many other ways of helping learning to happen. None of our programmes at Cranfield consist exclusively of this ritual involving arrows, boxes and circles. Many of them manage to be apparently highly effective and successful with hardly any arrows, boxes and circles in them at all. The point is not simply whether the arrows, boxes and circles quotient can be correlated with success; it is far more about the underlying assumptions upon which managerial learning has been founded over the years, and whether and to what extent those assumptions can be fully explained and validated.

Management and organisation development, like many practices, are not a static set of prescriptions. New ways of learning and new approaches to development keep us at Cranfield, and those elsewhere, constantly reviewing what we do, and how and why we do it. Sometimes, this kind of review is relatively superficial, taking stock of what is currently being done, and ascertaining whether any 'tweaking' needs to be done. But sometimes we undertake a much deeper and more significant review, in which we attempt to take as little as possible for granted, and go right back (as far as this is humanly possible) to 'basics'.

This book records such a review. It reflects what my colleagues and I have been asking about management and organisation development. It relates some of our current answers and what we have done with those answers. Although it is a work of theory, seeking to understand the whys and the whats of management and organisation development, it is also a book of practice, recording through large numbers of case studies how the theories we have been exploring have been put into practice.

Because I work in an institution which earns its keep in the down-to-earth world of real organisations and management, this book reflects two quite distinct driving forces. On the one hand, there is the deep curiosity about what makes managerial learning effective, as illustrated in my story of the arrows, boxes and circles. On the other hand, there is the drive, during times of challenge and change, to maintain an excellence in managerial learning for which Cranfield School of Management has gained a (what I naturally believe to be a well-deserved) reputation.

This second driver provides us with the chance to work collaboratively with managers to achieve and maintain their own excellence, leading, in turn, to their success in their own business ventures. Our role in this partnership centres upon how management and organisation development can enhance their 'knowhow'.

'Knowhow' may soon become to be seen as the only sustainable source of competitive advantage. In other words, whereas products and processes are rapidly imitable, knowledge of how to do things better than the competition may be much harder to replicate. Organisations whose people know more, are smarter, can adapt more, and can learn faster and more effectively will be those who will stay ahead and remain in business.

However, not many managers are 'experts' in learning. Most have their anecdotes and preferences; and many learning activities are designed around such glimpses into what works and what is disliked about learning. These are analogous to organisations' approaches in former times to disciplines such as marketing, for example.

Years ago, people 'did' marketing largely on the basis of what 'stands to reason' in the minds of a few senior managers. The boss would suggest a product be made because he would buy one if he were a customer; or a sales strategy would be based upon some interest of the Sales Director. These days, of course, successful organisations 'do' marketing significantly more rigorously; most managers would accept that marketing is too important to be left to ill-formed prejudice. Marketing has become almost a 'science' with a marketing planning toolkit of hundreds of techniques and methods. It is acknowledged as one of the most important aspects of many organisations' business.

But unlike management and organisation development, marketing does not directly deal with 'knowhow'. Ironically, management and organisation development is a poor relation to marketing, often delegated to a small band of 'trainers', who are, themselves, rarely lionised by the organisation's senior stars.

One possible reason for the success of marketing and the relatively lowly status of management and organisation development is that marketing appears to get results. Many management and organisation development activities, on the other hand, produce a few good intentions, a relatively smaller number of good ideas, and hardly any lasting impact. Consequently, some people doubt whether management and organisation development leads to 'knowhow'.

My colleagues and I are firmly convinced that management and organisation development does have the potential significantly to enhance an organisation's 'knowhow', and thereby to enable the development of sustainable competitive advantage. That it has not often done so in the past is due, I believe, largely to a deep and fundamental misunderstanding of the processes of managerial learning. Buried under the surface of a great deal of 'folk' theorising about what constitutes good management and organisation development are an interconnected series of outmoded and inappropriate models of organisations, of management and of how mature people learn. Innovations in management and organisation development often fail to make much of an impact upon this subterranean set of foundations simply because these innovations are themselves either built upon those same foundations, or because their potential efficacy cannot be reconciled with the 'folk' theories.

For managers seeking to develop strategies for management and organisation development – strategies to enhance organisational 'knowhow' – there are many books and models to turn to. But none, so far as I am aware, have been developed in the light of radical reappraisals of what other sciences have been telling us about organisations, about the mind, about the brain and learning, and about many other perspectives. Much of this research does not directly relate to management and organisation development; but much of it has implicitly posed some fundamental challenges to how we have traditionally gone about management and organisation development.

Which brings me back to the arrows, boxes and circles. I wanted to check out, among all the other key questions which formed the basis of our fundamental review, the robustness of these visual icons. Could these screen-projected images stand up to this interdisciplinary scrutiny? And if they were to do so, what would this tell us about effective managerial learning? To answer such questions, we had to seek out some fundamental principles concerning managerial learning, and test them out in practice. This we have now done.

The principles help us answer some of the basic questions which many managers who need to understand how 'knowhow' can be acquired will need to be able to answer for themselves:

- ❏ Why do some apparently successful approaches to management and organisation development suddenly appear to fail?
- ❏ How should management and organisation development connect to an organisation's strategy?
- ❏ How important is it that managers should want change to happen?
- ❏ What is 'unlearning', and what does it tell us about successful change and competitive advantage?
- ❏ Should 'knowhow' be gained on the job only, like apprenticeship?
- ❏ Is outdoors development a waste of time and resources?
- ❏ How do you make 'learning' stick?
- ❏ Is 'lifelong learning' just another consultants' fad?
- ❏ Is learning about *knowledge*, about *understanding*, about *need* or about something else?
- ❏ Does everyone learn in the same way?
- ❏ How can organisations capitalise upon managerial learning as a source of sustainable competitive advantage?
- ❏ Will the arrows, boxes and circles remain a key part of managerial learning into the future? In fifty years time, will a similarly ethnographically minded person look through those windows and still see the same cultural icons, and the same learning rituals taking place?

None of these questions has an absolutely 'right' answer. But there are some clearly wrong answers. Our practical research is based upon collaborative work with thousands of managers worldwide. It enables us to get better answers to these questions than we had just five years ago. That is what this book is about.

The views expressed in the book are those of the author and do not necessarily represent the views of other members of Cranfield School of Management.

KEITH PATCHING

Note: MBTI® and Myers–Briggs Type Indicator® are registered trademarks of Consulting Psychologists Press, Palo Alto, California.

Introduction

WHAT THIS BOOK IS ABOUT

This book is about management and organisation development. More specifically, it is about activities which organisations engage in to help achieve specific business goals. We may wish to argue with the simplistic certainty of the assertion that 'the only sustainable competitive advantage is an organisation's ability to learn', but, being in the business of management and organisation development, we are wholeheartedly in support of its broad ethos. There is an increasing belief that organisational success relates to the ways in which senior people 'think': that it is the ability or willingness to change cognitions which distinguishes successful from failing companies (Barr *et al.* 1993).

In the mid to late 1990s the notion of 'development' as applied to managers and organisations has become 'strategically important'. The relatively humble status of 'training' is contrasted to the burgeoning business of 'development' in all its myriad forms.

Management development within a single-company context refers to activities which gather together numbers of managers from an organisation in order to 'learn'. From learning together, behaviours will be different; from those different behaviours will flow, it is hoped, better business performance. The perceived issues may be about organisational strategy, the product portfolio, better customer focus, or increased performance of certain business processes. The list is potentially endless. In every case, however, managers of the organisation have to do something different to make whatever needs to be done happen.

This book is an exploration of what happens when this kind of activity takes place. Sometimes the activities seem to work well; at others, little of value seems to come out of them. As professionals in the field, we strive for ever improved management learning activities; and we believe that we have got significantly better over the past few years.

I shall undertake this exploration on two levels. The first is practical; it describes the work we have actually done, and what seems to work better, what seems to be less effective. At this level, we offer examples and cases which we hope will be of immediate benefit to readers. The cases cited are real; only the names have been changed. In some situations, the cases show shortcomings in our approaches in the past – this is especially true of the core

1

case which forms the Appendix. I am happy to describe our less successful interventions because we have learnt from them.

The second level is 'theoretical'; it seeks to explain why some activities work better than others. In trying to explain, I recognise that management and organisation development is not and cannot be a 'science'. There are no 'right answers', as I shall argue in some detail in Chapter 1. But this does not mean that we cannot learn. The argument of the book as a whole will call upon what we have learnt not only from our own work with managers, but also from a variety of other disciplines such as psychology, neurophysiology, and others. In drawing on these disciplines, I shall occasionally use models. But I should like to stress now that models used in the book are tools for thinking; they are not attempts to 'map reality'.

Finally, this is not a 'how to . . .' book. Although I shall refer to many techniques and methods we use in our management and organisation development work, this is not a management and organisation development 'manual'. It is a thorough reappraisal of some of the assumptions and practices of management and organisation development as a discipline.

THE PURPOSE OF THE BOOK

During the past few years the Management Development Unit at Cranfield School of Management has worked with a large number of organisations, designing, developing and delivering 'organisational and management development interventions'. These interventions range from residential 'courses' of two or three weeks' duration, to one day workshops; from locally run seminars to consultancy exercises. Some of the organisations we have worked with are relatively small, with only a few hundred employees; others are very large multinationals. Some are in the high technology businesses; others deal with more down-to-earth products and services. Some are public sector organisations; others highly commercialised.

What they have in common, apart from having worked with us, is that each has recognised a business need, and has taken steps to help meet that business need through 'management and organisation development' activities

During these years we have learnt a lot about what works and what does not work in this kind of activity. Four years ago, we did a reasonable job; now, we are told by our clients that, more often than not, we do an excellent job. But this book is not an attempt to 'advertise' our expertise. One of the most important lessons we have learnt over the years is how much more there is for us to learn about what we do.

We have learnt a great deal, which has been and continues to be of practical benefit to the clients we work with. This book is first a record of what we have learnt, mostly to share this learning with managers and Management or

Organisation Development specialists who have similar jobs to do, but also partly for our own purposes – it helps add value to learning if you organise what you think you have learnt.

But the book is secondly about the things we do not yet know enough about – a kind of research agenda. Being a university-based School of Management we are fortunate to work in a culture which asks questions, and will not allow answers which are not supported by good data. The Management Development Unit not only helps deliver organisational and management development activities, it also, at the same time, undertakes research into those activities – action research which has contributed enormously to the transformation of the quality of what we do.

Virtually all of the 'research' upon which this book has been based is 'action research', gleaned from practical experience in working with managers on management and organisation development projects and programmes.

Only a small proportion of what we are researching is 'finished'; this book is a record of where we are in the late 1990s. Further publications will focus on other things we are confident we shall learn as we continue with our work.

Our purpose, then, is to take stock, to share our learning to date, and to map out the territories we shall be continuing to explore during the coming years. We hope that it produces a number of responses. First, we hope that readers will find within it things which will help them in their organisational and management development activities. Second, that it will generate debate – we welcome feedback (indeed, as we suggest at various points in the book, feedback is what we live on). Third, that it will simply remind some people about some of things they already know, but may have forgotten. And fourth, that it will demonstrate to those who may still doubt, that the practices and principles of organisational and management development are rigorously researched and developed; they are no longer based on the "put them in a classroom, teach them about marketing, that ought to do the job" approach, nor on the "get them to build a bridge – that'll teach them about teamworking" style. We believe that organisational and management development are important enough to all our futures to be treated with the respect and authority which comes from a spirit of continuous improvement and rigorous research.

THE SCOPE OF THE BOOK

This book is about 'development', but it is not an attempt to deal with every aspect of this topic. Its major focus is that field of activities which we describe as 'organisational and management development' undertaken consciously and collectively within a single organisation or business.

In other words, we are not primarily concentrating upon activities such as public 'courses' or conferences or seminars which people attend as individuals, meeting and mixing with people from different companies and organisations. These do themselves provide a perfectly fruitful sphere of research, but we realise that much of what we have learnt may not be accurately applied to 'public' events. It has not been part of our plan to attempt to 'validate' our learning within the context of 'public', multiorganisation activities. The broad principles we have learnt have been acquired by working in situations in which there has been at least a nominal link between all participants involved in the activities we describe. In other words, all participants within each of the interventions we have used as our research base have 'come from' the same organisation. (What we can legitimately call 'an organisation' is not unproblematic; this issue is taken up in Chapter 1.)

Many of the terms I shall be using in the book cannot be 'defined' in the sense that there is '*a definition*' for each. Terms such as 'development', 'manager', and 'programme' can mean different things to different people. Many attempts to define them end up in fruitless arguments about terminology, deflecting focus from the issues in hand. However, I should like to attempt some descriptions of the terms we use.

The book's sphere of interest can be loosely defined as those activities which an organisation decides to undertake in the belief that, by developing managers' knowledge, skills or attitudes, this will have a beneficial impact upon the business, and make any investments of time, resources and money they make into 'management and organisation development' worth while.

By 'management and organisation development' we mean any activity undertaken within an organisation whose goal is, by developing how people think and do things, to improve, or 'develop' the organisation. We do not strictly differentiate between 'organisation development' and 'management development', although we do recognise that parts of their respective semantic fields do not overlap. However, because of our exclusive focus on activities undertaken within single organisations, from an outcomes point of view, these two concepts are sufficiently similar to be treated together. 'Management' is developed to help the organisation as a whole to improve; but organisations are, more or less, managed by people, who, in so managing, are the organisation's 'management'.

Our search for a term which is sufficiently broad to capture the essence of a whole variety of activities, plans, and so on has led us to use the word 'intervention'. By this we mean all those courses, consultancy exercises, seminars, workshops, and so on, which comprise the kinds of things organisations do to execute some kind of organisation or management development. Interventions do not have to involve outsiders; they can be self-managed by individuals (through self-learning, groups, through self-managed workshops and so on), or by an organisation, perhaps with help from their in-house Management Development department or equivalent. Most of our research is based upon interventions from the outside – by ourselves; but we have attempted to supplement this data, where appropriate, with data from other sources. Given that this book is mostly about what we have learnt, we do not feel that our bias in data gathering is a problem.

By 'development' we mean something different from 'training' or even 'education'. By 'training' we mean those highly focused learning activities which enable someone to perform a set of procedures or tasks in a pre-defined way. Our definition of training implies a narrowing of options; it implies that there is one right way to do something, and training instils that one right way to the exclusions of others. From training we learn to do something because that is the way to do it.

However, the problem with training in its pure form is that it closes off options, and utilises only a very small part of the essentially creative and innovative nature of people. Clearly, there is value in helping managers settle into what has been shown to be the most efficient ways of doing tasks, and in establishing a high degree of commonality on the ways in which tasks are performed. Training helps develop that kind of efficiency celebrated in the very earliest days of 'management science' by Taylor and Weber. Through training, we ensure that managers do not have constantly to reinvent the wheel. In so doing, managers become efficient components in a well-run machine.

By 'education' we mean a much broader approach to learning – almost 'learning for its own sake'. Education does not seek an immediate practical application, but has the primary function of broadening the mind, of adding new perspectives. It asks more questions than it answers; shows up short-comings in poorly considered views; concentrates on strong links between theory and evidence; and encourages people to say "I don't know, but I'll try to find out." From education we learn to do something only after we have weighed up all the evidence, considered all the angles, and asked ourselves deep questions concerning the assumptions we may have made in arriving at our conclusions. It is primarily about new ideas and new knowledge, and not about doing things differently.

'Development' takes yet a different stance, which synthesises the advantages of both the training and the education approaches. From training, development takes the focus, the sense of purpose, and the practicality of application. For each development opportunity there is a goal, an aim, which is achievable, and delivers benefits both to the individual and to the organisation is a timescale which is 'reasonable'.

From education, development takes the questioning, the willingness to explore new and radical ways of thinking, the demand for rigour in establishing a case, the willingness to accept fallibility in our own thinking, and seek inputs from elsewhere. In this, education provides a great deal of what we believe today's management and organisation development needs. We suspect that a fair amount of what is preventing organisations and managers to develop as effectively as they might stems from a perception by many manager we meet that, in management, there is a 'right' way; that the job of management and organisation development is to identify that 'right' way, so that managers can go back home and implement it. A 'training' mindset would reinforce that; and 'education' mindset would help to remove it.

Because there is no 'right' mix of the training and education approaches to any management and organisation development intervention, one of the challenges of this discipline is to find, for each and every case, a balance between the essentially prescriptive 'training' approach ('This is how to market these kinds of goods in this kind of market place') and the essentially questioning 'education' approach ('What would you need to do to find out how to market your goods in this kind of market place?').

From development we learn to do something because we have explored the alternatives, but also recognised the value to ourselves and our organisation of people sharing a common language, culture and approach. We learn that essential tension between conservation and change which lies at the heart of organisational life. In so doing managers become practical social scientists, coping with the uncertainties which go with attempting to understand human behaviour and organisational realities, while attempting to make a living out of decisions and actions which are based on what we understand today, which may be very different from what we understand tomorrow.

A significant amount of this book is about how we have attempted to accept and learn from this kind of challenge. One thing we think we have learnt is that there is no 'right' balance; that part of our job is to work with our clients to design interventions with a synthesis of elements which does as good a job as we believe can be done for that situation. And by 'those elements' we mean far more than simply training and education. The book is in part a catalogue of those many variables we have found to be significant to the successful design, development and delivery of management and organisation development interventions. The more we learn, the more variables we seem to recognise. The more we recognise these variables, the more we learn about their roles both in interventions, and in the wider realities of organisational life. One of the things we have to try to do is to manage all of those variables differently as best suits each organisation, and each intervention within that organisation.

We can never 'know' that we have got it right. The data suggests, however, we get closer to what people need the more we learn.

MANAGEMENT AND ORGANISATION DEVELOPMENT IN CONTEXT: WHY DO WE DO IT?

Given that the focus of this book is what we have described as 'in-company' management and organisation development, finding reasons why such activities are pursued apparently takes us out of the realm of personal interest and individual development, and into what can broadly be termed the 'political'. It is usually the case that the kind of investment an organisation makes in programmes of management and organisation development are expensive enough, and involve sufficiently large numbers of influential people that there has to be at least superficial agreement on a number of fronts that there is a good reason for the activity.

I use the term "superficial" deliberately. In the case study which forms the Appendix, I explore a programme which was provided for the top nineteen managers of a small, technically oriented company facing challenging times. Some years after the programme was run, we undertook follow up research with those managers. One of the most fascinating quotes from this research was from one of these very managers who said of the programme, "I think one of the big questions and I guess we'll never know the answer, is why we decided to have the course in the first place. I mean the fundamental reasons behind it, and not the obvious reasons." Even three years after the programme started, the managers of this organisation did not know why it had taken place. We suspect that this case is not unique. Why we do management development is not a simple question.

In the past, a 'good reason' for 'doing organisation or management development' may have been simply that 'managers need it'; it is not too many years since there was a kind of 'blind faith' that, if you put managers through a training programme, it must be good for the organisation as a whole. These days, we expect there to be an underlying drive for management and organisation development which, however well or poorly, links the goals of the organisation to the anticipated benefits from the programme itself.

There is, then, some kind of supposition that it is possible to help organisations achieve business goals through programmes of activity which involve numbers of managers learning together. In many cases, the gap between the business goals and the impact of a development programme is entirely the responsibility of the provider of the programme: these are the people with the 'expertise'. Given that many such gaps are filled by apparently 'bizarre' activities, such as teams of managers crossing car parks without touching the ground, individuals hanging by ropes from mountain tops, or people sitting in lecture rooms listening to the reminiscences of academics, we have to accept that many of the expectations which are placed upon management and organisation development are still based more upon faith than upon any quasi-scientific demonstration of efficacy.

As we in the business of management and organisation development ourselves learn more about our craft, so we have to accept that there is still a long way to go before we can be really confident about such efficacy. Dealing as we are with people rather than inanimate objects, we cannot hope to draw up a body of 'scientific' evidence as such. Our learning is the learning of the humanities, subject to differing interpretations, and coloured by perceptions which are part of the discussion rather than beyond it.

It is for this reason that we have chosen, throughout this book, to eschew attempts to draw up 'laws' for our discipline. We take an essentially ethnographic approach which presents the reader with as clear a picture of what we have seen, along with conclusions which we draw from those pictures. If these conclusions are found to be useful, then the book will have served its purpose. We prefer, therefore, to use looser terms, such a 'principles'. These are descriptions of what we believe we have learnt from our experiences and reflection, and which we use to guide us in our continuing work with organisations. Because they are for guidance rather than constraint, we feel comfortable questioning them each time we use them.

There is a philosophical argument at the heart of the book, which concerns the question of how generalisable learning from one human experience can be. We believe that there are generalisable principles, but that these are in no way universal. We have neither achieved, nor do we seek for, a 'methodology' for organisation or management development. We can find aspects of management and organisation development which lend themselves more readily to a 'methodological' approach. But we believe that it is in the very nature of a 'methodology' to constrain behaviours. We suspect that, at present, the most urgent need in business and management is not for constraint, but for liberation of many of the creative and collaborative behaviours which our institutions and businesses successfully suppress in our children and young managers.

However, these are matters for later in the book. For the moment, the challenge of effective management and organisation development seems to be to identify how to interrelate the uniques of any situation with the kinds of learning activities which have helped elsewhere. What makes this such a difficult challenge lies in the ways in which, as part of our culture, we find ourselves trying to 'prove' the link between the organisations' needs and the application of specific learning activities. In the past, we were relatively comfortable with this. 'Proving' the link depended solely on the scores on the review forms which accompanied the end of each event. Where those review forms contained numerically based evaluations, it was possible to arrive at apparent certainty regarding the effectiveness of the activities in question. High scores 'proved' success; low scores demanded rethinking.

But the purpose of management and organisation development activities is not to gain high scores on review forms. It is to have some kind of beneficial impact on the organisation. And since management and organisation development does not take place in a vacuum; and since it may well take time for that beneficial impact to take effect, 'proving' effectiveness becomes fraught with all kinds of complications so long as we continue to position management and organisation development within some kind of causal framework.

The study of in-company management and organisation development is essentially a study of how specific organisations have or have not changed over a period of time during which that organisation, among other things, took on board one or several initiatives which fall within the broad rubric of 'management and organisation development'. Whether any beneficial changes can ever be fully ascribed to a management and organisation development intervention is questionable. But in order to make as sure as we can that those benefits are likely to accrue, we need as good an understanding as we can get of what we are doing when we undertake management and organisation development.

That is what this book is all about. It is an attempt to get as good a grip as we can, at this stage of our own learning about management and organisation development, on the what and the why of management and organisation development.

1 Management Development: Organisation Development

INTRODUCTION

The relationship which my colleagues and I have with client organisations is one of partnership. Managers have as their primary brief to take decisions and actions which help to make their organisations become and remain successful. They stay firmly at the 'coalface' of their organisations. Most try to learn from their own and their immediate colleagues' experience, and to use that learning to carry on the constant fight against organisational entropy. But increasingly rapid change and complexity make it hard for individual managers, or even groups of managers, to gather even a small proportion of the facts and ideas which comprise the sum of all managerial learning. Most managers can gather only a limited view of the world. The immediacy of direct involvement in their own challenges, and the narrowness of perspective which any single organisational situation provides, make it impossible for them to gather for themselves the broader, more objective view which many feel they need for effective decision-making.

There are a number of reasons why managers may think that their immediate experience may be insufficient for their purposes:

- ❑ situations change – what worked before, and from which they have learnt, may not work now because the circumstances may not be the same
- ❑ new challenges emerge – managers may not have experienced a 'new' kind of situation, and be afraid of 'working in the dark'
- ❑ only a limited number of managers in the organisation may have what is believed to be relevant experience, and they may be unskilled in transferring their experience to others
- ❑ perceptions differ – different people may have different views about what were the factors which made for success in the past
- ❑ what works for one person does not necessarily work for another

Organisations such as Cranfield School of Management attempt to glean a broader view. By working directly with a variety of organisations, by undertaking first-hand research on organisational and management issues, and by keeping in touch through academic processes with research being undertaken by others in these and related fields, we are in a position to bring a level of 'expertise' into the partnerships we form with our clients. This expertise, however, is far more to do with the processes of managerial learning within a client organisation, than it is about bringing to the partnership 'the truth' about organisations and management.

There are no 'absolute right answers' which we can provide to our clients; what our contribution to the partnership will be varies according to the specific circumstances of the client organisation, and the individual styles and characteristics of its employees. There may have been a time when 'experts' could feel confident that their role was simply to draw up the 'magic formula', and then apply it to whatever organisational challenge came their way. But this was illusory. Despite their best efforts, no-one can say with certainty that this or that way of managing is the 'right' way for any situation. Organisational life is 'fuzzy' (Kosko 1994: passim). All we can do is to consider evidence and try to minimise error. In so doing, we undertake activities which are, in principle, no different from what any thoughtful manager should do every day. The practical differences lie in:

❑ the breadth of data and experience which we can call upon to work with
❑ the quality and rigour of the theorising we apply to those data
❑ the rigour and breadth of opportunity with which we are able to test out the theories which we and others develop
❑ the 'objectivity' with which we explore the theories with our clients

All managers who think about what they do are practical students of organisational theory. Theory is not something unique to academics, but something we all work with in arriving at our attitudes, beliefs and decisions as managers. It seems obvious to most of us that some theories are better than others. Many managerial discussions which we undertake in meetings focus upon trying to agree upon which theory will be best for a particular decision. A Boardroom discussion on whether or not to buy another company will often be a debate about theory. Clearly, 'facts' will be brought into the equation, such as the target company's market share, the size of its workforce, key financial ratios, and so on. But lying behind the exploration of these 'facts' will be theories concerning the importance of these facts. Buying big companies is good, since we acquire much more; buying big companies is bad because we have bigger problems with integration, and so on.

When we praise an employee, we appeal (more or less consciously) to a theory about how praise enhances self-esteem and produces better relationships. When we flatten our hierarchies, we work on the theory that this will reduce costs while enabling employees to become more empowered in their working lives. When we take over another company, we bank on the theory that buying in the expertise, or the products, or the customers, or whatever of the company we buy will increase shareholder value. From the mundane to the strategic, we take decisions based upon more or less articulated theories. In many cases, we look for evidence to support those theories: personal experience of giving and receiving praise; literature on organisations which have flattened their hierarchies; share-value trends of companies which have engaged in takeovers.

In many cases, then, the role my colleagues and I at the School undertake is in helping explore theories and their application with our clients. Those theories may come from us, or they may already be in the minds of people we are working with, as the following case demonstrates.

A MINOR CASE OF THEORY IN USE

Recently I was working with a group of American managers, putting together a workshop aimed at helping senior managers explore their roles in the introduction of a new process into their organisation. One of the managers from the company who was present to help us focus the style and content of the workshop on the needs of the participants was clearly frustrated at some of the ideas we were proposing.

We had been working on ways of involving the senior managers once the workshop got underway, ways which included engaging in a dialogue concerning some of the ground rules which may be set for each workshop. This manager clearly felt that setting ground rules by dialogue was inappropriate. Interrupting our presentation, the manager in question banged his fist on the table. 'This is all a waste of time,' he said. 'I know these people. You gotta be tough; you gotta be brutal. That's how to get them to listen and take notice.'

His observation was based on his personal experience of having worked with these senior managers. I do not think he felt that he was engaged in a theoretical debate – he was 'telling it like it is'. Yet even within this brief set of exhortations lies a potential wealth of theory. His approach was based upon the theory that being brutal with senior managers in the company gets them to listen. It may also have been based upon a deeper theory that, if you get people to listen they learn better. Was there also the theory that telling is better than involving? Could he also be working on an assumption (also a theory) that managers respect outside consultants better if those consultants exercise their authority in unequivocal ways, such as setting ground rules themselves?

Whatever was driving his assertion, there were implicit in his approach some kinds of 'If you do X, then Y . . .' rules which, for him, were valid at least for each application of the workshop.

Not all of the theories which drive our assertions and decisions operate at a conscious level. So part of our job is to help surface the kinds of underlying theories which managers use, more or less consciously, and to help apply to these theories the kind of rigour which we feel should be applied to a theory-in-use (Argyris 1992: 89) which may influence action and decision-making within a client organisation.

Theories of what does or does not work successfully can come, therefore, from practising managers or from ourselves as academics. The fact that an academic has come up with a theory does not, of itself, make it a better theory. It simply suggests that it is more overtly stated and (one hopes) more rigorously tested. But even these criteria do not provide guarantees. If our practical partnerships are to be of value to our clients, theories which we embody within our interventions need to be of relevance to their situation; they also have to be recognised as approximations rather than as 'scientific' truths; and they have to be translated into practical learning for managers within our client organisations.

Chapters 2 to the end of this book is all about the third of these requirements, practical learning. The remainder of this chapter deals with the first two: theories and approximations.

The Academic Research 'Industry' – The Question of Relevance

The vast majority of scientists who ever lived are still alive (and many of them still working) today; I suspect that the same applies to organisational scientists, if the steady outpouring of papers and books is anything to go by. There is an 'industry' of academic research, which is producing significantly more 'information' than any practising manager could hope to keep up with: 'Learning from the well of wisdom once required serious effort. Now it more resembles taking a drink from a fire hydrant' (Parikh 1994: 14). As with other academic disciplines, much of what is published takes the form of challenge to the writings of other academics, attempts to refine or even to refute what has gone before. What are they all doing? Why can't they agree? Why do so many of them seem to delight in 'disproving' hitherto received wisdom? Why can't they make more sense? What relevance does much of their research have to practising managers?

Part of the problem seems to lie in the increasing specialisation of organisational scientific research. Just as natural scientists' zones of interest become more and more specialised, and research projects find out more and more about less and less, so the published works of organisational scientists become more and more precise and focused, and, in many cases less and less accessible. As with many other academic disciplines, organisational 'science' is suffering from the 'principle of incompatibility' (Zadeh 1987), which simply states that the more precise our research activities, the less relevance it has for practical managers. Career organisational scientists often turn their attention to the problems of publishing and research more than to the challenges of practical managers, with the result that while 'The product of science is knowledge; the product of scientists is reputation,' (Kosko 1994: 40). It is this kind of phenomenon which often makes practising managers wary of working with academics, and with good reason. For many academic researchers into organisations and management, the customers are no longer managers, but other academics. My colleagues and I remain clear on this issue: the customer is the client organisation.

But it is not theory as such which makes many academics' work irrelevant to practising managers; it is the degree to which theories can be articulated cogently and applied effectively to organisational activities and change. Another of our roles in our partnerships, therefore, has to be to act as filters, translators, interpreters, summarisers and synthesisers of an increasing volume of research output. This demands that we recognise as accurately as possible, for any management and organisation development intervention, how fine a filter we apply. Too little filtering throws irrelevant research into the partnership; too much produces the 'quick fix' solutions of the 'one-minute manager' or the 'balanced scorecard'. Part of our added value stems from the rigour with which we explore and match this filtering process, situation by situation.

Seeking 'Right' Answers

Although one of the motivators for the volume of research on organisational and managerial issues is career enhancement for those engaged in that research, another is the search for the 'truth'. This is expressed clearly in the following: 'The social sciences have great power to get at how things really are, both through research and through eliciting the dynamics of situations.' (Klein and Eason 1991: xiii). Unfortunately, it is this kind of assertion which can easily mislead both managers and academics alike. It rests upon the assumption that, in the study of organisation and management, which is one of the social sciences, 'how things really are' can, ultimately, and with sufficient research, be 'got at'. This assumption is wrong.

To illustrate this point, I shall summarise a true case of an organisational 'problem' and its outcome.

THE COLLAPSE OF A COMPANY

In the mid-1990s the Chief Executive Officer of a relatively large information systems company took the company through a flotation on the stock market which turned out to be a 'full-blown disaster', according to the newspaper reports of the time. It led to his departure under a cloud of resentment and blame. In the year after flotation, shares had fallen to a quarter of their value at flotation, and investors lost £260 million in a few months.

The Chief Executive had been in information technology all his life, having been a successful salesman in his time, good at closing deals. He had a forceful personality and had risen to the top of what, prior to flotation had become a relatively strong company with a large and loyal customer base, and good turnover and profit figures. He had recognised, during his tenure, that the industry was undergoing some significant changes. Largely a hardware-oriented company, it was suffering, like its competitors, from shrinking margins, and mature markets. The Chief Executive had overseen a shift in focus from hardware to long term software contracts.

He had, two years earlier, led a management buyout, and was therefore, along with his fellow managers, in a good position to profit from selling his shares at flotation. Yet despite the share price being set on a valuation of the company 18.2 times its earning, double its valuation only one year previously, he did not do so. Large profits were made, however, by the other venture capitalists in the buyout, including £48 million by the Capital Investment arm of the same bank which was the company's adviser on the flotation.

The collapse in share price was due to a succession of profit warnings in the months after flotation. First-half results were down by 33%, and there was little sign of an improvement as targets were successively reduced. Many argued that the appropriate financial controls had not been put in place to cater for the fundamental shift in the nature of the business, and estimates suggested that such controls would not be in place for another 18 months. As the share prices continued to fall, the Chief Executive Officer resigned.

This kind of story is not uncommon. Buried within the story is a great deal of what management is all about – decisions, deals, estimates, prices, profits and so on. And individual careers. Somewhere along the line, the Chief Executive Officer got it wrong. But what it was that he got wrong is, in principle, a matter of opinion. It is not because we cannot gather enough evidence to settle the matter once and for all, or because we do not have the ability to compute all the information with sufficient accuracy, but because management is implicitly ambiguous and paradoxical. There is, within this and virtually all other stories about management and organisations, no 'how things really are' to be unearthed. Trying to find 'the truth' about such situations is a reasonable but mistaken venture.

It is reasonable, because, especially in western culture, we are 'trained' to look for black-and-white answers to well-formed questions such as 'what did he do wrong?' (Kosko 1994: 23). In Chapter 7, which deals with how people learn, I shall explore in some depth how we learn to look for such answers. For this chapter, however, it is more important to establish that management and organisation development is not about finding 'the truth', but about helping shape perceptions of the complex and ambiguous world of organisational life.

To help in this process, I shall construct a 'model'. This is a tool for thinking, a construct which is not an attempt to map the real world, but simply to help draw out some factors in understanding managerial questions. It is a simple, relatively crude model, which, having used it to do a job, I shall put aside. It loosely models some aspects of western legal processes. I use this approach because we may find ourselves, as we search for answers such as those concerning our case study, more or less consciously following legal precedent. Over hundreds of years, the law has been used to settle matters of blame and responsibility; many of our attempts to learn from organisational and managerial experience may find themselves mirroring such processes.

A TEMPORARY MODEL FOR GETTING ANSWERS TO ORGANISATIONAL QUESTIONS

The model separates out four elements which make up the search for judgements on complex matters. We need the facts of the case; we wish to know what the person in question (in this case, the Chief Executive Officer of the organisation in question) intended by his or her actions; we then find ourselves evaluating the situation; finally, we pronounce sentence – we make a judgement. The following is an exploration of how we may use this process in more depth.

Part 1 – Facts

The first part of the process is the exploration of the physical 'facts' or circumstances. 'Were you there, did you do so and so?' In a legal case this phase seeks simply to establish whether certain acts took place. For this part, what is required is 'hard' evidence, and the more evidence there is that the act in question took place, the more likely it is that we would believe it to be true. In our case study, the facts are manifold – share prices, profits, turnover, decisions, and so on. But facts by themselves mean nothing. A share price of 70p means nothing in itself. Facts take on significance only when we put some kind of evaluation upon them. Similarly, the 'fact' that the Chief Executive Officer put in place a process of a fundamental shift in the nature of the company's business is not in doubt. But this decision only makes sense in the broader context of why, and what the consequences were.

Part 2 – Intentions

The second part of the model takes into account our intentions. What did we mean, or intend, by the decisions and actions we undertook? Although the

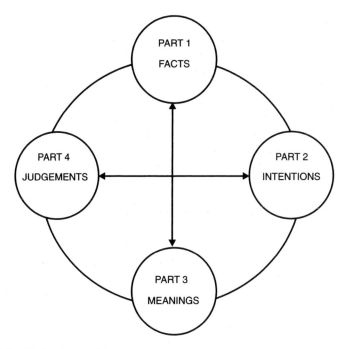

Figure 1.1   *Evaluation model*

outcomes of a situation may be the most important in management, we still recognise that our evaluations of such situations will vary according to those intentions. In law, the intention of an accused will help decide whether we call an act one of manslaughter or murder. In management, it can help us decide between incompetence and scheming. Both the law and management are about people, and people have intentions (Dennett 1987) and motives. There is the added complication that people may not always be fully aware of their intentions and motives, but I shall leave this observation aside until later chapters.

Part 3 – Meanings

The influence of the second part of the model on the third has already been suggested. The third part concerns fitting the circumstances and intention to a matter of law – whether, in this case, this constitutes an example of murder or manslaughter, theft or whatever; incompetence or self-seeking, courageous leadership or abdication of responsibility, and so on. In law, this is a matter which we have delegated to parliament – to establish the law's rules and principles (Dworkin 1968); and to the legal profession, to interpret in cases of doubt what the law 'means' in this case. But in management, we have no legal precedent to rely on, no legislation to fall back on, so we look to 'management science' to bridge the gap. We talk of takeover, appraisal, markets, consumers, share-prices, and so on; organisational equivalents of the legal terms such as murder, fraud, incest and criminal negligence.

What makes these *legal* terms 'real' is legislation. Other societies and other cultures use different ways of defining their own 'legal' terms. The very fact that, in our society, we have so many people spending so much time defining legal terms, framing and passing new laws tells us that we are now in the realm of choices, and not of trying to match terms against an unquestioned 'reality'. What makes something murder or manslaughter or incest or fraud is what we, as a society, choose it to be; and those choices continue to change with time, social attitudes, demographic changes and a whole host of other determinants. There is no such 'thing' as murder beyond what a society decides to call it. Continuing debates over abortion testify to the scope available for differently defining both murder, and associated concepts such as 'viable' and 'life'.

For a variety of reasons we do not have the organisational or managerial equivalent of law-making. We do not have an 'authority' such as the law, which acts as the ultimate arbiter of what constitutes an instance of an organisation, a merger, an appraisal, a consumer, and so on. There are some terms we use in business which are defined by law; most are not. Even if they were, they would still be a matter of some choice, but those empowered to choose would be only those with the given authority to do so. To what extent does being an academic researcher into organisations and management give the right to arbitrate on such matters?

Clearly not much. If an academic consultant is brought in to evaluate a situation – to arrive at some kind of decision as to the nature of a decision or series or decisions – that evaluation has authority only in so far as those being consulted choose to accept it. And as Grossberg (1982) and others have shown, managers' (and other people's) preparedness to accept such ideas vary according to how it resonates with what they expect to hear or think.

This part of the process – putting labels and evaluations upon situations, and thereby creating some kind of meaning, something from which we can learn – is and must always be a matter of opinion. And it is so because the 'variables' in our evaluative equations are concepts, not visible entities, abstractions from immediate perceptions, not the things we immediately experience. We can immediately perceive a wedding but not a marriage; we can immediately perceive people in rooms, but not organisations; we can immediately perceive a balance sheet but not a profit; we can immediately perceive a person talking to others, but not charisma; we can immediately perceive a person doing tasks, but not a manager. In each case, the second of those pairs is inferred from what we see, and from what we have learnt to infer.

Organisations, and many others of the kinds of concepts which managers work with cannot provide 'right' and 'wrong' answers because, they only *exist* in a conceptual sense (Burrell and Morgan 1979: 32), or as 'in-the-head fictions' (Fineman 1993: 11), or 'in-the-mind' (Stokes 1994: 121). Although it can be helpful to practical managers to operate as if they were 'objective' entities, it is unhelpful if academic researchers try to find out about their 'essential' nature as thought they had existence in any other form than the conceptual. Organisations, leadership, management, and so on cannot be studied except through people's perceptions and attitudes to them. People and their opinions are what give organisations existence; people and their opinions are not experimental 'noise' to be eliminated in order to study the phenomena more 'objectively'.

Therefore, the only sense which can be made of the assertions that 'The social sciences have great power to get at how things really are' (Klein and Eason 1991: xiii) is that the social sciences can gather more information on how people 'construct' their own pictures, images, concepts, meanings, attitudes and opinions of 'things'.

In our case study, debates about the nature of the Chief Executive's actions remain matters of opinion. Academic research could provide more facts about the situation, and even, through interviews, about the Chief Executive's motivations; but it cannot provide a 'right' answer to many of the elements of this third and vital stage of the evaluative process. Better informed analysis, perhaps, but better, not because it gets closer to some absolute 'truth', but because, possibly, it can bring into the debate a greater rigour in dealing with the inherent complexity.

Part 4 – Judgements

The fourth part of the model deals with how people would wish to deal with the situation. In law, this involves questions such as 'Does this warrant a harsh sentence, or is it a matter of such triviality that no further action is deemed necessary?' This, in law, we have largely delegated to someone else, the judiciary, although judges must frequently be aware that such delegation is given reluctantly by many in our society who would like, in many cases, to take upon themselves this part of the process. In management, such judgements are made by those with authority. It is partly in the nature of how we 'construct' management that it involves the 'right' to pass judgements. Hiring and firing are the extremes in the canon of managerial sanctions, although rewards, punishments and other kinds of positive and negative motivators belong to how we choose to define 'management'.

In our case study, because of the protocols of senior management, the Chief Executive resigned. Whether he 'jumped' or 'was pushed' is less important than the general consensus that 'he had to go'. But this is a consensus, and not a 'scientific' truth. It was true because a lot of powerful people said it to be so. Like judges, at this stage of the process, we all have to take judgements about the right outcome; but like judges, we are more or less aware that this stage of the process calls upon a moral rather than a logical kind of decision.

Putting The Pieces Back Together Again – Synthesis

There are at least two inherent problems with models such as this. The first is summarised as 'the map is not the territory'. In other words, this is just a model. It is sometimes tempting to use such tools for thinking as though they represented some kind of higher 'reality' than they do. They can become reified: people can be led to 'celebrate the map itself' (Quinn 1988: 29). Chapter 7 explores some of the reasons why people can become so attached to such models, and begin to see the world through the filters that such models provide. Models make a lot of sense to us, and can help in our understanding of the complexities we have to deal with. But to a man with a hammer, everything looks like a nail. Our evaluation model is crude, simple and has limited use. It is a tool for structuring our thinking, and not an 'answer'.

Another problem with such models is that they are essentially analytical; they dissect, and in so doing, tend to sever connections between their elements. But managerial life is experienced as a synthesis of such elements. Take, for example, a statement by the CEO of an organisation: 'I want to get our share price up.' Implied within this statement is: (part one) the share price is low; (part two) he or she intends to do something about it; (part three) share price is an appropriate focus for the organisation and for action; (part four) the level of share price has been judged to be unacceptable. There are only eight words in the CEO's statement – the explicit is sparse. But within those eight words lie a whole host of implicit meanings; many if not most CEOs make such statements, in which there are many implicit meanings. Indeed, most people in most cultures do precisely the same (Douglas 1975). It is in the nature of how people think and speak. The problem with models such as this one is that they may suggest that it would be better for all concerned if we tried to make explicit everything which we implicitly intend by our statements. That would be a mistaken view of human behaviour.

The pictorial representation of the model I have used so far reinforces this separation, and deliberately so. But models, like other tools, may have a number of ways of being used. The following is the same model represented to suggest the interactions between the four parts:

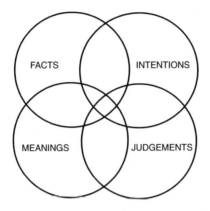

Figure 1.2 *Interaction of the elements*

We do not tend to deal with legal or managerial issues thus sequentially, and even if we attempt to do so consciously, we are unlikely to be able completely to separate out each element from the others. The facts which we seek to gather will be more or less consciously influenced by our prejudices, attitudes, opinions and values; the level of credence we give to others' stated intentions will be coloured by our expectations of the individual in question; our own motives and intentions will be unconsciously influenced by our background and experience; our evaluations will vary according to significantly more than 'the pertinent facts', and so on. These are all issues which are dealt with in some depth in Chapter 7.

The purpose of the model has been to illustrate how it is that, despite the availability of a great deal of data, and despite the energies of large numbers of researchers into organisations and management, it is inappropriate to expect to find absolute answers at the end of the 'road to discovery'. Because all of our managerial judgements, decisions and subsequent actions involve inferences and interpretations as well as 'verifiable facts', there will always be elements of managerial life which are not susceptible to such external 'verifiability'.

Much of management is about decisions and actions. Decisions call for judgements, which, in turn, discourage equivocation. The Chief Executive in our case study had to stay or he had to go; there was no room for 'on balance', or for 'grey areas' kinds of solution. Management is often about making 'hard' decisions; one reason why they are so hard is that there are very few situations involving people, motives or evaluations which are 'absolutely' clear cut. There is almost always room for the 'neither wholly right nor wholly wrong' (this is also true in science and even in mathematics – Kosko 1994, passim). Making decisions, especially hard decisions, causes stress (Jaynes 1990: 92–3). No wonder people imagine a world in which 'how things really are' could be sorted out once and for all. For this would take the stress out of decision-making. Management would become easy.

'A primary characteristic of managing, particularly at higher levels, is the confrontation of change, ambiguity and contradiction. Managers spend much of their time living in fields of perceived tensions' (Quinn 1988: 3). Teasing out a 'typical' case of organisational and managerial life through our temporary model has illustrated one view of why ambiguity and contradiction are an essential part of the realities of management. It would be naive, mistaken, misleading, and arrogant of management and organisation development 'experts' to bring to their partnerships with clients the notion that this expertise brought with it a closer approximation to some kind of absolute 'truth' about organisations and management. The fact that some 'experts' act as though they had access to 'the answers' is a measure not of their effectiveness as partners, but of their ineffectiveness.

If there were some set of absolute 'truths' concerning organisations and management to be discovered out there our role with our clients would not be a partnership. That 'truth' would be a commodity to be sold on the open market to the highest bidder; our role would be one of supplier to customer, and our product, that 'truth'. Because what constitutes 'the right answer' depends upon each situation, depends upon opinions and what people 'mean by' key concepts, and so on, our role has to be in working through the inherent and resulting paradoxes of management with our clients: 'A research and intervention approach which explicitly seeks to sensitise to this paradoxical nature is therefore more appropriate than approaches emphasising linearity and consistency,' (de Cock and Rickards 1996: 238). Partnership means working together to explore what decisions and actions our clients will take as a result of exploring these paradoxes and complexities.

The Role of the 'Expert' in a Management and Organisation Development Partnership

Social scientists, organisational scientists, researchers into management take a professional interest in understanding the worlds in which managers work and try to succeed. My colleagues and I believe that our interventions into organisations make a positive difference, and much of this is based upon the enormous wealth of experience and research which is collectively available within the University, and through publications (in all forms) available in the wider, global community of management research. We, and our colleagues are, in one sense, 'experts' in the field.

But we are not 'experts' in the more traditional sense of the word, that of 'discovering' truths and passing such truths on to managers. Our expertise lies more in working alongside practising managers, trying to make sense of the complexities of their organisations and the aims they are trying to achieve through their actions. As Grint puts it (Grint 1995: 61) 'what managers do is to construct their world through language, and what management researchers do is (re)construct managers' worlds through both managers' words and their own (re)wording'.

Put into the context of our temporary evaluation model, this can be represented as four interrelated areas of help.

By undertaking research, we can find out about what organisations are doing, what seems to be working in various situations, and so on. This is straightforward information. But we can also help managers become more acutely aware of what is going on around them. Part of our role in part one of the model is about helping the managers we work with become more observant. One way of doing this is in helping them see the 'same' reality through a number of different perceptions. To do so, we need input from the other three elements of the model.

Our role in part 2 of the model is to help managers become more introspective and self-aware; to be clearer about what it is they intend to do, both within a specific business situation, and within a series of broader perspectives, such as their current job roles, their career with their existing organisation, and the broader stage in which they act out their personal careers. Again, this cannot work without explicit reference to the other parts of the model.

It is in the area covered by part three of the model that a great deal of the 'expertise' manifests itself in the wider academic community. Here, researchers are engaged in the seemingly endless task of exploring businesses and markets, strategy and product development, human resources and empowerment. The reason that it can be never ending lies in that, in principle, infinity of choices about how we classify the conceptual world.

Rather than getting closer to a 'truth', researchers are more often offering new ways in which we could look at organisations and management. They are not (or ought not to be) saying, 'This is the way the world of organisations and management is;' they are saying (or ought to be), 'Try looking at it this way, now that way, now another way.' In so doing new words and concepts are brought into the language. 'Unconscious', 'consumer', 'class', 'feminism' 'value chain', 'organisational culture', 'systems thinking', are a very small subset of the words, phrases and concepts which have been brought into being by the deliberate acts of 'experts'. Their purpose is to help managers make sense of situations; to provide a way of thinking about situations; to help define, in the first place, what a situation 'is'. The measure of their value as contributors to the search for positive managerial action is simply how useful they appear; how much they actually do help to make sense.

The contribution of the 'experts' to the territory covered by part four of the model is mixed. Some try to remain 'neutral' and quote facts and statistics to allow managers to make their own choices; others, often the higher profile 'experts' and gurus who command large audiences and sell millions of books, unashamedly advocate judgements and courses of action which positively encourage listeners and readers to follow or be damned.

To illustrate these points, I shall briefly explore two sample articles from an issue of *The British Journal of Management*, a respected publication dealing with the kinds of issues which confront managers in their daily activities.

'Stuck in the Middle'

One of the pieces of received wisdom in strategic management is taken from the work of Michael Porter (1980). It seems to suggest that it is bad news for a firm to be 'stuck in the middle'. At the risk of oversimplification, this says that firms, or their brands, or their products, do better if they are either cost-leaders (cheaper than their competitors), differentiated (better than their competitors), or niche players (working in specialist markets where there are few direct competitors). But as is pointed out by Cronshaw *et al.* (1994: 29), Sainsbury's seems to do well while occupying a market or brand position which is 'stuck in the middle'. So have they successfully disproved Porter's thesis? And if so, what should practising managers do? Should they be debating their own corporate or brand strategies?

The authors conclude that many people who have used Porter's model in the past have confused 'two types of knowledge which *exist* in business strategy' (op. cit. 31, my emphasis). They go on to point out that 'stuck in the middle' is 'essentially taxonomic', in other words, it is, as with part three of our model, simply a way of looking at corporate or product strategies (themselves, of course, essentially conceptual); however, 'what ought to be a taxonomy of generic strategies has been used as a basis for . . . assertions about the everyday business environment' (ibid.). In other words, people have used the framework as a basis for propositions meant to guide strategic action. The paper continues that 'None of the extensive literature on 'stuck in the middle' which we have surveyed produces serious evidence in support of these propositions' (ibid.). Put into terms we have been using, the authors claim that writers on the topic have confused parts three and four of our model: meanings (what 'stuck in the middle' means) and judgements (what should we do about it).

Mobility Barriers in the Grocery Industry

The other sample paper is entitled 'Assessing the Height of Mobility Barriers: A Methodology and Empirical Test in the UK Retail Grocery Industry'

(Carroll *et al.*: 1994). It contains a wealth of highly precise statistical information, based upon the examination of a significant range of variables taken through several canonical correlations, the third of which 'provides an example of how regression style coefficients can become inflated as a result of multicollinearity' (ibid. 10). The authors pick up where others have left their own analyses, identifying that they are going to explore the interactions between a number of 'units of analysis': 'entry barriers', 'mobility barriers', 'the niche', 'strategic groups', and 'the firm'.

One of the authors' main contributions to the debate is to introduce a further unit of analysis. As they write, 'Another way of approaching the issue is to study the absolute movement of firms', a concept they go on to define and explain: 'The firm's history provides the reference point. Movement is determined by changes in the firm's position regardless of the positioning of its competitors. The current study adopts this relatively novel approach' (1994: 3).

By so doing, the authors add another perspective: the 'here's another way of looking at it' approach. This is an element we have characterised as lying within part three of our model: it is another construction, a different interpretation. When used as another possible factor in organisational performance, as it is in the paper, it provides 'information' which managers could use 'to make more informed strategic choices' (op. cit. 17). This tempts managers to use the insights within the area of decision-making, which we have characterised as part four of the evaluation model.

Clearly, one aspect of making those choices is the degree to which such a construction of the 'reality' of the industry is useful. The paper's concluding paragraph reads:

> As industry observers have noted, the method did not generate any novel insights into the workings of the grocery retail industry. Consequently this study may be best thought of as a test of descriptive validity. It represents the initial empirical test of a complex and somewhat innovative method. While it may not have discovered new insights, it has demonstrated that it has charted a well-known area (grocery retailing) with acceptable accuracy. (ibid. 17).

In the end, what might have set out to be a contribution to parts three and four of the model for practising managers has provided more data, for part one, 'with acceptable accuracy'. This may be helpful to other academics; I am not sure how useful it will be to practising managers. As I suggested earlier, not all academics see operational organisations as their customers.

Finally, we return to our case study of the collapsing organisation. When and according to what criteria, or whose perceptions is an organisation a failing organisation? In the case there were different interpretations at play, including those of writers about the case. When things go wrong, many people seek explanations; we all want to learn from history. But such learning is not done in any 'pure' sense. It is done through the filters which our own experiences and our culture provide (Douglas 1992: 59). The different interpretations or perceptions about the case may have been of varying quality, with some perceptions being seen as more insightful than others. But they did not differ as a result of some being closer than others to some kind of 'ultimate truth' about the case.

Social Constructs and Management and Organisation Development

Those of us 'experts' who have the privilege of working closely with large numbers of practising managers, all of whom are looking for help, do well to manage both their own interventions and the expectations of the managers they work with. Despite the intimate interactions between the four elements of our evaluation model, our roles are different for each. In the heat of the moment; in the enthusiasm for getting it right; in the trust placed in us to help across the whole spectrum of the model; and in our own tendency, like anyone else's, occasionally to confuse interpretation with physical reality; we could kid ourselves and the managers we work with into thinking we have found 'the answer'.

One of the key areas in which this tendency may manifest itself is in ascribing causal relationships to categories we have created. The notion of cause carries with it the kind of certainty which, in organisational situations, is impossible to guarantee. We often seek 'laws', such as the laws of physics, which are summaries of what we know about what causes what. But we cannot even be sure of a 'law' that increasing prices causes reductions in sales. 'Being brutal' may or may not cause senior managers to take notice in a workshop; stripping out layers of management may or may not cause a company to become more efficient . . . The list of potential 'laws' is endless. But it is a spurious list simply because the 'entities' appearing in the list are not of the kind to which the notion of cause, as used in the physical sciences, is applicable. It is a fanciful notion, equivalent to the application of almost any other physical notion 'incorrectly'.

Constructs such as 'mission statement', 'market', 'strategy', and so on which are created by the 'experts' to provide props for the physical data they and we can see are like any other abstract concept. As words, they gather to them many nuances, sometimes even different meanings. As different people begin to make use of the concepts, each may place another nuance upon it; words and concepts can become highly rich in meaning over time. One of the reasons for this is that, as each construct is matched against different people's perceptions of physical 'reality' (often through the semantically rich medium of yet more such concepts), they suggest how those new nuances may be useful.

In this case, then, the role of the expert is to help us to avoid confusing physical facts with interpretations, or conceptual constructs with judgements about appropriate courses of action, which is largely what this chapter is about. What we have been exploring is the nature of the kinds of experience and learning we have been involved in over the past few years. It is important, as we describe and attempt to draw conclusions from that experience and learning in the main body of the book, that it is clear what we are claiming and what we are not claiming.

Management Development is Organisation Development

We are not claiming to have discovered hitherto hidden knowledge about management and organisation development; we shall be claiming that some of the constructs which we and other people have offered as ways of seeing management and organisation development may be very useful in helping managers make progress along the management and organisation development paths they wish to explore.

Management and organisation development interventions make no direct physical impact on organisations as such; they create no product; yet they change things. What they change is managers' minds, in ways which I shall describe in the later chapters of the book. And in changing managers' minds, such interventions thereby change those constructs which comprise organisations, markets, careers, and so on. In other words, as managers' minds change, so do their organisations.

The most powerful illustrations of this stem from the significant shaping of organisations which can come from the minds of strong and influential leaders. Not all leaders shape organisations in ways which they intend, as the Chief Executive Officer in the case earlier in this chapter found out, and as the case study in Chapter 9 illustrates. But organisations can become very clear reflections of the minds of individual leaders such as Frederick Taylor and Henry Ford (Morgan 1986), even reflecting specific aspects of those individuals' personalities (Kakar 1970). More recent research (Kakabadse 1996) demonstrates the significant impact on organisational success of the personal perception and interactions of members of the top team.

The impact people who are not at the top of organisations can have on the development of that organisation may appear to be less individually significant. Yet 'organisations will be shaped, in part, by the unconscious concerns of their members' (Fineman 1993: 25). Helping to manage those concerns, conscious and unconscious, means helping to develop the organisa-

tions themselves. When managers come to *realise* something, they do just that
– they make that which they have learnt become real.

Developing Our Understanding About Management and Organisation Development

The remainder of the book describes the principles upon which our interventions are based. In so doing, it covers all four elements which we gathered
together in our evaluation model: using cases to illustrate the 'facts' of some
of our experiences with organisations; exploring aims and intentions – ours
and those of our clients; offering concepts, models and definitions to help
clarify how we and our clients think about management and organisation
development; and offering advice, based upon what we have found to be
effective.

The thrust of this first chapter has been that in management and organisation development we have to recognise that there are no absolute 'truths'
concerning organisations and management; and that, as we engage in
attempting to learn from our own and others' experience, this process is
not simply one of gathering unproblematic 'facts', and piling them up into
some kind of intellectual haystack.

Learning about organisations and management is a complex process about
which we believe few people know a great deal. This is not because the
knowledge is still 'hidden', waiting to be 'discovered' by some pseudo-
scientific process of analytical research, but because we cannot in principle
disentangle ourselves from those perceptions and paradigms of our own
which determine which inferences and interpretations make sense for us. It is
important for us that we work on the specific issues of each organisational
challenge with the practising managers actually involved in those challenges;
we cannot make any sense out of an approach which treats practising
managers as laboratory rats, to be watched at their work – objects to be
studied.

The managers with whom we work are part of the process of *our* research –
a process which recognises that we are not seeking discovery, but trying to
make more sense:

> The world as seen by members is a world of 'here and now' objects, events
> and persons; an occasional world identified, recognised, made visible,
> created in and through the methods members have for making sense with
> each other. The work involved in making sense is, essentially, practical
> work directed towards realising aims and aspirations; the purpose is not
> knowledge for knowledge's sake. Moreover it is work done as interaction;
> as part of the activities it organises and of which it is constitutive. The

member is, above all, an investigator of his or her social world, as much concerned with how a social scene is organised, what kind of persons are party to it, what relationship they have with each other, what they are doing and why, as is the professional sociologist. (Benson and Hughes 1983: 195)

In summary, then, I am arguing that many of the 'things' which managers deal with day to day are 'constructs'. Because of the shared language and experience of managers within an organisational context, these constructs are 'socially constructed'; in other words, although organisations, markets, careers, and so on primarily exist in people's minds, it is not necessary for each manager to 'create' such constructs from scratch. Like all other abstract concepts in our daily lives – politics, savings, relationships – we learn them through the language we share with our colleagues, friends and families. Many such 'constructs' have been introduced to managers by academic 'experts'. Some disappear; others, such as 'organisational culture' seem to become part of the 'furniture'. In other words, some constructs resonate better, help make more sense of the ambiguities and complexities. But they are still constructs, concepts, abstract. 'Truths' about them are not found from experimentation in the 'real world', but from researching perceptions and mindsets of the people who use them.

Such an approach does not deny the value of rigour. I do not suggest that learning about organisations and management is a free-for-all in which what anyone says about anything is equally valid. Throughout the book, I shall be seeking ways in which rigour can be established by a variety of appropriate means.

Rigour and the Role of Definitions

For me, rigour comes from being able to make more and more sense of managerial learning and management and organisation development. It may now be clearer why I have not, like so many writers in their chosen fields, offered any definitions of such terms as 'managerial learning', 'management and organisation development', 'manager' or 'organisation'. When writers offer statements such as 'development *is* a continuing improvement of effectiveness within a particular system' they seem to imply that they have 'discovered' the true nature of 'development'. Although the implication may be simply that, for the purposes of the argument, and for the moment, this is what the author happens to mean by the term, it is very easy for readers to infer that this definition is the 'right' definition, that some kind of physical bedrock has been established upon which to build.

Clearly, the more people use words to mean the same things, the more likely they will be to make sense to one another, a point which I pursue in more depth in Chapter 5. The more people make sense to each other, the more likely it is that they will work effectively together. For me, this is the kind of territory in which I seek rigour – in the effectiveness of what is done, in the coherence and consistency which inform our management and organisation development activities. It does not reside in the apparent rigour of tight definitions. Commonality of meaning, and not of definition is what constitutes a more probable path to effectiveness. I could happily trot out a whole host of definitions of the key terms I use throughout the book. But I believe that this would hinder rather than help understanding.

The ambiguities of management and organisation development are confronted and explored throughout this book. What any of the key words and phrases I use in the book 'means' is 'defined' throughout both the book as a whole, and in each and every management and organisation development activity we share with our partners. The more we learn from these shared experiences, the more rigour we can apply to their use. And this is rigour based not upon limitation and restriction but based upon an ever-broadening set of experiences of what has helped, what has made sense, and, therefore, what is more likely to work and make sense in the future.

Making Management and Organisation Development Work

Situations such as that which confronted the Chief Executive Officer in our case study signal to managers that organisations do not always work as well as they would like them to. Sometimes my colleagues and I are called into organisations because they are seen to be falling behind in some way; at others, we are asked to work with senior managers to explore how to maintain a 'healthy' organisation – to keep it ahead of the game. It is clearly the case that some managers believe in, value and trust management and organisation development to be an effective part of either a cure or as prevention in terms of their organisational health.

For the sake of these and future partner managers it is important for us to be able to continue to address questions such as the following:

❑ Is management and organisation development simply a figment of someone's imagination – like the Emperor's new clothes?
❑ How does management and organisation development 'work'?
❑ Why does management and organisation development work?
❑ When is it appropriate and why does it sometimes fail to produce the desired results?
❑ Could we do it better? If so, how?

This book looks at ways in which we are continually seeking better and better answers to these questions. We believe those answers (none of which will ever be the 'right' answers) should be of interest not only to ourselves and our partners, but also to providers of management and organisation development and any practising manager interested in how to make people and organisations work better and smarter.

2 An Overview of the Management and Organisation Development Process

In this chapter I introduce a process which we currently follow in working in partnership with our clients to establish a programme of management and organisation development to help meet some specific aims.

Organising our thoughts in this complex area could be done in a variety of ways. I have chosen to do so round the chronological stages we often go through with a client. This is not because this is the best way, but because it may help keep track, and provide a set of guidelines which others may find useful. The framework is outlined in this chapter, and summarised at the end. It comprises 15 steps. I do not suggest that this framework reflects the 'right' way, and some readers will find it useful to modify the process to suit their local needs. We will probably continue to amend and refine the process as we continue to learn more.

The process 'model' is an 'ideal' representation. Few interventions follow this process exactly. In many cases, there are missing links and mismatches, often because some training managers are more driven by ticking the boxes of their training plan than by contributing to lasting change within their organisations. However, I present the model as such since it can be helpful to clients to recognise how management and organisation development can and should flow directly out of the business strategy.

Some steps in the process are simple, and are not the stuff of innovation; others, I believe, are complex, and represent areas of significant learning for us. These differences are reflected in the levels of detail I provide for each of the steps.

This chapter explores the outline and the early steps, up to the stage where it is important to delve deeper into the issues. Those more detailed, and subsequent, stages are explored in greater detail in the later chapters. (Chapter 1, in one sense, covered some of the issues of principle of step 1, for example.) But since the book is about the principles more than the practice of management and organisation development, it has not been written to follow the steps one by one, and in approximately equal detail. Therefore, this chapter provides an overview of those 15 steps.

1 ORGANISATION WANTS TO DO SOMETHING DIFFERENTLY (STRATEGY) OR SOLVE SOME CURRENT PROBLEM

Before any organisation invests in any kind of management and organisation development intervention which is likely to be considered 'successful', that there has to be some kind of recognition of where, as an organisation, it wishes to go. Given the 'constructed' nature of the organisation and its challenges (Chapter 1), this is not a simple matter of agreeing co-ordinates on a map; it is as much about exploring perceptions and meanings as it is about taking decisions about the future. Chapter 3 looks in more depth at some of these concerns.

One of the things I have learnt about management and organisation development interventions which have been considered successful has been that they happen far more frequently in organisations where the participating managers tend to be clearer and in greater agreement about the strategic thrust of the organisation, and how the intervention itself can be seen to put weight behind that thrust. This may sound trite, but I have come to recognise it as one of the most important critical success factors in programme design. Successful interventions are more likely to be aligned to the organisation's overall strategy. Many unsuccessful interventions appear to fail as a result of a lack of perceived fit between what the organisation is seeking to achieve in its broad strategy, and what goes into teaching and learning design.

2 ORGANISATION RECOGNISES ROLE FOR MANAGEMENT AND ORGANISATION DEVELOPMENT IN HELPING ACHIEVE STRATEGIC GOALS

For some organisations, this next step would be one of the 'natural' implications of a recognition that 'things have to change'. These would be organisations in which key decision makers believe in the significance of management and organisation development in helping to achieve corporate strategic change. People in such organisations are likely to believe also in the development and implementation of strategy for management and organisation development, with such a strategy being a clear adjunct to the broader corporate strategy discussed in step 1.

What Would a Strategy for Management Development Look Like?

For many organisations we have started to work with there is a puzzling gap: that between the core strategy the organisation is seeking to pursue, and the specific 'management and organisation development' activities available to them.

In the management and organisation development 'market' there are a whole host of management and organisation development 'products' and 'technologies' available, from courses on finance for non-financial managers to computer-based training in keyboard skills; from managerial effectiveness workshops for senior executives, to customer-care techniques for front-line staff. Sifting through these options without some strategic guidelines may not identify an appropriate or effective vehicle for addressing a specific need, nor a congenial 'supplier' from whom to purchase. Most 'products' have some merit; many 'suppliers' are worthy, experienced and well-meaning. However, fitting all these products and technologies together, and making sure that the results are directly in support of the corporate strategy demands some effort.

Some organisations employ in-house 'Management and Organisation Development' specialists for this very reason. Because it is potentially complex, and senior managers have too much else to do, the 'training' department or someone from Human Resources is seconded to the task of developing a 'strategy' for management and organisation development. In many cases, what the organisation ends up with is little more than a shopping list of items which have some resemblance to the stated organisational needs. Moreover, the in-house department can sometimes receive bitter criticism from people in the business because each 'course' fails to meet the expectations of managers who have, themselves, not taken sufficiently seriously their responsibility for helping set the broad, strategic agenda for development.

Most managers have had both good and bad experiences in learning situations. We frequently come across managers who insist that no programme they will be associated with should contain this or that element (often 'outdoor games', or 'academic theory'); or that every programme should be built around something they have found helpful (such as making people work into the early hours of the morning, or putting the key learning points on a plastic credit-card-sized 'crib sheet' for them to put in their wallets). This can all be very helpful, but our impression is that managers are often 'dabbling' in the 'technology', while leaving the 'strategy' to the experts. This seems to us to be the wrong way round.

Figure 2.1 provides a simple illustration of the relationships which we suggest should exist between Corporate, or Business Strategy; the organisation's Management Strategy; and its Management and Organisation Development Strategy.

Business Strategy

At this level, senior managers are responsible for setting the direction of the organisation, and putting in place the resourcing strategies to ensure that people can follow the chosen direction. It is the 'classic' territory of business

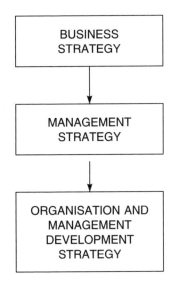

Figure 2.1 *Levels of strategy*

strategies, written about and developed widely in the 1980s and referred to in step 1 of our model. It is 'what' the organisation is trying to be or do.

It sets the *environment* for management and organisation development activities.

Management Strategy

Like most 'supporting' strategies, the Management Strategy concerns itself with the implications of the Business Strategy. It runs side by side with, and is as significant as the organisation's Marketing Strategy, its Operational Strategy, its Financial Strategy, its Information Systems Strategy, and so on. At this level, senior managers and specialists work together to decide the kinds of management processes, knowledge, skills, attitudes, competences, and so on which the organisation will need to have in place if it is to succeed in pursuit of the chosen Business Strategy. It is how the organisation will attempt to be or do what the Business Strategy defines.

It sets the demand for management and organisation development activities.

Management and Organisation Development Strategy

This is where the question 'How are we to develop those required processes, knowledge, skills, attitudes, competences for the appropriate people?' is addressed. This is where any discussions of the 'technologies' available is legitimate. It is an area in which, in our experience, senior managers often do not demonstrate the level of expertise they say they have.

It is the supply side of the management and organisation development activities.

Relating the Strategies Together: the Basics

Organisations which have recognised the differences between Management Strategies and Management and Organisation Development Strategies, can then segment their managers' activities appropriately. Senior managers need to take full responsibility for crafting the Management Strategies, in order, thereby, to provide clear direction for the 'providers' of management and organisation development activities. Those who fail to do so are asking too much of their Management Development or HR professionals. It is like asking your car dealer to provide you with the car he or she thinks you need, without clearly identifying where you may be wanting to drive, what size family you have, how much you are prepared to spend, whether you want a saloon, estate, off-road, or sports model, and so on. And then, when a vehicle is provided, based on the dealer's best guess, berating the dealer because the car does not have side-impact bars.

Broadly speaking, then, we believe that it is helpful if organisations recognise and respond to the need for senior management work at the Management Strategy level, to set out the 'demand' for management and organisation development, and then to take a co-operative role (rather than attempting to drive) in the supply side.

However, as with any 'systematic' approach, we also recognise that there needs to be a two-way flow between the levels of strategy. Although the primary drive is 'top down', much of what emerges from management and organisation development activities should have an impact on Corporate Strategy, and thereby on Management Strategy. It is not the purpose of the model to make management and organisation development totally subservient to the business. It is to help identify how, in both directions, links can be established and maintained between what an organisation wants to do as a business, and what actually takes place in the development of the people who make up the business at all levels.

Corporate Strategy or Business Unit Strategy?

Given the very different natures of organisations, it may be that there are different levels within those organisations for the focus of the 'corporate' strategy which drives the management and organisation development intervention. For a relatively small organisation like Relocation Ltd (case study in Chapter 4), the driving 'business strategy' relates to every aspect of the business; there were no subsidiary strategies at a lower level. When dealing with a much larger organisation, it may be necessary to take into account lower levels of strategy.

For example, we have done a great deal of work with Global Technologies. For some of this work we have to focus primarily on the overall corporate strategy: *a shift from product focus to customer focus* (see also pp. 290–2). However, for Corporate Liaisons, a business unit within Global Technologies, we needed to go down a level to explore how management and organisation development interventions may be able to help with their overall strategy: *customer solutions based upon strategic alliances*. Although part of Global Technologies, Corporate Liaisons is a Business Unit which has its own strategy to pursue; this strategy clearly supports the corporate direction, but has its own kind of focus.

Relating the Strategies Together: a Caveat

Clearly, this model is too simplistic to be applied as such without some recognition that, for example, some activities are better served by a more ad hoc approach. But we do recommend that such differences be seen as variations from the broad principle of the three levels of strategy development (Business Strategy, Management Strategy, Management and Organisation Development Strategy), rather than as the 'standard' approach. So long as the broad principle is applied as the 'default', then variations from that standard, such as those described in Chapters 3 and 4, are more likely to cohere as a strategy than to become a disconnected series of initiatives which could well work against one another.

There is an increasing number of organisations with whom we work which adopt this kind of 'segmentation' for their strategy development. The arguments of Chapter 1, and those embedded throughout the remainder of the book, suggest a number of reasons why this may be the case. The more that senior managers recognise the 'constructed' nature of the organisations, strategies, missions, markets, careers, and so on which they are tasked to manage, the more they will recognise the major significance to success of management and organisation development and other ways of exploring and managing these constructs.

As the Tech-Test case shows (in the Appendix, pp. 363–7), however, it may not always be the case that the identification of a role for management and organisation development in helping the organisation pursue its strategic goals is the result of a formal process such as the one we are describing. In many cases, what happens at this point depends upon the personal experiences of one or two of the key influencers. They may have been through, or they may know someone who has been through a positive learning experience, which, without a great stretch of the imagination, they can recognise as potentially the kind of experience which could help in dealing with whatever they see as the current strategic challenge.

The nature of this recognition is usually that managers in the organisation do not have the knowledge, skills or attitudes required to deal effectively with the implications of the corporate strategy. The 'solution' is to explore how management and organisation development may help deal with this challenge, often with 'expert' help.

3 ORGANISATION SELECTS A PARTNER TO HELP WITH THE MANAGEMENT AND ORGANISATION DEVELOPMENT ASPECTS OF THE STRATEGY

In some cases, senior managers may undertake to develop and run management and organisation development activities without any help from other people. In most cases, we expect senior managers to 'delegate' some aspects of such activities to people more in tune with what management and organisation development can offer.

Such people may be an organisation's own specialists. For a number of activities, these will be the partners who will work with the senior mangers to undertake the entire project or programme. Where, for whatever reason, external partnerships are sought to supplement in-house skills, it is often the case that such in-house specialists are delegated the task of setting up and managing those partnerships.

So far as this book is concerned, we shall have little to say which is directly based upon projects or programmes which have not directly involved us – programmes which may very successfully have been run by other external agencies or by in-house management and organisation development people. As explained in the Introduction to the book, our approach to learning about what we do is based upon action research rather than broadly based data gathering. Although this limits the quantity of situations from which we can seek to draw conclusions, we believe it vastly increases the quality of the information we learn from.

For the remainder of the process, therefore, I shall write from the point of view of what we have learnt from our own experiences of direct involvement in management and organisation development interventions with our client organisations.

4 ORGANISATION AND PARTNER CHECK THEIR MUTUAL UNDERSTANDING OF THE CHALLENGES AHEAD

Basic Background Data

Where a partner comes from outside the organisation in question, there is an inevitable understanding gap which has to be bridged before any progress can be made. It may also be the case that even where the partner is internal, the in-house management and organisation development department, for example, will have a gap to fill. In many cases, in-house consultants are not abreast of the latest thinking at the top of the organisation concerning corporate or management strategies. In-house partners may do well to check any assumptions concerning the business 'realities' as they are seen at the top of the organisation before proceeding; it is all too easy to be so close to a situation as to lose touch without realising it.

The partner has a clear responsibility to find out as much about the organisation and its circumstances as early as possible, and not simply to expect the managers within the organisation to provide all the necessary data. Obtaining and reading Company Accounts, official publications from the company such as brochures, and other background information is an important first step. But no matter how 'complete' this information may appear, it cannot tell 'the whole story'. Few published sources of information (including internal documentation such as Business Plans or even Invitations To Tender for management and organisation development projects) clearly set out how prospective management and organisation development activities link directly back through to the corporate strategy.

More importantly, official and internally-produced documentation are produced from a point of view which may, in itself, be 'part of the problem'. Management and organisation development interventions are about changing perceptions. Internally-produced documentation is likely to reflect some of those very perceptions which may need to change as part of the overall change process.

For example, a few years ago we were invited to work with a major multinational high-tech organisation which had decided that its competitive strategy was to be based upon a 'passionate' focus on customers. By the time we were called in, this 'strategy' had become 'the way we do things around here'. One of the documents we used to gain insight into the organisation was its Annual Report. Unfortunately, in all the 26 pages of its main section, customers were never mentioned. Instead, the 'heroes' were the technical experts who had produced the new products the company were trying to sell to these anonymous, invisible customers. The organisational culture shone through the document: pay lip-service to customers, but focus your attention on our products.

Broad Strategic Alignment

We have found it to be most helpful at this stage to ask our client sponsors to paint a very broad picture of their corporate strategy. By this we are not asking 'easy' questions, to be answered by Mission statements or by any other 'published' or 'official line'. We are asking the 'hard' questions, such as 'Why should your customers buy from you?' for a commercial organisation operating in a competitive market; or 'Why should your organisation not be scrapped?' for a public sector organisation or department. Unless the strategy as stated actually deals with these kinds of hard question, it is unlikely to be robust enough to support both a Management Strategy which makes sense and a Management and Organisation Development Strategy which will deliver any lasting value.

Hard though such questions are, they do not, at this stage of the partnership, need to produce complex answers. For Relocation Ltd, for example (case study in Chapter 4), the driving corporate strategy could be summarised as:

> Increasing margins from existing business activities, maintaining quality and customer focus as our key competitive strengths.

As the sample shows, the definition of the 'strategy' does not need to be detailed; it just needs to make sense in the light of the competitive and/or strategic position of the company or organisation. We are not advocating in-depth analysis of detailed business plans before moving on. The definition simply needs to enable all parties to be clear about the key issues, themes and priorities for the business, and for it to be possible to work towards a coherent set of management and organisation development aims and activities. In Relocation Ltd's case, one of the key aspects of the earlier stages of the intervention was work done on that very strategy by the senior management team. This work did not change the strategy; it helped validate it, and identify what needed to be done in order to help turn the strategy into reality.

Cascading from that corporate strategy, the management strategy which the intervention needed to relate to could similarly be stated briefly and succinctly:

> Managers will need to balance the needs of customers against the overall contribution to the business of their activities. This means seeking opportunities for working across teams within the business, and exploring at all times ways in which projects can be optimised to maintain quality while increasing margins.

Again, there is considerably more documentation which was available for examination at the time, and we clearly took note of the details contained in this documentation. But these few words provide a significant backdrop to the initial kinds of design and development considerations we have to make when assessing the enormous variety of ways in which we could occupy the time of the managers of the company. Such additional documentation would be reviewed during the iterative design stages (9 to 13 in our 15–step model); such detail at this stage would get in the way of establishing the broad principles for the partnership and potential intervention.

One further example to illustrate the simplicity which is required at this stage comes from our work with Corporate Liaisons, a subsidiary of Global Technologies (see Chapter 4 for the case study). The very broad corporate strategy for this group (*customer solutions based upon strategic alliances*) produced a coherent but simple top level management strategy: *the development of managers who are ready, willing and able to undertake the investigation, establishment, growth and nurture of selected strategic alliances.*

Clarity in Corporate Strategy

This is not a book about corporate strategy, although we hope that many of the issues explored within it will have an impact on how senior managers think about strategy formulation and implementation. However, it is clear to us that one of the key things which our management and organisation development process does highlight for our clients is the frequent lack of clarity concerning their overall strategy.

Most of our client organisations, by the time they come to us, have spent some time and effort on 'strategy'. Many have written documentation attesting to this effort, including Mission statements, Vision statements, Business Plans, and so on. In our experience, what is often lacking in organisations is clarity for managers concerning what these words actually mean in terms of what they should do in their daily jobs. This is especially the case for managers who have not been directly involved in developing such strategies.

In many cases, one of the key aims of a management and organisation development intervention is precisely to give such managers an opportunity to explore answers to this practical question. However, even in these kinds of intervention we do sometimes have to confront the fact that the corporate strategy is either short on detail, short on a sense of reality, or just plain unimplementable.

The Suitability of the Partnership

Based upon initial information, and upon clarification through conversations with the organisation's management and organisation development sponsors, the partner now has the opportunity to evaluate and report to the client on the feasibility and desirability (in the partner's opinion) of the management and organisation development programme. Such evaluation needs to be done with a high level of integrity, ideally using some kind of process such as the evaluation model we introduced in Chapter 1 as a means of checking understanding.

Initial reading and information-seeking questions will establish the 'facts' of the situation: organisation's size, market, espoused strategy, and so on. Intentions can then be explored, often in the form of questions about 'aims' for any management and organisation development intervention. Checking meanings, easily overlooked, helps reduce the chances of misunderstandings; for example, we often check our understanding of a client's situation by asking what would happen if the proposed intervention were not to take place. And answers to such questions help tease out the client's attitudes and judgements about the current situation and the broad picture of the world after the intervention has taken place.

By going through this simple evaluation model, we can expect to end up with a reasonably clear, if rather broad picture of what the client organisation is looking for. Not surprisingly, under almost all circumstances the client states that the intervention should improve matters. Having explored thus far, we have to decide whether we are in agreement with that judgement. Unless such a partner can support the organisation's strategies at all three levels, any subsequent intervention is likely to suffer from a lack of motivation and commitment.

Support may come in a number of forms. For example, at the cognitive level, the organisation's strategies may appear doomed to failure. The business strategy, for example, may appear to be far removed from any 'workable' approach. Desperate times may call for desperate measures, but if the chances of success appear to be very small then partnering with them in a management and organisation development venture would be, in our view, improper.

Most 'problems' at this stage, however, do not emanate from obviously 'crazy' strategies, but from 'flawed' strategies. An example may help:

INISYS CONSULTING: A CASE OF A 'FLAWED' BUSINESS STRATEGY

It was as I was writing the first draft of this section of this chapter that I received an enquiry from a prospective client. His business was Information Technology, largely specialising in systems integration. He said that it was becoming clear to the organisation that the systems integration business was in maturity, and that the future depended upon a shift of direction. His organisation's business strategy in response to this recognition was to move into broader-based Information Systems and Information Technology consultancy.

The implicit management strategy was based on existing consultants (with technical skills in systems integration) becoming skilled in this new kind of business venture. The implicit management and organisation development strategy was to develop skills in a number of defined consultancy areas, such as Feasibility Studies, Business Data Definition, and so on. According to our conversation, the client's existing consultants 'did not have a clue what a Feasibility Study looks like'. Consequently, the request was for a series of modules which would teach the consultants all about these consultancy activities.

All of which makes superficial sense; it may be challenging, but not impossible. However, when exploring what kinds of methodology the organisation had chosen to work to or to develop, and within which the consultants would develop their skills, it became clear that such a decision had not been taken. No problem, so long as selecting or defining such a set of methods would be part of the overall management and organisation development programme. It had not been seen to be, so far, part of that programme. Further investigation into why this might be, led back to the business strategy.

Deciding how to deal with the 'methodology' issue, we said, was dependent upon the organisation's competitive strategy. This relatively small organisation was going into a market place already populated by a fair number of experienced, professional, large and successful consultancies. If the competitive strategy was to compete against them on price, for example, then the selection of a methodology would be driven by acquisition of tools already designed, tried and tested, which enabled quick and efficient consultancy exercises in which, perhaps by handing most of the work to the end-user client, the consultancy project price could be kept to a minimum. If, again for example, the competitive strategy was to differentiate on the basis that each consultancy exercise would be a one-off, using none of those predefined methods which have been developed to deal with generic problems rather than the problems of this client at this time; that each project would be dealt with from first principles; then the 'selection' of a methodology would not form a prerequisite for the management and organisation development intervention. Rather, in this case, one would need to explore the feasibility of such a strategy actually working.

In this case, having explored one or two other potential strategic scenarios, our prospect went back to his management to find answers. The strategic decisions may have been taken; there may have already been clarity in the minds of these senior managers about how they were going to take on the competition. But since that strategy was not informing either the management strategy or the consequent management and organisation development strategy, it might just as well not exist. And as a non-existent strategy, in practice, it could not form the basis from which to take further steps.

Even if the business strategy is sound and consistent, the organisation may be firmly set upon a management strategy which is singularly inappropriate. Let us take another example:

GLOBAL TECHNOLOGIES: NORTH AMERICAN SALES DIVISION

It is often the case that, in times of financial difficulties, senior managers will revert to behaviours they feel comfortable with, and which they seem to trust to get them 'back on track'. It may be that they recognise that the behaviours which may have appeared to be successful in the past were so because they were performed in a very different kind of economic and social climate. However, during times of change, people often reinterpret both the present and the past in ways which may not always accord with all the evidence available.

In this case, which is an adjunct to the case on pages 112–14 in Chapter 4, the North American Sales Director decided to 'hijack' the workshop, and to use it to introduce what appeared to be a 'return' to the old style of command-and-control management. There had been, during the past two years, a lot of change within Global Technologies. Having come from a very traditional, hierarchical, functional, sales-oriented, numbers-driven, formal, efficient and tough culture, they had been trying to make a major turn towards customer focus, empowerment and process-orientation. According to some people in the company, the pendulum had swung way too far, and management had lost control; this was, they said, the reason why the company was haemorrhaging. Despite the research evidence which we and others had accrued to demonstrate the inefficacy of this style of management within a process-oriented organisation (Edwards and Peppard 1994), the North American Sales Director was sufficiently convinced of the need to swing the pendulum back that he rejected, for his patch, the workshop as designed.

By mutual consent, we withdrew from the North American round of the workshop. For the North American Sales Director our approach would be contradictory to what he wanted the workshop to say about managing. For us there was, in his redesign, a clear mismatch between business strategy (the overall agenda for change, built round process-orientation) and the management strategy he wished to pursue. There was, in consequence, an inherent contradiction in the redesigned workshop which we could not support.

But these kinds of concerns may not always close off the potential for collaboration. Where the soil is sufficiently fertile, we see management and organisation development starting as soon as we are in discussion with clients. And this is part of the same shift we discussed at the start of this chapter. Given that our focus is upon learning and not teaching, our role, and that of any others in a similar position, has also shifted: from provider of 'teaching products' to facilitators of learning. In other words, whatever we do to define a specific event or set of events for a client, the intervention has already started.

An analogy may help here. The traditional relationship between management and organisation development professionals and clients was predicated upon the client knowing what he or she wanted, and simply cataloguing the elements required. This was like a shopper buying cough medicine from a pharmacist. Research into management and organisation development continues to improve our understanding of what works and does not work for different kinds of organisational 'ills'. Clients ask for cough medicine, but we ask about the symptoms – hoping to get closer to causes. In situations where we believe that the problem may not be helped by the 'medicine' (as when a doctor diagnoses lung cancer, and advises significantly different treatment), we explore this with the client.

Some clients may wish to ignore the advice (as some patients wish to ignore a doctor's diagnosis); it is at this point that we have to withdraw. Others, however, may recognise that a great deal of the value gained from a management and organisation development intervention starts well before any formal events take place; it starts with an effective dialogue concerning the validity of the three levels of the client's strategy: business, management and management and organisation development. In many cases, the effectiveness of the dialogue undertaken at this point with an honest, objective outside agency can save the client organisation a great deal of wasted time and effort in pursuit of learning aims which are either unachievable, or are out of step with the needs of the organisation and its managers as they face up to their own organisational challenges.

There is, however, another possible reason why withdrawal may be necessary. This is where there is a lack of fit between the values of the organisation and the potential partner. Participants in any management and organisation development intervention are likely to be asked to question their own and their organisation's values if the intervention is to be more than a simple cosmetic exercise. Value clashes are among the most disruptive influences on effective learning. Not only should a partner in management and organisation development believe the brief, they must also believe *in* the brief.

At this point we need to be clear about the kind of thing the brief represents. In Chapter 3 we discuss some issues concerning the perceived aims of management and organisation development interventions. One key message in that chapter is to seek out and deal with what turn out to be incompatible aims within a single intervention. One of the purposes of the model we use at this point of the process (the Management Development Grid, Chapters 3 and 4) is to stimulate debate which is likely to tease out such incompatibilities. We shall return to this point when we explore step 8 of the 15-step process.

Confirming Broad Understanding

The other key purpose of the Management Development Grid is to help identify the kinds of principles which will most suitably be applied to best meet the aims implicit in the business and management strategies. As such, the Management Development Grid has become one of the simple 'technologies' we apply to the craft of management and organisation development, and as such, we use it in practice with clients to achieve mutual clarity concerning what it is the organisation is trying to do, and why they are trying to do it. As we suggest in Chapter 3, one of the most frequent questions we ask at this stage of the process is, 'What happens if you don't do this?'

The output from this kind of discussion leads to the setting of 'aims' for a management and organisation development intervention on two different levels. The first, which is the result of the conversation which the 'What happens if you don't do this?' kind of question opens up, sets a very broad agenda – almost a 'mission' for the intervention. It enables us to match this 'mission' against the kinds of 'driving forces' for that intervention.

Our experience is that this higher level of programme aims has often been overlooked until we raise the issue with clients. Typically, clients will have worked for some time on the next level – the more specific and detailed aims, which we explore when we look at step 8 of the process. But many are unprepared for this kind of higher-level analysis. It is often the case that the dialogue stimulated by this higher-level discussion is seen to be of significant value both to the client, who sees the challenge in a new and often clearer light, and, of course, to ourselves, as it enables us to have a much firmer handle on what the intervention is all about.

5   PERSON OR PERSONS TAKE PRIMARY RESPONSIBILITY FOR MANAGING THE MANAGEMENT AND ORGANISATION DEVELOPMENT PROGRAMME OR PROJECT

At one level, this is simply the normal practice of appointing a Project Manager for any project. At another, it is the establishment of a key relationship for both client and partner. My colleagues and I refer to this role as Management Development Consultant in our relationships with partners. The Management Development Consultant has a number of activities to peform, as follows:

❏   identify and clarify the client's requirements to ensure there is a close fit between the needs of the client and the competencies of the School;

❑ undertake an agreed number of days research with the client organisation, to determine the gap between current state and desired state that needs to be bridged through the management development programme;

❑ bring together a team of programme developers who have the requisite skills and experience to design a programme to meet the client's objectives;

❑ co-ordinate faculty, and resources for the successful delivery of the programme;

❑ facilitate on programmes to ensure effective learning;

❑ monitor the progress of managers during the programme in order to facilitate learning transfer and evaluate the programme input;

❑ conduct follow-up research and co-ordinate any further development work.

These activities are described in more depth throughout this chapter, and in other chapters.

6 DEFINITION OF THE 'DESIRED STATE' (WHAT MANAGERS WILL NEED TO DO DIFFERENTLY IN ORDER TO HELP ACHIEVE THE CHANGE DEFINED IN 1)

By this step of the process there is a clear intention by both partners to go ahead with some kind of management and organisation development intervention. Although neither partner at this stage can be sure what this intervention will look like (some inexperienced clients would dispute this, although those we have worked with for some time recognise that there is still a great deal of work to be done before any design activities take place), there is a broad recognition that exploring the potential for a management and organisation development intervention as a positive contributor to the organisation's strategic direction is worth an investment.

A management and organisation development intervention is a change project. As with any other kind of change project, it is helpful to be clear where we want to get to, and where we are starting from. By identifying these end and start positions, we can better understand the 'gap' between them, and put in place plans to bridge that gap. It will be in the later chapters of the book that we shall look at what we have learnt about building such bridges. For the remainder of this and in Chapter 5, we shall explore the two ends of this process – what we call the 'desired state' and the 'current state'. We explore the 'desired state' before the 'current state' because we take an outcomes-driven approach (see Chapter 3); what drives the process is where the client wants to get to, not what kinds of management and organisation development 'products' are available.

Strategic 'Themes'

Because of the dynamics of the changing market place of the mid- to late 1990s, it is not surprising that we come across some common themes in our exploration of these expressed 'desired states' with our clients. Many of them are focused on getting closer to customers; many recognise the need for managers to be 'more commercially aware'; many are advocating the benefits of 'teamworking' (although this means very different things to different people, and is, we believe, even among management and organisation development professionals, a poorly understood concept); and most talk about, even if they find it hard to implement, some kind of process orientation for the future. It is tempting, therefore, to treat this part of the intervention process lightly, to assume that, because we have heard the words before, we know, very quickly, where the client organisation wants to be.

Many such 'desired state' pictures are relatively abstract, based upon what managers broadly believe the picture needs to look like. For example, in the mid-1990s so many organisations include in their picture some kind of 'Teamworking'. Its inclusion is not by chance, the outcome from a thorough thinking through of a strategic situation with the result that 'Teamworking' is inevitable. Its inclusion is often because managers have 'been told' that 'Teamworking' is part of the future, and that if they don't 'do it' their organisation will not be able to compete.

So in many cases, we may have 'heard it all before', and therefore may wish to reach into our pockets and pull out the management and organisation development 'solution' which we have applied to the most recent 'Teamworking' story. Our experience is that this is inappropriate. As we progress further through the book, we shall see why such an approach is unlikely to be successful in terms of implementation. But even at this stage, as we work with our client to define the 'desired state' it is inadvisable to leave the picture so imprecise. The major risk lies in the fact that what we make of such a vague and abstract picture may be very different from what the client makes of it.

As an example, let us explore a phrase prospective clients often introduce into our early conversations: 'Business Process Redesign'. However precisely consultants and academics may try to define this term, it is made up of three very common words in our language. This, added to the apparent popularity of the broad 'idea' associated with the phrase (roughly, radical changes in the ways an organisation does its business – radical changes seem to be on many organisations' agendas, at least at the cognitive level), seems to have led to a proliferation of different ways in which people use the term (Edwards and Peppard 1994). No matter how hard we may try to legislate for the 'proper' meanings of words and phrases, once they are in common parlance, they take on a life of their own, being used in different ways by different people. Words and phrases which refer to socially constructed concepts, such as 'organisation' 'hierarchy', empowerment' and 'Business Process Redesign', will continue to behave in this way since they have no concrete 'reality' against which to be measured.

Therefore, when prospective clients introduce concepts such as these into our conversations, we have to do what we can to check what *they* mean. 'I want a transformational programme which enables our managers to become empowered to take a strategic focus for the global market,' may be offered by a prospective client as a succinct way, using language which people from a school of management ought to find familiar, to get straight to the point. When we pedantically ask the client what he or she means by all this, it may be that the client will think, 'Who is the stupid one here? You because you don't even understand your own language; or me, because you don't think I can speak it properly?' In either case, there is the risk that the client will feel rejected.

Living and working as we do in an environment where these concepts are being explored in depth, with many different organisations, and with a degree of rigour in their definitions, we are likely to see them differently from a manager who may be trying to 'picture' a relatively newly met idea in the context of her or his own organisation. The more vague the picture remains, the more likely it is that we shall see it differently. We work with the client, therefore, in refining these pictures. This does not necessarily mean 'lecturing' to the client on the relevant subject; it does mean exploring what, for this client and organisation, the application of such idea would look like on the ground.

Focus on Behaviours

At step 4 we will have had the opportunity to set out the broad background to the proposed intervention. In the sense that the strategies have been defined (especially the Management Strategy), thus far we have defined the 'desired state'. But 'background' is a good word for what we have done so far. All we have done is to provide the background to the picture; the backdrop to the stage upon which real managers will need to act out their roles for any strategic change to take place anywhere than within the imagination of the planners.

In exploring the 'desired state', therefore, we specifically try to focus upon what behaviours the client wants managers to exhibit as a direct result of the intervention; what should they do differently? This focus upon what managers should actually do helps focus on what the desired state would look like 'on the ground'. It is not always easy at first for our client sponsors to answer this kind of question at any length.

We focus on managerial behaviours primarily because, at a practical level, what matters to the client is what managers do, since it is what managers do which makes the business work. What managers think, what kind of 'culture' people infer from those behaviours, how an organisation is structured, and so on are all of potential significance, since they have an enormous influence, through influencing thoughts and feelings, on what managers do. And as we set about designing, developing and implementing a management and organisation development intervention, we shall have to move behind the 'facade' of perceived behaviours. But *at this stage of the process*, we remain firmly focused on behaviours.

This may seem perverse. After all, my colleagues and I work within one of the prime sources of the kind of constructs which have been developed precisely to explore the bases of organisational and managerial behaviours. So why this narrow focus, this rejection of such useful devices?

In practice, we do use them, but both with caution, and with our eyes focused on managerial behaviours. For example, should it appear appropriate, we may use McKinsey's 7S model (Waterman *et al.* 1980) as a prompt for the client to explore those desired behaviours as they relate to Staff, Skills, Style, and so on. Along with this, there are many other tools we can and do use which faculty at Cranfield have developed in their exploratory work. But in all cases, the aim remains to use them to help the client critically explore the changes in managerial behaviours which the intervention seeks to generate.

Unless we remain so focused, there is so much more room for misunderstanding. Valuable though such constructs as 'culture', 'structure' and 'style' may be, they remain constructs, and as such mean different things to different people. At this stage of the process, it is highly likely that what we mean by 'empowerment', for example, and what a client means by the same word will carry some very different connotations. The most effective ways in which we believe we can explore those different connotations is to ask the client to explain what he or she means by 'empowerment' in terms of what an empowered manager would or would not do. It may be one of the goals of a management and organisation development intervention to help generate a situation in which there is a high degree of common use of such key terms, and in Chapter 5 we shall reflect further on what such common use of constructs can tell us about people who work together. But at this stage, to avoid making potentially inaccurate assumptions about what such terms mean to different people (including ourselves), we focus as much as we can on behaviours.

As we suggested earlier, because we do not see ourselves in the business of providing management and organisation development 'products', helping to refine clients' thinking about changes in managerial behaviour is a legitimate part of our role. So long as we can establish this as a basis for us to work in the partnership, we can then get on with the job of helping the client become more confident in the behavioural outcomes desired from an intervention.

Confirming 'Desired State'

The outcome from this step of the process is provisional. It is an activity which will make more sense once we have undertaken the next step, which is to explore the 'current state'. It will be by comparing the desired state with the current state that we can identify the gaps, and use these as a basis for defining the broad learning aims for the intervention.

7 'CURRENT STATE' EXPLORED, WITH REVIEW OF THE GAP BETWEEN DESIRED AND CURRENT STATES

A client's definition of the 'desired state' is a construct, not a picture of 'reality'. But any picture of the 'current state' will also be a construct. In the sense established in Chapter 1 there is no 'current state' which exists to be studied. But there are perceptions: those of an organisation's customers, its shareholders and all the other key stakeholders. For the purposes of most management and organisation development activities, the perceptions of greatest concern are those of the sponsors, and of the 'target audience' of any proposed intervention.

The processes of researching and reporting on an organisation and its managers' current state are crucial to the design, development, delivery and evaluation of a management and organisation development intervention. They are processes which demand sensitivity and skill. They are processes in which my colleagues and I feel we have made a great deal of progress in recent years. The principles which we apply to these processes are fundamental to understanding our approach to management and organisation development, and are explored in depth in Chapter 5.

8 BROAD AIMS FOR A PROGRAMME DRAWN UP AND AGREED – PROGRAMME POSITIONED

The output from step 7 enables us to explore with the client the implications of the perceived gaps between the desired and current state. It is at this point that we can refine our initial understanding of the need, and make recommendations concerning what may be viable learning aims to bridge the gap. It is also at this point that we are able to return to some of the positioning frameworks, such as the Management Development Grid, to reinforce our mutual perceptions of the kind of intervention which is to be developed.

The other positioning activity which takes place at this point is positioning the proposed intervention within the broader management and organisational strategies of the organisation. It is often the case that many of the kinds of change the client is seeking to introduce are beyond the scope of any management and organisation development intervention. Where behavioural change is a desired outcome, the organisation will need to back up the learning from a management and organisation development intervention with appropriate supporting systems and so on. An organisation which wants to use management and organisation development to help its sales managers to establish long-term partnerships with customers, but which continues to reward those people solely on revenue earned on a quarterly basis will create problems for itself. Similarly, one which wants to introduce teamworking throughout, but makes no amendment to appraisal and reward systems which are individual and implicitly internally competitive will also be asking too much of management and organisation development.

Positioning a management and organisation development intervention within a broader management strategy means aligning the intervention with other aspects of that strategy. But not all those aspects may be immediately apparent to a client. Many management and organisation development interventions fail to achieve their aims because less tangible supporting changes may be missing from the management strategy. Among the most common of these is found among the managers of those participating in a management and organisation development intervention. Part of the positioning process is about these managers recognising and fulfilling their roles in both preparing participants and debriefing them on their return.

This is not just a cosmetic exercise, however. Especially in cases where participants are relatively senior and experienced, many management and organisation development activities generate significant motivation for, and suggestions how to implement change in line with the organisation's overt strategic goals. Yet many organisations remain almost completely unprepared for the energies which a management and organisation development intervention can unleash. Investing significant time and money in developing managers, only to greet returners with in-trays full of the past weeks' accumulated work, is likely to produce very low return on that investment.

Increasingly, management and organisation development is becoming an enormously potential vehicle for the kinds of strategic change which so many organisations are trying to implement. Effective positioning of such management and organisation development means being prepared to capitalise upon the investment in development rather than ignoring its messages.

In our experience, this remains one of the least understood and least developed areas of management and organisation development. Senior managers are only slowly realising how to harness the potential power of management and organisation development. Chapter 10 explores some of the principles behind this further.

9   BROAD CONCEPTUAL LEARNING DESIGN DRAWN UP AND AGREED

This process is driven by the kinds of behavioural outcomes which are agreed to be required to meet the learning aims. It starts with a broad set of sketches which take into account some of the parameters within which we are working. These will not only include the learning aims, and the current and desired state, but also some of the practical constraints, such as budgets, timescales, and participants' availability. They set the broad boundaries between the achievable and the desirable.

In Chapters 7, 8 and 10 of the book, I explore in depth some of the principles we apply to understanding and using managerial learning. It is at this point that, for example, we begin to agree the relative weightings to be placed upon such potential components as knowledge acquisition, understanding, organisational values, personal development, and so on. These are never completely separate from one another in how managers learn, but different interventions will demand different kinds of emphasis on these 'components'. It will be here, for example, that we will need to agree on such questions as, 'Does becoming more customer focused here mean knowing more about customers, understanding how to be customer focused, wanting to be more customer focused, or having a deep appreciation of customers and their needs?'

Questions such as these are not asked to find out 'the right' answers, but to test out our and the client's assumptions about the outcomes and the consequent learning aims. The better we can explore such questions, the more likely we are to create an intervention which actually achieves those aims. In the past, many of the less successful attempts to facilitate managerial learning failed simply because such questions were never asked.

The answers which we generate to these questions enable us to establish, in broad terms, what contributions we want from the 'experts' who will make up the tutorial team for a programme. It helps us select the 'right person for the job'. Colleagues of ours may be equally qualified in their subject matter, but they will differ according to their approaches to learning. We identify our team members on the basis of how well they will help achieve the outcomes as much as how well they 'know their subject'.

10   MICRO DESIGN (OF SEPARATE 'COMPONENTS') BY 'EXPERTS'

My colleagues and I in the Management Development Unit are not 'experts' in each of the disciplines represented by our Faculty. We defer to our peers on subject matter. But we work closely with our 'experts in their chosen field' in helping to maintain within the broad design a fully integrated learning experience for the participating managers.

In many cases, we are able to assemble our team of experts for a briefing before they each set out to design their individual contributions. These briefings have a number of aims:

❑ to share with the team members what we have agreed so far with the client, concerning the strategic context for the intervention, the current and desired states, the learning aims, and the broad conceptual design
❑ to check our mutual understanding of the purposes of the intervention and each team member's individual contribution (in terms of learning aims)
❑ to enable each team member to see where and how his or her contribution fits within the whole learning experience, and opportunities for synergy between the parts
❑ to provide an opportunity for further fine tuning of the conceptual design

This process enables each 'expert' to position his or her contribution within the broader contexts both of the intervention and of the organisation's programme(s) of change.

11   LEARNING INTEGRATION, BOTH BEFORE THE INTERVENTION (DESIGN), AND DURING THE INTERVENTION, AS NEW INSIGHTS ARE ACHIEVED

As the first run (sometimes a Pilot) of an event approaches, the Management Development Consultant brings all the resources together, and designs the components between the 'modules'.

The Management Development Consultant remains responsible for the entire learning event, even though some of the components are the primary responsibility of the 'experts'. No matter how well each contributor has prepared his or her contribution as part of an integrated whole, he or she will not witness the event over all. At the interfaces between the component parts (often at the beginning and end of each day), links between the overall learning activity and the various components need to be drawn together.

Participants will rarely have been involved in much of the learning design, and some may have difficulty building the overall picture – how what I have just experienced today both links with the other learning, and with my own role and learning needs.

The Management Development Consultant provides or facilitates those links, sometimes using vehicles such as 'learning points' sessions, or 'learning logs'. These serve to maintain managers' focus as much on the broader picture of why they are here, as upon the specific learning from each part of the programme. In most cases, the same Management Development Consultant will facilitate whatever 'action points' or 'implementation planning' sessions may be used to round off this stage of the learning process.

12   CHECKING AS WE GO HOW REALITY IS MATCHING DESIGN FOR LEARNING

This book is about people who happen to be managers. People are different from each other. No matter how much work we may have done before an event with the participating managers, the dynamics of individual personalities make every event different. Different questions will be asked, different concerns will be raised. This will mean that every event has the potential for deviating from expectations in different and unpredictable ways. The Management Development Consultant has to steer a course between those deviations and the planned programme, ensuring that deviations are productive and helpful, while maintaining the integrity of the overall learning design.

That is fine for the group as a whole. But groups of managers, even those from the same organisation, or even the same team within the same organisation, are comprised of individuals with personal concerns and perceptions. The group as a whole may be 'on track', but individuals may need extra help or attention. The Management Development Consultant spends social time with individuals, checking how they are doing. This means not just in terms of the learning aims, but also in terms of the managers as people. Being away from their normal environment often means being no longer 'in charge'; even senior and experienced managers can become 'institutionalised' if they are treated simply as 'empty vessels' to be filled with learning.

Our approach recognises the humanity of participants. Learning experiences are human experiences, and we deal with them as such. As client sponsors and managers themselves become more accustomed to this perception, we find ourselves incorporating into more of our events, one-to-one counselling sessions in which managers have the opportunity to explore on a personal basis the implications for them as people, as well as managers, of the learning they are going through.

13   PLANNING FOR IMPLEMENTATION

The dynamic and often interactive nature of a learning event produces potential outcomes which can be either foreseen or unexpected; and this can be both at the organisational and the individual level. Similarly, the wide variety of the kinds of aims from management and organisation development interventions means that planning for implementation of learning can take many forms.

The traditional 'action points' session is less common these days. In-company projects, too, are not so readily adopted as 'the' means of implementation, largely because so many such projects have produced disappointing results. This, in turn, is often the result of poor positioning of the intervention, as we discussed in Step 8.

Consequently, in practice, it is often at Step 8 that we plan with our client sponsors the kind of implementation strategy which should most fit the overall learning design in the context of the management and organisation strategies. In most cases, participants know in advance the broad strategic approach to implementation of learning which has been agreed, and start this planning at the beginning of an event, or, preferably, before that. It is increasingly the case that we work with managers on the basis that any specific learning event which we may work through together is seen as just one step along a continuing road of development. The management and organisation development intervention as a stand-alone activity is disappearing as we develop longer-term partnerships with our clients and the managers who work in their organisations.

Where, for example, managers document their learning and its implications in some form of 'personal strategy', this document will frequently have been developed before the intervention, and remain active long after it. Management and organisation development may receive significant enhancement from 'off-site' events, but they neither begin nor end at the School.

14   RE-ENTRY – DEBRIEFING AND LEARNING TRANSFER
STRATEGIES

As managers return to 'everyday life', the principles discussed in Step 8 become most urgent. The organisation, as constructed through the perceptions of the participating managers, will have been changed. But others' perceptions may not have changed. Managers are challenged at this point to continue the (re)construction process with their colleagues. Debriefing, 'cascading', Focus Groups, learning reports, and many other techniques are used to help this process. The better these can have been planned for and prepared, the more effective they will be. The sooner they can be implemented, the more likely they are to be effective.

This is because, on re-entry, there is a form of 'cognitive dissonance', between the perceptions managers bring back with them, and those they (and their colleagues) held before the event. Those who remained may be fearful of the threat to the integrity of their perceptions which returners pose (in ways which managers who attend events may themselves have been fearful – see the introduction to Chapter 7). This fear often takes the form of joking behaviour ('You've had a jolly, now it's back to reality'), or even of overt hostility, ('Don't try to brainwash me with your new Management School theories').

In Chapter 7, the learning process is recognised as more than simply intellectual. Re-entry strategies, to be effective, need to be built around the principles of learning, which this book is all about.

15 MONITORING, REINFORCING AND EVALUATING AGAINST STEP 1

Management and organisation development contributes to an organisation's overall strategy. If it has value, it is in this context that it does so. An event is not a stand-alone exercise, but an attempt to make a positive difference to an organisation's success. Monitoring, reinforcing and evaluating learning therefore only make sense in this context.

Yet many organisations persist in thinking of evaluating a management and organisation development intervention solely on the reactions of participants to the immediate experience of that event. Few such evaluations are capable even of taking into account the complexity of the learning process, and how that complexity will impact on managers' feelings about the event (see Chapters 7 and 10). Even fewer are likely to be able to evaluate the degree to which the broader aims of the intervention will be achieved.

There can be no 'absolute' measures for the effectiveness of management and organisation development. If an intervention is measured, this simply records managers' feelings about an experience they have had; if organisational effectiveness is measured, there will be many other contributory factors than management and organisation development to this effectiveness. Monitoring, reinforcing and evaluating, therefore, need to be continuous processes, integrated into the mainstream activities of an organisation, and not a separate exercise designed to try to isolate management and organisation development from these continuing activities.

Organisations with whom we have been able to partner for a number of years have been able, thereby, to work with us in effective processes of monitoring, reinforcing and evaluating management and organisation development. This has involved a variety of methods and techniques including

Follow-Up Workshops, questionnaires on specific issues, and in-depth interviews; in fact, those various methods by which we explore the 'current state'
(Chapter 5). Both before and after any management and organisation
development intervention, at any moment, our client organisations are in a
'current state'. The snapshot we develop before an intervention is one of
many which we can take – as many as are needed to monitor progress. The
more snapshots we take, the more each becomes like a frame in a moving
film.

There is nothing esoteric about evaluating learning. It is part of what
managing an organisation is all about, As our partners in management and
organisation development, our clients, more fully integrate management and
organisation development into their 'normal' operational activities, so continuing evaluation becomes another, integrated, part of that monitoring and
evaluating of the organisation and its managers which 'comes naturally' to
any well-managed organisation.

The world is never as tidy as the list suggests; like all such checklists it is an
approximation rather than a reflection of what happens in each case. What

---

**THE 15 STEPS OF A MANAGEMENT AND ORGANISATION
DEVELOPMENT INTERVENTION**

1 Organisation wants to do something differently (strategy) or solve a current problem

2 Organisation recognises role for management and organisation development in this

3 Organisation selects a partner to help with the management and organisation
development aspects of the strategy

4 Organisation and partner check their mutual understanding of the challenges ahead

5 Person or persons take primary responsibility for managing the management and
organisation development programme or project

6 Definition of the 'desired state' (what managers will need to do differently in order to
help achieve the change defined in 1)

7 'Current state' explored, with review of the gap between desired and current states

8 Broad aims for a programme drawn up and agreed – programme positioned

9 Broad conceptual learning design drawn up and agreed

10 Micro design (of separate 'components') by experts

11 Learning integration, both before the intervention (design), and during the intervention, as new insights are achieved

12 Checking as we go how reality is matching design for learning

13 Planning for implementation

14 Re-entry – debriefing, and learning transfer strategies

15 Monitoring, reinforcing and evaluating against 1

Figure 2.2   *The 15 steps of a management and organisation development intervention*

the list as presented also fails to highlight is the iterative nature of many parts of the process. As with most dynamic processes, there are feedback loops implicit throughout, loops which are both about levels of detail, and about the impact that later stages can have on former stages.

In the first instance, for example, it may be acceptable before the completion of step 7 (exploring the 'current state') to work with a highly abstracted set of definitions of 'strategy' for the client organisation. One of the purposes of step 7 is to explore the practical manifestations of strategy as they impact on the different levels of management within the organisation. Once such information has been obtained, one would return to step 4 (checking understanding) and integrate those insights into the mutual understanding of the challenges.

In the second instance, learning can take place at various stages throughout the process, and not just through the more formal 'programme'. The value added by many interventions begins well before managers 'start' to attend an event, and takes place in the dialogue we undertake with senior Management Development Consultants about their perceptions of the organisation and its challenges. As I suggested in Chapter 1, the fundamental contribution of management and organisation development interventions is in changing organisations by changing minds. It is in the early exploration of key stakeholders' constructions of the organisation, the problems, and so on, that we can, in partnership, become significantly more focused on what kinds of intervention are most likely to achieve the broad aims of our clients.

CONCLUSIONS

This chapter has been a brief overview of the place within an organisation's life which we believe management and organisation development should take, and of the kinds of activity which we undertake with clients to add value through management and organisation development.

Many aspects of what we have learnt about management and organisation development over the years have not been expanded upon here. That is what the rest of the book deals with. Management and organisation development has come a long way from its 'management training' roots. It is, for many of our partners, a fully integrated aspect of the continuing changes and challenges which confront them. Because of the complexities of those changes and challenges, management and organisation development has had to become a significantly more complex set of processes as well. This chapter sketches out the management and organisation development arena. The following chapters explore our responses to those complexities, and the principles which we have developed out of our own learning management and organisation development.

3 Types of Management and Organisation Development Interventions

INTRODUCTION

So far, we have raised some very basic questions concerning the nature of our understanding of management and organisations, and we have introduced a simple linear 15-step 'model' to separate out (for heuristic purposes) some of the key stages we may go through in establishing and managing our partnerships with clients. In addition, the Appendix explores in some depth a specific management and organisation development intervention. As we progress through the book, we shall revisit some of the more challenging questions, using Tech-Test (the organisation described in the Appendix) and other cases to illustrate what we believe we have learnt.

Some of what we have learnt is very simple, but effective. This chapter and the next sketch out some basic lessons we feel have been useful to us, and which, when we share them with our partners in our client organisations, have helped both sides to work towards greater effectiveness from our management and organisation development interventions. We therefore offer these two chapters as a review of some basic ways which readers may find helpful in applying to their own situations, of mapping out the management and organisation development territory.

'Maps' already exist of the territory we are calling 'management and organisation development'. But what 'maps' we have acquired over the years come from so many different sources, with so many different cartographic standards, that we cannot always read them effectively. Sometimes, we are not aware that the things we have can be used as maps of this territory. This may be partly because our 'classic' maps are often created and coloured by 'providers' of specific 'subject areas' within management training and education. The terrain which is marked out is identified as 'strategy', 'marketing', 'personal development', and so on, which some people may see as lying beyond the broad territory of management and organisation development. From our point of view, we plan to include within our exploration any activity which seeks to help improve organisational or managerial effectiveness, irrespective of whether such activity has been labelled 'management and organisation development'.

In this chapter I take a 'where are we trying to get to?' approach to the task of mapping the territory, rather than a 'what have we here?' approach. One major reason for doing so is that my colleagues and I have learnt the practical value of the former. Maps serve a number of purposes, among which are: as practical guides to getting somewhere; and as records of what 'exists'. One of the things we have learnt about management and organisation development is that, while more traditional academic activities favoured the 'record of what exists' approach (as in 'Here's what we have learnt about retail marketing, isn't it interesting?'), practising managers prefer, and often can get more value from the practical-guide approach.

In other words, where we have tried things, and they seem to work, our clients welcome sharing our crystallised experience. In terms of the evaluation model we introduced in Chapter 1, the following two chapters complete the cycle: we use 'facts' (the management and organisation development situations we have been involved in) as the basis for the development of our approach; we explore the stated intentions of the interested parties (especially where these refer to the 'aims' of specific interventions); we offer conceptual tools and frameworks which classify, characterise and group things, so as to make more sense of them (but not to say that this is the way the world of management and organisation development 'is'); and we take a largely prescriptive line, judging that through the application of the tools we have developed, people will be able to map out their own broad approaches to management and organisation development more effectively.

DEVISING A SHARED LANGUAGE

In the case study in the Appendix, we refer to the difficulties some of the participants on the Tech-Test management development programme had in identifying before the event what they wanted to get out of it. These difficulties were partly the result of a lack of experience on their part of any kind of management and organisation development activities in their past. But they were also partly the result of there being very little shared language available to them and the interviewers concerning such matters.

Whatever the reasons, the participants went into the programme with a wide and ambitious set of 'aims'. We shall suggest that this kind of disparity of aims can be counter-productive to management and organisation development activities, and can positively reduce the value of the learning experiences for both participants and facilitators. The Tech-Test case is not unique; we have learnt since then the value of recognising that 'management and organisation development' means very different things to different people. While people are working from very different definitions of apparently 'the same' thing, misunderstandings and frustrations are to be expected.

Generating a 'shared language' to address such situations brings with it the kinds of difficult questions which this book is seeking to address throughout. Because each of us, in some sense, experiences (and, to some extent, contructs) the world (which includes how we use language) in subtly different ways, how people experience a management and organisation development intervention will be different. There will, therefore, be no 'standard' experience (the management and organisation development event) against which to measure. Although there is a practical issue embedded here, and one which, as we move into the learning process itself (Chapter 7) we shall confront, there is also the unarguable point that language is, for our present purposes, the only vehicle for exploring such potential differences. And such exploration is logically impossible without an assumption that when we use a common language, despite room for misunderstanding, such misunderstanding is predicated upon the possibility of being able, in principle, to understand in the first place. And by 'understand' we mean 'make sense of'; in so far as that sense is common to people who use the words, thus far we are referring to 'common sense', and no more.

What follows in this chapter are some of the ideas with which we have been able to make more sense of the potentially confusing territory we know as 'management and organisation development'. None of what follows is sophisticated; most has been shamelessly borrowed from other disciplines and activities. They have been borrowed because they have been found to work; to be useful.

I suggested in Chapter 1 that the territory of management and organisation development, like many other aspects of human activity, could be mapped in an almost infinite number of ways. We also argued that, although it is unlikely that any one individual could come up with his or her unique way of mapping the territory, it is often the delegated role of academics to undertake such a task. This and the following chapter offer some of the basic aspects of how my colleagues and I work with clients to map out the management and organisation development territory, not because it is the right way, but because, in our experience, it helps us and them to achieve our mutual goals. As we progress through the book, we shall continue to propose that, in our view, a great deal of what makes for effectiveness in management is not predicated upon finding the 'right' or 'best' answer, but upon finding what works.

THE 'MANAGEMENT DEVELOPMENT GRID'

Programme Aims

Not all management development interventions are the same. The differences between them are of an almost infinite variety. Yet many debates we have had with people concerning 'management and organisation development' have been confused simply because we were unable to factor into those debates a common and shared 'map' of those very differences which lay at the heart of the debates. We clearly were in need of some, albeit crude, map which would start the process of reaching consensus. Our response was to develop one which took as the key bases of segmentation what people hoped to get out of management and organisation development activities.

We have, therefore, drawn a simple yet effective map which helps us to gain a broad understanding of what is required from any intervention. We have used it both in planning, and retrospectively to evaluate and assess previous activities. What it has told us is that there may have been incompatibilities in the aims of some programmes and activities. What we use it for now is to eliminate such incompatibilities before we proceed with any new interventions.

By 'incompatibilities' we mean aims, which may be more or less well articulated before the event, which, in practice, do not match each other. Few people would state incompatible aims deliberately. However, we have learnt that apparently compatible aims may not be compatible when we try to apply them. In the past, we have received feedback from participants on programmes that some approaches have not been 'relevant' to them or their situation – that we should ensure that in the future, we avoid using cases and examples from industries different from their own, and so on. This is fine as it stands. But we have received from other participants on the same programmes a demand to help them benchmark outside their own organisation or industry; to bring new knowledge and insights from situations which they cannot normally explore.

Neither of these approaches is right or wrong. They are simply hard to pursue at the same time. Similarly, we have been confronted, on the same event, with demands both to 'consolidate' and to 'change'; to 'stretch' and to 'unwind'; to 'look inside' and to 'take an external perspective'. Again, each aim is legitimate on its own, but they do not easily sit together.

In earlier days, like many others, we suspect, we simply noted these aims and attempted to deal with them all. After all, the amount of time many organisations were prepared to devote to management and organisation development was small enough; surely we should do as much with the precious commodity as possible? Similarly, was it not perfectly feasible to use different parts of the programme to deal with different aims?

Our belief now is that it is not feasible. This is not because we are incapable of providing 'product' like this, but because from an 'outcomes' point of view the attempt is fundamentally flawed. If we were to take a 'product' focus, we could design anything, and we could demonstrate to our clients that we had delivered what we said we would deliver; adding, to protect ourselves, 'If people cannot make much of what we have delivered, that's their problem.'

However, if we take an 'outcomes' focus, we have to recognise that some 'outcomes' cannot be achieved at the same time. For example, if two different people wanted as a result from the same programme that managers behave differently from each other, and that managers behave the same as each other, it is clear that every aspect of the programme which moved toward satisfying one person's aim would at the same time be a move away from satisfying the aim of the other. It would also confuse the participants.

It is up to each and every 'provider' in the management and organisation development 'business' to decide whether to take a primarily 'product-driven' or 'outcomes-driven' approach. From our the point of view, we have chosen to take an 'outcomes-driven' approach, thereby giving us the challenge of dealing with these kinds of inherent contradictions in aims. The reasons for doing so will, we hope, become increasingly clear as we explore throughout the book the kinds of learning we ourselves have gone through. And one step towards this clarity should come directly from the implications of the Management Development Grid.

THE MANAGEMENT DEVELOPMENT GRID: BASIC PRINCIPLES

The Management Development Grid helps us to recognise internal inconsistencies, and helps eliminate them at the outset, because it is not developed out of a 'product' focus, but from an 'outcomes' focus. At this stage the model is very simple; in future it may require further refinement, as organisations become increasingly sophisticated in their use of 'management and organisation development'. Currently, however, its very simplicity seems one of its strengths. At the very least, it helps us and our clients to realise that it is more helpful to talk about 'management and organisation development' as a series of different phenomena than to talk about it as a single phenomenon which has a variety of manifestations.

In its simplest format, which we focus on in this chapter, the grid is applied at the level of an overall intervention, rather than for a course or module. In other words, we use it to work with our clients to identify what, broadly, they want to achieve by the intervention of 'management and organisation development' activities as a whole. Although there may be a whole series of detailed 'desired outcomes', such as 'improved listening skills', 'better awareness of the market', and so on, there is usually an underlying 'why?' It is this 'why?' which we map onto the grid. And one of the most effective ways of unearthing the answer to the basic 'why?' is the question, 'What happens if you don't do this?'

The basic grid, then, helps work at the level of why an organisation wishes to invest time, energy and cost (a great deal of which is opportunity cost) in going through with an intervention. It tells us that we can segment the answers into four basic areas. As with any simple model, it could be replaced with others, which may segment the answers differently – into three or five areas, say; or even four areas which are fundamentally different from ours. We do not suggest that the map represents 'reality' better or worse than any other. Its purpose is not to tell, but to aid effective thinking and dialogue. Compared to what we may be using in years to come, it may be ridiculously crude; compared to what went before, it is extraordinarily helpful in improving what we and our clients do together to help managers and organisations learn.

Although the grid helps set the broad agenda for a management and organisation development intervention, its use in designing such an intervention is clearly very restricted. Even programmes which may have very different basic aims may nevertheless contain specific elements which look similar. In the next chapter we shall explore these and related issues in management and organisation development programme design. For the moment, our concern is not how to achieve learning goals, but what, overall, those learning goals should be. By keeping this stage of the process simple, we lay solid foundations for effective design.

The next section of this chapter explores a number of aspects of the Management Development Grid, and identifies why we feel it is so important to our understanding of what we are trying to do with and for our clients. I shall explore the grid and its implications first, and then look at how it has provided us with practical help with one of our recent clients, and finally how it may have helped in our work with Tech-Test, our case study in the Appendix.

Before proceeding, it is worth reminding the reader that this book is written from an organisational perspective, rather than for the purposes of the individual reader. Therefore, the lessons we have learnt from using the grid at an organisational level may not be particularly helpful to individuals seeking their own routes to development. At this stage, the book is more like a road atlas; the individual reader may need something which plots footpaths rather than motorways.

THE MANAGEMENT DEVELOPMENT GRID: BASIC STRUCTURE

The map is a simple one. The basic framework is a two-by-two matrix based on orthogonal axes, each of which relates to one key aspect of the overall intervention.

The first aspect is the degree to which the focus for management and organisation development is generic as opposed to specific to a particular organisation seeking such development for its managers. Drawn as a spectrum, at one end lie those activities which are concerned with addressing the specific needs and perceptions of the organisation itself; at the other end of the spectrum lie those activities which address generic management needs:

---

high   **low**

SPECIFICITY TO THE ORGANISATION

The other aspect concerns the degree of change to be aimed at from the activity or event. At one end of the spectrum are those activities which are designed to integrate managers within the principles and practices of management or of the organisation as they stand today – to make them work more effectively or efficiently within the current environment; in other words, to fit into the way one organisation currently works or how most, or 'the best', organisations currently operate. This does not imply significant change.

At the other end of this spectrum (the top on our grid, as this is the vertical axis) are those activities designed to introduce significant change into people or the organisation – to alter the status quo rather than accommodate to it:

---

today   **tomorrow**

FOCUS ON STATUS QUO OR CHANGE

Set orthogonally on a framework, with the extremes separated by dividing lines, gives us a grid which contains four generic areas for management and organisation development. The vertical axis is labelled 'Success through Change' at the top, and 'Success through Alignment' at the bottom, signifying a key difference between the key aims of each half of the grid.

At the bottom, the aims of programmes are focused upon taking what has been tried and tested, and helping managers align with that, either within their own organisation (left-hand side) or in other organisations (right-hand side). At the top, the aims of programmes are to change things, either throughout their own organisation (left-hand side) or, often as a 'pilot' or trial, among a few managers or a group (right-hand side).

Each one of the four resulting areas is fundamentally different in its aims, its activities, the most appropriate 'technologies', and so on. In order to be able to refer to each area uniquely, we have introduced labels.

'*Generic*' management and organisation development activities are those which seek to introduce to managers that knowledge, those skills, and those attitudes which seem necessary for the effective execution of management in almost any kind of organisation. The key aims of such activities are to increase managers' efficiency through increased skills and abilities in general management practices, such as marketing, accounting, or 'General Management'.

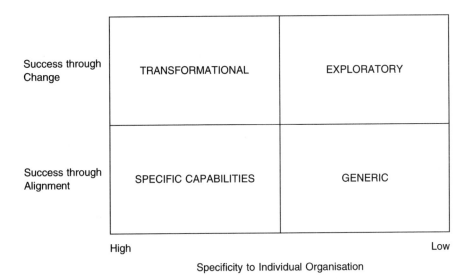

Figure 3.1 *The basic management development grid*

'*Specific Capabilities*' describe those management and organisation development activities designed to introduce to managers that knowledge, those skills, and those attitudes which are required specifically in one particular organisation, and are not the same from one organisation to another. The key aims of such activities are to defend the business position by increasing internal management effectiveness in core competencies specific to the business (or, in some cases, the industry).

'*Transformational*' management and organisation development activities describe those designed to introduce to managers that knowledge, those skills, and those attitudes which are required specifically to change one particular organisation, and are not the same from one organisation to another. The key aims of such activities are to gain and sustain competitive advantage by changing the styles and skills of managers within the organisation.

'*Exploratory*' management and organisation development activities describe those designed to introduce to managers that knowledge, those skills, and those attitudes which are required radically to change an individual, a group or, eventually, an entire organisation, but in ways which are not fully understood at present. The key aims of such activities are to introduce experimentation and innovation in management by learning new behaviours of various kinds.

These four kinds of management and organisation development activity comprise a 'portfolio'. We have learnt that activities in each quadrant of this portfolio are fundamentally different in their aims, what drives them, how they should be designed and evaluated and the kinds of activities best suited

Success through Change	Gaining and sustaining competitive advantage by changing the style and skills of managers	Experimentation and innovation in management, learning new behaviours of various kinds
	Transformational	Exploratory
Success through Alignment	Defending business position by increasing internal management effectiveness in core competencies specific to the business or industry	Increased efficiency through increased skills and abilities in general management
	Specific Capabilities	Generic

High   Low

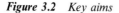

Specificity to Individual Organisation

Figure 3.2   *Key aims*

to those aims. The fact is that, in many cases, organisations invest in management and organisation development activities which are an unholy mixture of these types, with often very unsatisfactory results.

We start by exploring the portfolio model in a general sense. This will help us to identify design principles which we believe should be adopted in management and organisation development activities to enable the various benefits to be realised from each kind of activity as appropriate to the needs of organisations and individuals.

THE MODEL EXPLORED: DRIVING FORCES

The need for *Generic* management and organisation development activities is stimulated by a desire for greater efficiency in management. Higher productivity and better control of management processes are the kinds of output sought from investments in activities in this sector of the grid.

What drives activities to enhance *Specific Capabilities* will primarily be a desire for business consolidation. This demands integration of processes, practices and behaviours, as managers become more familiar and comfor-

Success through Change	Management vision Corporate strategy Key business goals Desire for 'culture change'	Breaking paradigms Desire for new models and concepts Need for more 'business', 'innovative', or 'entrepreneurial' thinking Challenging the norms
	Transformational	Exploratory
Success through Alignment	Business consolidation Integration of processes, practices and behaviours Need for common attitudes (e.g. 'Quality') Specific competences to focus on core activities	Need for greater efficiency in management Higher productivity and control
	Specific Capabilities	Generic

High   Low

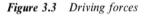

Specificity to Individual Organisation

Figure 3.3 *Driving forces*

table with 'the way we do things around here'. Sometimes, specific kinds of behaviours are addressed, as with 'Total Quality' initiatives, which seek to ensure that all managers follow a common and desired approach to their tasks. The focus is on those specific competencies which are critical to maintaining the style and quality of the business, and meeting the expectations of customers, internal and external.

Transformational management and organisation development programmes, on the other hand, are driven by a desire for change. They are the fruits of management vision and are critical to the successful implementation of corporate strategy. Changes in behaviour are sought to achieve key business goals, often anticipating fundamentally new ways of doing things. This is often wrapped up in a desire for 'culture change' within the organisation, as it faces increased competition, and a realisation that 'the way we do things around here' may be inappropriate for the changing realities in which the organisation is operating.

What drives *Exploratory* activities is less well defined, but still focused on change. Whereas *Transformational* activities are predicated on clearly defined new behaviours, linked closely to the Critical Success Factors (CSFs) of the changing business, *Exploratory* activities are more 'thematic'. They are driven by a desire for difference – almost of any kind. They seek to break the paradigms of the status quo; they seek new, as yet undefined, models and concepts. They are driven by such vagaries as a need for a more 'business-like', more 'entrepreneurial', more 'innovative' approach to the tasks of management. They seek to provide a challenge to the norms of the organisation, without necessarily having a clear picture of the results from such challenges. They may be more about unlearning than about learning.

TYPICAL KINDS OF PROGRAMME IN EACH SECTOR

Generic activities will encompass both General Management Programmes and specific skills programmes designed to enhance particular generic skills and knowledge. Where the approach is towards training and educational courses, the programmes which will be most cost effective will be open programmes, with the spin-off benefit of delegates meeting people from other organisations and enhancing their general knowledge about different industries. In other cases, open learning may be seen as the most cost-effective approach, allowing multiple access to teaching material which, once purchased, can be reused almost infinitely.

Such open approaches are less effective for the *Specific Capabilities* of an organisation. Although activities must be standardised to ensure commonality in behaviours and skills among the participants, they must also be tailored to the specific needs of the organisation. Least-cost, open programmes may introduce irrelevancies and even contradictions which could jeopardise the effectiveness of the programme as a whole. These activities, seeking as they do to arrive at a high degree of commonality in behaviours and attitudes, are likely to be open to very large numbers of managers within the organisation, and to focus on proven methods and models which ensure the effectiveness of the learning process.

Typically, induction programmes for new entrants will fall into this category, as will those 'rites of passage' which organisations provide for managers attaining or about to attain higher levels of management responsibility.

Tailoring is also necessary for the *Transformational* kind of management and organisation development activity, but here the tailoring is enhanced by the links to the specific goals of the organisation going through change. This kind of programme is focused on the key individuals within the organisation on whom the success of the strategy depends. It is not open to all managers, until, that is, the organisation has undergone sufficient change to make it 'the (new) way we do things around here'. At this point, the activity becomes a *Specific Capabilities* kind of programme, and subject to the kinds of approach described for that part of the portfolio.

The kinds of activity which typify the *Transformational* category are senior management workshops and what are sometimes referred to by terms such as 'culture change' programmes. Each of these aims to have a long-term pay-off, with deep effects on the future of the organisation.

It is hard to describe 'typical' *Exploratory* activities. They could encompass almost anything which falls outside the areas described for the other parts of the portfolio. Indeed, once the activity becomes 'typical', it is likely to fall within another category. But there are common features which can be identified here. The commonality lies in their exploratory use. Hence, an 'Outward Bound' programme for a small set of managers, designed to 'give them a bit of a shake-up' would classify as an *Exploratory* activity. The same kind of activity as part of a structured *Specific Capabilities* programme would have clearly defined desired outcomes, and therefore be classifiable in the bottom left of the grid. Similarly, T-group/encounter group activities and 'cross-cultural exchanges' can fall within several categories, depending on their aims, although the latter would be an unlikely candidate for the lower half of the grid.

Success through Change	Tailored and linked to specific corporate direction and initiatives Focused on key individuals likely to make strategy happen 'Culture change' programmes Senior executive workshops	Almost anything, including: Outward Bound T-group/encounter group 'Cross-cultural exchanges'
	Transformational	Exploratory
Success through Alignment	Standardised, tailored Open to most managers at appropriate levels Proven methods and models Induction programmes and other 'rites of passage'	General management programmes Open learning (where appropriate)
	Specific Capabilities	Generic

High   Low

Specificity to Individual Organisation

Figure 3.4 *Typical kinds of programme*

JUSTIFICATION AND EVALUATION

It may be stating the obvious to point out that it would be as inappropriate to ship in a Harvard professor to teach managers the basic skills of balance-sheet analysis as it would to attempt to implement culture change by getting senior managers to spend time with a teach-yourself guide to culture. But these extremes are simply caricatures of the kind of approaches which are incorrectly adopted all too frequently by unsophisticated managers and Human Resources people in attempting to get to grips with the best ways to deliver management and organisation development. We have had many experiences of similarly muddled thinking in attempting to help organisations address their management and organisation development needs.

It should be fairly clear from the above that the *Generic* activity is quite properly the kind of management and organisation development which lends itself to relatively measurable, tangible evaluation. And where evaluation is available in this form, so justification precedes it. Efficiencies can be measured both before and after management and organisation development. Such efficiencies can translate, without much interference, into financial returns. Costs can be similarly identified and measured. In this kind of activity, financial 'Return on Investment' (ROI) analysis is possible, perhaps desirable.

But with *Specific Capabilities* there is a greater degree of 'noise' in the calculation. It is perfectly possible to measure productivity before and after management and organisation development activities, but it is considerably more difficult to isolate the influences of the activities among the many other factors at work. Perhaps more important, however, is the issue of what effects can derive from not undertaking these activities. If knowing the procedures better does not easily translate into increased profitability, not knowing the procedures may lead to very uncomfortable results – lost sales, lost customers, lost opportunities.

How an organisation puts value on a common approach, a common language within the organisation, problem avoidance, collaboration and co-operation across functional boundaries will be a key element in the justification and evaluation of activities designed to enhance such management behaviours as will deliver these benefits. It is true that an effective management environment should produce increased profitability. But it may take a disaster or two to realise the value of investing in such relatively expensive management and organisation development. Tailoring and bringing in outside expertise do not come cheap. Short-term increases in profitability may not accrue. But in the longer term, building a 'winning culture' may mean the difference between survival and failure.

It is yet harder, by the same token, to justify and evaluate *Transformational* management and organisation development activities. These are likely to be among a set of CSFs for a changing corporate strategy. Here, measurement of success may simply be the achievement of that strategy, not a trivial matter, but one depending on a multifarious set of circumstances. Financial measures will be highly inappropriate, and one should be seeking measures of change in behaviours, in systems, in language, and in 'the way we do things around here'. Measuring a change in culture is not only extraordinarily difficult in itself, but is also a very long-term prospect, far removed from any specific management and organisation development activity for which a justification may be required before we start.

Again, the cost of not undertaking the activity may be a better starting point, and is likely to be a similar position taken for the other activities which comprise the strategy for change.

Justifying *Exploratory* management and organisation development, and its subsequent evaluation provides yet another set of problems. It may be necessary simply to point at those organisations which have an 'innovative culture' and beg leave to try to emulate them, by whatever means. And once activities have been sanctioned, it may be comforting, but of questionable value to count the number of new ideas generated, the hours spent on 'bootlegging', the numbers of instances of unexpected behaviours, and

	Achievement of movement towards Key Performance Indicators (KPIs) as drawn up from CSFs Changes in procedures, systems, language, behaviour A 'new culture'	New ideas tested/proven 'Bootlegging' activities Unexpected behaviours Challenges to the status quo
Success through Change		
	Transformational	Exploratory
Success through Alignment	Common language and behaviour Problem infrequency Collaboration and co-operation across the business	Measurable skills increase Efficiencies ROI
	Specific Capabilities	Generic

High   Low

Specificity to Individual Organisation

Figure 3.5   Measures/evaluation bases

challenges to the status quo. Whether these numbers are seen as better or worse the higher they climb is entirely dependent on the willingness of senior management to grasp the nettle and go for revolution as a means of coping with the ever-increasing pace of change.

BROAD STRATEGIES FOR MANAGEMENT AND ORGANISATION DEVELOPMENT ACTIVITIES

In Chapter 2 we suggested that it is helpful if organisations develop a strategic approach to management and organisation development based upon a clear delineation between Business Strategy, Management Strategy and Management and Organisation Development Strategy. The 'management development grid' introduces a new dimension to this basic model. What it suggests, broadly, is that at both the management and the management and organisation development levels, 'strategy' should read 'strategies'.

By this we mean that, for example, how one addresses the strategic links between business strategy and the consequent development activities which would be classified as *Transformational* will clearly be different from the 'strategic' approach to, say, any *Exploratory* activities. For some activities, the organisation will clearly need a high degree of integration with current practices, policies and processes; for others, such integration may severely limit the potential of the activity to achieve its 'paradigm-busting' aims.

Five Different Approaches to Management Development Strategy

It is often the case that different managers have different theories concerning how management and organisation development should be planned and brought about. In Chapter 1 we argued that all managers use theory, but that their theories may not be overtly expressed or even consciously known. Here we suggest that managers who have had any association with or have thought about any aspect of management and organisation development are likely to have views, or theories, concerning good and bad ways of thinking about the whole approach to management and organisation development.

Once again, such views will have similarities to and differences from each other. They are likely to cover a multi-dimensional spectrum. Our aim at this point is to offer another map: this time one into which many such views may be positioned. And once again, this map is not offered as the right or only way to plot these disparate views. It has, however, been found useful. In this case, our map has five different areas, which we describe only briefly here for the purposes of clarification.

The 'Top Down' approach

Some managers will take the view that, given how important management and organisation development is to the organisation, all management and organisation development activities should be part of a grand plan, which is directly driven from the top of the organisation; and in which senior managers have a direct and constant involvement. In this view, management and organisation development specialists are brought into management and organisation development projects which are owned and managed by line managers in the business, and which, collectively, form the totality of the organisation's investment in management and organisation development.

The 'Learning Vanguard' approach

Others see the Top Down kind of approach as too formal and grandiose. There will be those, for example, whose view will be that the only sustainable competitive advantage will come from the organisation's ability to learn, and that all management and organisation development activities should push people to the leading edge of learning. For these people, the key to management and organisation development strategies is how far ahead of the competition in 'learning' they can get; for them, any breakthrough in learning 'technologies' should be pursued before the competition get hold of it. They are likely to be the kinds of people who like to read the latest works by management 'gurus', or who are the first to advocate what others may see as 'management fads'.

The 'Empowerment' approach

Yet others will argue that the most appropriate strategy for management and organisation development must be based upon empowering managers at all levels to seek their own development as appropriate. In the view of this school of thought, you cannot force people to learn; therefore it is vital to cascade learning down to the lowest levels possible, and encourage all managers to take personal responsibility for their own learning and development. In this 'free market' approach, managers are free to seek help both from the in-house management and organisation development specialists, and from any outside source which they feel best meets their needs. They may advocate 'Learning Centres', or that the in-house training department compete with the external management and organisation development market by developing brochure-led 'open' programmes covering a wide range of potential development needs.

The 'Community' approach

Yet another approach often encountered comes from those who argue that organisations are best served by people who share the same language and follow the same processes in similar ways. For these people, helping everyone within the organisation to achieve the same levels of understanding and, to eliminate the confusion which stems from different uses of the same terms, different learning experiences, and so on, is the most crucial role of management and organisation development. For them, consistency, shared values and goals, and mutual understanding are crucial. And for people who wish to pursue this approach it is often recognised that the best repository of this consistency is the in-house department responsible for management and organisation development. 'What is the use of having such a department if we don't empower them, as the experts in the field, to develop standards, policies, procedures and a language which we all can share and agree?' For these people, everything should be co-ordinated by one single group of professionals tasked solely to achieve internal consistency and standards.

The 'Financial' approach

Finally, yet another approach may be favoured by a different set of managers. This approach recognises that management and organisation development like any other activity within an organisation, requires investment, not only of time, but also of money – the cost of doing the activities, and the opportunity costs involved while managers are not doing what they 'should be' doing. For these people, the simple approach is to pitch management and organisation development 'projects' against other potentially competing projects. For some, management and organisation development investments simply compete against each other. For others, they compete against everything else the organisation may wish to invest time and money into, such as new plant and equipment, developing new products, market research activities, increased salaries and bonuses for senior executives. Each project (either all management and organisation development projects, or, in the more extreme case, all corporate projects of any kind) has to be presented as a business case, with the key justification being ROI. Competing projects are assessed according to the comparatively beneficial rate of return they are expected to produce. Any management and organisation development project which can be favourably compared in terms of its ROI to other, competing, demands for corporate funding should go ahead. Those which cannot be justified in these terms should be abandoned in favour of those activities and projects which will produce a better ROI. After all, say this group of managers, the purpose of business is to produce a profit, not to spend money.

Reconciling Different Approaches

We believe that there is nothing fundamentally 'wrong' with any of the five quite distinct approaches described above. None of them seem, however, to deal adequately with all the complex needs of management and organisation development strategies. Many management boards spend long hours debating the relative merits of these approaches, often with little real progress being made. Indeed, we suspect that, for some organisations, it has been the very frustration of seeking to reconcile these effectively irreconcilable approaches which has led to that very abdication of responsibility for strategic management and organisation development planning to the specialists we alluded to in Chapter 2.

So long as these different approaches *compete* with each other for senior management attention and agreement, it is clear that resolution of their inherent differences is likely to depend more on the political astuteness of their respective 'champions' than on their respective merits as approaches for the organisation. However, we believe that in the 'management development grid' we have found a way in which these very different approaches can be reconciled, and their respective advantages be applied as appropriate to the different sectors of the management and organisation development needs of an organisation.

In this section, we shall explore some of the strategy and policy implications of adopting a portfolio approach to management and organisation development strategies, and show why it is possible, and often desirable, for organisations to apply these different policies and approaches to different elements of their management and organisation development strategies.

The skills which fall within the domain of *Generic* management and organisation development activities are widely known, and can be acquired through a number of different routes, many of them tried and tested. More than any other kind of management and organisation development, these skills are relatively susceptible of testing by results. The development of these skills is more like a commodity product than the others and therefore there is usually significant choice in the selection of such products. Given these factors, there is merit in treating this kind of management and organisation development activity as a regular investment with a recognised desired return.

It should therefore be relatively easy to explore ways in which a budget for this kind of development can be identified and spent in the most cost-effective way. The classic 'training budget', usually a proportion of turnover, can be parcelled out in pursuit of efficiency in meeting the training need.

In this sense, *Generic* activities are those to which the Financial approach is best suited. One could argue that, if there are many tried and tested approaches to this kind of learning on the market, the Financial approach is the one which will most likely encourage people to invest in the most cost-effective methods of gaining that leaning. There is a very good argument against people developing yet another course on telephone techniques, or finance for non-financial managers, or interviewing skills. In-house management and organisation development specialists caught doing so may quite reasonably be accused of wasting corporate funds which are better spent elsewhere within the portfolio.

Similarly, it is important to ensure that managers' scarce time is not wasted sending them on courses and training activities which, although nice to have, do not actually increase their abilities to function in their roles commensurate with the investment they have made. The basic principle of the *Generic* part of the portfolio is 'prove that it's worth it!'

This is less likely to be the case for an organisation's *Specific Capabilities*. The very uniqueness of an organisation's policies and practices, upon which it depends for its success in its market place, make such an approach as described for *Generic* activities less appropriate. The *Specific Capabilities* are a vital part of delivering the goods, and are of little effect if treated in isolation from other, related activities within the organisation. Here, integration with career management, progression plans, and rewards for contribution is essential. Integration also with other aspects of the business, such as operating procedures, manufacturing strategy, and so on, are just as vital. It is therefore necessary to design these activities within the organisation's overall Human Resource strategy, its manufacturing strategy, its Information Systems strategy, and so on, rather than as a separate, funds-led purchase of skills of the *Generic* kind.

It is for this reason that this part of the portfolio lends itself so well to the Community approach described above. In these vital aspects of the core business, eliminating the inefficiencies which can arise from different meanings, different styles, different languages, and so on, are crucial to the effective running of the organisation. The 'guardians' of the standards of process and language do not have to be the in-house management and organisation development people, but someone has to do it; and, in most cases, we can see little reason why this should not be a key part of the role of this department.

Managing a strategic change, in which *Transformational* management and organisation development activities play a critical part, demands even more close integration. But this time, the integration should be with the corporate strategy itself. A Top-Down planning process should lie at the heart of the development of *Transformational* programmes, linking management and organisation development intimately with the other CSFs for the Business Strategy. It is no longer, in this part of the grid, appropriate to hand over the task to the Human Resources professionals. They may be able very successfully to manage other kinds of management and organisation development, but, where the future of the business depends upon such development activities being in complete harmony with the other elements of the change strategy, involvement, commitment and management of the change process must lie with management of the organisation at the very highest levels.

Exploratory management and organisation development activities, being significantly less well defined, demand a yet different approach. Being by its very nature a leap into the unknown, it demands freedom from detailed planning. Nobody in the organisation is to be discounted as a source of the kinds of innovative approach that this kind of activity demands, and therefore it is important to free this kind of activity from the constraints of both current Human Resources procedures and the rigours of strategic planning.

The Empowerment approach, allowing individuals or departments to explore new avenues, is more likely to stumble on the critical idea which the organisation seeks. Similarly, introducing Learning Vanguard thinking into niches within the organisation will allow the kind of experimentation which this kind of activity demands. There is, however, a need for financial restraint; huge sums of money can be frittered away in 'playing' with new ideas. Like the R&D function in many organisations, this approach, if not

Success through Change	Top-down planning, linking programmes to business strategy via CSF analysis, etc. Senior management-driven and involvement	Individual or departmental search for exciting new activities No specific need for planning or co-ordination Working in small groups with the very latest in management development
	Transformational (Top down)	**Exploratory (Empowerment) (Learning Vanguard)**
Success through Alignment	Planned and managed as part of HR and other strategies HR/Management Development department as focal point/ co-ordinator	Funds-led, with appropriate percentage of turnover devoted to purchase of cost-effective methods of skill transfer
	Specific Capabilities (Community)	**Generic (Financial)**

High   Low

Specificity to Individual Organisation

Figure 3.6   *Broad strategies*

given some financial guidelines, can become a black hole from which nothing of longer-term value emerges. And, like R&D, there needs to be an ability to reject those projects which will not produce value, well before they have eaten up the potential profits to be gained from change. 3M's 'bootlegging' philosophy seems the most appropriate to apply to these activities.

SPECIFYING AND PROVIDING ACTIVITIES

In preparing to adopt a management and organisation development activity, it is clearly valuable to specify what is required. And here, again, the portfolio approach can be very useful. It is easy to attempt to specify the wrong kind of activity, creating confusions in the minds of those responsible for providing the activity, and false expectations in the minds of the participants. Many management and organisation development activities founder on differing expectations not only between the providers and the participants, but also among the participants themselves. In such situations, providers of management and organisation development activities can find themselves in a dilemma, as one group of participants begs for more relevance to its own needs from the programme, while another revels in the destruction of the paradigms which it realises are hampering its ability to change.

Specifying *Generic* activities is often a relatively simple task. So long as the providers of these activities are well respected in their field, and have a good track record, it is unnecessary, and costly, to devote too much energy in detailed specification of programmes. Successful providers have acquired experience in the most cost-effective ways of achieving the aims of such activities, and can usually be relied upon to deliver the goods. There is, therefore, little point in 'reinventing the wheel' for this kind of management and organisation development; select the most cost-effective provider, and state the skills required, and then get on with more important matters.

Providing *Generic* management and organisation development activities is often best left to the professionals in their field. In certain cases this may still require the intervention of relatively costly providers. Best practice starts somewhere, and for some organisations, it may be important to ensure that, although not necessarily the basis of potential competitive advantage for them, the skills of their people will need to be at a level which will justify expenditure on high quality *Generic* providers. Consultancies, for example, may find it necessary to ensure that, because of their high profile with clients whose impression of them will be based as much on their basic activities as upon their specialist skills, their staff are brought to a higher-than-average standard, even in basic areas such as customer care, invoice management and market intelligence.

However, for many *Generic* programmes it will be appropriate to go to training establishments and the less prestigious consultancies and business schools which specialise in cost-effective skills transfer. Open learning and 'teach yourself' methods, such as Computer Based Training, often offer the best approach to this kind of activity, as they rely on economies of scale entirely appropriate to the task. The use of in-house training and mentoring may also be considered, but they may be less cost-effective, relying as they do on relatively expensive resources whose knowledge of the organisation may be more effectively channelled into *Specific Capabilities* activities.

A different set of criteria is demanded for these *Specific Capabilities*. Detailed specifications are critical. Time spent on designing and developing activities in advance of delivery will be rewarded handsomely. An intimate knowledge of the 'way we do things around here' is a necessary condition for success with this kind of activity, as is a detailed knowledge of the specific procedures and language of the organisation. Learning can be severely hampered by the use of inappropriate language to describe processes which have their own jargon and acronymic vocabulary in different organisations.

The internal knowledge of and commitment to the organisation of the in-house Human Resources or Training function provide an ideal source of supply for *Specific Capabilities* activities. In situations where the skills of the in-house people are inadequate for the task of delivering the activities themselves, their role should be to manage the provision of activities from business schools or consultancies. That management demands both a detailed specification of the activities, and ensuring that adequate briefing in the specific language and 'culture' of the organisation is provided.

An alternative approach favoured by the Japanese is on-the-job mentoring. This is highly appropriate for the 'typical' Japanese organisation in which intimate commitment to the organisation, often associated with a 'cradle to grave' approach to employment, is a primary factor in the effectiveness with which managers carry out their tasks. The use of this approach demands, however, attitudes and skills on the part of the mentor which are not always available in UK organisations.

Specifying the *Transformational* activity is far less easy. Many of the behaviours demanded by the kinds of changes this kind of activity is seeking are known, in theory, to the organisation. But they are not practised – if they were, the activity would be a *Specific Capabilities* activity and not *Transformational*. Now the value of the activity becomes a split between the acquisition of new skills and behaviours and the very definition of those skills and behaviours most appropriate to the achievement of the strategic goals of the organisation. Overspecification leads to a narrowing of opportunities for change which can severely reduce the chances of success.

Outside and expert help is critical for *Transformational* activities, as the implications of the corporate plans are iteratively explored and developed.

Success through Change	Value is split between the activity itself and the development of 'ideal' models Suppliers as consultants Links to other activities modified as procedures change to fit the future strategy	No specification at all – high risk but high potential reward Links to other activities discovered as part of activity
	Transformational	Exploratory
Success through Alignment	Detailed specification and intimate knowledge of organisation required On-the-job links Links with other existing procedures	Less detailed specification – rely on suppliers to help identify areas of need and how to meet them Filling the knowledge/skills gap
	Specific Capabilities	Generic

High   Low

Specificity to Individual Organisation

Figure 3.7 *Specifying the activities*

This is the part of the portfolio in which we know what we want, but are not certain how we get there. For this reason, leading business schools and consultancies are often relied upon to act as partners in change management, helping to identify, step by step, the ways in which management needs to adjust to each stage of the implementation of the strategy.

Part of the learning process is adjusting to each new stage of the situation, and not attempting to implement too much too soon. New processes are tried out and integrated; new relationships forged within the organisation; new structures are implemented; and new rules developed for the changed environment. It would be both unfair and risky to expect the in-house trainers to take on such a task, steeped as they will be in the existing ways of doing things. Similarly, 'commodity' providers, such as those appropriately delivering *Generic* activities, will apply disastrous methods.

Exploratory activities can hardly be specified at all. The mere act of specification draws boundaries which such activities are aimed at breaking down. This is a high-risk area, and must be approached as such. The potential rewards can be similarly high. It is for these activities that it can be appropriate to delve into the esoterica of universities and 'fringe' consultancies. Behavioural psychologists, anthropologists, conferences on marginally

	Specific Capabilities	Generic
Success through Change	Leading business schools High-calibre consultants	Universities 'Fringe' consultancies Behavioural psychologists Seminars/conferences, etc.
	Transformational	Exploratory
Success through Alignment	In-house training department Business schools/consultants as sub-contractors to in-house departments On-the-job mentoring	Training establishments Cheaper consultants and Business schools Open University/distance learning organisations 'Teach-yourself' methods In-house training/mentoring
	Specific Capabilities	Generic

High   Low

Specificity to Individual Organisation

Figure 3.8   *Sources of supply*

related topics are all potential sources of new thinking. Direct relevance is not what is being sought – not at this stage; making new ideas relevant brings the activity out of this area and into another part of the portfolio.

A PORTFOLIO APPROACH TO MANAGEMENT AND ORGANISATION DEVELOPMENT

One final factor to consider in this introductory exploration of the portfolio model is the tendency for items in the various quadrants to move round from quadrant to quadrant. In the classic case, the *Exploratory* activity of today becomes the *Transformational* activity of tomorrow, and thence to the *Specific Capabilities* activity of the new organisation. After this, with increasing expectations from the market place for such things a 'quality', even *Specific Capabilities* can become *Generic*. The message is that approaches to the different kinds of activity may need to change with time. Consequently, management and organisation development specialists within the organisation, along with senior managers, may need constantly to be reviewing the role and function of various management and organisation development initiatives within their own portfolios. Where an activity has undergone this kind of change in broad aims or significance, the organisation would be well advised to rethink its style, provisioning, and so on, in order to ensure that they are getting the appropriate value for the appropriate cost.

In some cases, especially where we are dealing with activities at the top of the grid, the definition of the kind of event can change in-flight. Here is a simple case to illustrate such a move.

THE 'GOOD TEAM' TO 'GREAT TEAM' WORKSHOP

On of our clients came to us to ask for a workshop specifically designed to 'explore' opportunities for better interworking among his top team. The team had been together for some months, but the nature of the business was changing rapidly, and he and his colleagues in the team felt that they were 'a good team' but needed to be a 'great team' if they were to move ahead as fast as they needed.

The workshop was to be run for the 8 members of the team which ran a services operation within a multinational business. It was to take place at a very comfortable management centre on the edge of town in a mid-Western city in the USA. My colleague and I were to spend a few days with the team members in advance of the workshop, gaining insights into how the team worked, and gathering ideas from team members on what the workshop should look like. We would then have about half a day on our own to pull the structure together.

This is classic *Exploratory* territory. None of the team members had any clear ideas about what they wanted to get from the workshop, but all agreed that it was worth spending 3 days together finding out about themselves as a team, and how they could harness their collective strengths and talents.

As the 3 days progressed, and as the team members got to know each other better, it became increasingly clear what they had to do to be successful in the future. As the future grew clearer for the team, we started to build a stronger sense of direction and structure for the workshop. By the latter stages, there was an air of excitement as the team moved from open exploration and into strategic thinking about their own purpose, direction and strategy. The workshop had imperceptibly moved from *Exploratory* to *Transformational*.

As is so often the case in these days of rapid change, the team did not have time to implement all they set out to do at the workshop. The parent organisation took a significant turn of its own, and the team fragmented. It was gratifying, however, when I was invited to meet with a new version of the team three years later to hear that, for those who had been at the workshop, the learning had been carried forward into the new environment, and they had been able to apply the lessons to the new team's needs.

However, not all activities move in the classic manner. It may be that a change in organisational strategy – an attempt to gain competitive advantage through extraordinary focus on customers, for example – demands that managers previously kept at arm's length from customers find themselves in the front line, needing to acquire those *Specific Capabilities* which will form the backbone of the strategy. At this point a hitherto *Generic* activity, such as a basic introduction to customer care, is likely to be insufficient for the new environment, and a new activity may be required, which is tailored and very specific to the organisation. Unless this change of requirement is recognised, communicated, justified and acted on, the strategic intent can become a very embarrassing failure.

For any organisation, as it grows and develops, there will be a constantly changing portfolio of 'management and organisation development' needs; some will be *Generic*, some *Specific Capabilities*, some *Transformational* and others, perhaps, *Exploratory*. One of the key roles of management and organisation development professionals should be to help the organisation develop a strategic approach to these needs, and thereby to avoid the risks of haphazard investments of time and money in activities which may deliver a relatively poor return.

However, the key point we have learnt is to ensure that, despite the mix of needs an organisation may have over time, each specific 'programme' needs to be clearly positioned within the portfolio well before any tactical decisions regarding funding, design, and so on, are taken. It is this clarity of positioning which we feel many organisations miss, and which thereby, in many cases, leads us to the mixed expectations and demands which single programmes often fail to meet.

REWARDCO: A CASE OF MIXED EXPECTATIONS

In one example, we missed the opportunity clearly and overtly to explore this issue with our client, and thereby with the participants on the programme, with uncomfortable consequences.

We were approached by Rewardco (an alias), an organisation in a specialist consultancy business. Our client asked us to develop a modular programme aimed at helping their leading consultants to take a broader view. The reason for this was that the client felt that the traditional market in which Rewardco operated was becoming mature, and that it offered few opportunities for growth. They had already introduced new consultancy 'products' and were in the process of bringing from the outside specialists in these new but related fields.

Although the Business Strategy had not been fully developed at the time, it was clearly part of that strategy that Rewardco was going to broaden its portfolio of products and services, and that their key markets for these new products were their existing clients. The consequent Management Strategy demanded, therefore, that their senior consultants (who were also managers of the business at local levels) acquire the knowledge, skills and attitudes to 'cross-sell' the new products.

This led to the definition of the management and organisation development need. Put briefly, consultants were to be helped to take a wider perspective of their clients' businesses so that they could recognise and take advantage of any opportunities they and/or their clients identified for the new products. The key to this was to enable the consultants to reposition themselves in the eyes of their clients from specialist experts in a narrow field, to 'business-focused' generalists whom their clients would entrust with a wider portfolio of concerns and opportunities.

As such, this was not a fundamentally new direction for the business. They would remain primarily in the same business field as they were, and their basis of competing would not change. The core business would continue as was, but with a broader base. The key differences lay in the ability and willingness of the consultants to widen the portfolio, and to engage the new consultant specialists in Rewardco with the needs of their own clients.

We believed, therefore, we had a clear brief, which we could easily recognise as one for a *Generic* programme. The degree of change to the organisation as a whole, and indeed to the individual consultants on the programmes was relatively low; while the knowledge, skills and attitudes required for broadening from specialist to cross-selling were neither particularly esoteric nor specific to this organisation's needs. For us it was clearly a *Generic* programme. We recognised also that, although we had not gone through the process formally of exploring the management development grid with the senior managers at Rewardco, they saw it as a *Generic* programme too.

We assumed that the consultants who would attend the programme would also see it in the same way. In this we were mistaken. It became clear, rather late in the day, that many of them saw the programme differently. Some did see it as *Generic*, and were relatively happy with the design and execution. Others, however, saw it more as a *Specific Capabilities*, or even as a *Transformational* programme, and this had potentially disastrous effects on their perceptions of the quality of what they were experiencing.

It was during a module focused on the kinds of issues their clients would be facing that the mixed expectations emerged. Our design had been based partly on the recognition that, in this business, personal relationships with senior managers and directors in their client businesses were the basis upon which they worked. Rewardco's Management Strategy was to broaden the base of the consultants' relationships in the client accounts, by getting them to develop relationships not just with the one Director (who was the Director who bought their 'traditional' product) but also with other Directors (who would be more concerned with issues related to the organisation's 'new' products and services).

To this end, we were running a series of sessions entitled, 'The XX Director's Perspective'. Each was aimed at helping Rewardco's consultants to get closer to the kinds of issues and concerns which each of these 'kinds of' Directors (HR Director, Information Systems Director, Finance Director, and so on) have to deal with. Our faculty members responsible for delivering these sessions are familiar with many such directors, and we were confident that, in terms of the brief, this was as good a way as any to meet the learning aims at this stage.

In order to help the learning, we had encouraged our faculty to provide a whole range of case studies and examples from many industries and market sectors. Because we were helping consultants who work in many such sectors, the wider the perspective, the better the breadth of learning. This is one of the basic tenets of *Generic* programme design. However, it was at this point that hitherto hidden expectations emerged. Some of the consultants had come to the programme not 'wearing their consultants' hats' but 'wearing their middle managers' hats'. They saw the programme as being positioned fairly and squarely at the internal business of Rewardco. Its aim was to sharpen up, or even to transform the practices and processes of their own organisation, not of their clients' organisations. And for this reason, they were only interested in taking the tools, models, frameworks and principles, and applying them to a critical examination of Rewardco as a business.

The ensuing debate took a while to sort out; it demanded considerable rethinking and realignment. In the end, the consultants (in some cases reluctantly) agreed that the programme should remain positioned as *Generic*. (This time we did take the trouble to explore the management development grid with the clients.)

With the benefit of hindsight, we recognise how easy it should have been to spot the potential for mixed expectations. The consultants we were working with were mostly long-servers whose personal needs were well met by the existing business. Many told us, one way or another, during our precourse interviews, that Rewardco's success depended upon their personal skills at selling to 'their' clients. There was both a sense of ownership of the client, and a sense of personal satisfaction that each consultant could manage quite well on his or her own. The new products and services spelt the introduction of new faces into their accounts, new faces who were a personal threat to the relationships and dependencies which the consultants had built up. In our interviews the consultants hedged round their views of Rewardco's new strategy. But for them, the course was a great forum for attacking senior management in Rewardco, and pushing back on the changes which many of them were quite likely to feel considerably threatened by. For this reason, it was even more important for us to deal with consequential assumptions, and mixed expectations by seeking everyone's agreement to the positioning of the programme.

We like to think of this as a good reinforcing learning experience.

GETTING PROGRAMMES CORRECTLY POSITIONED

In principle, we believe that each area of the grid provides its own perfectly valuable set of opportunities to help individuals and organisations develop. Some may seem more exciting than others; some may seem to have more impact than others. For each of us, our own personalities and what excites us will 'drag' us towards one sector more than another. This being so, we urge everyone to be careful not to categorise programmes as what they want them to be instead of what they are. That way lies an almost inevitable conclusion: a 'failed' programme.

An example may help here.

POSITIONING THE INSCO MANAGEMENT PROGRAMME

We were approached by the UK subsidiary of an international insurance company who had already engaged another provider to deliver a programme of management and organisation development for all its managers at the level immediately below the board. The programme they were going through was modular, with three-day modules spread over two years covering a whole range of managerial topics. Managers were grouped into 'teams' of about 15, with each team going through the programme, module by module, together. By the time we were approached, most teams had made a start, and had attended their first module. Some had attended one or two more; others were still waiting to go forward. It was a well-structured programme of activities.

Although the overall programme design was in place, the detailed design of some of the later modules remained unfinished. Some concerns had been expressed by managers who had been on more than one module that the quality of the providers was not up to the standard they wanted. We were given the chance to design and deliver two of the remaining modules, with a possibility of taking over the entire programme, should those modules be 'up to scratch'.

Our key contact at the client organisation was Neil Puget, the project manager for the programme. He was a very outgoing, energetic and ambitious young man who created a lot of excitement about the programme, and its role in the organisation's future. He had not been present at the programme's original inception, having been brought into the company after the early developments had taken place. This may have been one reason why he missed the overall point of the programme.

Having looked closely at the original brief, and checked some assumptions concerning the overall aims of the programme, we realised that this was clearly a *Generic* programme. But it took us some time, and a meeting with Puget and his own manager, finally to convince him that he was actually project managing this kind of programme. He had been acting as though the programme was *Transformational.* For him, the excitement of change, of being a key agent of change, and of influencing senior managers to transform the sleepy business into a bright new future was too attractive to allow him to see the 'truth'. Added to which, there was a lot of change going on (or being attempted). There was an aggressive and domineering new General Manager; there were a number of Change Projects on the go (these were being run by Board members and were not associated with the management development programme); and the mood in the company was that change had to happen.

So Puget assumed that his programme was part of that change process, and approached the programme with all the trappings of managing and delivering a *Transformational* event. He, himself, took the lead on the introductory module, which was all about helping the 'teams' to work together effectively. After all, they were going to go through a series of learning experiences together over the coming two years. He set the scene, set expectations and witnessed significant disappointments.

Many of the managers were quite clear that this programme was not part of the change process, especially those who had been involved in the early discussions which led up to its being started. Other managers may have been caught on the tide of Puget's enthusiasm, and expected something radical. What they were getting was something which had started life as a *Generic* programme (although, clearly, this term was not used in defining the programme), and which was being hijacked by Puget's own involvement. The result was very messy.

At the time of writing, the programme looks much healthier (if somewhat more 'dull' than Puget would have liked). Puget has resigned from Insco, presumably seeking an organisation which is genuinely interested in running a *Transformational* programme.

The lesson from the case is that it is important to be honest about what a programme is actually all about. For Insco, change was on the agenda. But the Management Programme was a precursor to change. It had been realised that most managers needed some significant improvements in basic managerial skills before they could become an active part in radical change. Rightly or wrongly, the senior executive wanted basic, generic management development, in preparation for change, but not the change process itself at this stage.

Our experience is that this kind of misunderstanding, often driven by what one or two individuals 'want' to see rather than what has been agreed and decided, can play havoc with management and organisation development programmes. Our view is that, even if it has been excellently designed, and is delivered with consummate skill, a programme which is not in line with the expectations of both the sponsors and the participants is, at the very least, at serious risk of failure. What we have learnt is that the very first stage in successful management and organisation development interventions is to agree clearly and concisely what the intervention is all about. The Management Development Grid is of great help in achieving this agreement. Until this is done, any other developmental work, no matter how good, could be a complete waste of time.

THE TECH-TEST PROGRAMME AND THE MANAGEMENT DEVELOPMENT GRID

What kind of programme was the Tech-Test event (see the Appendix for the Tech-Test case study)? To answer this, we need to go back to the two models we have explored in this and the previous chapter: the 'levels of strategy' model, and the management development grid.

So far as the Business Strategy of Tech-Test is concerned, the key issue is one of increasing commercialisation of the business as it moves from what has been a largely reactive, technically focused organisation, to one which actively seeks out new business, and competes on quality against an increasingly aggressive set of global competitors. They too, like Rewardco, are seeking to broaden the base of their business from a core, based in Tech-Test's case upon a specialised testing capability.

The Management Strategy to support the Business Strategy is implicit in several references to Michael Pope's, the Chief Executive's 'Tech-Test Strategy' referred to in the Appendix. Given the criticality of achieving ISO9000 accreditation to the Business Strategy, a key platform for the Management Strategy has to be, in his words, 'Reshaping the working methods of Tech-Test to embrace the principles of Total Quality Management (TQM)...' The Management Strategy is one which requires constant improvement in working practices and recognition of the customer's role in survival and success.

Extrapolating from the Strategy Document, the Management and Organisation Development Strategy was aimed at developing the knowledge, skills and attitudes of managers to support these higher level strategies. As he writes, 'staff have developed good skills as specialists but have tended to be narrow in experience. There has been almost no management training of middle level and senior staff and historically there has been relatively limited delegation of authority.' He recognised that 'a sustained effort is needed to rebuild morale and team spirit and it will be a long slow haul to achieve the standards of programme and cost control across the company that are needed to keep Tech-Test competitive.'

For Michael Pope, then a key element in the Management and Organisation Development Strategy is 'to increase the motivation and job satisfaction of every individual in the company, to provide the necessary training and to ensure that responsibilities are delegated in a way which makes use of the full potential of every member of staff'.

Although these views were not set out within our framework of the three levels of strategy, because of the clarity of approach which is characteristic of Michael Pope, it is not difficult to extrapolate from his single document the interrelationships as they relate to this model. It is quite clear from his point of view that the kinds of management and organisation development activities which are very broadly 'specified' in the document are a necessary condition for the survival of the company. There is a direct and clear link between management and organisation development and the Business Strategy.

The key issues for management and organisation development, in Michael Pope's view, were clearly pointing to a *Specific Capabilities* programme. Managers of a specialist business had to be able to manage the core processes significantly better, and to quality standards which demanded consistency and alignment with the unique operations of their organisation. Everyone needed to grow in motivation and everyone needed to be willing and able to delegate and to be delegated to. This was not a matter simply of some basic management skills, but of the very way in which the business is run. Nor was it a matter of changing the nature of the business or of transforming the basis of competing. They simply had to get better at what they are in business to do, or they would lose their market.

When he was interviewed prior to the event, Michael Pope's stated aims for the programme largely reinforced his consistent views of what was needed. He spoke of the need for a 'commonality of approach' among the management team; of managers acquiring skills to implement *in-house* projects; and of a 'disciplined regime'. This was, for Michael Pope, a 'classic' *Specific Capabilities* programme; or it would have been, had we had the model to explore with him at the time.

But Michael Pope was neither the buyer (that was primarily Bill Gillies), nor the sole participant on the programme. Extrapolating from the interviews with the participants we can see that not all of the managers at Tech-Test had such clarity and consistency in their views concerning the aims and approach of the programme.

Some of Roger Wales' comments hinted more of a *Transformational* approach than anything else, and it is certainly true to say that the impression conveyed by the mood of the original meeting which stimulated the whole exercise (see Appendix) was one in which genuine and radical change was being asked for. These all point to some aims being set within the top half of the portfolio.

Meanwhile, many of the other, more specific stated 'aims' for the programme were clearly of the *Generic* kind: Norman Castle referred to 'advice on improving efficiency and delegation . . . how to run a business;' while Derek Stubbs and Victor Parrot made similarly general comments. Nobody seemed to be seeking an *Exploratory* kind of programme.

Consequently, one of the ingredients which we now recognise as crucial to successful interventions was missing. That is an agreed set of aims, set within an explanatory framework which *makes sense* of those aims.

The programme did have a set of words which were defined as the programme's aims. These were

> To enhance the general commercial and managerial capabilities and competencies of senior staff via the recognition and application of suitable management styles

Those words were 'agreed' by all 19 participants. The question which remains open at this stage is whether that set of words meant the same thing to them all. Our suspicion is that they did not. In terms of the language of the Management Development Grid, these aims most closely represent those we would associate with a Generic programme. They make no reference to Tech-Test as an organisation (which programmes positioned on the left of the grid would surely do), and do not suggest significant change (which one would expect from a programme aimed at the top of the grid). These words convey very little about the kinds of driving forces which led up to the development of the programme, especially about the intense pressure which some managers were expressing concerning their perceived need for radical change in the organisation (so, again, they point away from both the left-hand side and the top of the model). And yet they were agreed and accepted.

This implies one of two possible interpretations. The first is that they were 'neutral' enough to allow all participants, whatever their own hopes and aspirations for the programme, which were, as we have seen, diverse, to interpret the aims differently, and, for each, as though they meant the kinds of things they had talked about in the lead up to the programme itself. This could be described as the 'I know what it says, but what it means is...' interpretation.

The second interpretation is that participants to some extent recognised that the 'aims' did not reflect what they had asked for, but were prepared, for whatever reasons, to 'go along with' the aims as written. This could be summarised as the 'it doesn't matter what it says, it's what happens that counts' interpretation.

In practice, we are unable to resolve this problem. Even if we were to return to the participants with the direct question 'Which is the correct interpretation for you?', we should do well to take the answers with a very significant degree of caution. It seems to us that, in the absence of any clearly validatable data, we should pass over this problem and move on. The academic persona of the Management Development Unit shrugs his shoulders and looks for the next intellectual challenge; the change agent makes a commitment not to allow such a potentially wide range of expectations to go unchecked in the future.

The next port of call may need to be what happened rather than what people may remember about what they wanted to happen before the event started. So what of the programme itself? If the basic statement of aims, or the broad positioning of the programme may have left some people short of clarity or comfort that this was going to meet their needs, how did they actually receive the programme? Surely it would have been the case that, if the programme aims were not commensurate with what they wanted, then the programme delivery would have highlighted this. One could ask the obvious question, *As soon as it became clear to participants that the programme was not going broadly 'their' way, that their own interpretation of those broad aims were not being addressed, did they draw attention to it there and then, and if not why not?*

The fact is that they did not. Does this mean that, in fact, the programme did deliver to their respective needs?

The data gathered from the follow-up activities at Tech-Test seem to suggest that there were some serious mismatches between individuals' hopes and expectations and the 'reality' which unfolded after the event. Whatever actually happened on the programme itself, we suggest that the managers may not have been able clearly to identify how well the various programme elements were working towards their own views of the programme aims.

The first point to stress is that none of the people involved, including the lecturers and facilitators, had gone through the kind of analysis which the grid provides. From everyone's point of view there may well have been an assumption that what was going on was the best way to achieve the aims of the programme. The fact that different people may have had different interpretations of those aims also allows that they had different interpretations of what was actually going on during the programme, and how that was moving towards those aims.

Secondly, although the statement quoted above was the overall 'aim' of the programme, it was supported by more detailed aims for each of the four modules. For the first module, which is the crucial one so far as this issue is concerned, it was agreed that

'the module should be directed towards the following aims:

❑ Building on the recent strategy formulation for Tech-Test, to examine the strategic management process and to address the effective implementation of strategic direction

❑ To understand and apply a kitbag of managerial tools, techniques and frameworks to increase interpersonal and managerial effectiveness

❑ To examine the role of the top team within an organisation and to facilitate team building within that context. To address the implementation and communication of policy making

❑ To examine managerial styles such as leadership roles and decision-making, communication and delegation

❑ To develop the ability of senior staff to exercise managerial style in line with structural change and to assist and support individual managers with their own agenda for action'

It is very likely that each individual manager could find within those more detailed aims something which looked likely to deal with his or her particular hopes for the programme. And for those who would search in vain, there were still three modules to go.

The third point is that few of the participants had had any previous experience of management and organisation development. Few would have felt 'qualified', at least in the early stages of the programme, to judge how effective the activities were likely to be toward achieving their respective aims.

Finally, it may not be very easy for anyone unfamiliar to the processes of managerial learning quickly to identify the differences between programmes designed for each quadrant of the grid. In the next chapter we shall explore these differences. In so doing, we shall suggest that there may be very large numbers of 'management and organisation development' activities which have missed, and, in some cases continue to miss the crude but essential point that fundamentally different aims may need different approaches. Those differences may be subtle, but they can be very significant in their effects.

In conclusion, we suggest that the dominant mood, or interpretation of what was happening was that, somehow or other, the programme was going to do what each manager had, in his or her preliminary interview, asked for it to do. The fact that the initial statements of intent, as encapsulated in the 'aims' did not explicitly link with each manager's different hopes and perspectives was not, apparently, an issue. And as the programme progressed, what was actually going on could easily have been seen as, somehow, building toward what each manager was hoping for. If anyone did identify, during the programme, a problem in aligning his or her personal aims with what was going on, it may have been easier to wait for the next day, or the next module than to speak out. And by the end of the programme overall, it was clearly too late.

None of this implies that the programme was 'doomed' from the start, The data gathered since the programme clearly shows that there was some value to be had for all from the programme. But we believe that the strong possibility that different people went into the programme with very different sets of expectations, which were not challenged, and which may have coloured their interpretations of what actually took place, may have had a significant impact on how they have been able to use, or been prevented from using, the learning back at Tech-Test itself.

As we shall argue throughout the book, although what is designed into programmes, and what programmes deliver are crucial elements in successful management and organisation development, they are not the only elements to take into account. The next few chapters will provide us with, we hope, the means to explore the Tech-Test case much more effectively than we are able to do at this early stage in the book.

So this chapter has not been an attempt to 'prove' that the Tech-Test programme 'would have been better' had we used the grid to position it before we ran it. We are simply suggesting that we may have enabled a better dialogue between ourselves and the managers of Tech-Test had we had the language of the grid available to us. We also like to think that this would have helped us with other aspects of the programme, aspects which we shall explore in the following chapters.

CONCLUSIONS

The model explored in this chapter is simple. Of themselves models can do little to deal with the more subtle issues in managerial learning which we shall address in more depth as the book progresses. But as practical maps to show us one broad view of the territory we are trying to occupy, and thereby to eliminate some of the basic risks and threats to effective in-company management and organisation development, they do a similar job to those pages at the front of most atlases which attempt to map the entire world (or the entire universe) on a single page. They are good for positioning the big things (the continents or galaxies), but as practical tools to get from A to B they need supplementing with maps on a smaller scale. The following chapters will take us down to these more precise levels, and show how the large-scale maps from this chapter, used in conjunction with smaller-scale maps of the same territory can get us much closer to our aims of using management and organisation development genuinely to help people in organisations to be more effective and fulfilled.

4 Key Components and Assumptions

I suggested in the previous chapter than it may be helpful to think of 'management and organisation development' as four distinct kinds of activity (*Generic, Specific Capabilities, Transformational,* and *Exploratory*) rather than as one. The reason for doing so is that it helps us to take fundamentally different approaches to each. This, I argued, is appropriate, since, for each, we are trying to achieve something very different.

The first question I should like to address in this chapter is why, if these are so different, this has not been identified before. I believe that this is partly due to the relative newness of management and organisation development (especially when compared to other kinds of education); although managers have been 'educated' or 'trained' for some time, the idea of 'management and organisation development' as some kind of discipline is relatively recent. In situations such as these, it takes time for people to be in a position to develop helpful and agreed pictures, models or maps of the territory.

But another reason why we do not always find it easy to identify these different kinds of activity as so different lies in the fact that programmes within each quadrant are likely to contain 'the same' kinds of elements, and this can disguise those essential differences. An analogy may help clarify this point:

Although they are all motor vehicles, most people we know, including young children, would be able to tell the difference between a tractor, a racing car, a big family saloon car, and a van. Yet each of these vehicles contains an engine, a steering wheel, gearbox, driver's seat, and so on. What makes them so different does not start from what goes into them, but what they are to be used for. It is their differences in use which determine what kinds of component take precedence in overall design. For example, what makes tractors so different may be the size of their wheels: having big wheels may be more important than the comfort of the driver's seat; for a racing car, the performance of the engine and gearbox, working together may be the critical factors. Over the years we have learnt about these fundamental differences, and motor vehicle manufacturers have recognised the relative significance of the 'shared' components. Very early motor vehicles were far less differentiated by their 'aims'. Many 'management and organisation development' programmes are a little like these early vehicles: portmanteau efforts, and worthy, but soon to be superseded by vehicles more suited to their aims.

In some ways, people in management and organisation development, and the managers who represent their 'customer base' already seek to make these kinds of differentiation. However, if they are not already relatively clear about whether they are designing a tractor or a racing car, they may produce a vehicle which does not deliver what people wanted. We have often come across situations in which even people engaged in management and organisation development have not been able to see this point clearly, have, by trial and error, developed a relatively successful 'tractor' programme, but been very puzzled when this programme has failed to translate into what is superficially a similar set of needs, but has been, in fact, a completely different learning challenge. As one colleague put it, 'I can't understand why this programme has bombed out; when I did it for that other company, they loved it.' This was our cue to introduce the grid, and what it tells us about modifying the 'components' of our products to meet what can be very different needs.

In this chapter I shall explore how good management and organisation development design relates to this kind of essential modification of basic 'technologies', and why some programmes, for example, need to focus heavily on shifting participants' paradigms, while others need to major on the acquisition of shared language and processes.

'MUSIC' IN MANAGEMENT AND ORGANISATION DEVELOPMENT

As with our overall design of the Management Development Grid, our attempt at breaking down the key 'components' of a management and organisation development intervention is but one way of doing the job. It may not be the 'best' way, but it seems to be helpful. As a design guide, we recognise that its primary purpose is to help ensure that we focus upon the whole vehicle and not just one or two parts thereof.

The simple model explored in this chapter introduces, but does not pursue some important issues in managerial learning; those issues are pursued later. The reason for this is that the book is intended to be both practically useful as well as a deeper exploration of managerial learning. The model explored in this chapter helps, makes sense and is useful. My colleagues and I are continually at work designing and developing new tools based upon our continual learning. But, again, at this stage, we feel a relatively crude tool is better than none.

The elements within this tool can be summarised via the acronym MUSIC:

MOTIVATION
UNLEARNING
SKILLS, KNOWLEDGE AND ATTITUDES
IMPLEMENTATION
CONTINUOUS IMPROVEMENT

Although explored separately, we recognise that, as with the various elements in a motor vehicle, it is important for them to be connected together to produce an integrated whole if the programme is to be effective. Unfortunately, we have often come across examples of programmes which have been little more than 'construction kits'; providers seem to be able to get away with this approach more than we would have expected. Our view is that, these days, we ought to be able, even for a Generic programme, where the issue is least pressing, to design something more integrated that this. We believe that 'users' of programmes (the participants and the sponsors), just as drivers of motor vehicles do not need to know the details of how the engine and gearbox are linked, should not need to know how each component works in detail for the programme to do its job effectively.

Secondly, we do recognise that some 'technologies' may be able to do more than one job at the same time. For example, a session showing managers how their current behaviours, which are shown to be directly contributing to their organisation's competitive disadvantage, could be substituted for different behaviours, which would improve the organisation's chances of success, could have both a motivational and an unlearning role within an event. As I explore the 'technologies' in this chapter I shall focus in many cases on their primary use; this does not, of itself, preclude other functions for the same kind of activity. However, I would refer the reader to the section towards the end of this chapter, entitled, 'Approaches do not always translate', which, to follow our analogy, reinforces the point that a tractor gearbox placed in a racing car is not good design.

Finally, it is not our belief that good programme design takes each element in turn, deals with it, and then moves on (Monday is motivation; Tuesday unlearning; and so on). In many cases, motivation may need to precede other aspects of a programme, otherwise, little learning will take place; implementation does seem to come naturally towards the end of the sequence. But even the sequencing of these components, we have found, needs to be considered afresh for each design exercise, often changing in line with the specific needs of the participants, and the aims of the programme.

THE KEY ELEMENTS

In this chapter I have deliberately taken a practical rather than a philosophical approach to concepts such as motivation and unlearning. This is to enable us quickly to cover the broad territory of management and organisation development interventions. However, these concepts are not unproblematic, and will be more thoroughly questioned in Chapter 7, in which I explore research into some of the underlying processes which take place as managers learn.

Motivation

This is the part of any learning experience which deals with the 'why should I?' It is painfully obvious that nobody in the management and organisation development business can make learning happen. It is entirely up to learners to learn. However, it may be an important part of any intervention to help people to recognise that going through a learning experience may be of value to them. We suspect that, for quite a number of our activities, and for a whole variety of reasons, we may be required to devote energy and thought to helping people find their answers to this question.

As with the other elements, the *motivation* part or parts of the programme will look very different depending on a number of factors. Our belief is that one of these key factors will be the positioning of the respective intervention within the management development grid, as I shall explore in more depth throughout this chapter.

Unlearning

By this I mean the ways in which ingrained behaviours and perceptions may need to be abandoned before space can be created for new learning. Within this element we include activities which help people become aware of and question basic assumptions and paradigms which may be getting in the way of seeing the value or sense of new ways of thinking or behaving. Within unlearning I include everything from the way in which physicists had to abandon some of the assumptions underlying Newtonian physics before they were able to appreciate Einstein's point regarding the general theory of relativity, to the way in which some managers have had to abandon the assumption that people need to be forced by fear to contribute to the well-being of an organisation before these managers can get the point of 'empowerment'.

Skills, Attitudes and Knowledge

The core part of many traditional interventions, this deals with the acquisition of skills like balance-sheet analysis, attitudes such as a willingness to listen, and knowledge such as the actual percentage factory of output which is exported.

Implementation

There is a sense in which learning cannot be said to have taken place until it is used in a practical context. This sense is reinforced in the world I am dealing with in this book by the fact that the vast majority of the learning experiences which relate to in-company management and organisation development programmes are done for more than the good of the souls of the participating managers. This element, then, is the part which helps managers to find ways of behaving differently back at work, and in ways which are commensurate with the aims of a programme. Implementation is the part of a programme which deals with the 'That's all very well, but how can I make it work in my job?' kinds of questions

Continuous Improvement

Most of what we do in management and organisation development is not aimed at a one-time effect, but at helping managers continue to be able to gain value from their investment of time and effort in learning. Our suspicion is that a significant amount of what is 'learnt' on many management and organisation development activities is soon lost or forgotten. Finding ways of increasing the 'shelf-life' of managerial learning is a key part of effective management and organisation development. It is this which we believe is the least well understood of the five elements we work with.

HOW THESE ELEMENTS MAP ONTO THE MANAGEMENT DEVELOPMENT GRID

I believe that almost every management and organisation development intervention demands a contribution from each of our MUSIC elements. What makes programmes in different quadrants of the Management Development Grid fundamentally different from each other is their fundamentally different aims, and this is likely to have an impact on both the relative importance of each element within different parts of the grid, and the ways in which each is integrated into the whole learning design.

The 'extended' grid in Figure 4.1 illustrates approximately our thoughts on the relative mix of four of the five elements for each kind of programme. The relative size of each element in the four boxes symbolises its relative importance for each kind of programme. For example, finding ways of *implementing* the learning from an *Exploratory* programme may be a 'smaller' issue than it will be on a *Specific Capabilities* programme. But *unlearning* may be of vital importance for an *Exploratory* programme, while of relatively small significance on a *Generic* programme.

The centre of the diagram represents the centrality of the skills (and attitudes and knowledge) element to each kind of programme. I suspect that,

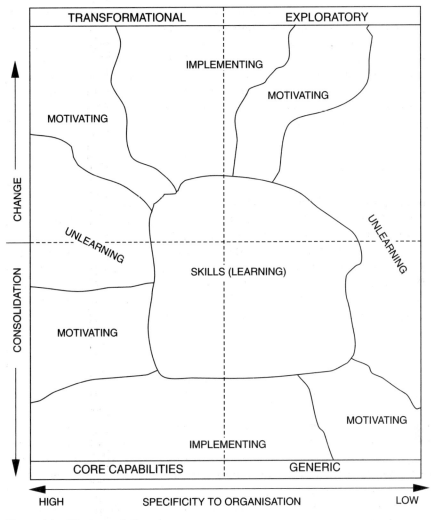

Figure 4.1   *The 'extended' grid*

of the four elements, this is the least affected by the 'nature' of the programme (its position on the grid); in one sense, balance-sheet analysis is balance-sheet analysis, whatever you want to do with it. But its centrality is ameliorated in the diagram by the retention of the dividing lines between the boxes. Good design still demands that we take into account, even in this core part of a programme, that managers will be using the skills, attitudes and knowledge to achieve very different kinds of goals.

SOME PRACTICAL LEARNING TRANSFER TECHNIQUES PLAY 'MUSIC' IN THE GRID

In the following section I shall briefly explore each quadrant of the grid, and each of the programme elements within each quadrant, identifying some of the design principles and practical learning transfer techniques this mapping process has helped us to identify. For more detailed exploration of these kinds of practical learning techniques, refer to Stuart 1984. Chapter 10 explores these issues in significantly greater depth.

I include a small case study for each quadrant of the Management Development Grid. The studies are based on our and others' recent work in management and organisation development and illustrate how, in practice, these principles have been applied to real learning events.

The placing of the 'techniques' is not absolutely exclusive; some techniques or activities will apply to more than one kind of programme. However, the aim is to provide insight into the most relevant or practical kinds of design principle and learning transfer technique for each. Nor is this meant to be a complete listing of the learning design principles we have developed. Further work on practical learning design will be explored later in the book.

GENERIC PROGRAMMES

Generic programmes are about gaining insights into existing and best practice within a variety of different industries and organisations. I believe, therefore, that *Generic* programmes are aimed at focusing more on the *skills*, attitudes and knowledge elements than the other elements.

Motivation

Motivation in *Generic* programmes is very often relatively straightforward: for example, it may often be closely linked to a 'you know it makes sense' kind of approach, as in, 'in order to maintain our position as an organisation, we need to continue to ensure that our managerial skills are reinforced, enhanced and matched against those in other organisations'.

Many *motivation* difficulties we may have to confront in this kind of programme are likely to come from differences in perception regarding the 'need' for such enhancement. Some managers express resentment, for example, that, by implication, they 'need' improving. Where the 'motivational' part of the programme is delivered with a 'remedial' slant, such resentment could be anticipated; where the 'motivation' is focused on 'keeping fit' in the managerial sense, we have found this to be more acceptable.

The kinds of device for *motivating* within a *Generic* programme, therefore, are often most effective at the individual level. Managers can often recognise the opportunity for personal growth, or for career development which *Generic* programmes offer. The individual's line manager can play a key role in helping develop this approach, as can, in certain circumstances, senior management, who can identify how the development of individual managers through this kind of programme can benefit everyone within the organisation; keeping it more efficient and effective through managerial best practice. The importance of the 'provider' in delivering or creating participant motivation within a *Generic* programme is often fairly low, with much of that motivation being delivered almost 'subliminally', for example, by exploring the implications for the organisation of the comparative materials used during the event. Where, for example, managers from a car manufacturer are confronted with the realisation that a Japanese manufacturer can retool and produce on the same production line one-off vehicles in the same time as it takes to mass produce the same model, this in itself may motivate them to seek ways of emulating this ability. (It could also *de*motivate – but this is a risk implicit in this style of programme.)

Unlearning

Within *Generic* programmes, we have found the *unlearning* elements also to be *relatively* easy to cope with. Given the relatively low focus on change from these programmes, the aim is more about building incrementally upon existing skills, attitudes and knowledge than about unlearning skills, attitudes and knowledge, although, we do stress that this is relative to other kinds of programme. In some cases, we may have to help people to 'unlearn' some assumptions regarding how to manage staff, or that having the best products guarantees success, and so on. But compared to the challenges of *unlearning* in other sectors of the portfolio, these are comparatively simple tasks to achieve.

Generic programmes pose a relatively low level of 'threat' to managers, compared to the other three kinds of programme. *Transformational* and *Exploratory* programmes threaten through change; *Specific Capabilities* programmes threaten to take away individual choice and identity. (These points are developed in much greater depth in Chapter 7). *Generic* programmes are, in consequence, much more likely to be dealt with by participants at a rational, cognitive, intellectual level. Distancing himself or herself from the emotional implications of what is being learnt, the individual manager may be able, objectively, to deal with his or her own unlearning through exposure to 'the reason why it would be better if . . .' or to techniques such as 'lateral thinking' or 'creativity indexes', and so on.

Skills, Attitudes and Knowledge

The *skills*, attitudes and knowledge components of a *Generic* programme are frequently the most significant. We suspect that many of the traditional means of delivering learning have emerged from the kinds of activity which were originally designed for *Generic* programmes. At Cranfield, for example, many members of faculty learnt their own teaching craft from working on MBA programmes. These, although not strictly part of this 'atlas', being public courses and not in-company activities, are very closely associated with what I have called *Generic* programmes. Lectures about managerial theory, case studies from a variety of industries, Study Groups of people from as varied a set of backgrounds as possible working together to bring different views to the same problem, and so on, are the stuff of this kind of programme.

What is also part of the set of design assumptions traditionally associated with this kind of 'Generic' programme is that bringing all the 'facts' together into an integrated, continuous story is not a vital role for the provider. Built around the 'Nine o'clock economics; ten o'clock strategy' model of the traditional MBA, many Generic programmes have offered managers a whole cupboard full of ingredients, in no particular order, which they can take away with them to cook up into whatever recipes they choose. We do not subscribe to this as an appropriate way to design or deliver any in-company management and organisation development intervention.

Implementation

Thus, the role of *implementation*, in our classification, is one which, for *Generic* programmes, remains relatively uncharted territory, and reasonably so, given that it is one of the core defining factors of a *Generic* programme that the learning aims should not be focused too much on the specifics of a single organisation. Many *Generic* in-company programmes maintain their generic nature by mixing managers from many different parts of the organisation on the same programme, or iteration of the programme. This mixing creates a challenge concerning the *implementation* of learning which most providers deal with by focusing upon helping the individual managers develop their own personal organisers of learning, such as 'Learning Logs', 'Personal Action Plans', or any other kind of device. In some cases, regrouping of the set of people sharing a course is mooted, but, in our experience, this does not happen very often, especially for *Generic* programmes.

A more accessible *implementation* device is the debrief of the participant by her or his immediate line manager or mentor. As part of this debrief, or separate from it, there is also the creation for the participating manager of opportunities for implementing the learning, again, probably with help from the line manager. This may depend for success on the participating manager sharing with the line manager the learning record, as captured in the Learning Log or Action Plan, so that both parties are agreed about what has been learnt, and how to apply the learning. Our experience is that this kind of *implementation* activity does not happen frequently.

Later in the book I shall attempt to understand why this may be the case. For now, it is worth recording that, in many cases, this implies that the onus for *continuous improvement* is placed upon the individual manager. Not all organisations we have talked to fully appreciate the implications of this.

Continuous Improvement

As we continue to learn (often at second or third hand) the lessons which our competitors on the Pacific Rim have learnt, we attempt to instil within all our organisations something resembling *kaizen*, or, as we have loosely translated it in this book, continuous improvement. *Generic* programmes often introduce ways of doing things which represent the current view of 'best practice'. Many aspects of this learning quickly go out of date. Companies which invest in *Generic* programmes do well to recognise the importance of keeping the learning going after the formal activities, through such devices as 'Quality Circles'. Most of these related 'technologies' (Crosby 1984; Deming 1988; Macdonald and Piggott 1990) are appropriate devices for the *continuous improvement* elements of *Generic* programmes.

RELOCATION LTD: A GENERIC PROGRAMME

This small but talented organisation recognised a need for improvements in some of the ways in which managers interacted within the business. More efficient and effective communication was needed, along with a wider recognition of the business realities. Technically sound, managers were in need of a supplementary competence in recognising the cost, profit and resource implications of their decisions.

However, that need was not to be met by the introduction of any specific processes or behaviours. What was being asked for was a greater awareness of what constitutes good management, so that the managerial roles of the senior people could be executed more professionally. As some of the participants said before the programme was run, 'We have never had any management training.'

Aims

The aims of the programme were clearly commensurate with those of a *Generic* event. They were simply stated, and focused upon improving the basic understanding by the participants of the nature of business, and of the implications of decisions on other parts of the organisation. The overall aim was to turn technically competent people into better managers.

Motivation

Two key means were used for this. The first was a series of one-to-one interviews with each of the participants undertaken by members of the Management Development Unit team from Cranfield School of Management. This gave each of them their chance to explore their own views of the business and to respond to questions concerning both the future of the business as they saw it and the issues to be confronted to achieve success in the future. The personal sense of involvement people gain from this active role in defining the issue to be addressed by a programme seems to us to be an effective vehicle for *motivation*, especially for *Generic* programmes.

The second vehicle used for *motivation* on this programme was a 'strategy' workshop. The management team attended a brief workshop in advance of the main programme, and identified through the application of analytical tools to the business, the key elements of their future competitive strategy. The first day of the full programme then provided participants with an opportunity to go through a similar experience, and to recognise the nature of the competitive environment; their company's strengths, weaknesses, opportunities and threats; the options available to them as a company; and the rationale for the strategy actually adopted. This set the agenda for the managerial behaviours required to operationalise the strategy.

Unlearning

Much of the *unlearning* requirement centred upon the ways in which managers tended to look after their own projects, staff and customers, often to the disadvantage of their colleagues, and to the business as a whole. The managers from this organisation were particularly astute intellectually, so there was a strong suspicion on our part, which proved to be correct as it happened, that they would very quickly recognise at a cognitive level their non-collaborative behaviours, but find it difficult, in practice, to shed them. We therefore used two consecutive exercises to deal with this issue.

The first was a standard, brief 'Prisoner's Dilemma' kind of exercise, which made the point very bluntly that it was more 'natural' for them to adopt competitive than collaborative stances, and to follow self-destructive strategies (supported, for some, by blatant lies). The second exercise was one we have devised ourselves, which sought to reinforce what steps are needed to unlearn 'natural' internally competitive behaviours.

We have recognised over the years that it pays huge dividends to design such exercises or simulations ourselves. There are many such exercises and simulations on the market, but challenges such as this one for Relocation Ltd.

are best met by exercises which provide an appropriate resonance with the participants' own style, culture and business. This belief was well rewarded in this case, as the participants drew upon their own skills and knowledge to confront the issues which the exercise raised for them.

Skills

The rest of the programme was relatively standard, as befits a *Generic* event. We covered the key lessons of strategy, marketing, finance and project management. What made the event successful for them, however, was not so much the 'content', as represented by these inputs, but the 'impact' on their behaviours which this new knowledge was to make.

Implementation

The final session of the programme was an Action Planning session. Because the organisation is quite small, it was possible to involve participants in a shared set of action plans. This meant that, because of the shared responsibility for successful implementation, there was greater chance of the actions being achieved.

Continuous Improvement

Relocation Ltd took a novel approach to this part of the programme: they offered full-time employment to the Cranfield Management Development Consultant who had run the programme for them, and gave him the job of helping the company to continue to apply the learning over the coming years. We do not recommend this as a standard way of dealing with this element of programme execution, as we have a limited supply of good Management Development Consultants!

SPECIFIC CAPABILITIES PROGRAMMES

Specific Capabilities programmes are focused upon building and integrating a common set of language and behaviours among managers. This implies to us that the key component of the set is likely to be implementing.

Motivation

For these kinds of programme, the *motivation* aspect will, or ought to, look very different from those for a *Generic* programme. Especially in these days of 'individualism', there may be a significant job to be done within a *Specific Capabilities* programme in helping managers to recognise the value of adopting language and behaviours which are shared across the entire organisation. Some managers we talk to express discomfort at what they see as this kind of 'brainwashing' and some express a great deal of satisfaction with the current downturn in the state of the Japanese economy. They are pleased that the kinds of slavish 'loyalty' to the organisation, which they perceive to be the norm in Japan, does not guarantee long-term success. I do not wish to comment on the validity of these perceptions; but do recognise implications for those of us involved in any kind of management development activities which could be interpreted as attempts to replicate this 'Japanese myth'.

Consequently, although the opportunities for personal growth and career enhancement which were a key part of the motivation for *Generic* programmes remain relevant to *Specific Capabilities* programmes, the motivational aspects of these opportunities are significantly less compelling here. In *Specific Capabilities* programmes, not only is there a focus on 'standardising' behaviours (getting on not from personal worth, but from following the rules), but these behaviours may not always build upon the personal strengths and preferences of individual managers on a programme.

The focus of a great deal of the *motivation* in a *Specific Capabilities* programme is therefore more likely to be on the community aspects of corporate life. Here, senior management are likely to be required to illustrate how the desired behaviours are in line with the organisation's strategy – are, in fact, a necessary condition for the strategy to succeed. This needs to be reinforced by evidence that the strategy is appropriate and, through success stories of other organisations who have successfully adopted similar approaches, tried and tested. There will also need to be clear indications of how the desired behaviours are to be rewarded on an ongoing basis and in line with the reward systems, the reporting structures, and so on, of the organisation as it is today.

Unlearning

Unlearning as part of *Specific Capabilities* programmes means helping managers to stop doing what they may have been doing for many years. The success of such unlearning depends upon supporting and reinforcing structures within the business, otherwise any good work which may be achieved during an intervention could soon be lost.

We recognise that one of the most effective ways of focusing managers on unlearning in a *Specific Capabilities* programme is by celebrating and reinforcing the differences between people. Given that the aim of a programme in this category is to produce similar behaviours and language, it seems psychologically valuable to get to those commonalities via the uniqueness of the individual, and by emphasising the compatibility of such uniqueness with the programme's aims. One possible vehicle for this would be the use of psychological profiling (see Chapter 9).

On a programme for a single organisation wishing to adopt a relatively narrow set of processes and behaviours, for example, we may use the insights into each participant's personality as a means of helping each of them to anticipate which elements of the process and behaviours he or she will find easy, valuable and 'sensible', and which will appear difficult, pointless and 'bureaucratic' (or some other negative perceptions). This kind of approach helps us to help managers realise why some behaviours are relatively hard to 'unlearn', because those behaviours make use of parts of their personality which they are relatively comfortable with; as compared with the 'new' behaviours, which may call upon parts of their personality with which they are less comfortable.

There is still a valuable role also for the more 'objective' approaches to unlearning. A great deal of the reinforcement to *Specific Capabilities* kinds of events are the 'you know it makes sense' kinds of message. Exercises which illustrate the effectiveness of managers working to a common set of terms and processes compared to those following different agendas reinforce that it is better to have a less-than-perfect process in place than to have no process at all (or, what is more often the case, as many processes as there are managers).

Skills, Attitudes and Knowledge

Some of the skills, attitudes and knowledge elements of a *Specific Capabilities* programme will be similar to those on other kinds of programmes. But the key difference will be that most *Specific Capabilities* programmes will contain a high proportion of 'this is how we do this' kinds of activities. This demands, for effective learning, a good mix of the overview (theory) with plenty of practice. Whereas many *Generic* programmes can be highly effective with very little practical work (by which we mean such activities as role plays, piloting processes, and so on), few *Specific Capabilities* programmes will work well unless managers have tried and explored what it feels like actually to adopt the required behaviours and language. For these programmes the process of implementation is so significant that few skills elements will make sense outside activities aimed at bringing the learning to reality through implementation.

Implementation

Given that many *Specific Capabilities* programmes are about adopting language and behaviours which relate to processes and activities which are already in existence (even if only as prototypes), one of the key goals must be to ground the learning into those realities as quickly and firmly as possible. It is more important here to ensure that the language and behaviours become the ways in which managers operate than to dwell on 'why this language' or 'why these behaviours'. This points firmly towards experiential learning and reinforcement.

Let us take the English language as a case. English is the standard language in this country, and to get on, most of us find it easier if we adopt it as spoken. As with any language, words do not 'mean what I want them to mean', but are standard (with variations, some of which are deliberately developed to confuse, as with the common practice in 'youth culture' to redefine the meanings of words in ways which 'exclude' the older generation). There is no good reason why we should use the word 'dog' rather than any other monosyllable to identify that animal; but there is also no good reason not to. Successful use of language depends upon suppressing a tendency constantly to ask why such and such a word is used, but simply to use it in as recognisable form as possible, and to get on with more practical matters.

A great deal of what we do in ordinary life, from the use of words in our language to the fact that we walk on two legs rather than four could be different. When we learn to speak, to behave, to walk, we learn by practice, not from theory. If our analogy holds, the kinds of learning which are appropriate for *Specific Capabilities* programmes may also need primarily to be by practice rather than theory. It may be necessary, to satisfy curiosity, to be prepared to explore the underlying 'theory'. But we suspect that this should support the primary, practical, experiential flavour of this kind of programme rather than take the lead.

Finally, suppose the chosen set of behaviours turns out to be less effective than a different set. For example, an organisation may adopt a process which could be improved upon. If a *Specific Capabilities* programme is being used to 'train' managers to use an ineffective process, is that acceptable, even if the resulting behaviours are highly tuned to that process and its needs? This is where continuous improvement plays a role.

Continuous Improvement

Although programmes in the bottom half of the management development grid are primarily about consolidation rather than change, they do not imply complete cessation of change activities. For the *Specific Capabilities* kind of programme, however, the principle is one of consolidation rather than change. In practice, room has to be made for improvement where change is beneficial. What an organisation cannot live with, however, is the core processes being changed willy-nilly.

Managers will frequently take very different views concerning the effectiveness, appropriateness, feasibility, and so on of any 'ways we do things round here'. The more a process becomes standardised, the more one group will support it for 'tidying up the mess we have been living with for years', while another will bemoan the 'onward march of bureaucracy'. How can any organisation satisfactorily reconcile such perceptions?

The chances are that it cannot, which may be no bad thing. But what it can do is to harness the skills of evaluation and creativity of managers involved in processes, collectively to maintain a continuing review of how effectively a process is achieving its goals. To do so, there has to be some kind of trade-off. The trade-off consists on the one hand of an agreement by all managers to follow the letter and spirit of the law in using a process for an agreed period of time. During that time, they need to record in as objective a fashion as possible how the process is working: time taken to use it; time taken to get output from it, and so on. During this time no tinkering is allowed.

The reason for this is that during this period the organisation is gathering as much data as possible, from as many different viewpoints as possible, concerning the same thing, which is the process in use as defined. Like scientists attempting to test scientific theories, the aim has to be as close an approximation as is feasible to the same test conditions for each evaluation. Clearly, it is almost impossible even for scientists, in laboratory conditions, to create absolute replications of 'the same' experiment. It is therefore that much harder for managers to do the same with process testing. There are two possible conclusions to draw from this: either to work even harder to ensure that unseen variables are eliminated from the 'experiment'; or to abandon the attempt altogether and to admit that the job is too difficult, so we should never try.

Our view is that, so long as managers recognise the limitations of the task, and do not act as though any conclusions they reach are thereby irrefutable, but the best they can come up with at present, it is always worth the effort to provide as well-thought-out and evaluated process environments for managers as is reasonably possible.

The other side of the trade-off is, therefore, an agreement to review the outcomes of the 'experiment' as often as is agreed to be appropriate, and to act on the results of the investigations. So long as managers are confident that genuine shortcomings in a process will be identified, quantified and rectified within a reasonable timescale, they should be more prepared to work within the kinds of 'way we do things round here' frameworks characteristic of *Specific Capabilities* programmes.

GLOBAL TECHNOLOGIES: A SPECIFIC CAPABILITIES WORKSHOP

Global Technologies is a multinational organisation going through significant change. In this case a workshop was designed to help senior managers appreciate and manage within a new sales process which was to replace a series of departmentally dominated activities. The aim of the process was to get product to the customer more quickly and efficiently. The workshop was designed for senior sales managers worldwide.

Aims

The aims of the workshop were as follows:

- Identify and reinforce positive coaching behaviors
- Clarify the nature of the coaching role in support of the new Customer Focused Sales Process
- Share best practise/ideas to resolve implementation issues

Motivation

The workshop designers, the internal 'sales training' organisation, were relying on the very senior management of each country organisation to drive the motivating aspects of the workshop. Their presence at the workshop would be preceded by briefings and discussions to get the senior sales managers to 'buy into' their roles with regard to the process.

Additionally, one module of the workshop was built round research into organisations which had adopted a process-orientation, and the lessons which had been learnt about how to operate successfully in this way. The basic message of the research was that, although fraught with risks, adopting this orientation, if done properly, can bring significant rewards.

Unlearning

Global Technologies had traditionally been a sales-oriented company. Although in the midst of major strategic change at the time this workshop was designed, it was clear to the designers that the sales 'culture' remained powerful. Most of the target managers for this workshop were themselves ex-salespeople and had learnt their craft and therefore what behaviours had made them successful within that culture. 'In their day', working from one's own initiative, often against the existing procedures, was not only perceived to be necessary, in order to cut through the 'bureaucracy', but also proof of the 'machismo' which the archetypal salesman displayed (the vast majority of the sales force was male; women often adopted 'masculine' behaviours in order to survive – see Chapter 2 for more on the 'culture' of Global Technologies).

Moreover, the traditional Global Technologies senior manager had been hard, uncompromising, ruthless, data-driven and possessive of his power (there were even fewer female senior managers than sales people). The new process (as well as many other aspects of the changes going on in the company) called for a different style of senior management, one which more closely represented coaching than controlling, and one which recognised the value of collaborative rather than competitive behaviours.

Therefore, the unlearning part of the workshop was part of a broader set of unlearning opportunities for the senior managers. This had the advantage of being consistent with other initiatives; and the disadvantage of being 'the same old hype from Head Office'. For this reason, we could not rely for unlearning on exhortation; it had to come from 'within' the managers themselves. The bad news was that, because this was a global programme, and only one part of a whole series of other initiatives going on at the same time, the workshop was limited to a day and a half over all – clearly not enough time for effective personal learning based upon good quality psychometrics.

In this case we therefore focused attention exclusively on one aspect of the overall unlearning need: the role of unchecked inferences in traditional management behaviours, how these can lead to conflicting perceptions of 'the same' reality, and how, in a process-driven, collaborative, coaching style environment, the confrontational, controlling and uncollaborative style of the traditional managers would reduce the effectiveness of the process overall. This was achieved through a mix of activity (managers commenting on a 'live' role play – a scripted interchange between manager and subordinate, in which the manager's behaviour is commented on, producing all sorts of unchecked inferences from the workshop participants), personal questionnaire on how each participant saw his or her favoured approach to resolving differences of opinion, and a co-coaching exercise on what each planned to do in the future to enhance his or her skills in coaching, which enabled participants to role model and practice 'more appropriate' behaviours.

Skills (including attitudes – crucial for this event, and knowledge)

This element required careful handling. The process itself was for sales people, but not these managers to use; the sales people would receive their own training separately. Managers would require only an overview of the process, sufficient to make sense of the opportunities it would provide for coaching the sales people. Managers who retained a 'command and control' mindset would clearly want a much more detailed picture of the process, helping them to identify points at which they would be able to 'check' their sales people. Although the process was to be automated, the workshop did not provide a copy of the software for practice (for the sales people's version of the programme, copies would need to be provided for everyone to practise). The managers were provided with a brief overview of what each part of the process did, and they then spent the majority of the 'skills' time in small groups exploring the implications for them as individuals and as representatives of the company. The focus was on 'How do I coach my staff at this stage of the process?'

Implementation

Throughout the entire workshop, managers were encouraged to focus most of their time and attention to the implications for them as 'coaches' to their sales staff. Significant amounts of time were 'breakouts' aimed at helping develop action plans.

Continuous Improvement

The learning from this workshop was aimed at being integrated into the wider programme of change activities within the company. At the time of writing, these are continuing, making it impossible for us to comment on the longer term impact of this workshop.

TRANSFORMATIONAL PROGRAMMES

Transformational programmes are designed to facilitate significant change within an organisation, through developing the thinking and behaviours of key people. This book is not specifically about organisational change as such, so we shall not attempt to replicate the good work which already exists on the subject (Burnes 1992; Grundy 1993; Mabey and Mayon-White 1993; Clarke 1994). However, the potential which management development provides in helping to transform an organisation does deserve closer attention.

For these programmes, motivating, unlearning and implementation are all crucial elements.

Motivation

Motivation has to deal with all those risk factors which are inherent in significant organisational change, and helping people through organisational change is a key role for facilitators of management development. Clearly, many of the opportunities which present themselves to be involved with a *transformational* programme will mean dealing with people at the top of the organisation, helping them, in real time, to 'create' the new organisation, crafting the strategy, designing the structure, drafting the systems, developing shared values, and so on. For the people at the top, *motivation* is unlikely to be a matter of helping them to 'see the point'; it is more likely to be a matter of providing both challenge to go the extra distance to validate their ideas, and support to encourage them to continue with what is often a very difficult process.

As Figure 4.2 shows, providing appropriate levels of supporting behaviours and challenging behaviours can create a stretching and stimulating environment. Facilitators who challenge without supporting create threat, and will find themselves being challenged in return. This can lead to the focus of an event being taken away from the issues facing the participants, and onto the process itself; many inexperienced facilitators have found themselves spending valuable time justifying themselves when they should be helping.

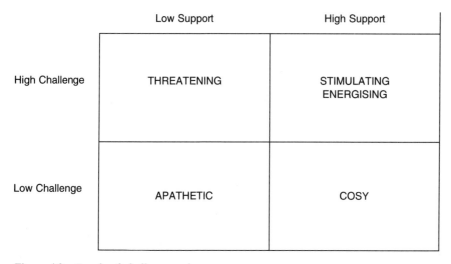

Figure 4.2   *Levels of challenge and support*

Similarly, supporting without challenging can be counter-productive. Facilitators who have learnt how important it is to listen and to empathise can waste time 'caring' for participants when they should be pushing them to confront their key issues. The environment becomes cosy, with the safety of the participants overriding the need for progress. Very poor facilitators fail either to challenge or to support, bring to the event a sense of apathy.

Where the managers on a *transformational* programme are not the key decision makers, but are important to the implementation of successful change, *motivation* becomes different. Here, previous work on all aspects of the strategic change needs to be made available, so that managers can see how what they are learning fits into the future. As Hope and Hailey (1995) has pointed out, 'culture change' programmes do not work. Transforming an organisation has to have a firm business basis. Unless there is a clear vision, and a relatively clear route to achieving that vision, the chances of this kind of programme succeeding are reduced. And by 'strategy' we mean more than just the words. To use the McKinsey 7S model as a reference point, we believe that, unless some careful thought has already been put into all seven aspects of the change, the programme could be at risk.

However, we do recognise that managing such a risk is almost inevitable. We have said that, ideally, these issues will have been dealt with before managers start work on their *transformational* events. Organisational change, however, is rarely as tidy as this, and our experience is that, in most cases, there will be many unanswered questions as we launch ourselves into almost any transformational management development intervention. Many of the fears and uncertainties associated with change will therefore be evident, manifested in such common phenomena as a lack of faith in the competence of senior management, and projected into a lack of belief in the strategy.

We recognise that different individuals will respond to change in very different ways. I shall return to this kind of issue in Chapter 9, as I delve even deeper into how managers cope with management development.

Transformational programmes are inherently more difficult from the motivational point of view in that they are, to some extent, leaps into the dark. We always encourage the mentors or line managers of any participants about to attend such an intervention to spend time preparing and motivating, by reinforcing the organisation's plans for the future. We encourage participants to read widely (we frequently provide copious pre-event reading for *transformational* programmes) on relevant change issues, including case studies. During times of change, many managers want as much information as they can lay their hands on. The more everyone involved can satisfy that want, the more we are helping to deal with the *motivation* aspect of these programmes.

Finally, because of the uncertainty, managers have to recognise that they also have a key part to play in both challenging and supporting senior executives as they, in turn, struggle with the change. Changing an organisation demands an almost infinitely complex set of calculations. The most senior managers have neither the wisdom nor the data to guarantee that their many decisions will be effective. Managers involved in learning their roles in the change, which is one of the key aims of a *transformational* programme, can provide both extra insights and ideas, and additional data to those calculations for change. Part of the motivational aspects of a transformational programme depends upon the willingness of senior management to involve these managers in the change process by being prepared to take on board ideas and approaches developed during a *transformational* programme.

Many *transformational* programmes, even where run for managers who are not directly responsible for driving the organisational change, provide significant input to the plans for change. A key motivator may be building into the learning design a role for managers either as individuals (often in the form of a 'learning contract') or (as is more common) as 'project teams' in identifying elements of the change process which they can actively play a part in implementing. This enables a shift from a feeling of powerlessness through change, to becoming, albeit in a limited way, an agent of change.

Unlearning

The *unlearning* aspects of *transformational* programmes can be among the most challenging and rewarding. It has now become commonplace that organisational change is easy at the 'hard' end: changing structure, and even systems, demands simply a set of decisions and relatively mechanistic actions. Changing behaviour, however, is not so simple or quick. A great deal of the success of a *transformational* programme will, we believe, depend upon excellence in the design and delivery of those aspects of the programme which help managers get to the roots of their assumptions and behaviours, and enable them to start the process of significant change.

Our experience to date is that almost any tool, device, method or means of unlearning is appropriate to *transformational* programmes, so long as they are used as part of that overall learning design which we believe to be so important, especially in this segment of the grid. Personality profiling, explicit exploration of learning theories, the experiential uncovering of paradigms at both organisational and individual levels, are all legitimate means of helping unlearning to take place. Once again, this is so important a topic that I shall not attempt to explore it in any depth here, but return to it in Chapter 9.

Skills, Attitudes and Knowledge

It is through the very acquisition (and implementation) of new skills, attitudes and knowledge on the part of managers within the organisation, that any genuine transformation will happen. What those skills, attitudes and knowledge may be could vary widely with the specific strategies being pursued by each organisation. In many cases, it is not a simple job identifying precisely how these will look; if they were already well defined, it is unlikely that they would be of much help in giving the organisation any kind of competitive edge through their implementation.

For this reason, a significant element within *transformational* programmes is 'discovery'. By this I mean that the identification and development of the skills, attitudes and knowledge appropriate to such a programme may not be predefined, even by 'expert' providers. This means that such providers themselves will need more in the way of skills of facilitation of learning than of 'teaching'. It will be largely by working together, participants and facilitators, that any picture of the skills, attitudes and knowledge which will form the organisational and management 'realities' of the future will be sketched out. (By the time the picture becomes detailed or 'finished', the organisation may be ready for a *Specific Capabilities* programme to seed them throughout the organisation, rather than a *transformational* programme to develop them.)

However, there are trends. As I write, in the late 1990s, I recognise a number of key areas in which successful *transformational* programmes tend to focus. They suggest that organisational transformation for success in the competitive environments of the day depends, to some extent, on the organisation's ability to help managers acquire some specific skills. Clearly, although acquiring such skills as these may help organisations differentiate themselves today, if they are truly part of what gives an organisation competitive edge, and thereby helps in its success, they will soon become commonplace. This would mean that their role in giving organisations a competitive edge will have disappeared, and they will be more likely to appear as elements in programmes which appear in the bottom half of the portfolio, to be replaced as *transformational* skills, attitudes and knowledge by some other set which we may not yet be conscious of.

Four *skill* sets seem to recur in what is currently the *transformational* area. The first (but I suspect soon to be shifted below the line) concerns strategic thinking or analysis. Despite the huge growth in 'strategy' during the 1980s, we still find many organisations being hampered in their attempts to undergo major change by a general lack of strategic thinking by middle and even quite senior managers. We suspect that, of the four kinds of management development programme, *transformational* programmes are the only ones which actually *depend* upon this skill being on the agenda. Given the centrality of the 'behavioural change follows strategy' argument, without appreciating the underlying strategic thinking and analysis, managers will be at a significant disadvantage in adopting this motivational device.

The second key area is in 'change management'. The enormous growth in change which has overtaken organisations and management in the past few years has generated a similarly enormous amount of data related to successful and unsuccessful change management. Although academics are likely to continue squabbling over some of the finer points concerning change management for many years to come, we believe that quite a lot of good practical learning has gone on which is of vital importance to a successful *transformational* programme. It is in the nature of *transformational* programmes that they exist and are part of a major set of changes. Managers who attend such programmes will be both agents of change and 'victims' of change. The more they can learn about their roles in personal and organisational change, the more likely the organisation is to achieve a successful transformation.

The third area of significance in transformational *skills* is that set of skills, attitudes and knowledge we collectively refer to as 'coaching'. Many of today's transformations are of such size that managers will be 'managing' staff who are doing things these managers have never, themselves, done. Much of the 'authority' of traditional managers, which gave them the mandate for command and control, was built upon the fact that they had been through and learnt from experiences just like those of their staff. The gradual attrition of this 'reality' which is going on simply through the changes taking place in the organisational world anyway, is given an enormous boost when an organisation chooses to go through the kind of change which accompanies a *transformational* programme. Senior managers can no longer put aside the implications of this change of relationship between themselves and their staff. This is the ideal time for managers to get to grips with coaching people who may be (and probably are, as in the case of many sporting coach/player relationships) better at their jobs than they are themselves.

The fourth *skill* set is closely related to coaching. We refer to the skills, attitudes and knowledge which managers need to acquire in order to help people (themselves, their staff, their colleagues and their own managers) to learn. Given that this is what this whole book is about, I shall not attempt here to summarise all that this skill set implies.

Implementing

Implementing the learning from a *transformational* programme will be a continuing process, so there is likely to be some overlap between *implementing* and *continuous improvement*, in terms of our classification. However, such overlaps are not a problem; the five elements are not discrete, but identified simply to help put structure on complexity.

We believe that a post-programme debrief is of major importance to *transformational* programmes. For other kinds of programme, having a debrief with one's immediate line manager is valuable, and can reinforce learning in a number of ways. If such a debrief does not happen, it does not seem to cause major disadvantages. *Generic* programmes often provide learning which may take years to have an opportunity for use; *Specific Capability* programmes are likely to be but one part of a whole host of reinforcing and integrating learning opportunities; *Exploratory* programmes may also take time to make sense, even to the participants, let alone their managers. But *Transformational* programmes are a key part of a confusing time of change, and it is important for both participant and manager to make sense, together, of the learning acquired, so that its place in the implementation of change can be agreed and acted upon.

We have found that one of the most helpful vehicles for both the debrief and for many other aspects of *implementation* is the 'Personal Strategy'. This 'document', which, in other situations we have come across under a number of different names, attempts to do a number of things. It helps participants capture ideas and learning; it helps order their thoughts; it focuses their minds on how to use the learning; it helps many of them to take stock of their lives and personal futures; and, for those who choose to share the document with others, it is a means of communicating. Our own style in using personal strategies for *transformational* programmes is to provide minimal advice on structure and content (enabling the freer format to generate the kinds of innovative thinking and approaches an organisation needs to encourage during times of change), and to treat the documents as confidential except in circumstances where writers have expressly given permission for their strategies to be made public (either to help others in the development of their own strategies, or as repositories of perceptions and ideas which others may wish to explore).

Another valuable use for the Personal Strategy has been in following up after a more formal event, such as a workshop or course. Between six and eighteen months after participants return to their place of work, we have occasionally had the opportunity to visit those workplaces, and have meetings with individuals or groups. Such Follow-Up Workshops can be a mix of activities.

In some instances, a fair amount of time is devoted to one-to-one conversations with individuals about their own progress. Here, the Personal Strategy is useful as a shared document to seek out blockers and drivers to the actions and intentions set out in the Strategy. Small groups can also get together to talk about coping with situations in which they have similar experiences of barriers to progress. Or larger groups can get together to take the learning forward by discussion, workshop, or even more input from the outside. In all cases, the sharing of experiences, especially of success stories, can be a powerful aid to implementing learning.

These are relatively unstructured regroupings; in contrast, some *implementation* activities centre upon Change Projects. These are groups which form during a *transformational* event, and set about a project which is in line with the kind of transformation the organisation is going through, and which builds upon the group's learning during the event. The group generally has a specific target to achieve within a relatively short timescale, and aims to deliver to senior management, according to that target, fully worked ideas or suggestions concerning some aspect of organisational change which will help the overall transformation.

Continuous Improvement

Some longer-term projects emanate from these activities, tending to take them into the realms of *continuous improvement*. Here these projects may be joined by other activities and structures, such as Alumni. These are groups of past participants on a *transformational* programme who meet on a regular basis to continue to offer to each other mutual support and reinforcement of learning. Either as part of this or as a separate initiative, we have helped set up co-coaching pairs of individuals, often with very different personal styles, or who have established some kind of 'bond' during a programme. These people will continue their mutual coaching of each other for an unspecified, open-ended period.

In so doing, the individuals are also engaged in another of the *continuous improvement* techniques which are valuable for *transformational* programmes, and that is 'role modelling'. Although concentrated activities, such as those which take place during an intervention, can make significant contributions to change, the kinds of constant reinforcement of appropriate behaviours which come from 'walking the talk', or 'role modelling' play a vital role in determining the 'shelf-life' of the learning: either the new behaviours become the reality, or, if the role models clearly indicate that 'it's not what we say but what we do that counts', they die away within a few weeks, at most.

Maintaining momentum is often difficult. During times of significant change, especially when not all of the systems or structural changes have been brought about to support the strategic direction, it is very easy for managers to return to what they are familiar with. One device for maintaining momentum is the 'organisational health check'. Undertaken on a regular basis, this can be a powerful stimulus to continuous improvement. However, it needs to be done with sensitivity and care, lest it become the regular round of the 'cultural revolution monitors', looking for people to pick out and punish for not following the party line with sufficient zeal.

CORPORATE LIAISONS: A TRANSFORMATIONAL PROGRAMME

Corporate Liaisons is part of Global Technologies (see Chapter 2), and has been established to support one of the key arms of the Global Technologies broad strategic change. Corporate Liaisons is responsible for a shift from 'self-sufficiency', which, in practice meant an arrogant isolation, to a series of collaborations with companies in related but synergistic fields. Global Technologies wished to become a 'solutions' provider; not having 'solutions' within its own portfolio of products and services, it was crucial to strategic success that strategic alliances be established with partners who could, along with Global, provide a full solution set.

Aims

The programme aimed to take managers most of whom, were existing managers within Global and who had sales and marketing experience, and help them appreciate and understand how the 'partnership' business was essentially different from what they had become accustomed to, and help them behave in a partnership-focused way.

Motivation

Because of the criticality of the roles of these managers to the success of Global Technologies, part of the motivation had to be driven by reinforcement of that strategy from senior management within the company. As it happened, we could have hoped for a greater degree of input from such senior management than was provided for these managers. Although the words pointed towards the centrality of partnerships in the corporate strategy, for a number of reasons, the programme itself started life in a relatively low-key way, sponsorship coming from a level of management lower than was strictly required. This led, in practice, to the programme's first iteration, even after a successful pilot, being postponed for lack of interest from the field.

One of the reasons we believe the programme survived these early setbacks was the work we had already been doing in other parts of Global Technologies, work which had achieved a high reputation. This reinforces for us the recognition that the respect which the 'provider' of a *transformational* programme is given by key influencers within an organisation may be a very significant motivator. It may also make a significant difference to the ways in which participants experience the programme itself.

Meanwhile, internal 'research' activity was adding to the motivation through people in Head Office identifying and relaying to potential participants and their managers evidence from a number of sources within and beyond the business how important successful alliance management was to the long-term success of the partnerships themselves, a point strongly reinforced on the programme itself.

Further motivational elements came from a powerful set of case studies, based on real situations faced by these managers themselves (the most important being a case which chronicled the decline and fall of an alliance due to poor liaison management).

However, in this case, we recognised that a great deal of the motivational factors would need to be integrated into the crucial unlearning elements, the success of which would determine whether or not the organisation's transformation would actually take place.

Unlearning

Most managers on this programme were senior and experienced. This had the advantage that they were mature and knowledgeable. It had the potential disadvantage that they were so deeply steeped in the culture and behaviours of the traditional organisation, that they would be unable, within the short space of the two weeks of the programme, to go through sufficient change themselves to be able to adopt the fundamentally new skills and attitudes needed. Because of the significant amount of unlearning this demanded from the programme, we built 'unlearning' into almost every element of the first two-thirds of the fortnight.

At a cognitive level, the programme dismantled assumptions about the strategic bases for alliances, about the nature of their core business, about the significance of organisational culture in successful partnerships, and about the role of the 'Account Manager' or 'Partner Manager' in the successful marketing of relationships.

At the behavioural level we identified how their 'learnt' managerial behaviours were, in fact, counter-productive to successful partnerships, and how they 'naturally' focused so heavily on their own gain, that the partner and the end customer were practically omitted from the equation. We also helped them to unlearn some preconceptions about the role of leadership in working in teams across organisations.

Skills

For each 'unlearning' experience, the programme offered the opportunity for the participants to develop their ideas as to how they would replace those 'lost' ideas and behaviours. Some broad guidance was provided through a relatively structured 'competences' exercise, and some insights were shared regarding approaches which other alliance-focused organisations had used. At the personal level, personality profiling gave participants insights into how to develop their own strengths and where their personal shortcomings could be coming from (to help develop skills in those areas), while there were plenty of opportunities for the development of skills of listening, and giving and receiving feedback.

However, because of the nature of the programme, a great deal of the 'skills' element required input from the participants themselves. It is in the nature of *Transformational* programmes to be built round 'discovery'. The organisation may be going in directions which others have followed, but the paths are still poorly defined, and it is crucial in this kind of event to recognise that what may work for others could be disastrous for Global Technologies. All 'skills' applications had to be developed as part of an implementation plan which would need to be constantly monitored and validated.

Implementation

Which led us inevitably to a significant focus on implementation. The chosen vehicle was the Personal Strategy, since many of the participants were coming 'alone'. This means that many of them would be members of very small local teams. Global Technologies is a truly global organisation, in which Corporate Liaisons was a small, if growing, part. For some of the countries represented, the Liaison 'team' would have only one or two members. The onus for developing the liaison business, and, by implication, for implementing the learning, was largely on the shoulders of the participants themselves.

The Personal Strategy model seemed the best for the job at the time, and a significant amount of time, especially from the middle of the second week, was devoted to the development of these implementation plans. Individuals worked largely alone, but were encouraged to continue to develop and use their co-coaching skills to help each other in their planning processes. Each participant also had at least one (mandatory) and in some cases several (optional) session(s) with members of faculty from Cranfield. The mandatory session was a counselling and coaching session focused on the entire programme; the optional sessions allowed individuals to seek out specialist members of faculty to explore in more depth one or more of the specific issues which had been important to them as learners.

Continuous Improvement

Many of the continuous improvement approaches which will become important to Corporate Liaisons have yet to be developed. At the time of writing, only a small proportion of the target population (which itself is a growing constituency) have been involved, and we as well as they are still learning a great deal about the ways in which the business will work in the future. At present, one of the most important vehicles for continuous improvement lies with participants from this programme linking up with other Global Technologies people who have been through an equivalent *transformational* event for sales and customer service staff.

EXPLORATORY PROGRAMMES

Exploratory programmes are focused upon challenging and changing individuals and groups in order to introduce radical approaches and novel ways of thinking and doing into an organisation. There may, at this stage, be no clear idea about how to make use of the learning which accompanies this kind of programme. They are often largely speculative. This implies to us that the key component of the set is likely to be *unlearning*.

Motivation

Among the most powerful of the *motivational* techniques for an *Exploratory* programme may be the very uncertainty and attraction of the unknown which will often surround them. Some providers of *Exploratory* kinds of activity deliberately capitalise on this element of 'mystery', and keep participants in the dark about as much as they can – until 'all' is revealed at the appropriate moment. However, this can have the effect of turning such an experience into a kind of competitive 'game', in which the impact of the learning is swamped by the thrill of 'beating' the facilitators. For some managers, also, being forced to confront the unknown is counter-motivational, so it is a highly questionable approach.

Our experience is that, even for *Exploratory* programmes, positive, open and honest *motivation* is most effective. Opportunities for personal growth, leading to a contribution to organisational growth seem more consistently to achieve commitment from participants.

We are increasingly attracted to the notion of the 'group learning contract' in this kind of context. Especially where we are working with people who know each other, at least superficially, before the event takes place, we find that an honest and open admission that we, like they, are about to embark upon a journey for which we do not have an accurate map, helps in the group's acceptance of their own responsibility for learning. Although, as we suggest in Chapter 10, responsibility for learning always belongs to the learner, it sometimes takes time to turn that into practical reality. For an *Exploratory* programme, participants must accept that responsibility very early, since here a great deal of the value added by the facilitator of learning will be just that: facilitation. Whereas, in other kinds of programme, learners can rely for a while on the facilitator 'spoon-feeding' them with data, models, and so on, such behaviours on an *Exploratory* programme merely delay learning.

Therefore, such preliminary, or 'warm-up' activities as setting ground rules (which on some other kinds of programme may, justifiably, appear to be little more than 'pious' attempts at involving people) may be helpful in leading a group quickly to agreement over what they will do, how they will do it, and so on, with the facilitator acting as process consultant rather than expert. Such guidance as is given would clearly be in helping the group towards a contract which most effectively addresses the unlearning aspects of the programme.

Unlearning

A significant amount of any *Exploratory* programme will be built around experiential learning, action learning and opportunities for giving and receiving feedback. It is tempting, at times, to suggest that, so long as it is moral and legal, anything goes in our search for *unlearning*; after all, it is hard to get people to break out of their paradigms. The problem is that, although we can define 'legal' relatively clearly, people in management development seem to have very different interpretations concerning what is 'moral'. For some, the ends justify the means; and these providers will not flinch from putting managers through extreme mental and physical discomfort if they believe that it will be 'good for them'. Others believe unlearning can be achieved without recourse so such dissonance, and limit their activities to those which, although providing surprises, do not rely upon shocks.

Skills, Attitudes and Knowledge

The *skills*, *attitudes* and *knowledge* elements of *Exploratory* programmes will often be in direct support of the unlearning. Personality profiling may be used to help provide an organiser for the revelations of the experiences; models of creativity and innovation may reinforce action learning activities; coaching and guidance in giving and receiving feedback may be helpful in adding to the potency of feedback received, and thereby, to the personal learning. Finally, given the role of change in these programmes, learning about managing personal and organisational change is a valuable additional element, as is any additional learning about helping others to learn.

Implementation

Given the highly experimental nature of *Exploratory* programmes, it may be very difficult to identify, especially in advance, any clear opportunities for *implementation*. However, also, given the potentially disorienting nature of such experiences, it is possible at the very least to anticipate a need for careful handling of 're-entry' into the 'normal' world.

THE TAVISTOCK 'CONFERENCE' ON GROUP LEARNING

This case study is neither one of Cranfield's nor, strictly, an *Exploratory* programme in our terms, since it was a public event, not an in-company event. However, since it captures a great deal of the essence of such programmes, we should like to include it.

The 'conference' was a loosely structured gathering of 24 participants. There were six facilitators, all of whom were primarily psychologists rather than management development specialists. The event lasted five days, from Sunday afternoon to Friday lunchtime. It had very little in the way of structure, although there were some check-points during the week which helped the process along.

Aims

The programme aims are broad and were written as a descriptive list of 5 key areas, covering (in summary) the following:

- ❏ internal and external forces on behaviours
- ❏ the 'seemingly irrational' forces, and ways of dealing with these
- ❏ surfacing and making more explicit those forces
- ❏ groups and boundaries
- ❏ consultative capabilities

Motivation

Participants were given plenty of opportunity to define their own personal aims, and to provide whatever structure they felt necessary. However, as it quickly transpired, the key working groups were three groups of eight, with two facilitators per group (one male, one female); individuals who attempted to 'impose' structure had to deal with the concerns of the other seven members of their group. Motivation quickly became for some, one of trying to find out what was 'actually' going on.

However, we believe that as is often the case with *Exploratory* programmes, the key driver for many participants was the motivation to find out about themselves. The ways in which the groups developed into 'entities' tended to fuel that motivation.

Unlearning

In this example, no formal approach to unlearning was used. Everything centred upon feedback. The facilitators, as qualified psychologists, provided role models of effective and insightful feedback, which participants followed. The unlearning which took place therefore was focused on individuals unlearning things about their own behaviours and impact; and upon some 'models' of how groups work in practice being slowly but comprehensively dismantled.

Skills

Again, no formal models were used; only experience. The focus was interpersonal skills within and across groups. Although the majority of the time was spent in the groups of eight, this pattern was interrupted by occasional one-to-one sessions (in triads, with an observer, who then rotated roles with one of the pair) on topics of participants' own choosing; and by 'visits' by one member of each group to each of the other two groups.

Implementation and Continuous Improvement

The 'conference' is for many, an intense experience which can lead to strong feelings of commitment to fellow group members. Plans are often placed for regrouping; we are not aware of how frequently these are followed through. The facilitators also provided a few words concerning re-entry, which are difficult to apply, given that few colleagues in the work environment which participants re-enter can appreciate the ways in which the highly personal learning impacts on them. However, as this is not an in-company event, this part of the case is the least relevant.

In Figure 4.3 I have attempted to capture a fair amount of what this chapter has been about. It does not represent every 'learning transfer technique' appropriate to each subsector of each of the four areas of the management development grid. But what it does show are some of the styles and approaches we have found helpful, and where we have found them to have the most beneficial impact.

What the figure brings out is how activities on the right-hand side of the grid (*Exploratory* and *Generic* programmes) have a primarily individual growth focus – that the individual manager is at the centre of the action; while on the left hand side (*Transformational* and *Specific Capabilities* programmes), activities have a primarily organisational growth focus, with the development of the organisation being the key to success. If 'organisational learning' means anything, it clearly points us towards the left-hand side of our grid. And if programmes are to be sharply focused in their aims, they will take these differences into account from the start.

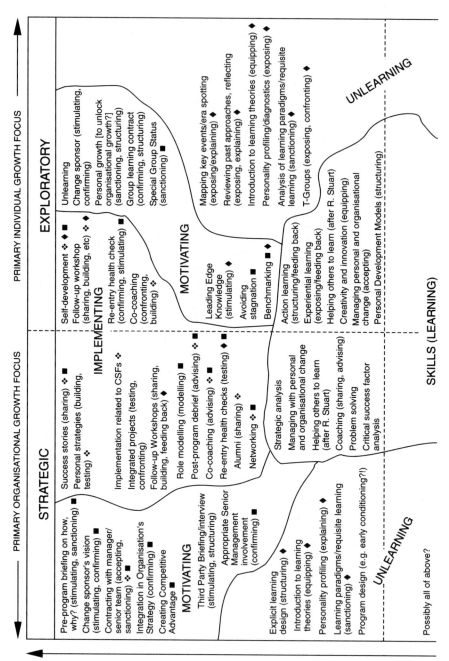

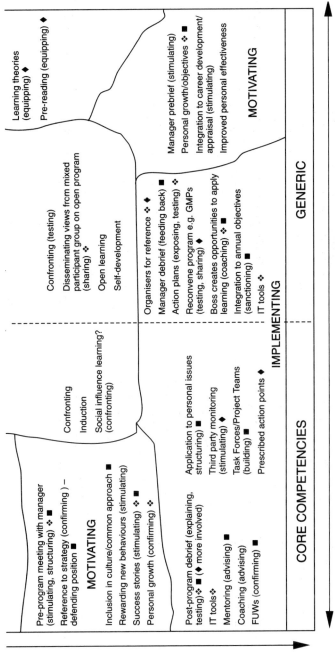

Figure 4.3 *Practical learning transfer techniques and the management development grid*

APPROACHES DO NOT ALWAYS TRANSLATE

In our 'whistle-stop tour' of the Management Development Grid, I have glanced at a number of tools and approaches which we have found to be beneficial. I shall delve a little deeper into the use of some of these in later chapters. For the moment, I wish simply to reiterate one of the key points we learnt from working with Tech-Test, as described in Chapter 3. That point is that, because the four quadrants of the grid map out very different territories, approaches which work well in one area may not work well in another. This we have learnt, again, the hard way, through experience. As I said at the start of this chapter, putting a tractor gearbox into a racing car is not good design; while slick racing car tyres just will not fit on a tractor's wheels.

It is important in the broad, conceptual design of any programme not to be tempted by the success in other contexts of any of our tools or technologies. Our belief is that each intervention needs to be redesigned from scratch. Just because an idea worked for one vehicle, does not mean it is right for another.

Take, for example, the post-event 'Change Project'. This is often a valuable means of involving managers in a complex and challenging change process. As part of a *transformational* programme, it frequently adds considerable value. However, the idea does not always translate well across the grid. In the past we have tried to facilitate the 'Change Project' approach as part of both *Generic* and *Specific Capabilities* programmes (as well as within the Tech-Test programme). In most cases, the efforts of the managers on the teams were 'heroic'. The work they did was often very insightful, and the analyses were precise. But most of the work went unused, because it represented too significant a series of changes. Projects which offered only marginal change were often better received than those which may have given significant benefits in the long run, but only at the cost of some radical reworking of structures or product lines.

It is not in the nature of programmes in the bottom half of the portfolio to bring about significant change. Our experience is that programmes of these kinds do well not to use the 'Change Project' as part of their design for implementation, unless the project teams are very clear that their primary focus is upon consolidation or incremental improvement, and not on radical change.

The 'Change Project' idea does have some validity for an *Exploratory* programme, but is likely to look different from those for a *Transformational* programme. In the latter case, there needs to be a means of identifying how each project aligns both to the organisation's strategy and to all other projects (thereby avoiding adding to the confusion inherent in any major change process). There also needs to be a spirit in the team of genuinely wanting to make the project work, of 'winning against the odds', and so on. However, projects emerging from *Exploratory* programmes do not have to align with organisational strategy – in some respects it is better if they do not. They do not have to align with each other – in some cases it may be better if they appear to be going in quite different directions. And the team spirit needs to be far less 'win at all costs' and more 'suck it and see'. Should the 'crazy' idea clearly be going nowhere, team members must not feel they have failed in their project; they must feel they have succeeded in trying an idea.

'MUSIC' AND THE TECH-TEST PROGRAMME

In Chapter 3 I identified that the Tech-Test programme did not sit comfortably into the management development grid. What impact did this have on the ways in which the five key elements of the programme (*motivation, unlearning, skills, implementation,* and *continuous improvement*) were built into the programme?

Unlearning was rapidly brought into the learning design by the introduction, on the first Monday afternoon, of the 'outdoors' exercise. The aim of the exercise was to involve them in group work, and to show through experience how working together, planning, communicating, and so on, are important to success. According to the feedback from the participants, this was a largely enjoyable and fruitful activity, despite its being very different from what they had been expecting from the first day and a half. It helped to challenge assumptions about working together (and what a management development programme is all about), and thus far, helped with the unlearning process.

The programme as a whole contained considerable inputs on *skills, knowledge* and *attitudes*. It is interesting to note that these were a very broad mix of generic approaches (general inputs on what strategy is all about, for example), and highly specific work on the business issues of Tech-Test as a company.

The programme focused a great deal on issues in *implementation*. The many projects and other initiatives which were spun off from the programme are a clear indicator that bringing the learning back home was a very important part of the design.

There is very little evidence, beyond the projects and initiatives themselves, of any concerted focus on *continuous improvement*. For some people, activities such as the projects which Tech-Test took home with them are enough to ensure that *continuous improvement* will take place. But *continuous improvement* demands more than being busy; it also involves an 'action learning' mindset. This means being both busy doing, and being busy learning while doing. The fact that learning while doing does not necessarily come naturally – that many managers become so embroiled in 'the task' that they lose sight of what they can learn by reviewing 'the process' – is one of the main reasons for the management and organisation development industry, as discussed in more depth in Chapter 10. Tech-Test's projects were not set up as action learning projects.

But the real challenge seems to me to have been with the *motivation* element. I believe that the programme designers relied upon the business imperatives to deliver the necessary motivation. And to a certain extent, one could say that, by their attendance, their interest and enthusiasm for the new ideas (as shown in the feedback from each module), motivation had been achieved. But I believe that this was motivation at the intellectual level only. In later chapters, I explore the impact of this 'superficial' intellectual buy-in. For now, I shall focus only on the fact that, despite everyone's good intentions, many (if not most) of the participants went with unclear expectations. Their role as partners in learning was therefore difficult to fulfil. They became (I believe) passive recipients rather than full partners. They went as willing, but naive, individuals.

In consequence, although 19 managers from Tech-Test went through an experience which shared the same broad physical space and time, from the point of view of how what happened related to what they anticipated, expected, were prepared to experience, and, therefore, to some extent, did experience, there may well have been some significant disjoints. So much research tells us that, to a very large extent, we see what we expect to see, whether we are managers or research scientists (Kuhn 1970). We suspect that this was the case for the managers of Tech-Test.

The data gathered from the follow up activities seems to suggest that there were some serious mismatches between individuals' hopes and expectations as they stood at the end of the programme, and the 'reality' which unfolded after the event. Could this be, even in some small part, explained by how they experienced the programme itself?

There is a sense in which all 19 participants had different experiences; but all 19 were prepared to act 'as though' they had all had 'the same' experience. In so far we 'learn from experience' there is, consequently, a sense in which the participants all 'thought' they had learnt the same things, but had, in that sense 'learnt' different things. Unaware of these differences, they were unable to make them fit together when they tried to do so back at work. And part of the reason for this is that very unawareness that they had parts to 19 different 'jigsaw puzzles' rather than to 'the same' puzzle.

Could the Management Development Grid have helped? From certain perspectives, one could argue that the essentially unique nature of personal experience makes the intervention of such a simplistic model irrelevant. From others, however, any moves made towards a shared set of expectations and a shared language are to be welcomed. Our position in this book is that it is possible, but more difficult than we may initially assume, to bring about shared experiences, and thereby shared learning. Philosophically, it must be possible, if language and learning are to mean anything at all. Practically, it appears from what we have learnt over the past few years that it is very much more elusive a target that we may have supposed.

For Tech-Test managers, the very debate and dialogue which an exploration of the grid may have engendered ought to have helped bring their expectations closer together. We believe that this would (or at least could) have brought their actual experiences and thereby their learning closer together.

The journey we shall take through the rest of this book will be one in which we recognise that, in one sense, the kind of essential difference in experience, and therefore in learning which we suspect the managers of Tech-Test went through, is unavoidable. However, what we have learnt through our own (shared and individual) experience is that it is possible to reduce the effects of this phenomenon. If we are to be successful and effective in our endeavours to help managers to learn, and thereby to make their organisations more effective and better places to be, then we have to use whatever means we can to facilitate an ever-increasingly shared set of experiences and learning among those managers with whom we work.

SUMMARY

This chapter has been a relatively superficial introduction to some of the practical learning approaches which lend themselves to different parts of the territory we call management and organisation development. None of these approaches has been explored in depth in this chapter; that activity depends upon smaller scale maps than this chapter has provided. Later chapters will provide this kind of more detailed examination of some approaches we have found to be of particular help.

However, my colleagues and I have found that even by the application of the relatively simple tools explored so far in the book, we have been able to make significant improvements in the effectiveness with which we work together with our client organisations.

5   Starting from Where?

INTRODUCTION

The previous two chapters dealt with the stages of the 15-step process which help us to clarify with the client what he or she wants to see as outcomes from a management and organisation development intervention. Broadly, what we have covered so far takes us to the first iteration of step 6 in the process, normally couched in terms of desired behavioural outcomes. Step 7 attempts to explore how far away from those behaviours are the ways in which managers actually operate now. This will enable us, with the client, to 'measure' the gap between what happens now and what the client wants to happen, enabling us then to draw up some learning aims, and a learning design to meet those aims.

Defining the Current State and Gap – a Naive Approach

The 'classic' approach to this step in our process is often summarised in the phrase 'training needs analysis', so well known by providers of management education and training that they all recognise and use the acronym TNA. At the simplest level, TNA is expressed as an equation: desired knowledge, skills and attitudes minus current knowledge, skills and attitudes equals training need (Cole 1986: 149). Finding out what are the current knowledge, skills and attitudes is achieved through 'training needs surveys'.

There have been developed over the years a wide range of methods which, according to perceived need, are available as contributing to such training needs surveys:

Recorded data:
- ❑ Personnel statistics
- ❑ Job descriptions
- ❑ Appraisal records
- ❑ Time and Method Study data
- ❑ Training reports
- ❑ Production records
- ❑ Marketing statistics

Interviews:
- ❑ with immediate staff
- ❑ with their managers
- ❑ with relevant specialist staff

Questionnaires:
- ❑ to immediate staff
- ❑ to their managers

Observation:
- ❑ by Work Study or O&M staff
- ❑ by managers of those concerned
- ❑ by trainers or other specialists

Aptitude tests:
- ❑ for relevant work-groups
- ❑ for potential work-group members

Group Discussion:
- ❑ via Quality Circles
- ❑ via 'brainstorming' sessions
- ❑ via other work-groups (ibid.)

In other words, there are a whole host of 'technologies' which management and organisation development specialists can apply to the challenge of establishing training needs.

With such a richness of choice, one may be tempted to explore ways in which such technologies might be broadened to the task of a 'wider' kind of TNA. In terms of our own acronym, MUSIC, we may think of using such methods to assess not only the 'S' of MUSIC, but also Motivation and the need for Unlearning. We might even explore the use of such a survey as a means of assessing the current situation in the context of how we may think about Implementing the learning, and setting up some kind of Continuous learning environment. With such a wide range of methods available, none of this seems beyond our ingenuity. We appear to be able to measure anything.

Following the TNA route, once we have the data we require from the survey, we simply analyse the data, comparing existing levels of knowledge, skills and attitude against required levels. For example, if we are measuring managers' skills in negotiating, in an environment where such skills are crucial to future success, we may use some kind of scaling, something like 0 for 'no skill' to 4 for 'expertise' in negotiating (and should we use this approach, 4 would equate to our 'desired state'). By matching individual managers' scores for their current skills against that requisite '4', we can arrive at how much negotiation training the manager needs.

CURRENT STATE IS NOT A TRAINING NEEDS ANALYSIS

There are a number of potential shortcomings with this kind of approach to training needs, especially if it is applied to the broad territory we are exploring in this book. Although some organisations may be able to use many aspects of training needs analyses to provide insights which they find helpful, for our purposes these potential shortcomings are sufficiently significant for us to be very concerned if our clients ask us to work within this kind of framework with them. Let us explore some reasons why our concerns amount to more than simply an unwillingness to use other people's 'research data'.

Getting Carried Away with the 'Technology'

Tools and methods such as those we have seen being brought to bear on the training needs analysis can be very seductive in their apparent precision and efficiency. As with any battery of tools and techniques, it is very easy for users to become mesmerised by the processes they are going through, and lose sight of the overall goal. In terms of this risk, management educators are experiencing a situation analogous to that faced by information technology specialists a few years ago.

In the mid-1980s managers were confronted with enormous opportunities to use information technology. Hitherto, computers had been the responsibility of the computer department; managers knew very little about processors, discs, programs and databases. The arrival of the personal computer and specially written software made it possible for managers to have computers on their desks. At the same time, the massively increased processing power of the large computers still being run by the information technology specialists allowed for a similar increase in the ways in which information processing could be made available to the business. Managers were bombarded with technology; information technology specialists promised all kinds of new opportunities. When managers, as they frequently did, did not jump at every one of these opportunities, the providers were puzzled – they accused managers of 'technophobia', and got on with the job of finding yet more ways of getting managers to see what they were missing.

What was missing in many of these situations was not always vision or flexibility or courage on the part of the 'luddite' managers, but the direct links between corporate strategy and the kinds of 'benefit' which information technology providers were insisting their new technology could provide. In sales terms, the new technologies often could not deliver 'benefits' to managers, only 'advantages' – things which are nice to have but which do not meet explicit needs as defined in where and how a manager is contributing directly to achieving either personal or organisational goals.

In some situations my colleagues and I have experienced, a similar story is being enacted by management trainers. Armed with questionnaires and tests, they are offering managers the chance to generate masses of training needs data. Their analyses are detailed, and can often be presented in very impressive graphical formats. They make a telling point. But in many cases, they make a telling point not about what are the training needs of managers or the organisation, but about how busy management trainers have been, and how sophisticated are their technologies.

This potential shortcoming is clearly less likely in organisations which have gone through the process of defining those three levels of strategy we introduced in Chapter 2. Where this has taken place, at the very least, any training needs analysis technologies should be focused upon management behaviours which have clearly been identified as supporting the broad organisational strategy. However, focus is not enough.

The Illusion of Behavioural Measurement

The second major area of risk in the use of these tools and methods lies in the susceptibility to measurement of the 'things' people are trying to measure. In Chapter 1 we argued that a significant number of the concepts people use when they work within a management and organisation development setting are socially constructed concepts. As such they do not reflect an independently available 'reality' against which people can match their 'discoveries'. It is similarly the case that many of the aspects of knowledge, skills and attitude we may wish to evaluate within our 'current state' activities will be socially constructed as well. Such concepts will be very hard to measure with any degree of 'objectivity'.

Let us take 'leadership' as an example. Some training needs analyses seek managers' 'leadership qualities' to assess whether managers so assessed need leadership training. Grint (1995: 124–61), in an extended analysis of what I shall try to summarise here, argues that 'leadership' is not an 'essence' which managers either have or have not, and which could, therefore be 'objectively' studied and measured, but is a socially constructed concept which says far more about people who follow than about people who lead. 'when . . . a leader does 'exert power' it is subordinate others, not him or herself, that actually engage in action. If the subordinates do not act, then the leader has no power; only as a *consequence* of subordinate actions can leaders be deemed to have power.' (op. cit. 154). There is, therefore, a significant contextual element to how such a concept can reasonably be used. This contextual content makes it difficult to apply sensible measures to such concepts as leadership.

However, this argument, presented so baldly, is in danger of raising the question – what is it about some people that makes them more likely to stimulate good follower behaviour than others? It does not seem to be a matter of complete chance that some people get followers and others do not. Clearly, it is what a 'leader' does (or at least what a leader says) that stimulates that engagement in action by others, which then makes what the leader has done or said an example of leadership behaviour.

Even here, however, there is a significant interpretative element to the ascription of 'leadership' to what the leader does. Why should what the leader does or says be interpreted as *leadership* behaviour?

Such interpretations of behaviours, especially as they relate to whether an example be characterised as 'leadership behaviour', are likely to be significantly influenced by outcomes. Someone who gets to the top of an organisation which is profitable is more likely to be described as a good leader than someone who presides over the total collapse of an organisation. Yet we are all aware that the risks taken, the decisions made, the options chosen by leaders are only a part of the complex set of circumstances which bring about success or collapse. For this reason, it is perfectly possible for success to be put down as much to good luck as to good leadership: 'He should never have got away with it; it was a stupid risk, not good leadership.' And it is perfectly possible for failure similarly to be argued away – there are plenty of people who would argue that it was bad luck rather than poor leadership which best explains the stories of Freddy Laker, Gerald Ratner, Ernest Saunders, Don Burr and the Chief Executive Officer of the organisation in our case study in Chapter 1. In one sense, what makes something an act of leadership is what people subsequently call it, and there may be a strong link between this ascription, and the interpreter's view of the outcome of that behaviour.

So any attempt to measure people's leadership skills is a highly complex process. This is not to say that it is absolutely 'impossible', but that the risks such an attempt carries with it need to be factored into the measurement process, if that process is to be anything more than a superficial activity generating spurious numbers. One way of highlighting the complexity, and how that complexity might be managed is to explore this process through the evaluation model we introduced in Chapter 1.

If I am asked to evaluate either myself or another manager in terms of 'leadership skills', I need to be able to identify from my experience relevant events ('facts') in which the subject of the evaluation did things. But as we said in Chapter 1, what we select will have a significant influence on the outcome of this process. This is because the 'facts' are already informed by the filtering process of our search for 'meanings' – we are looking for behaviours which may or may not be good instances of what we, as individuals, mean by 'leadership' on the part of the subject, and we shall therefore be highly selective. In this kind of task – searching for evidence to 'prove' or demonstrate good or bad leadership, our use of the model must start at part 3 – at meanings. Unless we are clear what such behaviours mean, we cannot pursue the task effectively.

Therefore, what specific evidence ('facts') we select will clearly depend upon our own idea of what constitutes leadership; what 'leadership' means for me. In the absence of any 'objective' yardsticks of what leadership 'means', two

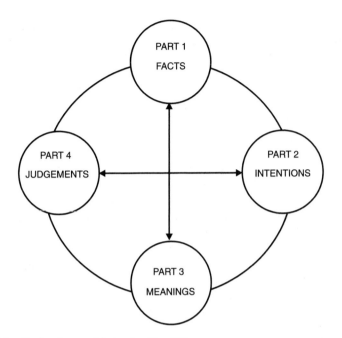

Figure 5.1 *Evaluation model: leadership skills*

different people may select from 'the same' managerial career completely different historic events to illustrate their point.

When I went to school, 'history' meant kings and queens, battles and treaties; to my children's generation, 'history' means how the common people lived. Part of my 'skill' at history was my ability to recite all the monarchs of England from William the Conqueror to the present day; to my children's generation this kind of skill has nothing to do with 'real' history. Someone who was 'good at' history in my day, may not be seen as 'good at' history now. And just as what 'history' means in our schools is influenced by what groups of people see as important, so 'leadership' is influenced by just the same kinds of selection process. For one person, instances of 'strength in making unpopular decisions' may be the relevant 'facts'; for another, instances of achieving consensus. Indeed, for each, the 'facts' chosen by the other in support of 'leadership skills' may be precisely those which would illustrate 'poor leadership' for them. One person's strength and determination may be another's arrogant blindness; one person's search for harmony may be another's lack of conviction.

A great deal of this selectivity is the result of the potential influence of part 4 of our evaluation model ('judgements') on all other parts. In the absence of any other constraints, our own perceptions of what constitutes good or bad behaviour by managers will influence how we 'define' leadership; how we select supporting evidence or data; and, in many cases, how we interpret what the manager in question's motives were in carrying out those behaviours.

In summary, then, evaluating behaviours, such as 'leadership' as part of a training needs analysis may not be anything like an 'objective' process of identifying an individual's 'needs'. It may be much more a survey of what different people in the organisation mean by the terms used in the survey than it is a survey of managers' knowledge, skills and attitudes.

The 'Competencies' Approach

These risks may be known to those who are responsible for developing measures as part of training needs analysis, and for any other aspects of management and organisation development. For this reason they will attempt to eliminate the negative aspects of this 'subjectivity' by introducing tighter definitions, greater focus upon behaviours rather than evaluations, and so on, into relevant elements of the survey activities. For example, one of the ways in which people are attempting to get to grips with these risks is through the introduction of behavioural 'standards' often described as 'competencies'.

Managers can be measured. Should we wish to do so, we could measure and record the height and weight of each manager within an organisation. As we become more concerned with healthy bodies for healthy managers, such measures are not completely irrelevant to this section; one of our management and organisation development 'gaps' may be that between 'desired' weight and 'current weight'.

The reason we can rely on such measures is that we have clear and agreed standards for measuring height and weight. The key question for a 'competencies' approach is whether such 'standards' can be produced for what managers do, as opposed to how much they weigh. The key answer is that, *in principle*, such standards can be so produced.

The fact that a process, such as that summarised in our evaluation model, can fail to achieve the evaluations people may wish to get out of it does not invalidate it as a process. The fact that we can misunderstand what someone says to us does not imply that we misunderstand everything which is said to us. The very act of misunderstanding only makes sense when contrasted with understanding. It is simply philosophical casuistry which extrapolates this point to argue that we can never understand anything. What we can never do is be certain that we understand in any particular instance. But this uncertainty makes sense only in the context of a basic principle of understanding.

So the potential shortcomings inherent in measuring managerial behaviours should not prevent us from pursuing such measures so long as we are conscious of the risks, and do whatever is appropriate both to minimise those risks, and to minimise the potential impact of resulting 'inaccuracies'. We may get data out of the exercise, and those data may be helpful in identifying traits, trends, and so on. Whether these are the best way of representing the 'current state' remains open to question; as we delve deeper into the ways in which we go about exploring current state, this question will be reopened. Before that, however, let us look at some of the contributions a 'competences' approach might make.

Making Sense of 'Competencies'

We have argued that one of the main problems with attempts to measure managerial behaviours stems from the impact of widely different perceptions that different people will have of 'the same' situations and behaviours, and how those perceptions will manifest themselves in what people say. In trying to measure a manager's 'leadership skills', we may simply be measuring what people we involve in the process 'mean by' leadership far more that measuring anything about the specific manager in question.

In a management and organisation development context, however, this itself may provide us with a great deal of value. Suppose we went ahead with such a measuring process, asking a range of managers to evaluate the 'leadership competency' of a number of their colleagues, discovering at the end that there were very widely differing views about a particular manager. At the very least we could conclude from this that it is likely that, among the population of respondents, there are several different ways in which the word 'leadership' is being used. In consequence, we may reasonably infer that 'leadership' means different things to those respondents.

If, within its definition of 'desired state', the organisation wants people to demonstrate a consistent set of leadership behaviours, we may conclude in this instance that a significant part of the challenge in getting there will revolve around dealing with the different perceptions the respondents have about what they see as leadership, especially those who may not see the 'desired' behaviours as commensurate with their sense of what leadership is. The challenge may be much more about managers' perceptions of what leadership 'is' than about 'developing' leadership in them as managers. In other words, developing managers to adopt a specific approach to and style of leadership, without helping managers within the organisation to recognise these as 'leadership' behaviours, may not be effective in achieving the desired follower behaviours in many of the respondents.

In passing, it is worth noting here that it is possible that this point may help to explain the relative lack of success of certain 'leadership' programmes. Focusing as they do on the behaviours of 'leaders' rather than the perceptions of 'followers', they may have been successful in changing the behaviours of those 'leaders'. However, unless those changes were in line with what 'followers' saw as 'leadership', according to their own definitions and meanings, those behavioural changes would not have achieved their goals. Sometimes 'management development' (in terms of developing individual managers) may not be the 'answer'.

Where a training-needs survey of the current 'leadership skills' of individual managers ended up with a highly consistent set of responses about a particular manager, we could, at least, infer that there is a degree of consistency in respondents' use of the term, and a corresponding likelihood that they would respond consistently to any manifestations of the 'desired' leadership behaviours. What this consistency of response might be would have to remain at the level of guesswork, however, because consistency in the use of a term in such situations does not imply consistency in resulting behaviours. For example, a survey of many people may produce the broad agreement that, in what she did, Margaret Thatcher demonstrated clear leadership competency. However, this does not mean that, translated into the workplace, and manifested by their own line managers, the same people would be willing to be led like this in practice.

For many people, these kinds of shortcoming are best dealt with by applying greater and greater degrees of precision to the survey methods. Instead of allowing respondents the 'luxury' of interpreting broad terms such as leadership in their own ways, these analysts will focus on more and more narrow 'facts': how many times did a manager take decisions which were 'officially' deemed to be 'good decisions'; has this manager at any time actually talked to you about the corporate 'vision'; do you have clearly defined and measurable objectives which the manager agrees with you at the start of each year? The more one eliminates the opportunities for 'subjectivity', the more 'accurately' one gets results. The only remaining problem is that such accuracy may miss the 'point' of the exercise.

Management is unlikely to be effective if it is manifested in 'cloned', mechanical, rote-learned pursuit of such standards. Of course one can measure the number of times a manager talks to a subordinate about the corporate vision; but what we ought to be interested in is not what a manager 'does' alone, but in the impact this has on those managed, and upon all others, both within and outside the organisation, who are affected by this manager. And what this impact will be cannot always be inferred from surveys.

Individual Feedback and Development Needs

In our exploration of the potential role of 'surveys' and other techniques used in training needs analysis, we have suggested so far that their only 'real' value may lie in what the collective results tell us about the respondents rather than about the 'subjects'. Does this mean that we do not believe such methods have any validity in their 'primary' purpose, which is to give data on the individuals about whom questions are being asked, rather than on the respondents?

Such techniques clearly can provide us with such insights into individuals. Where, to continue our 'leadership' analogy, there is a consistently 'negative' response about a certain individual, one can reasonably conclude that, in the current climate of the organisation, and given the prevailing 'meaning' of leadership, this individual is not conforming to the behaviours associated with such meanings. One can readily anticipate, therefore, that such an individual will have great difficulty in achieving from others the kinds of 'follower' behaviours which would actualise his or her 'leadership'. To that extent, we have gleaned some data about the individual in question.

In the event that there are no such clear and unequivocal responses, where respondents disagree over an individual's 'leadership skills', then we have to take great care in interpreting such data for what they are. We have to recognise that such data cannot be taken 'at face value'.

This is because, like all data gathered in the search for some kind of understanding of behaviour, it is not simply a collection of 'facts' about the individuals being assessed. Like all such data-gathering exercises, the gathering of data through a training-needs analysis or similar kind of activity is, whether we call it such, to engage in 'social science'. The reason we have been so apparently pedantic about the aspects of training-needs analysis we have chosen to explore (and there are many others we could similarly question) is that our experience tells us that much of what goes on under the broad rubric of training-needs analysis is poor social science masquerading as rigorous research.

Current State is Not Just About Managers

Let us summarise what we have explored so far in this chapter. We recognise that it is important to be able to assess the current state as compared to the desired state, and that some kind of measure may be helpful. We have argued that this measure should focus primarily upon behaviours, but that, because behaviours may be interpreted and described differently by different people, there may be merit in using 'standard' terminology, such as that used in the 'competencies' approach. However, what we may be measuring through this process is not any 'absolute' competencies as demonstrated by individual managers, but the degree to which respondents, when asked to evaluate colleagues' behaviours, are consistent in their use and application of the terms. In so far as consistency in the use (or meaning) of competency terms tells us something about the current state of the organisation, we have successfully gathered some data. But we have also highlighted a broader issue, and that is that there may be risks in pursuing the path of apparent objectivity, since this may lead us to miss the point altogether.

So far, however, we have simply been exploring some of the more basic and practical issues in one way of looking at the of 'current state': the 'training-needs analysis'. Our concerns have been focused almost exclusively on potential shortcomings with this kind of approach, but we have not yet offered any alternative versions of the process. Such alternatives depend upon a more general point concerning how, in principle, one may legitimately say anything about a 'current state'.

CURRENT-STATE INVESTIGATION AS SOCIAL SCIENCE

It is at this step in our 15-step process that we come face to face with the practical implications of the issues we introduced in Chapter 1. There we argued that organisations and management were realms in which the notion of 'discovery', of finding out the 'truth' of situations, was inappropriate. Yet if we are to make any headway with our desired state/current state comparisons, we do need some kind of current-state picture against which to compare our desired state. How can we get such a picture if, as we argue, there is no 'right' picture to be painted?

There may be no one 'right' picture, but, so long as we approach the problem with a degree of accord over what would constitute a satisfactory kind of answer, then we can go ahead. In partnership with our clients, we have to make some choices about what kind of frameworks and data will help us to arrive at an appropriate (rather than correct) picture of the current state.

In the past we have borrowed concepts and frameworks from current-state analysis from a number of different academic disciplines, and have learnt from doing so. We still do recognise the enormous value of the learning we can get from all those disciplines pertinent to our understanding of the social life which characterises much of what goes on in organisations: the social life which we, as people working in management and organisation development, not only have to understand, but help to enhance or even change.

Borrowing, however, is different from shifting promiscuously from one framework to another. We believe that it is important to have a 'base' from which to borrow; otherwise one will end up 'talking' in a random mix of languages (the 'languages' which characterise the different disciplines), and talking none of them well. Instead of being a polyglot, comfortably able to converse in many languages, one becomes incomprehensible in any one language.

Management and organisation development does not have much of a language of its own; there is some 'jargon', such as the TNA we discussed briefly above. But as a framework for dealing with the complexities we have to confront when trying to achieve the kinds of goals we and our clients set ourselves, it falls well short of the task. We have had, therefore, to review how we go about helping our clients to deal with this key social scientific element of the management and organisation development process.

We have argued throughout that management and organisation development has to be about behaviour. But management is behaviour with other people; and that behaviour is focused to a greater or lesser extent on an organisational setting – the 'organisation' provides some kind of bounded social space in which, for the present at least, most managers can tell the difference between what lies within their organisational scope, and what lies outside. Moreover, many writers of recent years have argued that one of the key influencers on how managers actually behave in these organisationally bounded social settings is strongly influenced by the 'culture' of their organisations.

Culture, Subculture and Boundaries

Because of the constructed nature of the concept of 'culture', we are unable to 'discover' what constitutes a culture, where one culture ends and another begins, or how many 'subcultures' there are within any specific culture. There are no absolute boundaries, and therefore no definitions. Whether a group of actuaries within an insurance business are a core part of the organisation's culture (the 'extended family'), are a subculture within the broader organisational culture (the 'nuclear' family within the extended family), or form a culture of their own (a different, unrelated family) is not a matter which can be proven scientifically – it is largely a matter of what makes more sense, of what is going to be the most helpful way of defining their part in the picture.

When drawing these pictures within an organisational context, it is often the complexities, ambiguities and inner contradictions which tell most about the current state. Complexity in organisational culture attracts academics to introduce analytical models, such as the 'culture web' (Johnson and Scholes 1988) which sees culture as a complex 'web' of interacting and mutually reinforcing social phenomena. One cannot extract culture from a social situation and study it in isolation. What we mean by 'culture' is simply a way of showing how language, rituals, processes, structures, and so on provide a multitude of facets of social experience. In organisational terms, these mutually reinforcing social phenomena have sometimes been summarised within such concepts as the 'paradigm' of an organisation.

An associated point has been raised by many writers, and that concerns ways in which this interdependence of cultural facets acts as a brake on change. The steady accretion of local constructs, language and meanings become mutually reinforcing in their significance and authorisation of specific behaviours and ways of seeing the organisation and its challenges.

Writers on management have advocated for many years that change in one aspect of an organisation may require supporting change in another (Waterman *et al.* 1980), and I am sure that, at this very moment, there are management researchers single-mindedly working on the 'definitive checklist' of everything you have to take into account when introducing organisational change. My guess is that, soon after it is published, someone will come along with a better list, with even more checkpoints on it.

Even without wanting to pursue the chimera of such a complete checklist, we do recognise that the depth of reinforcement providing resistance to change does imply that management and organisation development interventions which we characterise within the top two quadrants of the Management Development Grid, where the focus is on change, will need to take the *unlearning* aspect of the learning process very seriously if such an intervention is to be successful.

Another key point made by most writers is that this complex, this paradigm, these various social experiences work together to minimise, or limit, or constrain, or circumscribe individuals' behaviours. The ways in which such implicit constraints are expressed vary widely, from the 'managers in this situation are incapable of seeing things from any other point of view' kind of determinism to the 'although I cannot speak in another language, I can express myself perfectly adequately in English' school of thought. This latter kind of approach takes a positive view of such constraints, in the same way as we recognise that, for example, gravity acts as a constraint on our ability to fly (a constraint we have had the wit to overcome through technology), but it also keeps things on shelves and in cups.

So if 'culture' acts as a some kind of constraint on behaviour, are those constraints different in 'different cultures'? In other words, when we are exploring the 'current state' in an organisation, are there 'common' factors and 'unique' factors? Is our current-state activity designed to separate out those cultural phenomena which are found in 'most' organisations from those which are 'unique', so that we can compare these unique features to the 'unique' features dreamed up in our 'desired state'? Tempting though it is to provide a glib answer to this question, the reply has to be, frustratingly, 'It depends upon how you define those features in the first place.' In other words, the 'discovery' of some social phenomenon which is common to all organisations tells us more about the 'research method' which made that 'discovery' than it tells us about organisations.

The Methods of Current-State Exploration

Traditional social science can provide us with a wide range of tools and methods for current-state exploration. Many of these have been adopted by people developing approaches to training-needs analysis (above, pp 134–5). Despite the richness of opportunity, my colleagues and I do not use most of these approaches. If we are trying to make sense of a current situation within an organisation, we find that many of the tools offer far too much scope for misunderstanding – for not making sense at all.

The reason for this is that there is no 'current state' to analyse. 'Current state' is a construct, a shorthand phrase to summarise one or more perceptions of the range of behaviours, attitudes and expectations of a finite number of people who are 'united' in being managers within what (another construct) we call an organisation. Similarly, there is no 'competency' to analyse. 'Competency' is a construct which summarises one or more perceptions of the range of the ways in which the behaviours (including what is said) of selected individuals is interpreted and measured against some kind of 'ideal' model.

In certain situations, as we have seen, people may mean very similar things when they use the same term to describe a specific competency. To that extent, those people can be said to share a 'common culture'. In many cases, however, we find that people make assumptions about how such terms are used by individuals, and do not make a great deal of effort to check those assumptions. In terms of our three levels of strategy (Chapter 2), the middle level, Management Strategy, would be the focus for both establishing clear definitions, and for developing ways of ensuring that people understand and follow such definitions – that key words mean the same to them. Few organisations seem to have made much progress in this kind of activity.

Neither of these points makes it impossible for any of us to talk about, evaluate, find shortcomings with, or otherwise 'measure' how we feel about the 'current state' of an organisation or the 'competencies' of managers. But what differentiates our approach to these tasks from the 'traditional' training-needs analysis kind of approach is this basic underlying assumption – where we start from. We and those following the more traditional route may both end up talking to managers; but we are likely to be undertaking such conversations from very different 'paradigms'.

The 'Scientific' Approach to Current-State Analysis

One of the key ways in which these paradigms may manifest themselves is in the assumptions we bring to our respective approaches to the 'research' into the current state. It is implicit in the 'scientific' approach that one of the main purposes of research is to produce data against which to measure the validity of a hypothesis. For example, in the non-managerial context, a social scientist may wish to test the hypothesis that the young are more disenchanted with the future than they were in a previous generation; so the data to be sought would be that which either validates or denies a sense of disenchantment on the part of youth. In a managerial context, a researcher may wish to explore the hypothesis that, in a particular organisation, empowerment has not yet taken off in the ways anticipated; here the researcher should be seeking evidence of empowered and non-empowered behaviours.

In such cases, the research has a clear purpose, and it is this purpose which enables researchers to be very precise in the ways in which they seek evidence. Their goal is to discover how much disenchantment, how much empowerment 'exists'; and if the level of disenchantment or empowerment is what they anticipated, the researchers can feel good about their hypothesis.

As researchers go about administering this research activity they can anticipate that respondents are likely to raise objections. Respondents may not understand a specific question; they may take an exception to the method (perhaps it feels intrusive); and they may wish to point out that, so far as they are concerned 'disenchantment' or 'empowerment' are not the issue. 'Scientific' methods are designed round the elimination of such distractions – it is no surprise that the laboratory is where so much science takes place, as it is within such controlled surroundings that scientists can most powerfully eliminate any extraneous 'noise' from the single-minded focus on the hypothesis in question.

People who pursue the 'scientific' approach similarly treat distractions as 'noise' and find ways in which they can be eliminated. One of the most powerful tools for eliminating such noise is the questionnaire.

Questionnaires

In our experience, questionnaires are normally designed to be completed by respondents by themselves. It is often taken as a sign of weak questionnaire design if respondents cannot complete them without help from the administrator. 'Good' design enables the researcher to separate him or herself from the respondent, to allow the respondent to get on with the job of providing data uninterrupted, and to eliminate the opportunities for the respondent to create 'noise'. With no researcher to talk to, respondents' concerns, questions and issues go unspoken. The data remain untainted.

One of the most irritating aspects of 'noise' is the way in which it can upset the analysis. In the search for scientific rigour, many questionnaires only allow respondents to answer questions with 'yes' or 'no', or with some kind of numerical assessment. By adding together the responses from a number of respondents, researchers can produce averages and aggregates, apparently objective pictures of situations in which the 'peculiarities' of one individual's views are minimised by the averaging or aggregating process. If respondents do not reply 'properly' by giving the required 'yes' or 'no', then this interferes; in many research processes, non-standard responses are omitted altogether.

Returning briefly to our simple evaluation model, it seems that it is in the nature of the questionnaire, in principle, to operate on a south-to-north axis:

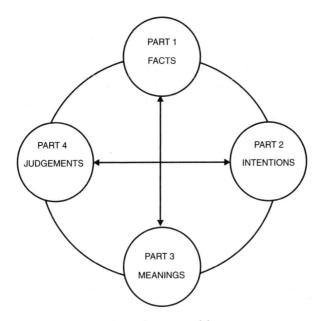

Figure 5.2 *Questionnaires and the evaluation model*

Here, the thrust of the activity is that the researcher says, 'This is what is meant by Competency X; now how much of it is there?' Scientific rigour seeks suppression of such messy stuff as 'judgements', which are 'purely' subjective; and 'intentions' which are irrelevant.

But the more one tries to understand a situation by forcing people to respond to tightly defined questions, the more one is likely to be asking 'Have you stopped beating your wife, yet?' kind of questions. This is not to say that all such questionnaires in use for training-needs analysis or for related explorations of current states contain such impossible questions. But the thrust is, in our view, incorrect in principle for this purpose. So long as one is attempting to 'test' some kind of hypothesis, it is the research or the researcher which drives the activity. Respondents are of use only in so far as they can be 'trained' to answer the researcher's questions. This is not partnership in action. Questionnaires rarely leave room for people to say,

'But I have never beaten my wife; have no wife to beat'; and so on. Many that do leave such space do so not because the data will be taken into account, but as a place for respondents to let off steam; what they write will be discarded as 'noise'.

Even if questionnaires are redesigned to eliminate many of these kinds of risk, it is in the very nature of the pre-defined question that the problem seems to us to lie. And this is because it takes two steps in one. We suggest that a better job is done when these two steps are taken separately.

Separating Current-State Exploration from Gap Analysis

The first step of the pair is 'Where are we?'; the second step is 'And how does this compare to our desired state?' So long as we do not separate these two steps, so long as we try to find out where we are only in respect to where we say we want to be, we run the very grave risk of getting a misleading bearing. In our focused search for comparison to the desired state, we may completely overlook perceptions, issues and observations which, in practical terms, could have a much greater bearing upon achieving the stated goals than any of the comparative data we may generate.

This is equivalent to asking 'How far to the oasis?', and discounting as irrelevant our respondent's point that, although it is ten miles, he has plenty of water available here. If we are not open to the unexpected, we face a potentially long, thirsty, and perhaps unnecessary, trek.

So long as we are open to the unexpected, and do treat the 15 steps as an iterative process, we may find that information which emerges from the current state exploration significantly influences our views on the 'desired state'. The point is that any activity which takes as its starting point a comparison with a desired state will have a significant impact on the quality of the data it generates. Clearly, this point is best made in the context of the box-ticking kind of questionnaire. But its principle remains in a search for 'competency' measures, or in any other process which predefines what it is we want respondents to tell us.

This is not to say that we should always and at all times reject any predefined exploration tools. It is to say that the use of such tools may be best approached from a paradigm which is completely at odds with the 'scientific' approach we have discussed so far, but which is in harmony with the approach we have been following throughout the book.

Current-State Exploration – Starting with a Clean Sheet

Naive though it may sound, we take the view that the 'ideal' current-state exploration is one which poses no such questions at all; one that starts with the premise that it should be the respondents who decide what are the important issues. This is in line with the separation of current-state exploration from gap analysis.

It is also in line with our basic philosophical point, which is that there is no current state out there to discover. What we mean by current state is what people make of it. The people whose perceptions are important in building our picture of the current state will be primarily (but not exclusively) those for whom the prospective management and organisation development intervention is designed.

In order to explain why this should be, let us assume for the sake of simplicity that our sponsors and our target participants are the same people – in this case, we are working with senior managers on a prospective intervention for themselves. We have argued that 'organisation' is a construct, that there is no organisation as such, only what people construct to make sense of the day-to-day impressions they have of the interactions which take place between people, and between people and artefacts such as machines. We have said the same thing about 'management'.

Now if neither 'organisation' nor 'management' have any independent existence, how can we 'develop' them; what sense can we make of this phrase 'management and organisation development' which keeps appearing in the book? In one sense, management and organisation development is equivalent to whatever learning about themselves, about their 'management' and about their 'organisation' takes place. Through learning, managers enhance or change their perceptions about themselves as managers and about their organisations. Such learning in itself changes them and their organisations. In so far as both 'management' and 'organisation' are constructs, changes to those constructions in the minds and behaviour of those who construct them are changes to 'management' and to the 'organisation'.

Clearly, any 'organisation' is constructed and maintained by more than just the senior managers. Bankers, shareholders, customers, employees, academics and many others have a stake in the 'reality' of any specific organisation. To that extent management and organisation development is limited in its potential impact, especially on 'the organisation'. But whatever impact it will have, it will have it through alterations, first of all, to the constructs of the managers involved in the management and organisation development intervention in question.

It is for this reason primarily that our current-state exploration makes most sense when built around the perceptions (constructs) of the managers themselves. What it seeks to do, as far as is possible within the inevitable constraints of time and cost, is to see the organisation through the eyes of those managers. This is most likely to get us as close to the 'real' current state as we can get.

Such 'open-minded' exploration is what characterises ethnography. It is no surprise, therefore, to find more and more writers in the broad field of management and organisation development turning to social sciences such as ethnography, sociology and my own former discipline, social anthropology – the study of people in their social and cultural settings. If we are to be effective in achieving the kinds of goals which are set for management and organisation development, I believe we have to take a rigorous approach to understanding where we are starting from in any prospective management and organisation development intervention. And it will come as no surprise that I believe that such rigour will be best found in the principles and processes of social anthropology and ethnography as applied to the 'study' of managers in their organisational setting, otherwise known as 'current-state analysis'.

In the early days of ethnography, many fieldworkers went into the task with a 'scientific' attitude. They would go among a tribe to 'discover' what kind of 'superstitious beliefs', for example, these people 'had'. Not surprisingly, they were able to 'discover' all kinds of superstitious beliefs; anyone from an alien culture wanting to discover superstitious beliefs among the twentieth-century British would very easily find them. For example, the alien ethnographer could write a fascinating treatise on the superstitious belief which leads us, once every five years or so, to take ourselves one by one into small chambers to mark a piece of paper with a cross, so as to bring about the kind of society which we value. The ethnographer should have very little difficulty in demonstrating the causal inefficacy of any one of these millions of acts, and in proving, through cross-questioning, that the British believe in 'democracy', which is some kind of invisible spirit which is said to have its home in Westminster or ancient Greece.

Like ethnographers, we are susceptible to bias in our current-state work. There are a host of methodological pitfalls in store, which a separate book on methodology would be required to deal with thoroughly. Issues such as our own motives in undertaking the work, our own paradigms, interpersonal issues between interviewer and interviewee and 'creating' an organisational 'reality' which is 'non-existent' are far from simplistic. For practical purposes, however, our approach is to acknowledge these risks, to sensitise ourselves to them and, by raising them to consciousness, to ameliorate their impacts. In the end, the difference between ourselves and ethnographers is that we are there to make a difference, not to 'pretend to be invisible'.

Mapping Current-State 'Research' Techniques

One of the ways in which we can explore the impact of the potential influence of the researcher on what managers say about themselves and their organisation is by plotting the respective roles of 'researcher' and 'manager' on two axes: those of 'involvement' and 'control', as represented in another of our matrices:

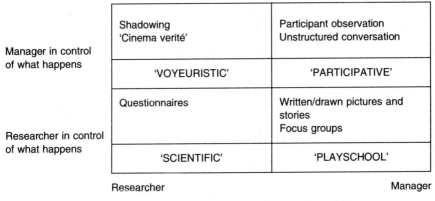

Figure 5.3   *Research methods and the role of the manager*

The two axes are approximations of the relative influence of the researcher and of managers within the organisation on what happens during a 'research activity', and on what data are generated.

The vertical axis defines the bottom of the grid as representing those situations in which the researcher has more control: the manager generally does (with differing degrees of grace) what he or she is told, such as filling in questionnaires or writing diaries. At the top of the grid are those situations in which the researcher follows the lead of the manager or managers. The horizontal axis characterises the left side of the grid as those situations or methods in which the researcher plays the major part in defining what data are important, either by designing an activity, or by selecting from an experience what seems to be important. The right side of the grid represents methods which give the manager or managers control of what data are generated or recorded.

In the bottom-left corner of this matrix, therefore, lie methods and techniques such as the questionnaire which we explored in the earlier section of this chapter, and which we have called the 'Scientific' approach. Typically in this quadrant, the researcher defines what questions are asked, and what kinds of reply are legitimate. The only involvement from the manager is in activities such as filling in numbers, ticks or other predefined fields. The only control the manager has on how the data are captured is in not filling in any parts of the form.

One possible way of giving managers more involvement in this kind of technique for data gathering is to involve them in designing the questionnaire, but this raises the question of the value of the questionnaire which emerges from the process. For those who are involved in design, there will be less artificial and constraining ways of getting their views. So far as managers who are not personally involved in design are concerned, those managers who have been involved in design will have simply become honorary researchers, and the 'problems' remain the same.

The bottom-right of the matrix represents those kinds of approach which allow managers much freer rein in capturing their views and perspectives. Here, we may find managers being asked to keep diaries, write stories, attend facilitated Focus Group meetings, and so on. The aim is to involve managers in processes which are normally the idea of researchers.

Many managers feel uncomfortable with this kind of activity, partly because it is uncharacteristically reflective rather than active. This is not to say that there is anything 'wrong' with the approaches; but it does mean that managers may well be motivated by the unnaturalness of the situation to write, draw or say what they think they ought to say, what will shock the researchers, what they do not necessarily think, but it fills in an otherwise uncomfortable blank, and so on. This is one reason why I have characterised this quadrant the 'Playschool' approach. Researchers are wellmeaning, and are often trying to capitalise on some very powerful routes through to managers' perceptions (Morgan 1993); but, unless handled very carefully, this kind of activity can spark off some very suspicious responses. (In one case, a colleague tells me of a senior manager from a relatively staid organisation who, on being asked to draw a picture which represented his views of the organisation, became very angry indeed. He accused the 'researcher' of treating him like a child, refused to co-operate in any further activities, and walked out, saying he would write in protest to the 'highest authorities' and complain about being treated with such complete lack of tact and dignity.)

The top-left quadrant of the grid represents managers more in their 'natural state'. Typified by 'shadowing' or by some kind of silent recording of 'what goes on', here managers get on with their jobs while researchers watch and draw conclusions, hence the word 'Voyeuristic' to characterise this kind of organisation and management research. Managers are deliberately not involved in the research process, in order to try to get them to 'act naturally'; if they thought that what they did from moment to moment was going to form some kind of picture of the current state, they may 'act to the camera'.

Therefore, in this approach, managers are asked to 'forget' the presence of the researcher or the camera, and simply get on with doing what they normally do. This places most of the responsibility for selecting what is important from the rich pool of resulting data with the researcher. Clearly, this can be modified should the record (especially if this is video or audio tape) be subsequently explored by researcher and manager together. This subsequent activity would then sit within the top right of the matrix.

Apart from any such collaborative exploration of recorded data, other kinds of activity in the top-right box include unstructured conversations with managers about how they see their organisation, their own roles within it, and so on. Managers spend a great deal of their time engaged in this kind of conversation. Where a researcher asks as few 'leading questions' as possible, and allows the manager to pursue lines of interest and avenues of concern which are stimulated by the manager her or himself, that manager is both fully involved, and largely in control of the lines of enquiry. From the perspective we have been advocating throughout the book, in which what constitutes an organisation's current state (a socially constructed concept) is precisely what is in the minds of those within the organisation, this kind of situation seems most likely to produce accurate and relevant pictures of an organisation's current state. We call it the 'Participative' approach.

The Role of the 'Interview'

Missing so far from this model is the 'interview', one of the most ubiquitous of ethnographic methods. We have left it until now largely because of its very broad potential range of manifestations. 'Interview' can be used to describe activities all the way from the bottom-left of our model to the top-right.

At the lower left extreme of our model, interviews are highly structured; in effect they become verbal questionnaires, and thereby suffer most of the problems which questionnaires carry with them as providers of information. Halfway up the diagonal we meet the 'semi-structured' interview, an attempt to provide a happy medium between the apparent rigidity of the question-naire-form of interview, and what some interviewers regard as the anarchic free-format of the extreme top-right. At the top-right, we meet the apotheosis of the 'subjective'; here, the interviewer takes as little control as possible, and allows the interviewee to range freely across whatever territory he or she wished to cover. The chances of extracting from such 'interviews' any 'comparative' data are very slim indeed.

Things which may be called 'interviews' may be found, it seems, at all points on the grid. Therefore, we need to clarify what we mean when we refer to interviews. Since 'interviews' can feature both in training-needs analysis and the ethnographic current-state exploration, it is possible that these apparently 'same' things – interviews – are very different in their meanings.

Once again, we are not planning here to review the entire topic of interviewing as a method in the social sciences. Works such as Kahn and Cannell (1952), Becker and Geer (1970), Phillips (1971), and Converse and Schuman (1974) provide plenty of advice on interviewing, including 'rules' for successful interviewing. Our concern is much more with the potential role of the interview to provide us with the primary route into effective exploration of the 'current state' of an organisation or, at least, of those parts of such an organisation which may have a bearing upon any prospective management and organisation development intervention.

The interview is not, implicitly, devoid of potential methodological problems, which may 'arise from the fact that, as a method, it aims at producing verbal reports about social phenomena rather than directly observing them' (Benson and Hughes 1983: 82). This point is closely related to another, often made by 'traditional' social theorists: that what an interviewee says is not important in itself, but only as an indicator of some more significant 'truth' (Mehan and Wood 1975). What is said in an interview, according to these views, is seen to stand, more or less, for something else, the 'reality'. This 'reality' is something which is said not to be directly observable through an interview.

If the interview is said, by some writers, to 'stand between' the researcher and the reality which the researcher wishes to understand, the only solution seems to be to eliminate all such barriers and to get involved in that reality first hand; to engage in what is described as 'participant observation' (Benson and Hughes 1983: 82–3). We have recognised that, unless we focus upon activities which firmly lie in the top-right hand quadrant of our 'methods' model, we stand every chance of missing the point in current-state exploration. But we believe that our approach to the 'interview' is, itself, a form of participant observation which meets many of the objections to the interview which those who reject the method in favour of the 'purer' participant observation proponents raise.

Our approach is to carry out our 'interviews' in the context of the top-right of the model; as 'social encounters' between professionals engaged in dialogue which is aimed at contributing to mutually beneficial goals. We refer to these social encounters overtly as 'conversations' rather than interviews, and attempt to establish with managers an agreement that the conversation is an instance of 'practical reasoning' (Garfinkel 1967); we are working together to make sense of the organisation from the point of view of the individual manager. We rarely use the actual term 'practical reasoning' as such, recognising that, to the practising manager it could sound like jargon. But we choose whatever language seems appropriate to establish that our conversation will involve us in working together to achieve some kind of common understanding of how that manager sees the relevant parts of her or his world.

The notion of working together, of using each other to achieve clarity in our mutual understanding of the managers' perceptions, means that, although we want managers to take the lead, our role is not one of trying to be 'invisible', as it would be in the top-left quadrant of the model. We act as 'sounding boards' for some; for others, our questions form part of 'a creative process in which the observer, through penetrating an alien mode of existence, enriches his own self-knowledge through acquiring knowledge of others' (Giddens 1976: 56). The conversation is a dynamic process of 'discovery' – but in this case it is not the 'discovery' of an external 'reality', but the discovery of how each manager contributes to the creation and maintenance of the socially constructed world which is the organisation in question.

The majority of managers with whom we deal are experienced and mature people, used to meeting with and talking to professional people. Indeed, a significant amount of what managers do is precisely this kind of thing. Rather than an encounter with another professional (albeit in management and organisation development rather than in, perhaps, more familiar managerial territory) being a strange, unusual, or artificial situation for a practising manager, it is part of his or her daily life – the 'reality' is not so different from the encounter. As Austin (1975) pointed out we 'do things with words'; what we say is not necessarily a precursor to what we do, but the doing itself. Just as the 'act' of a 'leader' is most likely to be what this leaders says, so a great deal of what managers do is with words not some other actions which somehow follow on from the words.

The 'reality' which an interview seeks to establish is intimately tied up with talk. We use talk to help managers say what they think, and through saying, demonstrate, create and recreate the very reality which current-state research is attempting to (re)construct.

Especially at the top-right end of our model, we therefore see the interview with the manager as a business-centred social encounter, much like many other such encounters, and therefore subject to the same rules, guidelines and considerations, such as the establishment of an appropriate atmosphere, and recognition of the ways in which the age, gender, ethnicity and social class of the 'interviewer' may have an impact on both the manager we are talking to and the 'interview' outcomes.

What may upset the potential harmony of this kind of social encounter may be the introduction of any 'artificiality'. For example, in our Tech-Test case in the Appendix, relatively inexperienced management and organisation development interviewers followed a semi-structured interview process focused upon 'development needs'. Given the almost complete lack of management and organisation development experience on the part of most of the managers interviewed, both parties to the interview were exploring territory neither felt at home in.

What we learn from this kind of situation is to remember the risks of using 'current state exploration' as a means of testing some kind of hypothesis about development needs for managers and for the organisation. How we operationalise the reduction of such risks is through consciously trying not to allow any of our questions to 'lead' the conversations we have with managers.

It has been noted by Cicourel (1973) and others that people can often respond to questions differently depending upon the context in which those questions have been asked. In sociological research, this has led to conflicting data over such issues as 'ideal' family size (respondents favouring large families when family meals was the topic being discussed, but favouring small families when costs were the current topic). In management and organisation development current-state research, we have to be conscious of the same tendency influencing managers' responses. 'People do not necessarily believe what their culture trains them to say' (Needham 1972: 5), and the fact that management and organisation development professionals may be asking questions concerning 'strategy', 'flatter structures', 'empowerment' and what needs improvement within their organisation could easily stimulate responses which do not accurately reflect managers' views.

In general, then, we do what we can to allow each manager to take as much of the lead in the conversations as possible. It would be naive to expect that we could avoid all reference to management and organisation development; if there were no management and organisation development considerations in the minds of our sponsors, it is most unlikely we should be there talking to these managers. So we do introduce the conversations with such references as are appropriate to set the scene. Thereafter, however, the kinds of rule we follow are simple:

1. The aim is to use the limited time as effectively as possible for the manager to explore freely her or his perceptions of all those aspects of the organisation and its management which she or he thinks are important enough to mention.
2. Ask as few questions as are necessary to stimulate the manager to talk.
3. Keep questions as open-ended as possible – allow the manager to decide what kind of answer is relevant.
4. Questions should primarily seek clarification, not confirmation.
5. Remain as impartial as possible – if a manager asks if his or her opinion is 'correct', the response should be along the lines of, 'I can't say until we have had the chance to explore all aspects of the situation.'
6. If in doubt, wait for the manager to say the next thing.

During a conversation, the 'interviewer' has two key roles: to participate in the dynamic process of helping the 'interviewee' to explore as widely and as freely as possible the 'intersubjective' world of her or his organisation; and to 'capture' what the manager says. We recognise the potential significance of everything that is said in such conversations, and frequently tape-record what is said in order to ensure that we miss nothing – neither text nor intonation. While actively involved in a conversation, we may still miss some of the significance of what may appear at the time to be of peripheral importance.

We acknowledge the potential for artificiality which a tape recorder introduces, and do everything we can to ensure that each manager is aware: first of the tape's presence; secondly, that the manager has the right of veto, and can stop the tape at any point if he or she wants to talk 'off the record'; and thirdly, that none of what he or she says will be reported back to his or her superiors in such a way that it could be traced back to him or her as an individual. We thereafter draw no further attention to the tape recorder, and we believe that many managers are soon unaware of any intrusion from the machine. Finally, we also recognise that an audio tape recorder misses the body language which a video recorder would be able to record. However, at this stage of our thinking, we do not believe that the gains made from the introduction of video recording our conversations would be worth the potential losses.

Limitations on the 'Ideal' Current-State Exploration

Our approach has been characterised as largely ethnographic. Yet in one major respect, and that is the amount of time we have to devote to the research, we cannot properly be said to be 'doing' ethnography. No ethnographer wishing to be taken seriously would expect to be able to come up with anything of value in the few days which we are normally given for our current-state work. Even the best of circumstances we can normally hope for is counted in weeks; ethnography is counted in years.

There is also the fact that, in some situations, we are unable to gain access to all relevant people to talk to them; even if we do have time, they may not, or they may be located physically far enough away for it to be uneconomic for us to meet.

Because of the practical nature of the relationship between ourselves and our clients, we do not use such limitations on the 'ideal' as a reason for not going ahead. By exploring the 'ideal', however, we remind ourselves of the need for increased vigilance in how we interpret the information which we are able to acquire. It is against this 'ideal' which we set the shortcomings we have to live with, and through which we monitor the risks we run.

It is therefore not unknown for us to use other methods for information gathering than our conversations. For example, we use questionnaires where we feel they may help us. Many of these will be 'hand-crafted', comprising, for example, a limited set of open-ended questions (or statements requiring completion, such as 'What I like most about working in my organisation is . . .'), concerned with how individual managers view their organisation and its management.

Other methods which we have found useful have been 'shadowing' and Focus Groups.

'Shadowing', which sits in the top-left quadrant of the 'research methods' model, is limited in its value in that the 'shadowed' manager has a relatively passive role in the research itself (the manager just gets on with her or his daily activities and tries to ignore the researcher). In most situations, apart from larger meetings and other more public activities, the manager is unlikely to be able to forget completely the researcher's presence, so it is 'better' for the researcher not to try to be too 'invisible'. In other words, we approach 'shadowing' from the right-hand margins of the quadrant, and encourage our shadowing researchers to take every opportunity to step over the edge of the middle line on the model into conversations with the shadowed manager. By this interaction of watching and checking, observing and asking, researchers are emulating the two key elements of 'classic' ethnography.

Focus Groups exemplify the bottom-right quadrant of our 'research methods' model. In terms of attempting to bring to life the 'intersubjective reality' of the organisation, gathering together a number of managers is potentially advantageous. And in so far as any influence which a dominant manager may have on the expressed views of others in the group is concerned, there are many who would argue that this reflects the 'political' realities of the organisation better than the individual interview, where 'weak' managers may overplay their 'real' contribution, free as they are from the chance of being 'corrected' by others.

The practical limitations with Focus Groups lie in the fact that they are convened specifically to explore a management and organisation development agenda. Although this is true also of the conversation we described above, such conversations can quickly become relatively relaxed meetings of minds between professionals reflecting upon and reviewing an individual's point of view. For a variety of reasons our experience is that this transformation is relatively difficult to bring about in a Focus Group; and is the more difficult the larger the group. It is as though the dynamics of 'the meeting' resist any attempt to 'unwind'. Maybe so many managers have spent so many hours feeling frustrated and alienated in ineffectively managed meetings that they cannot avoid putting up barriers to such openness and freedom from constraint. The 'rules' have told us that a meeting must have an agenda; that agenda for a Focus Group is management and organisation development, so we have to stick to it. And as we have argued above, while management and organisation development is so overtly on the agenda, it is that much harder to generate an 'unbiased' picture of the organisational 'realities'.

Focus Groups, therefore, have a role to play in meeting with, and giving 'air-time' to a larger number of managers than could be achieved in the same time through individual conversations. Given that there may be value in covering some fairly basic 'climate setting' within a group, and as an opportunity to get a very broad, if distorted view, we do occasionally have to resort to this rather artificial 'compromise'.

So long as we do not forget the significant distancing from 'reality' which such 'research methods' generate, and therefore, so long as we do not try to draw any 'scientific' conclusions from the results, we feel such tools, where we have no choice but to use something like them, can still introduce us to some aspects of the language and perceptions of managers within an organisation.

The key difference, even in the use of these devices, between our interpretative approach and the 'scientific' model is that we use them in support of our preferred 'subjective' mode, and treat the data they generate as less valuable than the records of our conversations. The scientific approach would view such devices as preferable to the highly subjective 'conversation', and treat the data that they generate as more significant than the 'unstructured ramblings' of the conversations.

In times of rapid change, such as those we are frequently told we are living through, organisational 'realities' are unlikely to remain unchanging for long. Even if it were practical for us to spend the kinds of extended time doing our current-state research that ethnographers spend with other cultures, it may be counter-productive. In so far as 'the organisation' and 'the management' are constructs, aggregations of the intersubjective perceptions of managers and other stakeholders, these 'realities' will be subject to change each time any participating manager or stakeholder changes his or her perceptions; which could happen almost on a daily basis. A 'complete' picture is therefore impossible. What we are seeking is as broad a picture as is useful in helping to understand where, for the most part, people are coming from.

It is certainly the case that we may be unable to spend as much time building an accurate picture as we should like; that we may have a distorting influence on what managers say about themselves and the organisation; that we do bring with us a whole host of our own perceptions which will influence how we interpret what we see and hear; and that we are unlikely to be able completely to ignore the management and organisation development agenda which drives almost all such current state explorations. It is in the very awareness of these limiting factors that lies our ability and willingness to devote time and effort in minimising, as far as is humanly possible, their potentially negative impact as we draw together the results of our work with the organisation's managers in exploring the current state.

COLLATING AND 'ANALYSING' THE DATA

While engaged in the 'data gathering' phase of the current state exploration, we can take a relatively minor role, especially if we follow the kinds of principles which we have associated with the top right quadrant of the 'research methods' model. We can quietly sit back and allow participating managers to explore through their own perceptions what are the important 'social facts' which characterise the organisation in which they work. But once we move on to attempting to bring together this data, and to draw some 'conclusions', we are forced to acknowledge even more overtly that we have an active role in this process, and that our own perceptions, paradigms, and so on will significantly affect what 'analysis' comes out at the end.

We are expected to, and will produce for most clients, some kind of documentary output from the current-state exploration. It is not uncommon for client sponsors to ask for this document to be brief, and to summarise 'what we have found' in as few words as possible. In many cases, there is an implicit or explicit demand for the kind of 'truth' which we have argued is inappropriate for the study of organisations and management. So if we believe that it is impossible to identify 'how things really are', to what extent could we be accused of dishonesty and expediency in our dealings at this point with our sponsors, if we go along with their demands for 'the truth'?

Reporting on the Organisation's Current State

It is often what is not said that provides people with the most information. The more we adopt an approach which is characterised in the top-right quadrant of our research methods model, the more it is up to managers to decide what gets said and what does not. Should we take a different approach we may get different data. Let us take an example.

CURRENT STATE WORK FOR GLOBAL TECHNOLOGIES

During the current state exploration I undertook for our first event for Global Technologies, I 'interviewed' about 30 senior sales people across continental Europe. Leading up to this had been the previous steps in our 15-step process:

1 *Organisation wants to do something differently (strategy)*
Global Technologies had recently introduced a whole new range of pro-ducts which would give it a technical lead over its competitors for a short while. However, to gain the benefit from this range of products, customers had to make large investments, adopting integrated technology strategies across their organisations. Global's strategy was to become the leading provider of integrated solutions to a selected number of large organisations.

2 *Organisation recognises role for management and organisation develop-ment in this*
Global had a large sales force, many of whom were experienced and mature people. Since the corporate strategy called for effective solutions selling across large organisations, sales people would need to talk to senior

business people within the customer organisations instead of to their traditional buyers, the Information Technology departments. The senior sales people would need help in shifting from a technology to a business focus, and this stimulated, in Europe, a search for a management and organisation development component to their change project.

3 *Organisation selects a partner to help with the management and organisation development aspects of the strategy*
Global Technologies chose to work with us at Cranfield.

4 *Organisation and partner check their mutual understanding of the challenges ahead*
We had a significant number of meetings during which we recognised the potential value of helping senior sales people through a change in focus for their activities.

5 *Person or persons take primary responsibility for managing the management and organisation development programme or project*
In this instance, I had the privilege of taking Client Management responsibility for the relationship and the project.

6 *Definition of the 'desired state' (what managers will need to do differently in order to help achieve the change defined in 1)*

We summarised the 'desired state' that we had gleaned from earlier discussions in the following:

CURRENT SITUATION	DESIRED SITUATION
Short-term focus/competition	Strategic focus and relationships
Technology-led culture	Business-led culture
'Features' selling	Benefits selling
Ad hoc competitive analysis	Clear view of Global's competitive advantage
Jungle fighters	Strategic planners
Reactive 'market-traders'	Proactive 'sales consultants'
Individuals	Teams

Although it was clear that there were those key areas for exploration within the current-state work, we avoided the temptation of focusing upon them. This enabled us to identify a factor which may otherwise have gone unnoticed, and that was the apparent lack of significance of the concept 'benefits' to the senior sales people. This factor was identified by the fact that not one of the 30 people talked to introduced the concept into the conversations, despite those conversations frequently being focused (through following the sales people's 'trains of thought') on topics in which one may have expected the notion of 'benefit' to emerge.

We drew an inference from the fact that not one respondent spontaneously introduced the idea into our conversations, which we shall explore towards the end of this case study. In making this inference, we were going beyond what a strictly interpretative approach may allow. How do we deal with this?

First it is unlikely that unless we had undertaken the 'research' as we did that we would have come to the conclusion we did. It is most likely that had we prepared a questionnaire, or a set of questions for a semi-structured interview, the data from this would have been all we would work on. The issue of 'benefits' could easily have been lost. This is because we either would have included questions on the topic or not.

Had we included such questions, our belief is now that the respondents would have been responded to in 'rote' fashion. Senior sales people know what they are expected to say about 'benefits', and as soon as you provide them with the cue, they can quickly and competently respond to that cue. Having worked subsequently for four years with many of these senior sales people, I am sure that, in response to any such cue, we should have had consistent (but, I believe, misleading) data concerning how important they all felt 'benefits' to be.

Had we not included any 'cues' on the topic of benefits, then the absence of data would have been down to our research design, and not to anything we could legitimately say about the people we talked to. We may have completely overlooked the issue, or, having raised it, but having no 'data' to go on, we are likely to have ignored it.

But this still leaves us with a great deal of uncertainty. Is it not highly speculative that we should infer from a lack of data (the fact that the topic was not mentioned) something about what goes on in the minds of these senior sales people? Should we not, following Argyris (1993: 83) have checked our inferences during the conversations?

In this, as with so many other uncertainties, I had to make a judgement which may not have been the 'best' way of dealing with the situation. In only two cases I did feed back to the sales person I talked to the fact that he had not brought up the topic of benefits, despite our conversation touching closely on areas where I might have expected 'benefits' to enter the debate. In both cases the response I received was what we should refer to as 'rationalisation': the individual had not talked about it because 'it was too obvious. .I refrained from further checking. Not only did I find the reactions unhelpful, but I was also aware that there was a possibility that individuals may see this as some kind of 'trick'. In this case, it would not take long before all future 'interviewees' were primed on the topic, and the 'data' would have been lost.

The situation continued as before, with references to benefits being conspicuous by their absence. We were left with the challenge of drawing some conclusions from what had not been said as much as we were looking at what had been said. We were led to infer from this lack of data that thinking in terms of benefits did not come 'naturally' to the sales people we had talked to.

This inference was important in our subsequent learning design and delivery, which we shall discuss in Chapter 10. We believe (but we would, wouldn't we?) that this small piece of data was highly significant in what we subsequently did with the people from the organisation, and that what we did was helpful in ways we may otherwise have missed. However, post hoc does not mean propter hoc, and one case does not 'prove' a point.

We characterise the situation described in the Global Technologies case as an example of the 'paradigm effect'. 'Training' in sales and marketing which had been provided, along with all the 'hype' from the centre of the organisation concerning the benefits to the customer of the organisation's major shift of focus seemed to have settled precariously upon a 'culture' in which 'benefits' were somewhat alien. Our contention is that, as with the 'benefits' issue for Global Technologies, part of our job in current state exploration is to go beyond the immediately available data, and even to go beyond checking inferences on site, and to present, where relevant, alternative pictures which may differ from those managers themselves would recognise. People may not be able to articulate their own culture in ways which an outsider, by drawing contrasts and comparisons, may be better suited to do.

But are we 'right' when we do so? Clearly, the answer has to be 'No'. Can our insights, our representations be helpful or revealing? Here I believe the answer is 'Yes'. But only if these representations are offered as alternative ways of seeing, rather that 'the truth' about the organisation. It is often a matter of 'What if?'

In the case of Global Technologies, we offered a 'What if?' What if the lack of spontaneous use of the concept 'benefits' were to be associated with a lack of focus on those benefits in dialogue with the customer? What if the 'lip-service' which may be associated with this apparent peripheral nature of the concept within the 'culture' of the sales people be visible to customers through the behaviours of those sales people? What if this small piece of data were to be a clue to sales people not 'being' as customer focused as they may say (believe?) they 'are'?

None of these kinds of 'what if' questions is susceptible of 'scientific proof'. But as pointers to where management and organisation development may be most helpful and effective, they can be valuable building blocks. Because management and organisation development is not a 'science' it is impossible to demonstrate any causal link between an intervention and positive organisational benefits. It seems important, therefore, to look for the kinds of clue which may not be immediately obvious, especially to people who inhabit the cultural milieu which is itself being explored.

Interpretation is not a 'Free-For-All'

Once a commentator, whether a management and organisation development professional with a 'mission' or any other person exploring people in a social setting, decides to interpret a situation in ways which have not explicitly been checked with those within the situation, there is the potential for the flood-gates to open. Statements beginning 'It's pretty obvious that . . .', 'What they don't understand is . . .' and 'The people believe . . .' can be powerful signals that what follows is unchecked inference presented as 'fact'. We have to recognise how easy it would be for us to wander off into the realms of 'fantasy' as we present bizarre images of organisations which are reflections of ourselves as 'researchers' far more than they are reflections of how people in the organisation present themselves. Just because we have the experience, the 'outsider' view, and the remit to unearth the unexpected does not give us the right to indulge in interpretative games.

One of the devices which helps us to take care in presenting an organisa-tion's current state is our evaluation model. We are aware that it is easy to bundle together 'facts', inferred or stated motives or intentions, meanings or classifications, and judgements or opinions, and Hammersley (1990: 31–51) provides a significant amount of evidence to suggest that ethnographers frequently do combine claims and conclusions, descriptions and predictions, explanations and evaluations, and so on, in ways which make it hard to separate the ethnographer from the data.

It is at the point where we are putting together our 'conclusions' from the current-state work that it helps to be able to use the evaluation model to check what we are saying against the data. For example, we try to spot instances in which judgements on our part may be read as though they were the views of one or more of the managers we have talked to. Where we introduce terms which may convey meanings which may be different from those commonly used within the organisation, we try to ensure we highlight these differences ('strategy' has been one of the most frequent sources of potential misunderstanding in recent years, soon to be overtaken, I suspect, by 'culture', 'empowerment' and 'coaching').

So we are in a position to 'map' out our data and conclusions within a loosely defined matrix (which we tend to use for planning rather than as a framework for presenting the results):

	Facts	Intentions	Meanings	Judgements
What managers said				
What we conclude				

What Current-State Work 'Finds Out'

At the time of writing, I believe that many of our current and potential sponsors are not prepared to recognise the enormous potential for rigour in management and organisation development interventions, which an effective current-state exploration can provide. For whatever reasons, most sponsors (and, regrettably many management and organisation development professionals) seem to take a very simplistic approach to current-state work, and appear to be happier hearing blunt, crude generalisations about their management and organisation than spending effort in exploring the nuances which effective research can generate. It is the kind of thinking which says, 'Give my managers a course, I'm sure something will rub off,' and 'They're all afraid of taking responsibility – I want them to be more proactive.' It is the same kind of approach which, rather than taking an interest in the finer details, simply asks the equivalent of us: 'Tell me, doctor, is my organisation going to live?'

In Chapter 1 I argued that all managers are students of organisations. Good current-state work provides significant clues about how an organisation works, the ways in which the 'culture' reinforces itself, the barriers to change, the limited potential impact of any management and organisation development intervention. It can be a highly effective design tool for a learning intervention. But if it is to become useful it has to be seen less as a 'traveller's tale' ('How interesting, how bizarre, what a shame it all has to change') and more as a set of insights into what is likely to work, and what is likely to be ineffective in any attempt at change, whether through a management and organisation development intervention or not.

But to appreciate fully the impact a 'good' current-state exploration can have on learning effectiveness, we have to be able to set it into the context of how learning takes place. Specifically we have to be able to recognise the influences on learning both of managers' individual styles and history, and of the organisation in which managers spend a great deal of their time, and which sponsors the management and organisation development intervention.

The case explored in the Appendix is a good illustration of this point. It was with the best of intentions that the current-state work was undertaken by the team, with willing co-operation from almost all the managers of the company. Yet I believe that a number of crucial elements were overlooked in that work, which had a significant impact on the outcomes of the programme as a whole. The most critical oversights are described in the Appendix, and at the end of Chapter 9.

REVIEW OF THE GAP BETWEEN DESIRED STATE AND CURRENT STATE

In classic management mode, the final part of this step is the comparison of the desired state with the current state, to 'measure' the gap.

It should be clear from everything which has been written both in this chapter and elsewhere that we do not believe that this 'gap analysis' is a simple matter of 'measurement'. We cannot say, for example, that we want managers to be 90% customer focused, compared to the 40% customer focus that they exhibit today. In that sense, what takes place here is not an 'analysis' at all, but review of the implications we and the sponsors draw from the differences we and they perceive between these two 'states'. If analysis means breaking things down into their component parts, then it is the wrong image for this process.

Because of the ways in which we focus our current-state work on the top-right box of our research methods model, we frequently find that there are few direct 'comparisons' which are immediately available between the two states. Were we to adopt any other approach, we could skew either the data gathering or the data analysis (or both, as would be the case for bottom-left techniques) so that the two states would be directly comparable. But we believe that the advantages this would provide would be superficial, representing an easy comparison of 'misleading' data.

Some managers would prefer such an 'easy' option. Used to simple models, and, in some cases, used to the direct comparisons which tend to emerge from traditional training-needs analyses, such managers want to be able to measure a distance and to evaluate how many steps per person-day's investment (of time and money) are required to 'do the job'. We believe that such an approach misrepresents the nature of the work we have described up to now.

Desired state and current state are not two points on a spectrum, separated by time and 'learning effort'. To look at them in this way is to misrepresent the learning process, to present it as a linear progression from one place to another. Even if very simplistic learning processes (such as the learning of motor skills) could be represented in this naive way, the kinds of learning which characterise effective management and organisation development are seriously misrepresented by this image.

In Chapters 7 and 10 I shall explore learning, and why it is misleading to see it as simple progression. For now, let us simply say of the comparison of desired state and current state that each represents a 'complete' picture in its own right. Comparing them may be better characterised as comparing a picture of a bungalow with a picture of a mansion. One represents what we have now; the other represents what we would like to have. But at this stage, we have no idea of how we may go about achieving the goal of the desired state. Whether we can keep some of the foundations, some of the window frames, most of the garden, and so on, are questions which remain to be explored. But they are clearly deeply dependent upon the accuracy of the picture of the current state we have generated.

When learning design starts, it is vital that we have this clarity of vision. Learning does not take place in a vacuum; the fact that most of the picture of the current state will have been 'drawn' by the participating managers themselves will help us to understand how those who we will be helping to learn see where they are coming from.

But until we have looked at learning, we can do no more than look at the two pictures and say, 'Do these two pictures represent as accurately as possible where you want to be (the mansion) and where we are today (the bungalow)?' Because if that is the case, then we have some idea of what the relevant management and organisation development challenge looks like.

CONCLUSIONS

Our journey has taken us quite a while, and we have not even started to design any management and organisation development interventions yet, let alone started a 'course'. Is all this really necessary? What happened to the happy-go-lucky management training approach which bundled a few 'rookies' into a room with a hastily conscripted old stager and let some of the learning rub off? It may have been a bit crude, but surely something good came out of it. Are we in danger of overanalysing, of analysis-paralysis? Does all this preparatory work really pay off?

There is no way of 'proving' anything in the social arena of human interaction. What we have set down so far has been a whole series of ideas which have been accumulated by many people in the broad territory of management and organisation development over a number of years, and crystallised by the intensive experiences my colleagues and I have shared with many managers going through learning in the more recent past.

What we can say with some conviction is that

❑ until recently many people working in management and organisation development have been working in the dark when it comes to finding answers to the big questions, such as 'why?' and 'how?' regarding managerial learning
❑ we have witnessed an apparent rapid improvement in the quality of learning which we have shared with managers from our client organisations
❑ we are beginning to understand some of the ways in which organisational culture, individual personalities, learning design, experience and reinforcement, and personal growth (among many others) can be seen as linked

together in a cohesive framework which makes a lot of sense in this
confusing world of management and organisation development
❑ understanding how managerial learning works, and therefore how to
  make it increasingly effective and lasting will be a vital part of our ability
  to compete in global markets in the twenty-first century
❑ if we stay where we are in terms of our understanding of all this, we shall
  fail

It is for these and many other reasons that we are prepared to grapple with
the challenges which have characterised the early chapters of this book. It is
for these and many other reasons that we feel it is vital to continue to explore
all aspects of the management and organisation development world. In
subsequent chapters I shall move beyond the 'preparation' stage which has
characterised Chapters 1 to 5, and dig deeper into what we currently think
managerial learning and management and organisation development are all
about, and what impact this has on our ability to work with organisations to
make them better at what they do, and better places to be.

6 Aiming for Learning

INTRODUCTION

In the previous chapter I explored some of the principles of diagnostics when attempting to find out where an organisation is trying to start a management and organisation development intervention from. Over the past few years, we have found this aspect of our work of increasing importance in creating successful activities. There is a very simple but powerful reason for this.

Traditionally, management and organisation development interventions have worked from aims which have almost exclusively been developed from what, in Chapter 5, we called the 'desired state':

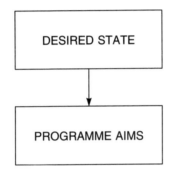

Figure 6.1   *Defining programme aims from the desired state*

In other words, it was enough simply to sketch out the kinds of behaviours and knowledge required to form the basis for a design activity. This is still the model many clients come to us with in the first instance. It seems to make sense; it looks forward rather than backwards.

CURRENT-STATE ANALYSIS

In other cases, clients bring with them their own 'current-state analysis' – derived from practices which may appear to be similar to those we have described in the previous chapter. However, we have found a common problem with this approach.

Current-State Analysis is part of the Process

The problem is that many of these client-generated analyses are built upon the kinds of error which we encountered in the previous chapter: managers may not be aware of what they do not know; they may have very flimsy criteria for assessing their levels of competence; they may not be encouraged to explore in any depth some of the underlying influences on their potential learning which we recognise as crucial (see Chapter 7 for details on this point). Similarly, many of those undertaking the analyses may not be familiar with the influences on learning which this book explores. In all, we have found that many such internally derived analyses are superficial, and built upon the very foundations which we have found to be at the heart of many well-meaning failures in management and organisation development.

The approach of clients undertaking their own 'current-state' analysis is understandable. They are internal 'informants' (developing the ethnographic analogy of Chapter 5), and may believe that they should be able to provide much more meaningful descriptions of their organisations than any outsider. Chapter 5 has questioned this assumption. But more importantly, they do so because the traditional 'model' of the role of a management and organisation development 'provider' is one which limits the external provider to the delivery of the 'training product'.

The partnership approach which we introduced at the start of Chapter 1 is more than a desire to 'grab' more of the 'relationship value chain'. It is about providing expertise in learning as well as in the embedded 'subjects', such as strategy, marketing and teamworking. It is about sharing responsibilities for more than the happiness of managers at the end of a 'course'. Making an impact depends upon helping clients throughout the learning process, and this means bringing the considerable learning we have acquired over the years to all elements in the learning process. This starts with high-quality current-state analysis.

What constitutes such an analysis will vary widely. But we believe it is inappropriate to start to define an intervention on the basis of, for example, a couple of lists of two- or three-word phrases covering 'issues' and 'topics'. In practice, this takes us straight back to the 'desired state' – 'learning aims' model which we introduced at the start of this chapter. The risk of failure in this approach is very high.

Aligning Learning Aims

The second common problem is that current state analyses are sometimes effectively overlooked in the development of learning aims. This may be the case even where rigorous and penetrating analyses have been achieved, as in the following case.

MISSING THE MARK: THE WDS SENIOR MANAGERS' SEMINAR

Early work undertaken within WDS had followed many of the current-state research principles which are explored in Chapter 5. It had produced a significant list of 'current state' issues, as well as a series of clear perspectives on the future. Among the key issues which we suspected would play a major part in the relative success of any subsequent management and organisation development intervention were some highly sensitive issues, which are summarised here as

❑ no common culture across the company
❑ transnational differences in conditions of service
❑ confusion concerning market developments
❑ the top team was not a team
❑ over-control of detail and lack of empowerment were commonplace experiences
❑ bosses did not value feedback
❑ top managers were individualistic and did not share ideas
❑ there were perceived barriers between different parts of the organisation

These were in direct contrast to the desired state, which included, among others, such aspects as

❑ common culture
❑ demonstrated teamwork among the top team
❑ barriers between parts of the organisation broken down
❑ trust replacing suspicion
❑ the boss as coach as well as the boss
❑ sharing and learning from each other

(I use these lists here for brevity, and not to suggest that, in practice, these can tell an adequate story.)

A number of management and organisation development initiatives grew out of this analysis, some of which adhered firmly to the process described in this book. However, at least one initiative 'got away'. Consequently, a seminar was set up for the tier of management immediately below the top team, with the following aims

❑ To enable WDS managers to consider ways in which their own businesses can be most effectively aligned to the WDS strategy
❑ To extend the emerging language about key changes within WDS at this level of management
❑ To consider ways in which managers at this level can facilitate and encourage their management team to apply ideas from other programmes

The seminar covered the following

❑ The Global Business Environment
❑ Developing Competitive Advantage
❑ Business Process Re-engineering

It was well presented and, in principle, well received. But there were problems with the seminar as a contributor to the relationship with WDS. The managers who attended had mixed views on the applicability of some of the ideas to their own circumstances. Others were unable to capitalise upon much of what was explored because they claimed to have no insight into the overall WDS strategy. And there were numerous other perceived mismatches, often related to individual managers' previous interactions with models and frameworks used in the seminar.

The source of the difficulty lay in a disengagement between the 'realities' identified in the current-state analysis and the ways in which the topics were dealt with. As a response to the 'desired state', the seminar was fine; as a 'product' in its own right, it was very good. But as part of the overall management and organisation development process, it did not achieve what many of the people involved would have wanted it to achieve.

In effect, the current-state work became lost, and the seminar became attached solely to the 'desired state', with the kinds of consequence which are highly probable when this is, in practice even if not in intention, the model driving the design and development of a management and organisation development intervention.

This case is one of many which we used to have to deal with. The 'solution' to such problems start with a redefinition of the links between current state, desired state and learning aims:

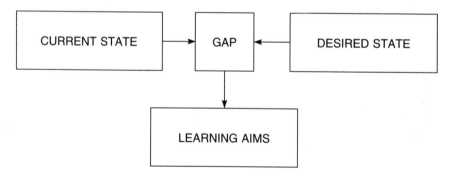

Figure 6.2   Defining learning aims from the gap

This redefinition is simple to draw as a diagram. It is much harder to replicate in establishing effective learning aims. However hard people try to set learning aims in the context of the gap between current and desired states, there seems an almost inexorable drift back to the earlier model of aims being driven exclusively by the desired state. It is in the very simplicity of the conceptual shift as illustrated in the diagram that the problem lies, because it both obscures the complex and sophisticated processes underlying the analysis and outcomes, and it rests upon a major shift in the underlying approach to learning.

Rigour in Defining Learning Aims

The first of these points was the central topic of Chapter 5. There it was suggested that current-state diagnostics and the subsequent analysis are not trivial activities which can be handled in a casual manner. The fact that they can appear to be accessible to anyone with a reasonable grasp of training (i.e. everyone who has ever attended a training event) means that some clients may want to handle the 'needs analysis' themselves. Their view is that 'external expertise' is confined largely to the provision of the learning event itself. Our view is that this provision is but a small part of the overall process, and that effective current-state and gap analysis (and the consequent definition of learning aims) demands at least as much rigour as the 'formal' parts of the intervention.

The impact of this upon what I have referred to as 'learning aims' (as opposed to programme aims) can be significant. Programme aims are often relatively vague reflections of some elements of the 'desired state'. Learning aims focus upon what, in the light of where people and the organisation are at the outset, needs to be done to get there. And this will be as much a function of the current state as it is of the desired state.

One of the most effective words which we use to maintain focus on learning aims is 'outcomes', against which we contrast 'inputs'. It is still true at the time of writing that some clients' approach to learning aims is dominated by their focus upon topics or themes. Some still bring their 'shopping list' of topics to the 'supermarket', and find it hard not to drift frequently into discussions on the need for 'strategy' or 'marketing'. Part of our job is to help them keep their minds upon the desired behavioural outcomes, rather than on the inputs which they suspect will achieve them.

Much of this book is devoted to removing some of the often crass prejudices about management development. As I suggested in the preface, and replay frequently throughout the book, the lack of in-depth research into managerial learning results in some highly questionable 'causal' beliefs. One of the most regular tasks we have to perform with clients is to challenge the naive assumption that, for example, teaching about strategy in a lecture room will necessarily produce strategically oriented behaviours in managers.

The Underlying 'Model' of Learning

As with so many aspects of management and organisation development, establishing learning aims, along with the processes which lead up to them, and the ways in which outcomes are planned to be monitored and measured, is often approached through a 'model' of learning which we believe to be false. This 'model' is rarely questioned; it forms an unconscious foundation to people's approaches to learning. By building upon this foundation, people can miss a fundamental point about managerial learning. That point is that managerial learning is not like filling an empty vessel. Nor is it even like adding to an already partly filled vessel.

The output from many 'needs analysis' exercises can be illustrated by the following metaphor:

Figure 6.3   *Filling the vessel*

The metaphor assumes that learning is analogous to some kind of 'substance' which is poured into a 'vessel', that vessel being the manager or his or her mind. It, in turn, depends upon a model of the human mind which is often referred to as the tabula rasa model, after the eighteenth century philosopher, John Locke, who suggested that we are born into the world with a mind like an empty slate, and onto which experience is etched over time.

Most people do not overtly articulate this model of the human mind, nor yet the model of learning which rests upon it. Yet it underpins many of the assumptions and practices of managerial learning. And in so doing, I believe, misrepresents the complexities and dynamics of such learning.

In this chapter I have touched upon the superficiality of many of the 'aims' which are set for management and organisation development interventions. I have suggested that this superficiality is supported by this unconscious model of learning. But the alternative model of learning which needs to replace the 'empty vessel' model cannot be represented by a simple diagram, or a few sentences. It is a fundamental reappraisal of how we think about learning. This is what Chapter 7 deals with.

7 The Myth of the 'Empty Vessel'

INTRODUCTION

It has become increasingly fashionable for management and organisation development providers to involve managers in the learning process. Many different reasons are suggested for this involvement, ranging from the idea that, by getting them active, managers will not lose interest in the proceedings, to the belief that managers already know what they have come to learn, and that management and organisation development activities simply bring out this knowledge and sort it out into 'the right order'. We share this approach of involvement. The reasons for this are brought out in this chapter.

The key, however, is not keeping managers' interest; it lies in the enormous amount of ideas, beliefs, experience, assumptions, values, attitudes, propensities to behave, cultural expectations and personality preferences which managers bring with them. Many of these will not be obvious, even to the managers themselves. Management development is a partnership between learners and providers in which 'new' ideas and ways of behaving are not simply added to the managers' stock of knowledge, but are (sometimes unconsciously) examined by managers to ascertain to what extent these ideas can be incorporated within an already extremely complex and busy mind.

Much of what constitutes the lack of success of management and organisation development interventions, when this happens, results from the 'new' not 'making sense'. This is not to say that, at the time, cognitively, intellectually, it does not make sense. But that, when managers try to implement what they think they have learnt, it does not work. People are not like vehicles, to be steered in new directions simply by turning the steering wheel. They need to have 'bought in' in many different ways before they can take on, and maintain, new behaviours. The new behaviours have to 'make sense' in the doing, and not just in the thinking.

This chapter explores some of the many different ways in which the ideas, concepts, suggestions, and new directions of any management and organisation development intervention have to 'make sense' to managers in order for learning to take place in anything but the most superficial meaning. It lays foundations for the remainder of the book. As such, it does not contain answers; it raises the questions some of which the subsequent chapters will seek to address. Those chapters will describe how we try to ensure that the new directions 'make sense' in as many ways as possible; this chapter simply describes the significant personal challenges which management and organisation development providers must confront if they are to do their jobs properly.

Learning and the 'Open Mind'

Although it seems that people like to learn in general, it is certainly not the case that every manager approaches managerial learning with an unmitigated thirst to absorb everything which can be 'provided'. Managers approach management and organisation development with 'mixed feelings'; some, like several of the Tech-Test managers, are, to certain degrees, fearful of processes associated with management and organisation development. Managers are not children: they do not arrive at a management and organisation development experience with no prior knowledge or attitudes. They come with a whole host of personal experiences, values, concerns, worries, and so on.

Because of the complexity of these factors, it can sometimes be tempting to ignore them, to act 'as if' managers had no previous thoughts, feelings, ideas, or values. Although most of us involved in management and organisation development try to take such factors into account, people are all so different that it seems an impossible task to design round the needs of each individual, with his or her unique history.

Responsibility for learning remains with the learner, and this is especially the case with mature and experienced managers. But this is different from saying that providers of management and organisation development have no responsibility for helping in this process. Like any good business, management and organisation development needs to be 'customer focused' rather than 'product focused'. It may have been the case some time ago that management and organisation development providers could simply trot out a few standard lectures, taking the attitude, 'There's the knowledge; it's not my problem if you can't learn from it.' We are still some way from knowing enough about managerial learning to be able confidently to issue warranties or guarantees that learning will be successfully implemented; but we can recognise that simply 'dumping' a product in front of managers and walking away is just not good enough. Learning is a collaborative process between learner and others; among those others are the teachers, lecturers, facilitators, and so on, who tend to make up the major part of the formalised human resources involved in management and organisation development activities.

One of the 'truths' of management and organisation development that does not need to be rigorously researched is that managers do not 'remember' everything from an intervention; that management and organisation development interventions are not always 'perfect' in what they seek to achieve. The learning 'process' is susceptible, like most processes, to 'continuous improvement'. This chapter seeks to explore ways in which we can understand and improve upon the processes we are involved in.

'Open Mind' or Empty Vessel?

When asked individually about their aims or aspirations from a management and organisation development intervention, some reply that they have come with an 'open mind'. This image is one which this chapter seeks to question deeply. It suggests a passive empty vessel into which knowledge can be poured. Learning is not like this, and managers (even those who make such statements) are more or less aware of this. Learning is not passively acquired, and it changes us (Donaldson 1992: 19).

Moreover, given that management and organisation development is often designed to change managers' behaviours, our interventions are, to some extent, attacks upon the personal integrity of those managers. As Nagel (1986: 191) says, 'If we are required to do certain things, then we are required to be the kinds of people who will do those things.' However conscious managers may be of this kind of potential impact, most will recognise to some extent that management and organisation development interventions are about changing them as people.

Managers adopt a number of strategies to cope with this realisation. Most, in our experience, adopt (at least at first, until they feel comfortable with the process) an 'intellectual' or 'rational' approach. This is an attempt to distance themselves (as people) from the process, and treat the learning as an abstract exercise in exploring the relative validity of the notions presented. They then evaluate these notions, dispassionately, and decide which to accept or reject. Messages may be retained but they do not have to be believed (Baddeley 1992: 32).

Such approaches are built upon a model of the self which allows for more or less complete detachment of the intellect from the person. This is a pretence, but one in which some management and organisation development providers go along with, largely because it allows them to remain similarly detached. The focus for the intervention then becomes not the managers but the models, ideas, knowledge, research, and so on of the 'expert'. This puts the 'expert' into a superior position (often symbolised and reinforced by the traditional 'habitat' of the lecture, in which the expert stands while the learners sit, the lecturer does most of the talking and manipulation of the 'tools' – OHP, white board, handouts – and the conceptual schemata used within the event are those of the expert, with a few concessions to the learners such as examples drawn from their organisation or industry).

Even if management and organisation development was only about such detached intellectualising, in which the goal was to convey ideas rather than change behaviour, the 'open mind filled by expert' model would still fail to match the ways in which learning takes place. People do not have 'open minds'. As we suggested in Chapter 1, people are theorists, a point which we shall be exploring in more depth within this chapter. No-one gets to middle or senior management positions without forming a great number of theories about the nature of business: what are appropriate and inappropriate decisions, what makes a good manager, and so on. Despite the best of intentions which the 'open minders' may have – intentions to listen and learn without prejudice – people are not always aware of the degree to which their existing beliefs, values and ideas act as filters to what is being presented to them.

'It seems to be a basic trait (though stronger in some than in others) to manage information selectively so as to confirm previous judgements and to reject information which contradicts them.' (Sillince 1995: 69; see also Nisbett and Ross 1980; Crockett 1965; Grossberg 1982). The history of science is replete with examples of hard-nosed, rational, intellectually well-developed scientists who had difficulty with this 'problem'; they just could not 'see' the evidence which contradicted their hypotheses (Kuhn 1970). It would be surprising if managers were better at being 'completely objective' than professional scientists, for whom 'the truth' is the ultimate goal. As we argued in Chapter 1, part of the problem is that, especially in organisational and management matters, this 'truth' is rarely likely to be forthcoming. Therefore, we should not be surprised by the widespread tendency for managers, like other people, to utilise the common 'mechanisms for maintaining beliefs and either avoiding or discrediting evidence which conflicts with those beliefs'. (Donaldson 1992: 82).

Clearly, it must be possible to break through these filters and barriers to learning, otherwise no-one would be able to continue learning beyond the point at which their first set of opinions were formed. It is the very fact that learning can continue throughout our lives that anyone has any faith at all in such activities as management and organisation development. But unless we are 'highly self aware, disciplined and scrupulous, then we may claim ourselves to be and believe ourselves to be reasoning rigorously when we are doing nothing of the kind'. (ibid.)

It may be the case that managers decide to 'set aside' their 'prejudices' when they become involved in a management and organisation development activity; that they intend wholeheartedly to be 'open minded'. I believe that this is almost as difficult as 'intending to set aside the influence of the force of gravity upon my person during the programme'. What we know, believe, value, suspect, and so on are not 'things' to be set on one side for the duration, but the context within which we learn. Like gravity, which can be harnessed to make cups and tyre treads work for us, what each of us has both innately within us, and have accumulated during our individual lives can be harnessed to 'make sense' of new learning. But to do this, it helps enormously if we can make ourselves as 'self aware' as is possible. If we don't know that we are filtering information, or how we are filtering information, we may find it impossible to manage that filtering process. We may be fooling ourselves about our 'open mindedness'.

How Well do we Know what's in Our Minds?

Once we introduce the notion of 'fooling ourselves' we invite reference to Freud, from whom we have learnt a great deal about the notion of the 'unconscious'. It is reasonable to assume these days that most educated people (a set which includes most managers) are prepared to accept that there may be parts of our knowledge, beliefs, values, attitudes, and so on which are not always and at will available to us; that some of our 'drives' remain more or less hidden from us in our unconscious. Freud called the processes by which we 'push' some things into our unconscious 'ego-defence mechanisms'. Processes such as projection, intellectualisation, displacement, reaction-formation, repression and denial (Stevens 1982: 235) are formed early in our development (Freud suggests the second year of life); they remain part of our defensive armoury well into our mature years, and frequently manifest themselves in managers with whom we work who are having difficulty confronting unwelcome feedback. One of the 'problems' with these processes is that they are not often consciously used; more often they 'happen to us' without us being aware.

All of this leads to a challenge for managers and for management and organisation development providers. A few simple scenarios will outline just a small part of the learning challenge. Let us take a case in which something is presented (either through telling or some experiential process) from which a manager could 'learn'. There are a number of possible outcomes:

❑ The manager consciously accepts the idea; it makes sense at the cognitive level, and the manager intends to implement the idea. At the same time, the idea fits into his or her unconscious beliefs, values, and so on sufficiently to allow for the idea truly to be implemented. With a bit of luck, and only a few removable barriers to such implementation, the idea may be carried into behaviour, and learning may therefore take place. However, such barriers are manifold, and there are no guarantees that these will be overcome early and easily enough for the learning to be consolidated before the momentum dies.

❑ The manager consciously accepts the idea; it makes sense at the cognitive level, and the manager intends to implement the idea. However, because it clashes in some way with his or her unconscious beliefs, values, and so on, it never gets implemented. Despite the good intentions, somehow the opportunity never seems to present itself; or, on reflection, it does not seem to be such a good idea after all. Learning is unlikely to take place.

❑ The manager consciously rejects the idea. This rejection is reinforced over time by the unconscious through a feeling that he or she was right to reject the idea as false. No learning is likely to take place.

❑ The manager consciously rejects the idea, even though it may fit well with his or her unconscious frameworks. This would be a clear case of denial. While that denial is allowed to persist, no learning is likely to take place. The best one could hope for would be that, over time, through repeated inputs or through introspection the manager would have a change of heart. (Later in the chapter we shall explore introspection and find that this is an unreliable vehicle for such changes of heart.)

In addition, in all of the above scenarios, the manager may say what he or she thinks (his or her conscious response), say the opposite of what he or she thinks, or say nothing. Unless we are capable of addressing the various elements of this challenge, management and organisation development will be a hit-and-miss affair.

Working with managers in a management and organisation development context means working with more than the overt, stated and intended; it means working with complex people who may be more or less aware of their own conscious and subconscious roles within the learning processes.

Learning – Researching and Defining

A significant subject such as 'learning' has, not surprisingly, been the subject of a considerable amount of research over the years. Like many research topics, the style or approach of the research has changed over the years, as trends or fashions influence researchers and their sponsors, or, more charitably, as discoveries enhance the steady evolution of our understanding of the subject. This is not a textbook, and I do not plan, therefore, to devote time rehearsing this research history. There are many works on the subject, such as Analoui (1993), which will provide a considerable amount of detail.

Little of the relevant research, however, has been undertaken specifically to explore the key questions we are seeking to answer, since most of it was not focused upon how managers learn. Scouring the literature, one discovers that many of the 'definitions' of learning which writers base their approaches upon have a pedigree which may not be directly pertinent to our subject. Many notions of learning are still based upon the early behavioural theories of Skinner, Hall and others, whose ideas about learning were based upon experiments with animals (usually rats in a maze: it is only the most extremely frustrated of managers who would value being paralleled with these!). Other notions are based upon models of memory, again built from the kinds of laboratory experimentation. Learning and memory are clearly related, but these experiments explore memory largely through remembering lists of unrelated words (Baddeley 1992: 20), and fail to provide us with helpful pictures of managers in action.

Yet more definitions are based upon training models, themselves often rooted in motor skills acquisition theory (Gibbs 1981). Learning how to type is very different from learning how to empower staff or how to develop marketing strategies. This is not to say that these research activities have nothing to say about managerial learning, but that we should be cautious about building strategies for management and organisation development on definitions of managerial learning which have their foundations rooted in inappropriate locations.

A great deal of research has been going on, meanwhile, in other disciplines which may raise questions concerning the very solidity of the foundations upon which some of the earlier ideas may have been based. Many of the social sciences (of which I argued in Chapter 1, management is an example) are in a state of flux. It would be naive for management and organisation development blithely to sail on, taking no notice of these developments, and working with definitions of learning which fail to take into account the complexities and subtleties of managerial work. We may need to rethink what we mean by managerial learning.

It does seem to be important that professionals in management and organisation development should be in a position to appreciate what goes on when managers bring their complex persons to a management and organisation development intervention. We are, in some respect, 'messing with their minds'. I, for one, would not want my car to be serviced by a mechanic who had little appreciation of how cars work. I therefore feel obliged to explore as rigorously as possible whatever is available to help me answer questions such as whether it is a good idea to take managers on an outward bound experience in order to enhance their effectiveness in decision-making. And to be able to answer these questions from a firmer base than what is fashionable in management and organisation development.

That fashion may influence such choices may be worrying to prospective 'customers' of management and organisation development providers. But it would be irresponsible to suggest that all management and organisation development professionals had a confident and agreed grasp on managerial learning, and what its understanding can tell us about good and bad choices in management and organisation development. Research (Wills 1994) suggests that, even at such an advanced institution as Ashridge, 'tutors' views on what constitutes learning varies according to the nature of his or her subject

discipline'. With a fair amount of 'leading edge' management and organisation development being provided by 'expert' researchers in their own disciplines, this state of affairs is not surprising; it is simply a reflection of what
goes on in any business organisation where senior people specialise (see, for
example, Bowman and Daniels 1995 on this phenomenon in industry). The
fact that it happens does not make it ideal.

What Do we Know so Far?

There are a few things we can say about managerial learning which, I believe,
are well established. The first is that managerial learning is not like the
'learning' we go through in our earliest infancy. When babies learn to walk
and speak, they do so from some innate set of drives which are far from the
kinds of drives and motivators we consciously adopt in later life. This is a
shame, since the learning capacity of young children is something to envy,
especially those of us who struggle to learn a foreign language in adulthood,
mastering the rudiments after hours and weeks of dedicated study, to be
humiliated by the fluency and accent of a young native speaker within
minutes of arriving in his or her country. There are few of us who can ever
overcome the strong 'foreign' accent with which we speak a new language
(Greene 1987: 151), a point which we shall return to when we consider the
adoption of 'foreign' behaviours.

Adult learning is not like the fluent and carefree learning of a child.
Consciousness, ego, experience, all play a part in affecting how we approach
the demands of new learning in our more mature years (Jones and Hendry
1994: 159). Without necessarily wanting to, we make the process highly
complex.

There are a good number of 'models' and analyses which are aimed at
clarifying or simplifying this complexity. For example, writers compartmen-
talise on different kinds of skills, showing how learning the Greek myths
differs from learning to write good essays, differs from learning to ride a bike
(Greene 1987: 137). Others simply describe 'three' (it often is three for some
reason) kinds of learning, the favourites being 'cognitive', 'affective', and
'motor skills'. More focused upon managerial learning, Wills' (1994) trio are
'cerebral', 'behavioural' and 'transformational', where transformational is
'best'. Others (for example Pedler and Boydell 1985), worried by the potential
taints from being associated with low level skills learning suggest that
management and organisation development are not really about 'learning'
at all, but about 'development' (a move towards a different state of being or
functioning), a distinction which simply begs the question about how
managers 'develop' to get there.

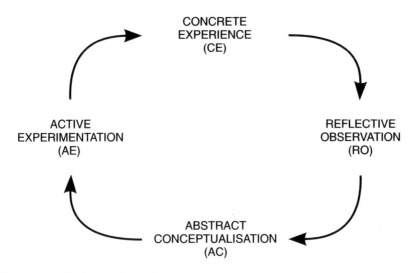

Figure 7.1   *Kolb's learning cycle*

There are a few 'analytical' ideas which do seem to have gained some wider currency. One, based upon the recognition that learning implies a number of different processes to be successful is Kolb's 'learning cycle' (Kolb 1983).

One of the strengths of Kolb's model lies in its recognition of the value of 'using language to monitor action and to debate new procedures [without which] behaviour would become routinised and teaching would be impossible. Human learning requires the ability to reconsider, and talk about, one's own actions' (Greene 1987: 160). And in this context, we can include in 'talking' the notion of 'talking to oneself' which, for some individuals, comprises a fair amount of the reflection which Kolb refers to.

The Lancaster Model of Learning

Some years ago, people at the Centre for the Study of Management Learning, University of Lancaster, pulled together many threads from earlier research and theories in learning, along with the insights from Kolb's model, and came up with their own 'model of learning', the Lancaster Model.

The Lancaster model provides us with a classification which differentiates three 'modes of learning': by discovery; by reflection; and by receipt of input.

Discovery, a learning mode which the model places primarily in the outer world, is a two-part process. The first part involves action – learning by doing, trying, and being open to the experience which such action provides. This closely parallels the top of Kolb's cycle. The second part involves feedback. This feedback can be generated by other people (as it always was

INNER WORLD

OUTER WORLD

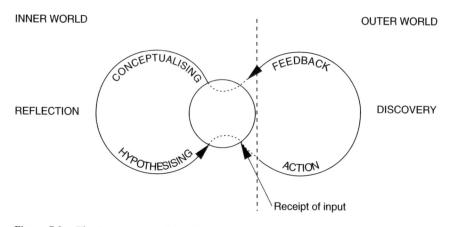

REFLECTION

DISCOVERY

Receipt of input

Figure 7.2   *The Lancaster model of learning*

with the 'conditioning' models of learning); or by self-reporting (as would be more likely in the 'cybernetic' kinds of learning model).

Reflection, on the other hand, takes place, in the Lancaster Model, in the inner world. It also consists of two parts. The first comprises putting together experiences and observations, of 'making sense', of conceptualising. The second is about generating theories and hypotheses concerning what has been and what will be.

The final element, receipt of input, is what happens when we are being told something, being given information based upon other people's experiences and so on.

As a heuristic device, the model is of significant value. By asking questions based upon the use of different combinations of the modes, different frequencies of the use of the modes, the relationships between the modes and learning aims, and so on, learning design can be significantly enhanced, as we shall explore in more depth in Chapter 10. But although it is a useful tool, it does not provide answers to some of the more basic 'why?' questions which this chapter is asking.

A Note on the Style and Approach of this Chapter

This chapter is not a critique of models such as the Lancaster Model. It is an attempt to take stock of the current state of research into many aspects of human minds and behaviour which can inform what we do as management and organisation development professionals. It ranges over a wide set of territories, building a picture in which each of the component parts is important to our rounded understanding of managerial learning.

There are few direct references within the chapter to immediate application of the ideas explored. These will be picked up in later chapters, drawing upon the theories from this chapter, and providing some clear answers to some important questions concerning the hows and whys of management and organisation development. There are two reasons for postponing reference to application of the theories.

The first is simply about the sheer length of the chapter. Should I try to provide examples of application for each of the key ideas in the chapter, it would become unbalanced in the context of the book as a whole. The second, and much more valid reason, is that it is only through the aggregation of the ideas, the joint application of the full set of notions, that we can provide the kinds of answers which we do. If we were to attempt to provide examples at every turn, we should need constantly to refer to ideas not yet fully explored within the chapter.

Managerial learning is a complex set of processes. It would be unforgivable to trivialise this complexity; it would also be mistaken. If we are to do the job properly, we shall have to avoid the kinds of oversimplification which tempt the production of the 'quick fixes' such as the 'one-minute manager'. Therefore I make no apology for the complexity of this chapter. But I would urge the reader who feels the arguments are getting nowhere near answering his or her questions about how to kick off a course next Monday morning to suspend judgement until we have both explored the ideas of this chapter, and provided examples in later chapters of how we can use these ideas to answer such questions.

For example, many management and organisation development professionals and many managers are currently vexed by the question of whether outdoors development is a valid and powerful means of managerial learning, or one of the most elaborate con-tricks ever played on managers. In Chapter 8 I shall address this question; in so doing, we shall draw upon the ideas and theories of this chapter. Practical application to managerial learning is the goal of the book. Full understanding of what we know about managerial learning is the means by which we shall go about it. This chapter is about gaining that understanding.

Managers, Minds and Learning

'This is a glorious time to be involved in research on the mind . . . the frontier of research in the mind is so wide open that there is almost no settled wisdom about what the right questions and answers are'. (Dennett 1991: 257). There has been an upheaval in many of the disciplines which can inform our understanding of managerial learning. It seems that the last few years have witnessed a fundamental questioning of much of the received wisdom in psychology, ethology, anthropology, neuroscience, ethnobiology and socio-biology, as well as that in social science and management. The boundaries have blurred, and we are in a position to dip into a number of previously closed and introspective sciences for insights which can help us understand different facets on the complex issues of managers and how they learn.

Few of the writers in these areas of research have anything directly to say about managers per se. But what they do say, I believe, can help us to re-examine and, where appropriate, modify what we do on management and organisation development. It will be the job of this and subsequent chapters to dip into some of this unrelated research and to show how that research can help us to do management and organisation development even better.

CONSCIOUSNESS AND LEARNING

I have already suggested that the unconscious minds of managers have a vital role in learning, and that we should not ignore the often unspoken and unseen influences of those managers' unconscious minds. Much of the rest of this chapter will be about this and other factors in managerial learning which we need to take into account in doing our jobs well.

One reason for taking note of the 'unconscious minds' of managers is that 'each of the 20 billion citizens of our brain is talking to at least 10000 others at least once and as often as 100 times a second' (Hunt 1989: 132). By 'citizens' Hunt is referring to the neurones which comprise the cells of the brain, and what he is saying about them is that they are in almost constant communication with each other. There is an enormous amount of 'chatter' going on in there. Yet our immediate impression of consciousness is of a relatively small amount of 'serial processing'; we don't hold onto many pieces of data *consciously* at any one time.

In other words, however complicated our conscious thoughts, and however elaborately we explore what's going on in our minds, what we are conscious of at any moment is a tiny fraction of the vast amount of automatic and unconscious activity in our brains. One analogy which some people find helpful is of thousands of radio signals which surround us (Parikh 1994: 44). As we turn the dial on our radio tuner, we pick up fragments of each signal. Sometimes we pay attention to one programme for a while, and listen to it exclusively. The other signals are still being broadcast; we simply cannot hear them while we are tuned into one station. Our consciousness is like this; most of us are able to 'tune into' more than one 'station' at a time; few of us can tune into more than seven. Seven is impressive, but orders of magnitude smaller than all the available 'frequencies' in our heads.

Trying or hoping to become consciously aware of everything going on in our unconscious minds would be hundreds times more difficult than the Chief Executive of a huge multinational organisation insisting upon reading and 'rubber-stamping' every single communication coming into, going out of and being sent within the organisation. Senior managers learn that they cannot know and assent to absolutely everything which is going on within the organisation. So they delegate. This is what our minds do. It enables our minds to deal with a great deal more than our consciousness can cope with alone.

Delegation is not abdication, nor is it denial of the existence of those activities which we do not directly manage. Being unable to be everywhere at once, managers learn strategies to keep in touch with what's going on elsewhere, to influence those activities which they cannot directly manipulate, and to be influenced by those activities where appropriate. A great deal of effective managerial learning is learning how to emulate this kind of approach to our minds.

EMOTIONS AND RATIONALITY

The Notion of Rational Decision-Making

People who have suffered damage to specific parts of the brain (the prefrontal/amygdala circuit) often notice no deleterious effect on their intelligence as measured by IQ tests, and by monitoring much of their 'rational' behaviour. Their cognitive abilities remain undamaged. Yet their decision-making is significantly flawed; they make highly questionable choices in both their personal and business lives, and can become obsessive about simple matters such as when to make appointments (Damasio 1994).

Although these people's problem is the result of specific damage to, or surgical removal of, part of their brains, and therefore suffer an extreme form of the decision-making disability, they are demonstrating a potential problem which can affect anyone to some extent. There are many people who have not suffered such physical damage, but who still make disastrous choices, time after time. All that is different about the patients referred to above is how specific damage significantly affects the degree to which they suffer from this lack of access to a crucial part of our ability to function normally, and, more disconcerting for them, their subsequent inability to do much about it. What studying this kind of brain damage helps us to do is to find out more about how we go about such activities as making good decisions. Managers' roles include a great deal of decision-making.

Some approaches to managerial learning appear to be based upon the notion that decision-making is a 'purely rational' process. Emotions have, to a large extent been left out of these approaches. However, if, as the research suggests, people can retain many of the features of 'rationality' but be bad at decision making, this shows that there is another factor in good decision-making, apparently influenced by other parts of the brain. Learning about decision-making means learning about more than 'purely rational' processes. It is also about recognising the emotional elements in decisions.

These emotional elements are not always consciously noticed. This may not be obvious, because the popular view of emotions is that, unless we are aware of them, they cannot be happening to us. Rational managers may argue that they know the difference between decisions taken 'in an emotional state', 'in the heat of the moment', for example (which may thereby be poor decisions), and those taken 'with a cool head'. Managerial maturity involves recognising and avoiding the kinds of emotional unbalancing which is variously described as 'emotional hijacking' (Goleman 1995); being 'in the grip' (Quenk 1993); 'out of the blue' (Modell 1993), and so on.

But these are the instances where our emotions are so strong that we cannot fail to attend to them. Research into brain and behaviour suggests that the underlying processes which produce these conscious manifestations are continuous, mostly unconscious, but highly influential on our attitudes and values. The choices we make between hierarchy and empowerment, whether an act is one of leadership or autocracy, and so on, are partly shaped by the rational discourse we have with ourselves and our colleagues. But they are more basically shaped by the underlying emotional architecture of our brains.

Attitude Formation

We frequently engage in conscious, rational evaluation of situations and form attitudes as a result. This is the 'model' which we often think characterises all our attitudes and values; it is one in which we see ourselves weighing up the pros and cons of a situation before making judgements. As managers, we learn how to do this overtly. But 'research has shown that in the first few milliseconds of our perceiving something we not only unconsciously comprehend what it is, but decide whether we like it or not; the 'cognitive unconscious' presents our awareness with not just the identity of what we see, but an opinion about it. Our emotions have a mind of their own, one which can hold views quite independently of our rational mind' (Goleman 1995: 20).

This kind of 'love (or hate) at first sight' has its roots in evolution, where knowing what attitude to take to something (fight, flight, feast or fornicate with) had survival value. It still happens to us now; we have not lost what evolution has given us. Humans have gained the ability consciously to explore attitudes. But this exploration is not done on neutral subjects. Conscious attitudes are edited versions of attitudes which we already have, but may not be aware of. We do not consciously 'rubber-stamp' every attitude we have.

Experiences in Childhood

Some of the attitudes which, according to many psychologists, continue to influence throughout our adult lives, are those formed in early childhood. In those early years, when the brain is still being formed, and before we have acquired the language with which to 'rubber-stamp' what we experience, what happens to us gets stored away in memory 'as rough, wordless blueprints for emotional life' (Goleman 1995: 22). Psychologists suggest that it may be impossible directly to access these early attitudes and memories through our conscious minds. To learn of their influences on our adult behaviour, we have to draw inferences from dreams, and from various forms of psychotherapy. But we may also draw inferences about them from observing our values, and asking questions about where these values may have come from.

We cannot hope to find 'the answer' about childhood, preconscious influences on our deeply ingrained values, nor of those influences which are formed through our innate processes of attitude formation. But acknowledging their influence on how we decide between options seems better than pretending that all our judgements are taken fully consciously, and without any bias. Sixty years of research show how the constructions we create from the data which surrounds us – our views of the world, including the world of organisations and management, are 'largely on the basis of . . . attitude' (Bartlett 1932), reinterpreted in the light of beliefs (Bruner 1990), and rebuilt on the basis of the 'must have been' (Jaynes 1990).

Emotions and Learning

Although managers may like to think of their minds being 'open' to learning, the emotions, attitudes and values which they bring with them, albeit often unconsciously, will significantly influence how they respond to the learning situation. Management and organisation development facilitators will be similarly influenced. The principle which we recommend is acknowledgement and awareness of manager's emotions rather than denial of the influence of those emotions.

People who can gain greater access to their emotional drivers not only benefit from being thus more aware. There is a more positive aspect to the acknowledgement of emotional drivers, and that is the opening up of alternative ways of seeing problems, challenges and opportunities. In many cases, alternative forms of problem solution may be unconsciously suppressed, being associated with what people may feel are inappropriate emotional connotations. The legitimization of emotional expression can free up new ways of seeing which 'provide options for alternative forms of organizing' (Putnam and Mumby 1993: 55).

UNCONSCIOUS 'TEMPLATES' IN THE MIND

Over a number of years, people at the Center for Creative Leadership have gathered data from large numbers of successful senior managers, gathering their views on lessons they have learnt about management from experience. Among their conclusions was that there is a small number of critical experiences from which learning the lessons of management are most likely to be drawn ('Some experiences simply pack more developmental wallop' McCall *et al.* 1988: 5), and that those lessons show some cohesion. In other words, if managers face these kinds of situation, they are likely to learn things, and what they learn is likely to be similar to what other managers faced with similar situations will learn. The key situations listed were

❑ challenging job assignments
❑ significant other people
❑ hardships and setbacks (such as personal mistakes and failures)
❑ coursework at pivotal moments

Is this 'new' knowledge about managerial learning, or is it something which many people have known for many years?

A number of writers (for example, Burnett 1995) have likened the 'journey' through managerial life with elements of similar ventures experienced by people from many cultures through myths and rituals. The commonality of themes of heroic journeys in myths from many cultures (Campbell 1972; 1993) suggests some kind of 'universality of experience': expectations that we shall all have to face challenges, learn from other people such as guides or mentors, have to deal with hardships and setbacks, and be presented with 'formalised' opportunities to learn a great deal in a short period of time. In other words, there is the possibility that the parallels between the kinds of experiences cited by the managers questioned by the researchers from the Center for Creative Leadership and those very situations which myths and rituals persistently focus upon, are no accident.

Explaining the close approximations of the managers' list and the common themes from myth and ritual could take two key directions, apart from writing them off as chance. The first would be to suppose that a significant number of the senior managers who answered the questions were familiar with the myths and rituals of many cultures and that, somehow, this knowledge influenced their answers; that they identified those four key kinds of learning experience because of some more or less conscious belief, drawn from their readings, that the parallels between the experiences of people from other cultures' learning from myth and ritual, and managers' learning from experience are valid. This seems highly unlikely.

The second hypothesis is that the parallels are there irrespective of any reading which these senior managers may or may not have done into the ethnographic literature; that the parallels have something to do with some kind of 'archetypes'.

Innate Propensities to Behave in Certain Ways

The instincts which we recognise in animals are 'hard wired' into their brains, and do not disappear over time. Research shows that instinctive fear of falcons has persisted in Galapagos Island finches over nearly a million years during which no falcons have been experienced by such birds (Stevens 1982: 48). Some patterns for survival are similarly innate in humans, such as a crawling baby's 'innate aversion to venturing out onto a supporting pane of glass, through which it can see a 'visual cliff' (Dennett 1996: 90). This is not to say that human behaviour is 'instinctive'; but what all humans seem to inherit 'is the potential to develop . . . behavioural systems' (Bowlby 1969: 45) which show cultural differences, but overlaid upon similar foundations. Such foundations are thought to persist in the same lower levels of the brain in which emotional memories are 'stored'. They are not directly accessible by consciousness; their influences can only be inferred from what happens, from what we do directly experience.

The idea of this kind of 'innateness' as related to human behaviour has been explored by researchers in a variety of different disciplines: ethology ('Innate Releasing Mechanisms')' psychology ('behavioural systems' and, more recently, 'aptic structures'), anthropology ('structuralism'), psycholinguistics ('deep structures'), sociobiology ('genetically transmitted response strategies' and 'epigenetic rules'), psychiatry ('psychobiological response patterns' and 'deeply homologous neural structures' and cognitive science ('Darwinian algorithms'), to cite just a few (Stevens 1995: 128, see also Fodor 1975 on innate ideas). All of these are akin to the idea of 'archetype' which Jung introduced earlier this century. The common theme from them all is that human development takes place against a more or less influential set of 'likelihoods', 'tendencies' and 'unconscious expectations'.

'Archetypal' Learning Situations

Returning to the Center for Creative Leadership research, it looks likely that, like any innate propensity, there are archetypal propensities to learn in certain situations – that certain situations kick off some kind of 'innate releasing mechanism'. When we meet those situations, we are 'naturally' more attentive to what is going on, and learn from them. This may be more complex, but it is related to the kinds of 'expectation to learn' which we see in other animals, as when vixens teach their cubs. What the archetype may be 'saying to us' is 'pay attention to this, you're going to learn something'; and in more cases than not, we do pay attention, and we learn.

This has implications for management and organisation development. Some of those implications, such as the potential for using outdoor management development somehow to 'replicate' the ritual context in which to learn, are already part of the portfolio of many management and organisation development interventions; and in the next chapter we shall explore ways in which management and organisation development providers can operationalise this kind of archetypal propensity to learn.

Projection

In psychology, a 'complex' is not a problem or disease, but simply the elaborate set of impressions, attitudes and images associated with a concept or idea, such as the concept or idea of 'father'. If an archetype is the foundations, a complex is the building. We cannot see the foundations; we infer them from the shape of the building. Similarly, although the foundations limit the scope of the building, they do not determine many aspects of that building, such as colour, materials, height and so on. The complex is what we see and live with in consciousness.

We carry with us a wide range of complexes, built from their respective (innate) archetypes and from the (often emotionally coloured, but to some degree unconscious) experiences of our lives. Our complexes are 'idealised' sets of impressions and expectations. 'Idealised' does not necessarily imply some kind of goodness or perfection. In some cases, as with our early impressions of our parents, our partners and our children, the innate tendency to love these people does bring with it a (sometimes temporary) image of such goodness or perfection. In other cases of complexes, 'idealised' approximates in meaning more to 'simplified' (a rough template for the concept against which to match people we happen to meet).

One manifestation of complexes is sometimes referred to as metonymy, in which one image 'stands for' something more abstract or general: 'Schweitzer becomes 'compassion'; Talleyrand 'shrewdness'; Napoleon's Russian campaign the tragedy of overreached ambition; the Congress of Vienna an exercise in imperial wheeling and dealing.' (Bruner 1990: 60). In the normal run of events, such complexes carry less emotional charge than 'mother', 'child' and so on, but it is in the nature of being human that all our complexes will bring with them more or less conscious attitudes, as we described earlier in the chapter. It is also likely that many such attitudes will be different for different people: if Sir John Harvey-Jones 'stands for' sound, practical management for one manager, he may 'stand for' outrageous ties, bad haircuts and self-aggrandisement for another.

In our daily lives, we meet and have attitudes (many unconscious) to many people. Many people try to act as though every relationship with every person is crafted anew, built on an objective evaluation of that other person. Managers are often charged with this kind of objectivity, when appraising staff, for example. But so long as managers remain unconscious of the psychological process which takes place as we respond to other people, they may forget the fragmentary nature of the ways in which we construct our impressions and attitudes to people. Not only do we have an instant attitude, generated by our limbic system within milliseconds, but we also tend to 'classify' people according to our underlying set of archetypal norms or ideals.

The data which we acquire concerning others remains, in all but a few cases, a very small set of 'excerpts' (Jaynes 1990: 62) from a life story. Just as our visual capabilities enable us to infer from small amounts of data what we are seeing (Dennett 1991: 344 et seq.), enabling to recognise a cube without having to see it from all sides, so, in a more complicated way, but using the same powers of inference, we find ourselves matching small pieces of behavioural data about other people against the set of expectations which are our complexes: innate 'ideals' modified through personal experience, which itself is emotionally charged, and values-rich.

The process of such matching is known to psychologists, both Freudian and Jungian, as 'projection'. Not only do we project our complexes of father, mother, and so on, onto those who fill those roles in our daily lives, but we also project onto people we meet in our managerial lives other complexes, such as mentor, enemy, and so on. This means projecting 'idealised' images onto those 'real' people, expecting them to match up to an 'ideal' (even an 'ideal' enemy).

This means that there are a number of 'characters' in our life whom we meet not simply as 'strangers' to be taken at face value, about whom we learn from scratch, their role and impact upon us being developed as though on a clean sheet of paper. Rather, they arrive on the scene already well defined by our complex; it is against the blueprint of the complex. We don't learn about our mothers solely from experience; we learn about them as *contrasts* to the idealised archetype of 'mother'. And our personal complex of mother develops out of modifications to that idealised model, not just from the 'neutral' set of experiences (facts) which happen as we grow.

What happens in the case of 'mother' happens with many other characters in our lives; indeed, there is a reasonable case for arguing that the number of significant people with whom we interact throughout our lives who are not (albeit unconsciously) being similarly matched against an 'idealised' complex is relatively small. When we interact with our boss, are we interacting solely with the individual person about whom all we know is what we have learnt by experience? Or are we also in some way interacting with the 'boss' complex, built as much by our archetype of 'superior in the hierarchy' (a character to be found in virtually all mammalian groups) as it is from 'objective' reality? It may be that it is in this very 'matching' of experience and archetype that we go through the 'learning' from 'significant other people', as the Center for Creative Leadership identified. We learn from them because we are paying attention to matches and mismatches between our innate expectations and the evidence of our senses.

In Chapter 5 'leadership' was described not as an 'essence' which managers either have or do not have, but as a socially constructed concept which says far more about people who follow than about people who lead. What it may say about those people who follow is that they have projected onto that individual the archetypal 'ideal' of 'leader'. Individuals can surely encourage us so to project our complexes, as is evidenced by the 'charisma' of leaders such as Hitler. But what makes leaders like Hitler so successful is that they have learnt the knack of getting many many people to project their complexes of 'leader' onto them. One of the keys to such projection is that they are projections from the unconscious, where rational argument has no role to play. Hitler, in the rational world, was just another man; to those on whom they projected their complexes of 'leader' he was significantly more than that.

The fact that we may not have to 'teach' managers about leadership, but simply help them to delve into their already rich vein of archetypal knowledge about leadership – and about a whole host of other managerial concepts – should have a profound impact on how we think about helping managers to learn.

STOCKTAKE

Where have we got to so far? We have suggested that the unconscious plays a potentially significant role in managerial learning. It does this in at least two ways.

The first is in the attitudes, of which managers may or may not be fully aware, with which managers evaluate what they are expected to learn. We have suggested that it is unlikely that any manager (or any other person for that matter) will not already have a whole set of attitudes to the kinds of non-concrete 'components' of the organisational and managerial worlds; that however 'objective' managers may like to think they are being about a situation, they will be reappraising 'new' information in the light of deeply held attitudes and values which may not present themselves consciously. There are potentially no 'value-free' topics in management and organisation development.

The second is in the 'innate ideas' or archetypes which colour actual experiences by matching situations and people to personal complexes built not just by experience, but by how that experience matches up to the 'idealised' archetype. And those archetypes are also 'value-laden'. There are no absolutely 'new' situations, no absolutely 'new' bosses, partners, subordinates, and so on. When we study 'leadership' we are not setting out onto uncharted waters, but comparing the territory with unconscious models which we all bring with us.

In principle, all of us, including and especially managers, have the ability to 'override' these influences. We feel that we can be 'objective' about situations and people; that we can set aside our prejudices and, harnessing the enormous power of reason and the intellect, take a 'fresh' and untainted look at what we are doing and learning. What gives us this confidence is that our conscious minds have power over the unconscious. By concentrating on the 'objective facts' we can consciously repress these unconscious influences. Consciousness is what has given us the edge over the rest of the animal world, and enabled us to create organisations and management in the first place.

If this were not largely true, then surely we would be unable to achieve what we do achieve through the arts and efforts of management. We do control our anger, we do change our minds about people, we do learn new ways of thinking about situations and things.

UNDERSTANDING SOMETHING

Wanting to Learn – Making Sense

The word 'emotion' is based upon the same root as 'motion' and 'motivate'. The constellation of related meanings remind us that the emotional or attitudinal roots in our brains system are not 'intellectual' – not about mulling over or simply sensing, but about doing something (in our evolutionary past, usually one of those four Fs – fight with, flee from, feast on or fornicate with). As humans evolved greater levels of consciousness, much of this 'movement' has been internalised, a kind of moving about within the neocortex, shaping and exploring ideas so as to 'make sense'. It is no accident that we don't tend to like things which don't make sense to us, or which we do not understand. In evolutionary terms, this has clear survival value: if I don't know how to react to (move in respect to) this thing I am aware of, how can I be sure that I am not going to 'kick in' the wrong F?

Understanding is a positive value, but it can appear to be hard work. In response to this hard work, during a management and organisation development event, for example, some managers will devote more effort than others to trying to understand. Some will adopt the 'flight' strategy. Managers do this by 'switching off', or, in extreme cases, leaving the event altogether, using phrases such as 'This is not doing anything for me.'

If we can understand more about understanding itself, this ought to help us to help managers learn. But understanding about understanding is in itself hard. Part of what makes it hard is that a great deal of the understanding process takes place out of reach of conscious will. We cannot 'make ourselves understand'; people who try are often at a loss to know how to go about it apart from 'concentrating'. As we shall see in this section and the next, this strategy for 'trying to understand' is probably not the best choice. Put crudely, conscious understanding depends upon prior unconscious 'understanding'; unless something 'fits' into our unconscious minds, it will not 'make sense' to our conscious minds, and irritate or worry us.

This section explores some of the neurophysiological foundations for the process which we call understanding.

Meaningful 'Maps' in the Brain

The numbers of connections between neurones in the brain is enormous but not limitless. Because not every neurone is connected to every other, some of the connections in each of our brains are different, even in identical twins. This is the result of what goes on inside the brain when we learn. Learning changes the connections in our heads (Edelman 1992: 101). What connections are actually made, reinforced and 'survive' depends upon a complex process which is analogous to, and may indeed be a direct development out of the evolutionary process of 'natural selection'. Natural selection is not a conscious or deliberate process (Dawkins 1976; 1995; 1996; Jones 1993: 167). It works by selection not instruction (Edelman 1992: 74). In other words, what gets learnt about and retained is not so much the result of 'deciding' to learn something, as the survival of knowledge or information within the brain because it is 'selected', favoured within the ecology of the brain. Because each of us has unique experiences, the connections each of us actually has within our heads are different from those of other people (Broadbent 1981; Harre 1995: 157).

Cells gather into groups, which Edelman calls 'neuronal groups'. Different sets of neuronal groups become interconnected and respond selectively to specific elemental categories such as 'movement' and 'colour'. The sets of groups which work together are what Edelman calls 'maps'. The more we use those maps, the more they become reinforced; their connections to other neuronal groups is strengthened and the better they survive.

At its simplest level, this means that the more we think about something, the stronger the maps which represent that thing will be in our brains, the more 'adapted' those maps will be to survival within the brain, the better we will have remembered or learnt that thing. Rote learning is the simplest manifestation of this; by constant repetition, we reinforce and strengthen the respective neuronal groups in the associated maps, and we thereby ensure the survival of that learning. But any new idea or set of concepts which we think about, mull over, ponder on, or even dream about will thereby be reinforced: 'It is quite common when encountering a new abstract structure in the world . . . to find yourself trudging back and forth over its paths, making mind-ruts for yourself – really digging in and making yourself at home' (Dennett 1991: 300).

There is common ground between the neurophysiological notion of 'maps' in the brain and the psychological notion of 'complex'. Each comprises an interrelated set of images and impressions, attitudes and connections which make up some of the 'ideas' with which we think. Psychological constructs – complexes – which relate to 'father', 'leaders', 'challenges' and 'journeys' can also be represented as neuronal groups or 'maps' within the brain. Each map carries with it an (in principle) almost infinite set of connections to the other maps and complexes within our minds.

Understanding and 'Relevance'

One of the tenets of good learning situations is that learning should in some sense be 'relevant', that learners should be able to 'ground' the learning in their own experience. In other words, unless what is being presented can be connected – the new idea with the maps managers have of the work situation – then it will not 'make sense'. One of the big risks with managerial learning is a lack of this kind of connectivity between the ideas being explored in the management and organisation development intervention and the subsequent behaviours of the managers doing the 'learning'.

When managers cannot see the connections between what is being explored, and their learning needs, dissonance occurs. Managers are prone to say 'I understand what you are trying to put across, I just do not understand the relevance.' Knowing what to do even with small pieces of data, such as that the share price of company X stands at 70p at the moment depends upon context, relevance. Managers' subconscious 'filing systems' are vast and complex, but they are still organised. If new data or ideas cannot immediately be attached to existing mental maps, but are expected simply to float in some kind of cerebral 'in-tray', this produces the kind of dissonance which we often describe as 'not understanding the relevance'.

In Chapters 3 and 4 it was suggested that what constitutes 'relevance' depends partly upon the learning aims of an intervention. For *Exploratory* activities, for example, 'relevance' may demand the use of a significantly greater number of such 'dissonant' situations. Here, the goal will be to increase the learner's motivation to 'struggle' with seemingly unconnected maps and complexes, to become more determined to increase the less familiar interconnections, and thereby be able to 'see things' in a fundamentally new light. This means making some big changes within the managers' mental maps. For a *Core Capabilities* event, however, too many such puzzles will distract the learner from the goal of 'trudging' over the familiar connections of 'how we do things around here' to make them almost 'second nature'; to make the link between given situations and proscribed behaviours so common that they do not have to call on the full resources of consciousness to make them happen.

Mental Maps and Metaphors

The brain works with millions of mental maps, actively making and maintaining multitrack connections, most of which we are rarely aware of – we just don't have time to explore all those billions of connections. What we can do is appreciate what the connections within neuronal groups 'feel like'. Chapter 1 introduced the notion that many of the 'things' which managers work with are constructions – abstract concepts which do not have physical reality. They still make a lot of sense, however, and have major influence on managers' lives. We feel we understand organisations, managers and profit. We understand them as metaphors.

Let us take some examples of how we talk about organisations and management: we set managers *goals* or *objectives*, and set them along the *path* towards those objectives. We talk about *how far along* we have got, what has *got in the way*, being *sidetracked* by unforeseen events, of *getting there*. In all these cases, there are no physical paths or goals, only abstractions. Similarly, we create *hierarchies*, with someone reporting *up* to the boss, or instructions being *cascaded down* through the *organisation*. We talk of *flattening* the *structure*, or of achieving a *balance* between *profit* and *customer care*. We talk of some actions as being *central* to a *strategy*, of *branches* being *out from the centre*. We talk about being *at the front* of the *race* for *market* domination, or of *holding back* plans. We talk of competitive *forces* and of *strategic links*. We talk of *coming into* profit and *getting out of* a market.

In the following brief statement, a whole set of metaphors are used to get a message across. The message makes sense; it can easily understood: 'Our *organization* will *enter* the *top end* of the market, using the *leverage* of our *partnership* with Company X to *harmonize* costs and revenues. *Head* Office will define the strategy for achieving our *goals* of getting *ahead of* the competition.'

In none of these common examples have I used any of the more fanciful images such as 'back burner', being 'up front', getting 'on' board or 'floating an idea'. Yet such ordinary management language is full of metaphors, many of which link with our mental maps of everyday bodily experience (Lakoff 1987: 267). As we build our pictures, constructing our 'truths' and 'false-hoods', we use metaphors which are based upon the common, everyday kinds of experiences of anyone, anywhere in the world. Because of the 'obvious' nature of many such metaphorical links (that more profit is represented as 'up' on a chart, rather than down), some people may not recognise them as metaphors, as acts of imagination. The fact that some writers focus upon deliberate attempts to surface metaphorical thinking in managers (Morgan 1986; 1993) may make these more mundane examples of metaphor seem somehow more 'real' than metaphorical.

Metaphorical links are not logical. They are not the kinds of things which one can prove or disprove. Metaphorical links exist because they make sense, they help us to understand. They are (strictly speaking) irrational and largely unconscious in how they operate. Unless brought to the surface, metaphors can constrain managerial behaviour, as in the following case:

SPACECO: UNCONSCIOUS REPLICATION OF OPERATIONAL MODELS

The Background

We have undertaken a number of interventions with Spaceco. At first, these were exploratory activities with the most senior managers in the company. To some extent, they were trying out management and organisation development to see if it helped them. Because it did seem to do so, it became accepted by the senior managers in the company that a programme for 'high potential' managers would be a good investment in the long term.

The Problems

The nature of the business of Spaceco is changing radically. In the past the key success factors were innovation, project management, and a scientific culture. They had plenty of guaranteed money, mostly from friendly govern-ments, which they could use to try out new technologies, new processes and new materials. All they had to do was to prove their technologies for the future. Now they are going through radical change. The technologies are proven; there are a number of commercially viable companies selling those technol-ogies. They succeed not on innovation, but on standardisation, robustness, and lower costs. Spaceco has to turn projects into process, scientists into production workers, disinterested curiosity into profit.

Spaceco is also a multinational and growing, which it has to be to achieve the critical mass to compete in global markets. As it does so, it faces the kinds of cross cultural problems which many global organisations face. How can managers from very different cultures work efficiently and effectively together? And how can they all, at the same time, be persuaded to change those very cultures which have established their success, but will be their downfall if they cannot change?

What Spaceco Wanted

The idea behind the 'high potential' managers was that they would be less resistant to change than the older, more senior people; and that they would be less set in their 'cultural' ways than the older managers. They would be the senior managers of the future. If Spaceco could use them as catalysts for change, and as the pioneers for cross cultural interworking, then, they argued, the change process would be enhanced. It may be too late for the senior people; but let the next generation be developed into international business managers before the 'culture' could get them.

They asked us to design and run a programme for these high potential managers which would help them become those international business managers of the future. The problem was that we would not be permitted to meet and interview any of these high potential managers, because, for the sake of maintaining morale among those managers not elected to the 'high potential' list, no such list was to be drawn up until virtually the eve of the programme, and no public announcement of the existence of such a list would be made.

Although we could not meet any of the target population, we were given free access to talk to the most senior managers within the company. This meant that we did, at least, have some clear impressions about the business imperatives, the indigenous cultures of the various sites, and so on.

What We Did

The fact that we could have no first-hand insight into who we were to be working with heightened our resolve to incorporate within the programme an experiential element which would bring to the surface any hidden factors which could affect the learning one way or the other. We also needed a means of creating some learning about working across cultures. By this time we had concluded (a point which was confirmed for us by most of the senior managers we interviewed) that the 'cultural' issues were primarily about different cultures at different sites, and not about different 'national' cultures. This was in line with previous observations we have made about cultural challenges within organisations: that 'national' cultural issues are very often manifestations of social stereotypes than they are about fundamental differences between nations. Degrees of difference within an organisation tend, in our experience, to narrow as one moves away from the individual, through the workgroup, through a location, and up to the national level.

Our aim was, therefore, not to build the learning around such stereotypes, but to go for 'blue-loop learning' (Ratui 1983). This is the idea that internationalism is not so much about knowing customs and mores (how much to tip the taxi driver in Paris; whether one toasts the host or vice versa in Denmark), but about having the interpersonal skills and sensitivities to 'fit in' in different cultural settings. Skills like active listening, watching carefully what is going on around one and knowing when and how to ask for explanations, are said to be far more effective bases for international success than checklists of things to do and not to do in Kuala Lumpur.

We therefore built an experiential module which would enable the managers to establish 'cultures of a kind' within small teams, learning about each other, and working together on managerial exercises. Then we would provide an exercise which called for interteam collaboration, as a metaphor for international collaboration.

What Happened

It worked quite well. But the key learning point was unexpected.

There were three teams; each had been working in its own syndicate room in our new Centre at Cranfield. These syndicate rooms are adjacent (none more than 5 m away from the other) and have glass walls (although blinds can be drawn across for privacy). During the 'collaborative' phase of the exercise each team sent one representative to an 'executive' which met to decide on financial and other resourcing issues, the representatives returning to their groups with the outcome of decisions, and to discuss the practical implications for them.

As facilitators, we occasionally have moments of powerful imagery. I had one of these as I sat with one of these teams. While their representative was outside, negotiating, the remaining four team members sat looking poignantly through the glass wall, waiting for his return; when he did so, there was frenetic activity; the team members seemed like fledglings in the nest, opening their beaks for the information which the 'parent' had brought back. It was not enough – questions remained. He went off again, and the team settled back to wait for their next 'information meal'.

The teams got on with their respective jobs, firmly rooted within their own syndicate rooms. They had recreated in miniature, a metaphorical replication of the functional hierarchy of Spaceco. The few metres and the glass walls which separated them were as powerful a division between them as hundreds of miles. No-one had told them to organise themselves in this way; they carried into the exercise the metaphors of Spaceco's 'structure' and 'cultures'.

Part of the 'problem' with Spaceco's approach was the implicit assumption that habits become hardened over time, and that these younger people would not have acquired those habits. This assumption is misleading largely because it is built upon a model of managerial learning and behaviour which is naive. It assumes that young managers remain relatively unaffected by the metaphors and models of an organisation, and can easily create new metaphors and models if given the chance. Clearly, all managers can change their minds, and in so doing, bring about change in their organisations. But to be able to do so, naive models of managerial learning will need to be replaced with models which take into account the deeply, largely unconscious metaphorical nature of managerial thinking and behaviour.

The Uniqueness of Our Personal Maps

Innate ideas, or archetypes, provide us with a common set of foundations for thinking and learning. Without them, it is unlikely that we could learn anything. Children, for example, learn their first language so easily because language learning comes naturally to all human babies. But the complexes or mental maps we construct are different for each individual. Same foundations, different buildings. Anyone involved in the facilitation of learning has to acknowledge the problem that we can never know, for any set of managers learning together, how much overlap exists between their mental maps. They often share a common language, but may use the words within that language in very different ways.

At this personal level *social stereotypes* will become *personal stereotypes*, and each of us will have our own complexes of 'ideal manager' or an 'ideal leader', and of paragons – individuals we have met or otherwise know about who represent for us those archetypal ideals, both 'good' and 'bad'. Although the society and organisational cultures in which we operate will have a major influence upon these categories, there will be uniques as well. It is often those uniques which are not recognised as such which can cause so much confusion for managers trying to work together and to learn.

We use metaphor and metonymy to short-cut what would otherwise be unbelievably tedious communications. 'I want you to show some leadership: to do a Parsons and work like a Trojan to wrap up the class A customers and bring in all the outstanding bread-and-butter business before end of year,' is the kind of conversational item a manager may have with a subordinate. Most of the time, there is an assumption that all these metaphors and metonymic references are fully understood, and have 'shared' meanings. But if, in interpreting the managerial instruction cited above, the subordinate's concept of Trojan means of 'single-minded, insensitive bully', while the manager has 'Trojan' down as a typical example of 'collaborative, hard-working, unassuming', that subordinate is likely to interpret the instruction very differently from its 'intended' meaning.

Unless assumptions are checked, this kind of misunderstanding is almost inevitable. It happens a lot in organisations.

Checking Assumptions

What stops us achieving absolute clarity of communication through checking the meanings of everything which is said to us are a number of factors, some more obvious and conscious than others.

The most naive reason is the belief that all words have single meanings, and therefore mean the same thing to all people. Most mature adults learnt that this is not the case.

However, not everyone has learnt that our mental maps, our metaphors and how meanings interrelate within our minds are uniquely interconnected for each of us. Ideas, images and concepts link together in our personal mental maps by being unconsciously suggested in a number of ways. This produces maps in which there are many 'related' ideas, images and concepts, but for which there is no single connecting theme. Wittgenstein described this kind of collection of related ideas, images and concepts as having 'family resemblances', as in the example of the concept 'game'. There is no single attribute of 'game' which every game shares; yet there are sets of traits which some games have and others do not. It is the complex, messy, yet 'motivated', set of connections which enable us comfortably to think of such different phenomena as hide-and-seek, ping-pong, chess, erotic teasing and the na-tional lottery all as games. Because there is no central, core, anchoring idea, individuals' mental maps evolve links which are both unique to them, and unconsciously formed.

Not only do people not know that others' minds are mapped differently, they do not even know a great deal about their own mental maps. Dreams, free association, word association, ink-blot exercises, and so on can all provide ways into our own mental maps. Most managers would see these activities as trivial and unimportant, compared to the 'real business' of learning about management. As a result, they may not stop to check assumptions about how others' mental maps, their meanings, differ from their own.

This could have unfortunate consequences in management and organisa-tion development activities. Recently I was a guest lecturer for a session towards the end of a general management programme which had been going on for the previous two weeks. It came as a shock both to me and to many of the managers attending that when I checked my assumptions about what they meant by such key concepts as 'management', 'leadership', 'vision' and 'strategy', those present had very widely varying ways of using these concepts. The problem was that many of these concepts had been used by a variety of 'experts' during the previous fortnight. What those managers were taking away from those experts was a range of very different, sometimes contradictory messages. Participants and providers alike had made assumptions which could have significantly affected the quality of learning.

A third reason for not checking assumptions in this way is that it threatens to lead to 'infinite regression'. 'By X, I mean Y' may help, but then we may have to ask, 'But what do you mean by Y?' Checking meanings is not an exact science. For some people, if you can't get an accurate answer, there's no point in asking the question in the first place.

Finally, people do not check every assumption because there just is not enough time to engage in what is an inexact science which can lead to infinite regression. This is not to say that people never check meanings, or assumptions. Only that many may do so less than may be helpful.

Understanding and 'Management and Organisation Development'

Those engaged in management and organisation development are in the business of communicating, of attempting to find shared meanings so that learning can take place. We seek to make managers understand ways of seeing. 'Understanding a thing is to arrive at a metaphor for that thing by substituting something more familiar to us. And the feeling of familiarity is the feeling of understanding' (Jaynes 1990:52). Management researchers and providers of management and organisation development use models and theories to help in this process. Models are representations which suggest 'Look at it this way, or that.' Models are neither true nor false, but simply constructs which make more or less sense to people, according to the degrees to which these images resonate with their existing mental maps. The degree to which a manager feels a similarity between a model and his or her view of the complicated data, which is where theory provides a metaphorical connection, is the degree to which understanding can be said to have taken place.

Models and theories add to the stock of the family resemblances between images, concepts, words, metaphors which we believe will 'make sense' to, and help change the behaviour of, managers. In so doing, we are making available to them new or revised sets of mental maps which we are urging managers to adopt, and to graft onto their own maps, and in so doing, make a difference to the profitability and happiness of the managers we work with.

THE RATIONAL MIND OF THE MANAGER

One of the 'problems' with all this focus on emotions, complexes, metaphors and models is that it does not seem to help us to get at 'the right answer'. For example, in an argument about John, one point of view may be that he is lacking in vision; the other may say, 'John's not lacking in vision, he's realistic.' Recognising that this kind of disagreement says more about those evaluating John than it does about John himself makes it difficult to decide what to do about John. Most people would agree that it is part of the portfolio of a manager's role to make decisions. And the more a manager can 'prove' the correctness of a decision, the better that manager will be.

The Intellectual Mode of Thought

There is a 'model' upon which managers can build, which does deal with such certainties; it is the model best exemplified by mathematics and logic, and which lies at the heart of most scientific endeavours – to get at 'the truth'. Its tools are logical reasoning, intellectual argument, and so on. It has triumphed in the western world by turning scientific 'truth' into computers, Boeing 747s, motor cars, and nuclear missiles. There is a very strong sense, therefore, in which we can talk of 'truth'.

As we have seen in Chapter 1, it is tempting for people to extrapolate from this kind of triumph of technology to the world of management; to look for the certainties which this model provides. For the purposes of this book, I refer to this mode of thinking as 'rational' or 'intellectual'. It is the part of our mind which deals with problem-solving in a focused, conscious and systematic way, and in so doing it relies significantly upon language and various kinds of written notation.

The use of language is a sequential, consecutive, time-constrained process, rather than one which is, like other aspects of our minds, parallel and simultaneous. It is in the nature of narrative that we are forced to sacrifice that simultaneity and multiplicity of connections which characterise the other activities of the mind for the precision which language provides. But this trade-off does not necessarily mean that our use of language remains unaffected by the emotional and metaphorical aspects of our minds. Our ordinary language about organisations and management retains imprecision largely because it rests, through metaphor, upon that complex set of neural networks which comprise our minds. And it reflects our attitudes and values in the often unconscious evaluative slants we give to our inferences.

A great deal of the use to which managers put language is in the telling of stories. We describe our decisions, explain our judgements, explore possible scenarios, and so on.

'In human beings, with their astonishing narrative gift, one of the principal forms of peacekeeping is the human gift for presenting, dramatizing, and explicating the mitigating circumstances surrounding conflict-threatening breaches in the ordinariness of life. The objective of such narrative is not to reconcile, not to legitimize, not even to excuse, but rather to explicate. And the explications offered in the ordinary telling of such narratives are not always forgiving of the protagonist depicted. Rather it is the narrator who usually comes off best' (Bruner 1990: 95–6).

The need managers have, in management and organisation development activities as with any other of their daily tasks, to 'come off best' is not just arrogance or 'ego'. It is simply the result of the myriad of attitudes and values which have formed the 'world-view', helped that manager in his or her construction of reality, in which how he or she feels about the component parts is the most basic and influential determinant of what to accept or to reject, what to agree with and what to deny, what to see as 'reality' and what to say is 'not true'. This, in part, is why different people from the same organisation can 'retell' events from such widely differing perspectives (Knights and Murray 1994: 177–8), and generate stories which people feel cannot all be 'true'.

Because our intellectual capabilities are so closely associated with our spoken and written language, a great deal of early research into the mind, learning, memory and so on concentrated upon this faculty rather than those I have been describing so far within this chapter. This is not surprising: if you can talk to people during an experiment into such topics, then research is made easier (Baddeley 1992: 20). Add to that the recognition that 'Education is far better at teaching facts than procedures for action' (Greene 1987: 228) and it is easy to see why so much management and organisation development has attended to this aspect of learning. Management research and education, for many of its earlier years, modelled itself upon the sciences, and formed a kind of 'conspiracy' with managers which allowed both providers and managers to 'forget' all other aspects of human learning, and focus exclusively upon 'teaching the hard facts about organisations and management'.

The 'intellectual' mode works 'best' when it does so in abstraction from meaning. In its pure form, it deals with one plus one equals two – not one manager plus one manager equals two managers, nor in 'proving' whether John is visionary or realistic. Its strength lies precisely in this abstraction.

This mode is, then, logical, objective, systematic, meaningless (in the sense that it is only when abstracted from 'things' to 'absolutes' that it works properly), value-free, and potentially infinite in its power. It deals with numbers (of which there are an infinity), abstract symbols, and absolute truths. For those who have been trained well in its use, it provides its own justification and value; it can be 'fun' simply playing with numbers, chess pieces, or computer programs. It is, while it remains in its own territory, harmless. No-one gets hurt by the square root of 49.

As I have argued in Chapter 1 and consistently throughout the book, however, the worlds of organisations and management are not just about numbers. They are about people, products, services, customers, and so on. Logic, the intellectual mode, the rational, cannot tell us anything about organisational and managerial decisions and actions without some idea of context, of meaning. This means that the rational has to be mixed with the 'emotional', affective, value-laden and meaningful. It is in this mixing that we can get into difficulties, if we are not careful. The intellect is in danger of becoming dangerous when it 'invades' territory which it does not 'understand'. Meaning (in the making sense, having value) and intellect just don't get on, unless carefully managed together.

'The Dictatorship of the Left Hemisphere'

The neocortex is split into two halves, called hemispheres, joined through a large bundle of nerve fibres called the corpus callosum. Most neuroscientists agree that the intellect 'resides' in the left hemisphere. Many of the intellectual skills we humans have, such as language use and literacy operate within this hemisphere. Compared to emotions or affects, complexes, and neuronal groups, the intellectual, conscious activities of the left hemisphere are relatively recent developments, which, though potentially powerful, do not operate independently from what goes on elsewhere in the human mind. Star Trek's Spock is a fiction. 'consciousness is a culturally learned event, balanced over the suppressed vestiges of an earlier mentality . . . [It can], in part, be culturally unlearned or arrested' (Jaynes 1990: 398).

However, some people suggest that, especially in western cultures, this 'new kid on the block', the intellect, can become a bit of a bully, tending 'takeover', to dominate, to 'dictate' (Stevens 1995: 341) on its own terms the way we humans will behave. Clearly, in many western cultures, it is having its way because of what it has given us in terms of technological superiority. For the intellect, the ends justifies the means, and if the ends are continued control of the environment, then the intellect has to be listened to. The implications of this dominance, however, are potentially very significant, including and especially for managers. Let us take just one example.

Americans are often said to be uncomfortable 'noticing themselves being inconsistent from one occasion to another, or possessing mutually inconsistent aims . . . In contrasting cultures, such as India, people have long been comfortable with the 'inconsistencies' of life and with context-sensitive behaviour . . .' (Much 1995: 106). Intellectual development (in the sense in which we have been referring to it – the separate development of the intellect from meaning) is a significantly stronger part of the American education system and culture than it is in India, where the development of intellect is harmonised with the development of other aspects of the personality (for more on this, see Goleman 1995).

For Americans much more than people from Asian cultures, including those from Japan and Malaysia, the mindset of there being one right approach, one right answer creates a tendency to infer that there must also be one right set of aims, one right set of truths. Inconsistency is 'bad news', therefore. The certainty which comes to be important to many Americans can have disastrous consequences when American companies try to manage their operations overseas in the one right way. Even in Europe (Kakabadse 1996), not noted for its 'eastern mysticism', American-owned and run companies can fail through a lack of sensitivity to the multiple 'cultural' factors in business. Or when American managers assert with absolute conviction 'You gotta be tough; you gotta be brutal' (see Chapter 1, p. 12).

Management is increasingly being recognised as being about coping with ambiguity and contradiction; about 'A and not-A' rather than 'A or not-A' (Kosko 1994). The intellectual mode finds this kind of ambiguity highly uncomfortable.

The Zone of Uncomfortable Debate

One of the biggest potential frustrations with being involved with management and organisation development interventions is the knowledge that many managers will nod sagely during an intellectually dominated exploration of topics such as strategy, and then go back to the office and do nothing. There's nothing wrong with the logic of what they have 'learnt'; but things will get in the way. The overt suppression of all but the intellectual in exploring organisational and managerial challenges often means that managers are not forced to confront the emotional, cultural, metaphorical and personal implications of what is being discussed.

To do the job of management and organisation development effectively demands entering what a colleague at Cranfield calls 'the zone of uncomfortable debate'. This is the zone in which managers have to confront the integration of logic with meaning. They have to deal with how they feel about ideas, what it all does and will mean to them, both in terms of thought and action. We have to acknowledge that the intellectual mode ignores the 'hard fact' that it is people, not intellects, who have to do things.

Entering the zone of uncomfortable debate is a potentially difficult experience, not only for the managers, but also, at times, for facilitators, as the following case describes.

**ENTERING THE ZONE OF UNCOMFORTABLE DEBATE:
THE SCANDBANK EXPERIENCE**

The Background

We were introduced to the top team of a Scandinavian Bank by one of the directors. She had joined the bank from a company with whom we had been doing some personal and team development work. She believed that the kinds of problems the top team of the bank were having were those which we may be able to help with. She had had quite a few moments in the 'zone' when she had attended with her former colleagues during her time with that company.

As is not uncommon with this kind of situation, not all of her new colleagues at the bank felt the same way about management and organisation development as a means of helping get to grips with their challenges. They were sceptical because, as they said, it is all too easy for managers who had had an emotional experience as she may have had, to become evangelists for this kind of 'touchy-feely' stuff. Whether their reluctance to go ahead with such an event stemmed from fear of having to enter the zone, I cannot say.

The Problem

The problem was presented to us in simplified form. Since we were unable, for practical reasons to do our own 'current state' research, we had to take the presentation of the problem at face value. This was that, when the members of the top team worked in smaller units of up to half a dozen, they worked very well together. However, the top team comprised 19 people; and when this group got together, they fought, argued, and generally created havoc. In consequence, 'corridor' management was the order of the day, with deals being struck, and bargaining taking place outside the legitimate forum of the whole team. This led to yet further suspicion and mistrust within the team, further fuelling the corridor meetings.

The obvious option, of reducing the size or scope of the top team was not available; nor was any other 'structural' solution. These had been vetoed. Our challenge was not to find yet another way round the problem, but to help them confront and deal with it head on.

The Risks

We had met only one or two members of this team before: the lady who had called us in, and another Director who, like her colleague, had moved from the company with whom we had worked before. It was the Director who called us in through whom all our investigations and discussions took place. There was a clear risk that the other team members would attend under duress, knowing very little about us or what we believed the aims of the event should be.

We were under major time constraints – we had just over two days (an evening and two full days) with the group – and they were all to be flown over to England for the event, whether they liked the idea of not. There was a real prospect of one or more team members slipping away to do shopping or sightseeing in nearby Oxford.

We had only second-hand information about the current state, in terms of the 'culture', the business issues, the individuals, and so on. Within the short time they were in England we had no chance to make use of any of the kinds of investigative tools or profiling instruments which frequently provide us with data on which to base our discussions with the managers. And we had no feel, from our own point of view, of the kinds or levels of dysfunction which pertained within the team. The 'reality' of dysfunction, being constructed, can be constructed very differently by different people. Were we facing the Vikings versus the Anglo-Saxons, or were they merely in need of some 'basic meetings management skills?

What Happened

We guessed that basic meetings management skills were not the solution, and that there were likely to be some fairly significant interpersonal issues which would not be resolved by an exploration of models of team development or discussions about team roles. We decided to take a risk and get them to reproduce, before our eyes, and without planning to do so, the very kind of situation which lay at the heart of the problem. We were a bit underhand in doing so, since we had implied in what we said in our introduction that the session would be conducted in smaller teams of six or seven, each with its own facilitator, and with very little interaction across the entire group. By mid-morning of the second full day it became clear to the small teams that they would have to collaborate with the others to achieve the goals we had set them in an exercise. When, as a result of attempting to build bridges between the groups, fundamentally different views about the basis upon which they should collaborate emerged, things began to get a bit fraught. The 'reality' of life in the office in Scandinavia had followed them to Oxfordshire, and it was painful.

There were moments when my colleagues and I in the facilitator team were sorely tempted to intervene and lay down the law, forcing them to find a solution; fortunately we resisted; and even more fortunately it worked.

The arguments which were being fought out around us, about sharing revenue, resources, payments for services rendered, and so on were surfacing many of the assumptions about the nature of business which had never surfaced in 'real life', since, in the professional and senior world of the boardroom, such basic questions were far too elementary to be given airtime. And, moreover, how would one of the team feel if views were aired, and he or she found that they were the only team member with those views? Clearly, these elementary questions, which had to be asked to find a solution to the exercise we had set within the time available, were being asked by these team members for the first time. It was painful for some; it became almost unbearable for one of the older members. This was when we had a slice of the kind of luck management and organisation development people need when we sail this close to the wind.

The manager in question found himself more and more isolated as he stuck out for an approach which others had either never taken (since it was not in line with their values and assumptions about how business should be conducted) or had abandoned after being convinced of the alternative approach which was being increasingly seen as the 'only way' forward. As he became more isolated, he became more emotional; he became more and more stubborn. Either way he was going to have to lose face. At this point the Managing Director, about whom we had known very little before the event, put his arm round the older man's shoulder, and walked slowly away with him, up a pathway, and away from the rest of the group.

They talked, one to one, for about half an hour. We extended the exercise deadline to accommodate this 'time out'. When they returned, the task was completed, the group became elated, and dialogue began across all 19 which, by their admission, was of a different order and quality than ever before. They had entered the zone of uncomfortable debate, and come out the other side feeling the better for it. Whether the improvement has stuck, I cannot say, since we have not yet been able to go back to see the team, and check on progress.

This case is not an unusual one. It simply reflects the many instances in which managers are brought face to face with the realisation that dealing with their managerial problems cannot be achieved as an intellectual exercise. It was only when managers 'let go' of approaches and ideas which they had an emotional attachment to that the team was able to move forward. It was painful for many of them. Intellectual ideas are not painful; genuinely altering maps in the mind can be painful. Managers know this. This is one of the reasons why some managers prefer not to commit themselves, but only their intellects to learning, and in so doing, severely limit what learning takes place.

Intellect and Gender

The implicit model of the 'rational manager' working unemotionally and calmly towards the right answers for any organisational challenge is one which underpins a great deal of the traditional approach to management and organisation development.

The traditional model of the rational manager is essentially masculine. The intellectual mode tends to be favoured by men rather than by women; in other words, men seem far more willing to work to an implicit model of the rational manager, while effectively denigrating the potential value, contributions, significance, and so on of all the other aspects of the human mind. This observation is not unique to management. For example, over the two thousand years or so of the development of philosophy in western cultures, most philosophers have been men. This has led to a 'masculine' approach to philosophy which has, according to Grimshaw (1986: 59), the following characteristics:

1. A denial of the social and interactive character of human development; a stress on the separateness or isolation of human beings.
2. Forms of individualism which stress autonomy, e.g. the autonomy of the individual will, or the autonomy of the knower.
3. Oppositions between mind and body; reason and passion; reason and sense.
4. Themes of mastery, domination and control of the body, the passions or the senses; and fears about the loss of control.
5. Fear of women and of anything that is seen to be associated with them; sexuality, nature, the body.
6. Devaluation of all that is associated with women and the need not to be dependent on it.

Many of these characteristics can be as accurately applied to the majority of our organisations. The intellectual is the dominant mode in organisations and in management thinking. There is nothing inherently wrong with the intellectual mode when it is used in harmony with the rest of our minds. The dangers lie in the very abstraction from meaning which is characteristic of an over-reliance on this mode.

In our western cultures, we teach a great deal in schools in the intellectual mode; very little in any other. This is largely continued in business schools (Martin 1993: 34). It has become the dominant mindset or paradigm of management. Like many such paradigms, it becomes 'invisible' in the sense that it is hard to question. Managers may be tempted to assume that many of the manifestations of the left hemisphere, such as aggression, intellectualisation, and so on, are 'human nature'. They will be tempted to follow the line that it is 'natural' to want to 'control' emotions and other potentially hazardous phenomena.

The perceived need by one sector of a community to 'control' another is not confined to traditional 'management', which has been seen as necessary to 'control' the unpredictable: the market (nature), and the staff (irrational and potentially disruptive people). Men in many communities seeing it as their job to 'control' the potentially 'wild' natures of dangerous things. In many societies this includes the need to control women for the benefit of culture as a whole. In other words, it is not only in our society and organisations that men patronise and oppress women.

Part of the danger of any paradigm is that it becomes so 'natural' a way of thinking and doing that it becomes almost impossible for people to imagine any other way, any alternative approach; or any reason to consider why such an alternative could or should be considered. Men can come to believe that it is 'human nature' to think and act like this (Chance 1988; de Waal 1989; Ortner 1974).

I was reminded of this recently when I facilitated a workshop for the top team of a UK bank. There were a number of strategic options on the table, but for the team members the only option they could consider pursuing was some kind of radical expansion. I asked one or two of the Directors why they felt they should go for this expansion. For most of them, the question did not see to make any sense; it was as though I was speaking some kind of nonsense. Every one of these Directors was a man; each of these Directors was so incapable of getting in touch with their own personal values, motivations, sense of purpose or sense of meaning, that being asked to match those senses against the chosen corporate strategy was too difficult for them. If growth was an option, then growth it had to be, irrespective of what (if anything) it meant for each of these individual humans sitting round the table. Highly paid and powerful they may have been, but the 'logic' of the situation gave them no real choice; and the personal implications for them – how this strategy fitted into each of their personal plans for their lives – were off the agenda. Pursuit of the logical can demand a high personal price (see also Patching and Chatham 1998).

Many of the implicit assumptions which lie behind traditional management and organisation development activities are embedded within this highly masculinised, but narrow, model of the manager. The alternative which is being explored in the second half of this book attempts to broaden the horizons, and to create a model which both takes on some of what women writers have helped to identify, and may help to enrich our concepts of management such that women will not need to become 'honorary men' in order for them to be recognised and valued in their own right as managers.

LEARNING WITH MORE THAN INTELLECT – PRELIMINARY CONCLUSIONS

Organisations are increasingly (albeit reluctantly, in some cases) recognising the imbalance that organisational theories based upon the rational model of the manager have generated over the years. More or less consciously, they are attempting to redress the bias against women. They are, at the same time, trying to get to grips with other 'threats' to the 'dictatorship' of the left hemisphere, introducing empowerment, teams, coaching, and so on. In so doing, they are calling upon the resources of the parts of the mind which we described in the first sections of the chapter: the emotions, the archetypes and the imagination.

They are also opening themselves up to risks. The 'proofs' of rationality may be spurious, but at least they are rigorous. One of the problems with 'engaging the right brain' (a blanket term for those other aspects of the mind which are not pure intellect) is that the kinds of checks and balances which have traditionally been put upon managerial decision-making do not seem to be so readily available. Managers may fear that they will become victims of cranks, mystics and all kinds of charlatans masquerading as guides into the 'age of Aquarius'.

I am sure that there are significant numbers of such charlatans operating within the arena of management and organisation development. Embracing the idea of involving more than the intellect of managers in management and organisation development does not imply a lack or rigour in learning design and implementation. 'Rigour' does not necessarily only mean 'intellectual rigour'.

On the other hand, like managers, management and organisation development providers will have to do more than nod sagely in agreement that people are not mere intellects, and then simply carry on delivering lectures. Management and organisation development which is built upon the model of managers which is being developed here needs to be very different in its basic assumptions about classes, lectures and all the other means of operationalising learning. And one aspect of this different model takes into account that management is not something which people do by themselves.

Managerial Learning is not a Solo Flight

Some people would like to think that they can learn alone. There are clearly some things which we can learn in this way; indeed, we can read books about many aspects of management, and get value from them. But management is primarily about working with, influencing, listening to, and instructing other people. How we come across to them, how likely people are to see us as credible and worthwhile partners, and as leaders, will need to be a partnership between ourselves as managers, and our colleagues, bosses and subordinates. Our own behaviours, how we present ourselves will be a key part in this partnership. The more managers know about themselves (their emotions, values, mental maps, implicit models of 'manager' and 'organisation') the better they are likely to take on learning.

In many of our activities with managers, we use another heuristic device first introduced by William James (James 1890) and subsequently explored by Modell (1993): the separation of what we call a manager's 'inner self' and his or her 'social self' (see Table 7.1).

This is not to say that there are two distinct 'beings', but that it is helpful for managers to remember that what they feel about themselves through introspection may be very different from the ways in which others see them. Introspection means discovering the 'inner self' simply by looking within. As I have been suggesting so far in this chapter, and will explore in more

Table 7.1 *'Inner self'* vs. *'social self'*

Inner Self	Social Self
• Consciousness	• May be unconscious
• Intentions	• Behaviours
• Desires/wishes/values/beliefs	• What goes to work
• Dreams	• Impact
• Reflections	• Varies in 'size'
• I feel I am the 'expert'	• Others really are the 'expert'
• Others infer and could be wrong	• I infer and could be wrong
• I build and 'own' this	• Others build and 'own' this

practical terms in subsequent chapters, becoming aware of what's going on inside (surfacing the unconscious) is very important.

Introspection is a process which will help managers to bring to the surface (into consciousness) some of those filters through which they will evaluate new learning. The more we can encourage managers to ask questions of themselves about patterns in their life choices, those incidents which have made significant impact on them, what they mean by some of the key concepts with which management deals, and so on, the more likely it is that they will be able to manage their emotional, value-driven, archetypal, and metaphorical responses to new experiences, concepts and models. The more a manager is encouraged, by becoming involved in talking about these matters, to confront his or her 'inner self' the more the conscious intellect can be harnessed effectively in evaluating learning. While those influences remain unconscious, they will still influence learning, but in ways in which a manager may not be aware of, and be unable to explore, confront and manage.

However, although introspection is a powerful tool in learning, it has its limitations. It is in the nature of our fragmented minds that introspection cannot guarantee access to the relevant parts of our minds. Even when looking for what may already have been stored within some corners of our mental maps, there may be no 'route' through from where we are exploring now to where the relevant information may be. Not every part of every map is linked to every other. Introspection is 'at best 'early retrospection', and subject to the same kinds of selectivity and construction' (Bruner 1990: 99) as other mental acts. In other words, we may 'fool ourselves' about '. . . the idea that the activity of introspection is ever a matter of just "looking and seeing". I suspect that when we claim to be just using our powers of inner *observation*, we are always actually engaging in a sort of impromptu *theorizing* – and we are remarkably gullible theorizers, precisely because there is so little to 'observe' and so much to pontificate about without fear of contradiction' (Dennett 1991: 67).

It seems helpful, therefore, for managers to engage in healthy dialogue about themselves with people whom they know and trust. By so doing, they gain access to alternative neural networks. Learning from other people is like hitch-hiking on someone else's neural networks, picking up links which we have not made, and thereby making our own 'copies' of those links. If we like them, we can 'trudge' back and forth over them until they become easy-access pathways of our own.

No two people have completely the same neural patterns in their minds. Yet many of our likes and dislikes, our values and attitudes, our metaphors and concepts, our preferences and complexes are so 'natural and obvious' to us (because many of them will have been stored without conscious review and consideration) that we may assume that others see the world as we do; and be surprised when we find out that they do not. However, in many cases, we may not find out, unless we check.

It is 'natural' to us to operate in a social context, alongside others of the same species (Humphrey 1986). It is also 'natural' to treat others as having the same motives, intentions, beliefs and desires as we do (Dennett 1987). Because a great deal of our 'understanding' of these 'inner states' of other people derives from inferences we draw from their behaviours, rather than from deep discussions concerning such matters, many such inferences can be misplaced. It is clear that those inferences, however, have a significant impact on how we see ourselves in relation to other people:

'[P]eople's self esteem and their self concept changed in sheer reaction to the kinds of people they found themselves among, and changed even more in response to the positive or negative remarks that people made to them. Even if they were asked merely to play a particular public role in a group, their self-image changed in a fashion to be congruent with that. Indeed, in the presence of others who were older or seen to be more powerful that they were, people would report on 'self' in a quite different and diminished way from their manner of seeing themselves when in the presence of younger or less-esteemed people' (Bruner 1990: 109, reporting on research by Gergen and others).

What happens during an in-company management and organisation development intervention, is that a 'social self' is built around each partici-pant, which is the creation not of his or her introspection, but of the aggregation of observations and inferences of those who are interacting with this manager. Although this 'social self' may not be like the various 'social selves' which have been developed round the manager at work, at home or in other public settings, it can provide an alternative insight for managers into 'how they come across'.

I may think that I am a caring, concerned listener to other people's ideas and problems. But if those people I manage all see me as an uncaring, unconcerned manager who does not listen at all, then this mismatch will cause practical problems. No matter how strongly I feel about my inner self, it is my social self which I take to work; it is this self which others deal with. Finding out about my social self demands looking in a mirror. We call this mirror 'feedback', and it can provide managers with insights into themselves which introspection alone cannot provide.

Many of things which a manager may say or do will be the more or less conscious outcomes from his or her complexes, emotions, values, metaphors, and so on. These cannot be seen directly either by a manager or by those with whom a manager works. Both the manager and his or her colleagues infer from patterns of behaviour what may be the underlying drivers. We encourage managers to recognise that, in the interpretation of an individual's behaviours, other people's inferences can, in principle, be more valuable than his or her own. Learning from other people is often about seeing our behaviours and the inferences which can be drawn from those behaviours through another's eyes.

Measuring Learning

Learning is a dynamic process which involves introspection, feedback, the deliberate surfacing of unconscious filters, and the conscious exploration of new information and ideas in the context of the whole self of the manager – in both the 'inner' and 'social' senses of 'self'. Introducing into the process those aspects of the mind which are not intellectual, linear and precise enriches the learning, but it also runs the risk that 'anything goes' in providing learning activities. In a sense, it implies that almost anything, whether it be introspection, talking, playing with lego bricks or going for a walk, delivers learning of a kind, since all experience is potentially learning experience.

Managers and management and organisation development providers may still want ways of ensuring that 'relevant', effective or 'real' learning has taken place. 'What gets measured gets done.' And to measure something, we have to contain it, to define it. So what is 'managerial learning', and how, in the light of this reappraisal of learning, can we be sure that it has happened?

I have not, and will not attempt to 'define' managerial learning. The reason for this is that there is no 'absolute', 'fundamental' or 'scientifically demonstrable' difference between, on the one hand, the learning which is going on continuously, largely unconsciously and by chance; and, on the other, the kinds of learning which management and organisation development interventions are designed to achieve. 'Learning' is socially constructed. What constitutes 'learning', therefore, is a matter of choice. Not of absolute choice, clearly. But, nevertheless, learning can, within limits, be what you want it to be. This is why, like so many of the kinds of concepts we discussed in Chapter 1, there can be so many different 'definitions' of learning. They are different not because they are more or less accurate in their capturing of the 'essence' of learning, but because there is no final arbiter, no authority against which one can match definitions and judge them to be closer or further from 'the truth'.

There is therefore no absolute sense in which one can say that 'learning' has happened. One of the reasons why it is so difficult to evaluate management and organisation development activities is that any measures used tend to be based upon a definition of what will, in this instance, constitute 'learning'. Measuring against that definition does not *necessarily* say whether anything has happened 'in the real world'. For many measures of management and organisation development interventions, this is precisely the case. Measuring how happy people are at the end of an event (which is largely what end-of-course review forms comprise, whatever their 'overt' objectives) says nothing about what will happen to the organisation as a result of this level of 'happiness'.

Our choices will reflect our meanings. Here are some of the options people have chosen.

What Learners Say – the Risks

There is one sense of 'learning' which is best served by asking the learner. We ask what conclusions managers have been able to draw from their experiences during a management and organisation development intervention. Bearing in mind that 'learning' is a constructed concept reflected in the neural networks in our minds, each manager is likely to mean different things by the word. For some, 'reinforcement' may not be what they mean by learning ('That's not learning, I knew that already!'); for others, 'learning' may be limited to those few major moments in life when their whole approach to management is 'turned upside down'. Yet more, however, may be comfortable with the idea that learning is as much about incremental steps as U-turns; that learning is about gradually becoming more and more skilled in the arts of management.

Managers may also be relatively unskilled in introspection, even some very successful senior managers. Despite their obvious facility with complexity, the ways in which they are able to handle a variety of different and often difficult situations with alacrity attests to the complex internal and social processes they are constantly managing. Yet many such people come out with the most trite and simplistic statements about what they heave learnt in life. It is often said that successful people are not always good at 'teaching' the sources of their success. When such highly successful executives turn to explaining the learning which has led to their success, they, too, can come unstuck.

In many cases, this is because what continues to make them successful is so ingrained in their behaviours that they are not able easily to bring it into consciousness. They are 'unconsciously competent', and as such, may be largely unaware of what it is they have, over their lifetime, learnt.

Many of the things which people may refer to as learning are inferential. Where we may be unable clearly to introspect about ourselves, we may infer from our own behaviour and others' responses to our behaviour what we have 'learnt' about ourselves. Feedback may change this perception. But if that feedback is not available, we may think we have learnt something about our social selves which is inaccurate or incomplete. The following case illustrates an example of this.

HOW INFERENCES INFLUENCE OUR LEARNING ABOUT OTHER PEOPLE

An event for learning about oneself

A large and growing UK-based conglomerate was working with us to help develop some of their middle to senior managers. I was involved in designing and helping to deliver an intervention whose purpose was primarily to give managers a chance to find out how they came across to their peers. This, in turn, should help them to be more sensitive to how they present themselves to different kinds of people at work, and thereby help them to manage their 'reputations' in the company.

We ran the event in facilitated groups of seven managers, introduced up front the idea of the 'social' and 'inner' selves, and gave the groups of managers a number of tasks to do, whose primary purpose was to generate data for the managers to talk about in review sessions. Because this was an event focused exclusively upon the impressions people made on each other, we 'formalised' and 'legitimised' the personal feedback process to ensure that each manager was presented with clear and comprehensive pictures of their 'social selves' as constructed by those with whom they worked for the three days they were together.

Peter, the Self-confessed 'JFDI'

We were not planning to use the language of the Myers-Briggs Type Indicator (MBTI see Chapter 9) on this event, but because it is used in some parts of the company, one of the managers dropped it into the conversation, hinting to one of his group that these two shared the same preferences. This was the cue for another manager, Peter Walpole, to say 'I'm a JFDI!' It was a succinct summary of the task-oriented behaviours he had exhibited so far. This took place in the first review, after one brief activity designed to get them started in the process.

The second task included the requirement for the separate groups to bid against each other at an auction. During one phase of the auction Peter Walpole was given the job of representing his group as bidder. The bidder's job was to carry out the group's agreed bidding strategy so far as was possible during the bidding session. This he did.

However, at the start of the review process which followed the completion of the task, Peter received, independently, from the three most open and erudite of his six colleagues the feedback that each had believed, as they approached the auction, that he, Peter, would not follow the agreed strategy, but would follow his own line. This was the first piece of feedback of the session. Each manager had spent an hour or so preparing, alone and from his or her own perceptions, what feedback they would give each other. As the first manager said to Peter what he believed Peter would do at the auction, the others looked on and nodded. The second then confirmed, 'That's what I have noted, too.' Then the third, 'I've said the same thing in my notes.'

Peter was visibly stunned. He was comforted to some extent by everyone's agreeing that he had not done what they feared he would do. But this did not eliminate the insight that half (at least) of his colleagues had, within the space of no more than a couple of hours' acquaintance, drawn the same inferences. He then had the chance to appreciate the impact of these inferences.

One of the other managers went on to describe how he had interpreted Peter's behaviour at a later stage in the task. At this point, the auctions were over, and participants were all preparing to go their separate ways to fulfil their subordinate tasks. As they gathered in their workroom, this manager suggested a quick 'time out'. He went on, 'When I suggested the time out, your shoulders dropped, Peter. I could see that you were in no way interested in a time out. You wanted to 'just do it'. This made me feel bad about calling the time out.' Peter responded. He said that he remembered his shoulders dropping not from frustration and impatience, but from relief that someone was trying to get a sense of order into the chaos which was ensuing at the time. I cannot say whether Peter's colleagues believed this explanation.

Refining Personal Learning through Constructive Dialogue

What differentiated these incidents from the general run of managerial life was not that people were making inferences, but that these inferences were being openly shared, checked and explored. Peter had to recognise that what was revealed to him about his social self by his colleagues here may be 'secretly held' inferences of almost anyone he works with – even those he only meets for an hour or so. By the end of the three days, the openness and honesty of the feedback process had enabled Peter's colleagues to check the inferences they drew about him, help Peter to adjust his behaviour to reduce the possibility of 'misinterpretation', and create an environment in which what people 'learnt' about themselves and each other could be enriched through constructive dialogue. Everyone Peter meets will have an attitude about him; those who he has worked closely with on this event have a shared, agreed and positive attitude which, they feel, is better than the six disparate sets of attitudes they will have taken away had they not had the chance to say what they felt, share their impressions and thereby shape and enrich their inferences about him, about each other and about themselves.

One of the most important factors about learning which the case highlights is that it is easy to draw inferences from limited data, and then to treat these inferences as 'learning'. The problem with a great deal of 'learning' which is not questioned and challenged is that it can simply be another way of describing the inferences we have drawn, and which we have not properly checked. Therefore, although we cannot say that unchecked inferences are not learning, while checked inferences are learning, the quality of learning, I suggest, is significantly enhanced through dialogue. In other words, until what someone 'thinks' they have learnt is subjected to debate, alternative interpretations and inferences, checked against other perspectives, and so on, then it is unhelpful to call these unchecked impressions 'learning'.

What Learners Say – the Learning Review

So, to get managers themselves to be 'better aware' of whether they have learnt anything means setting the scene in some way; it means exposing to the scrutiny of others, and in some sense gaining acceptance from them of the validity of the complex 'map' of 'family resemblances' which unite a whole series of 'kinds of meaning' for each individual. By motivating managers to reflect (ideally with others) on their experiences, we are helping to make managers more conscious of the ways in which their thoughts and ideas, images and concepts may have been influenced by the management and organisation development experience. This reflection is an important opportunity not only for the manager to become more aware of the (more or less conscious) conclusions he or she has been drawing, but is also an opportunity, if managers share a discussion on this point, to help clarify and crystallise for the other participants ideas which they have hitherto not grasped so clearly.

This kind of 'learning review' is, in one of the senses of the word 'learning', where much of the learning actually takes place for some managers, because it frequently surfaces to consciousness what they have failed to identify as learning. By dubbing the hitherto dimly perceived experience as a kind of learning – in other words, by consciously linking the two maps, 'learning' and 'this experience', these managers are elevating the status of the learning from 'just one of those things' to 'something I have learned'; the latter is much more likely to be called upon for future reference, and is, in that sense, better learning.

It is helpful, therefore, in such 'learning reviews', to introduce the idea of the multiple meanings of learning – perhaps simply by asking managers to 'brainstorm' all the kinds of learning they know. This legitimises many of the more 'obscure' meanings of learning which some managers may use, and enables a much greater degree of 'hitch-hiking on other people's ideas', significantly increasing the learning which is identified, acknowledged and therefore made more consciously available.

What if they have 'Learned' the Wrong Thing?

There are shortcomings to this 'definition' of learning, however. As we suggested at the beginning of the chapter, managers may lie, or they may fool themselves. They may get caught up on the tide of enthusiasm, and claim to have learnt things which are not much more than a set of words.

Moreover, they may draw conclusions which we do not want them to draw: 'I learnt not to trust anyone any more' may be an unwelcome conclusion from an intervention designed to enhance collaborative behaviours. Management and organisation development professionals are often tempted to tell people what they should have learnt in ways which suggest that this is what they will have learnt. This is unhelpful. But the more we step back from 'telling' and allow 'exploration' through an increase in experiential learning, the more we open up the possibility that managers will learn things which we neither believe in nor want them to learn.

Many people feel that something which they do not believe to be true cannot be 'learnt'. There is something not quite right about the statement 'I learnt that one plus one equals three'; it is not true. Therefore, although you can believe it, we feel that you can't learn it. When it comes to questions of whether it is right to trust people, there are no such truths. We have to recognise, therefore, that what we, as management and organisation development professionals, believe in, and what we facilitate managers to learn can only be the same if we 'manipulate' the learning experiences in some way to ensure that they do learn what we want them to learn.

This is an issue which we shall return to in our chapter on learning design, where the more practical aspects of the theories of learning from this chapter will be elaborated.

What Learners Do

An alternative approach is not to ask managers what they have learnt, but to monitor managers' subsequent behaviours. If it is the aim of an intervention to help managers become better coaches, then, surely, it is not what the managers say about what they have learnt which is most important, but what they do. We therefore need to ask their subordinates, peers and bosses whether they have become better coaches. Chapter 5 suggested that, in this kind of investigation, the more perspectives we can get, the better.

Even this approach has its limitations. The manager may be 'acting' – going through the motions, but not really believing in what he or she is doing; biding his or her time and gradually slipping back into the old ways while no-one is looking. Again, since those who would 'measure' the manager's changed behaviour are making inferences about the quality of that manager's coaching (many will also, more or less consciously, making inferences about the manager's 'sincerity', 'beliefs', and so on, thereby seriously influencing those perceptions), we are still not measuring 'reality', but only a number of people's perceptions.

The Potential Contradictions between these Two 'Measures' of Learning

It is possible that there could be a clear mismatch between what a manager says he or she has learnt and what others will infer from his or her behaviour. Managers have said that they have learnt, for example, to listen better, and that they have been able to put this learning into practice, while we have heard from colleagues that the manager is 'still the same old so-and-so, deaf to everything but his own voice'. In this situation, who should we believe? Has learning taken place or not?

The answer is that, it depends what you mean by 'learning'. The manager may genuinely believe he or she is listening better and, in one sense, this belief is the proof of the pudding. He or she is paying attention, focusing, concentrating. To that extent he or she has learnt to listen better.

The colleagues, on the other hand, may have difficulty in taking an 'objective' view of the manager's 'new' behaviours. Among those factors we have identified as potentially colouring the inferences they may draw could be

❑ a more or less conscious dislike of the manager, which will tend to obscure 'evidence' of good listening, and highlight 'evidence' of poor
❑ a 'complex' or 'ideal' image of what good listening looks like when it is observed, which the manager's behaviour does not match
❑ a sense of the term 'listening' which significantly differs from that of the manager
❑ a personality difference, which values 'listening' differently (as in 'That's not 'real' listening')

The 'reviewing' colleague may be more or less conscious of any or all of the above.

Can We Talk about Learning at All?

We can sensibly talk about managers learning. Management and organisation development depends upon this ability. But we need, if we are to do a professional job, to recognise the essentially fluid nature of both the learning processes and the ways in which we may wish to measure or assess learning outcomes. Many of the 'failures' of management and organisation development in the past, I believe, are the result of attempts to turn management and organisation development into some kind of science – to try to achieve hard, measurable, certain outcomes. This is not what people or learning are about.

This does not mean that management and organisation development is simply an 'act of faith'. It does, however, mean that it is part of the job of the management and organisation development professional to recognise and seek to work within the constraints which we have explored in this chapter and earlier chapters. We cannot rely simply on one kind of outcome (especially the end of course appraisal) to 'prove' the worth of any intervention. We have to work with managers to find strategies which, unlike the quick-fix, will enable managers, their bosses, their colleagues, their subordinates, their customers, and their families and friends to become aligned in agreement that learning has taken place. We have to create situations in which managers come back to us and say, 'I've just been to see my customer for the first time since the programme, and it's fantastic!'

This kind of evidence will not constitute 'proof' of learning, but it is worth much more than the spurious 'proof' of certificates and 'happiness sheets'. The world of management and organisation development is uncertain and ambiguous; but so is that of management. It is far more honest to admit to this uncertainty and ambiguity than to play the snake-oil salesman, and promise the kinds of certainty and proof which we cannot promise. The revised 'model' which this chapter has introduced is not compatible with simple, linear, numerical measures of managerial learning. The kinds of approach to measuring learning will be embedded in the kinds of approach we take to designing learning, which will be the subject of Chapter 10.

Involvement in Learning – Partnership in Practice

Learning changes minds; it alters people's mental maps. Learning is not a matter of pouring new knowledge into a passive vessel; to be effective it has to be a collaborative activity. This means engaging more of the learner's mind than his or her intellect. That intellect does not and cannot work in isolation from his or her emotions, values, and so on. Therefore, designing learning simply to appeal to the intellect is, at best, an inefficient process. At worst, it fools teacher and learner alike into assuming that learning is taking place, when all that is happening is an intellectual exercise. For some people this may be fun; for others it is clearly a pointless waste of time.

When management and organisation development providers start a session by engaging participants in a dialogue about the concepts which are to be explored ('What do we mean by leadership?') this can signal one or two different kinds of response, often depending on why the facilitator chooses to do so.

In some cases, this kind of activity is being used to clear out of the way all the 'wrong' definitions, to make way for the 'right' one which the facilitator will provide when he or she feels ready. In such cases, some managers may feel reluctant to join in with the exercise, knowing that 'the answer' will be revealed sometime soon, and, perhaps, unwilling to risk offering a definition which may differ from the 'truth'. This approach is predicated upon the whole set of assumptions constellated around 'truth', 'right', 'rational', 'masculine' and 'empty vessel learning'. The invitation being offered by the facilitator is to clear out from the manager's 'vessel' any 'rubbish' which may get in the way of the 'right answer' concerning leadership. Part of the problem in helping management and organisation development providers learn about learning is that many of these kinds of assumptions are paradigmatic, deeply held, and unconscious. Because they have for so long been shared with many managers attending management and organisation development events ('go ahead, teach me'), they have been reinforced as 'the right way' through positive responses from managers ('I have been successfully taught').

The alternative motivation for asking participating managers to explore their views on such matters as leadership is embedded within the alternative paradigm. The goal is not to show managers what leadership 'is' in some abstract sense, but to work with managers on how they, individually and collectively, understand leadership, and how to build upon that understanding to enrich their options in leading and being led in the future. This means encouraging managers to experience and talk about how they feel and have felt in the past about instances of leadership; why leadership means different things to different people; how leadership is associated with different models and concepts for different people; how leadership has manifested itself in different individuals and 'ideal types'. This is a process which deliberately and constructively engages emotions and values, imagination and 'irrationality'. And in so doing, it involves not just the narrow, serial, time-constrained, linear thinking processes of the intellect. It involves a broader spectrum of the manager's mind in the whole learning process.

If Chapters 1 to 6 of the book were about the partnership approach to the organisational challenges of management and organisation development, in which we form partnerships with sponsors of management and organisation development interventions, Chapters 7 to 11 are about taking this partnership approach into the intervention itself, forming partnerships between managers' intellects and the other aspects of their minds; and forming partnerships in learning between managers and facilitators. We cannot teach management; but we can help managers to continue to learn about themselves as people who happen to be managers.

This chapter has been about the principles of managerial learning, as they are based upon a different model of the person from that which underpins traditional management teaching. The rest of the book is about some of the broad ways in which this revised model helps us to help managers to learn in practice.

8 Is Outdoor Development a 'Clever Trick'?

INTRODUCTION – HOW DO YOU EVALUATE SUCH LEARNING?

This chapter is about justification. It seeks, by applying the theoretical frameworks of Chapter 7, to address questions concerning outdoors development for managers. In so doing, I do not intend to undertake a thorough literature review of all that has been written about the subject since Kurt Hahn. I shall refer, where appropriate to writers on the subject, but solely as illustrative of certain stances and ideas. In other words, it is not my intention to try to pass judgement on writers who have researched and worked in this field for many years. It is, however, my intention to say what my colleagues and I believe about the subject, and why.

It is a difficult subject because those of us in the management and organisation development profession do not agree on the subject. Our attitudes range from the almost evangelical – 'The potential . . . for building incredibly durable bonds and transforming communications to new levels is nothing short of magical' (Long 1987) – to the frankly dismissive (Mumford 1993: 43). Managers, too, have very mixed ideas about the subject; I can remember, in my early years in management and organisation development, the strong feelings of anxiety which used to well up inside me if and when the subject came up for the first time in conversation with a new client. Was this client an advocate or critic? It was important, since the subject seems to stir up considerably more violent responses than many other aspects of management and organisation development. On balance, it seems, managers are either converts or hate the idea with a deep loathing – and hate anyone associated with it as well.

Clearly, we are dealing with developmental dynamite here.

Why Can't We 'Prove' it One Way or the Other?

It would be wonderful if we could undertake a piece of rigorous research into outdoors development and 'prove' once and for all whether it works or not. People have, of course, undertaken many research projects in the area; my colleagues and I have done just that ourselves. But we still recognise that the question remains open. Chapters 1, 6 and 7 have provided arguments to show why we cannot find proof of this kind in research. Let us briefly rehearse these arguments.

The 'Scientific' Approach

We may try to undertake our research in a scientific way. This will demand the identification of a number of entities, and their separation into dependent and independent variables, followed by the measurement of hypothesised relationships between those variables. In the case of outdoors development, we may choose to identify, for example, seniority of managers and impact on organisational success from outdoors development. To be scientific, we should put large numbers of managers of all levels of seniority through 'the same' learning experience, while at the same time having at least two control groups: one to whom we pay 'the same level' of attention (to cope with the Hawthorn Effect), and the other who get no development or attention at all. We should then seek to measure corporate success.

There are problems here: 'seniority' means different things to different organisations; 'success' can be measured in different ways, because it really does mean different things to different organisations; 'the same' experience is clearly nonsense, because each manager brings a wealth of experience, expectations, attitudes; and so on. Researchers in management who seek to follow this path find themselves defining more and more tightly the variables they are measuring, and the measures they are applying until they reach the point at which the accuracy of the research is matched only by the triviality of the conclusions. This would lead to the 'principle of incompatibility' (Chapter 1, page 13). Scientific research will not answer such management and organisation development questions.

The Statistical Approach

If we cannot treat managers as objects to be experimented upon, we can ask them questions. And we can add up answers to such questions, comparing those answers to get conclusions of the kind that 70% of managers say that they benefited from outdoors development. Would this 'prove' that outdoors development is valid?

In order to produce data which can be classified together – counted up, subtracted, turned into percentages – you need comparable questions and answers. This leads to questionnaires. Questionnaires produce lots of data, but are limited in their ability to pick up what people mean. The fact that everyone's 'concepts' of leadership, learning and so on are built from neuronal maps, linked through metaphor into complexes of family resemblances means that when anyone says 'learning' or 'leadership', they 'mean' very different things. As people work closely together, as they do in organisations, their mental maps are likely to become more aligned – that is one of the drivers of organisational culture. But across organisations, there can remain very significant differences in what people mean by such terms.

Asking for comparative data, therefore, means either ignoring these differences in meaning (thereby rendering the data pointless), or creating data gathering devices of such complexity that the exercise becomes bogged down in its own processes. This was one of the points of Chapter 5.

But even assuming that we could overcome these problems of meaning; suppose that we could devise such data-gathering devices which gave us a great deal of confidence that the percentages made some kind of sense. Even in that unlikely event, we, as management and organisation development professionals could not, in good faith, put outdoors development permanently on the agenda. If it were the case that 70% of respondents said that they had learnt from outdoors development, this provides no predictive value for the next manager, for the next intervention or the next organisation. To say that John is 70% likely to turn into a delinquent is to say nothing about him at all (Allport 1937). Similarly, statistical surveys say a great deal about probabilities. But management and organisation development is about managers, not numbers.

Self-Reporting – Without the Statistics

Theoretically we could ask everyone who had ever been involved in outdoors development (and who is still alive) whether they had learnt from it. Everyone who goes through outdoors development learns a lot, in the sense that we all learn constantly. Again, there are likely to be relatively few who have gone through 'life-changing' experiences – what some may be tempted to call 'real learning'.

And some, also, may have learnt precisely what the organisation did not want them to learn. This may tempt us to take as valid only that 'learning' which managers admit to which is in line with the original aims of the intervention; but that would be cheating.

In any case, it seems to us from our own researches into managers' learning from various forms of outdoors development that such self-reporting would not provide us with the answer we are seeking. This is because, like management and organisation development professionals, those who have been on the receiving end seem also to have mixed feelings about the validity of the experience. Looking back over the experiences they have gone through, we may argue that the reason they have such mixed feelings is that the events were not as well designed and delivered as they may have been. But this is a different question, one to be addressed in Chapter 10. And such speculation cannot help us resolve the central question.

Have Managers Been Seen by their Colleagues to have Become Better Managers?

Further research could be (and has been, by many people) undertaken into the longer-term effects of outdoor development on perceived managerial behaviour. Much of this is anecdotal (Bank 1994) (and why not, since management is about people and telling the right stories to shareholders, staff, customers, and so on?); much of it is probably selective. Despite the large amount of evidence which can be accumulated by practitioners which demonstrates, through testimonials, how effective outdoor development has been for large numbers of people, there is always so much room for alternative interpretations, for the 'well you would say that, wouldn't you?' kinds of response that it remains perfectly feasible for people to deny the validity of the whole enterprise.

Management and organisation development is about long-term impact, about effective change, and so on. It takes place within a context of other changes within organisations and people's lives. Organisations which treat management and organisation development seriously recognise its role as just one vehicle for effective change, and adopt management and organisation development interventions in harness with many other initiatives designed to be mutually reinforcing for positive change. This means that there is so much 'noise' in the system that attempting to evaluate any aspect of the complex processes of change in isolation is likely to be difficult at the very least. Can changes in the behaviour of a particular manager be ascribed 'solely' to his or her participation in outdoor development; or is it likely that these perceived changes are as much the result of structural changes in the organization, for example?

Evaluation: Post Hoc or 'Making Sense'?

In this, outdoor development is no different from any other management and organisation development activity. In so far as evaluation is concerned, attempting to do so solely post hoc may be missing the point.

How do we go about evaluating other kinds of learning; for example, learning that it is not a good idea to cross busy roads with our eyes closed? Most of us would recognise that we do not need a research programme for this. We do not send blindfolded people scuttling across busy roads to test our hypotheses; we do not amass statistical evidence concerning how many blindfolded versus sighted people successfully get across; we do not have to ask each other, 'Have you truly learnt not to close your eyes when trying to cross a busy road?'; and we do not have to ask the same question of others about people they know. This is trivial, I know, compared to managerial learning, but it does, at least, demonstrate a principle: that we can evaluate learning by other than post hoc means.

Deciding to do something before you can 'prove' it will work means taking a risk. A great deal of good management is about tempering risks where possible: test marketing is a good example of post hoc validation; there is nothing inherently wrong with post hoc evaluation where it is available or where it makes sense – suitable rigorous research can, in principle, be undertaken. But there is also a great deal in management which is and will continue to be about risk. Minimizing this kind of risk is about being confident in the process – that it makes sense, not about trying it out first, and then seeing if it worked. Managers who have grown up with a succession of egocentric bosses may have learnt, post hoc, the art of flattery. This will not help them with a boss who hates 'yes men'. Finding this out is better done by understanding the new boss in advance, than by discovering through trial and error that flattery, in this case, will get you nowhere.

So another way of exploring outdoor development is by matching its assumptions, processes, and so on, to the principles and theories about learning we explored in the previous chapter. If outdoor development provides fertile soil in which learning can take place, then this will provide some level of justification of outdoor development in principle (although it will not say that all outdoor development is good). If it creates environments which appear inimical to learning, then we should conclude, with its critics, that it is a fad designed to satisfy the teacher more than the learner.

RAISING THE STAKES – GENERATING STRESS

What, if any, are the key differences between outdoor development and 'ordinary' management and organisation development? Various writers have helped answer this question in a variety of ways. There are many 'classificatory models' which point out some significant differences between kinds of outdoor development, often showing how different an experience an enforced night-time march is from a treasure hunt on a summer's day; an exercise in which participants never know when the next 'buggeration factor' will be thrown at them from one in which everything is fully defined and available from the start, and so on. There are as many different manifestations of outdoor management development as you can imagine.

There are also numbers of 'models' of outdoor development, which I do not intend to explore, since this will distract us from the aims of the chapter.

Those who wish to explore these in more depth will get a great deal from, inter alia, Bank (1994), Irvine and Wilson (1994), and Dainty and Lucas (1992).

At least one feature of outdoor development seems constant: that it is primarily directed towards 'experiential' learning (usually with some reflection). In terms of the Lancaster Model, it pairs the 'external world' loop of having an experience and getting feedback, with the 'inner world' loop of reflection and hypothesising about one's own behaviour and consequent learning. There is, at most, a minimal amount of 'input'. (How one achieves balance between these elements is a matter of learning design, to be explored in Chapter 10.)

It is of the essence of most outdoor development to be 'experiential' (this is not an exclusive feature of outdoor development – many 'indoor' interventions are also 'experiential' in approach). By this I simply mean that it is the intention of designers and providers of such learning that participants will primarily learn by having and reflecting upon their own experiences, rather than learning 'second-hand' through lectures, books or some other 'input' medium. This means that little or no 'teaching' goes on, apart from that which comes 'naturally' from the experiences themselves, and the reflection upon those experiences.

In focusing upon the outdoors as such, as opposed to the broader territory of 'experiential learning', I shall pick out just two features which seem to me to be highly pertinent to our understanding of the potential for learning provided differently by the outdoors than by 'ordinary', classroom-based or on-the-job management development. Neither of these is exclusively the prerogative of outdoors development (as they can be features of some 'ordinary' management development activities), but, in my experience of outdoor development activities of varying degrees of 'impact' they tend to be significant for many participants. They are probably not unrelated to each other.

The two features are 'visibility' and 'stress'.

'Visibility' and 'Stress'

Visibility seems to be an important factor in outdoor development. Participants tend to find it much harder to 'hide behind organizational and educational norms' (Dainty and Lucas 1992). In lectures, seminars, even in syndicate groups, there is room for anonymity; at least for switching off for a while. Although this can be true for outdoors development, it is less often the case. This may add to the second feature, stress, especially for more private managers.

Stress is a manager's response to pressure (Arroba and James 1992); pressure is often what managers feel under when in the outdoors. It is a combination of the visibility, the threat of the unknown, the novelty of the environment, the (sometimes) almost relentless time pressure, and any manner of other perceived risks: each manager will approach the outdoors in a different way. Many will feel relaxed, at least until the pressure is raised.

Many outdoor activities are designed to put pressure upon managers. The common argument for this lies in the idea that managers work best under 'just the right amount' of stress. Too little, and they become complacent and under-perform; too much, and they have too much to cope with, and, again, under-perform (ibid.: 3–4). Designers of outdoor interventions often deliberate on how they can create just the 'right amount' of stress to 'bring out the best' in managers. What would constitute the 'right amount' is one of those unanswerable questions with which this book has been dealing throughout; unfortunately, some management and organisation development providers seem to treat the question as one for which there is a right answer: it is the one they work to.

What Impact does Stress have on Learning?

Various writers have alluded to the impact of heightened arousal on performance, with a variety of conclusions; it could be inferred that stress both enhances and inhibits good performance. One of the more common themes seems to be that among the greatest of impacts of such stress is that made upon logical reasoning (Gilbert 1989: 312–13; see also, for example, Haber and Alpert 1958; Hunsley 1987). In other words, the most vulnerable aspect of our minds to the negative impact of stress is the intellect, or rationality, often associated with the left hemisphere of the brain. One of the effects of stress in the outdoors may be, therefore, to reduce participants' ability to 'rationalise', or 'intellectualise', even if they wanted to.

Now given that many of the kinds of aims of outdoor development are focused upon behavioural change rather than the acquisition of intellectual knowledge, a reduction in intellectual capability may be neutral – neither good nor bad. But according to what we explored in Chapter 7, concerning the dangers inherent in the 'dictatorship of the left hemisphere' (Stevens 1995: 341), reduction in intellectual capacity could be seen as an opportunity to increase focus on other parts of the mind, brain or personality. Would this help?

Many writers argue that effectiveness in learning is enhanced by 'making the associations as wide as possible, clothing them not just with visual and auditory features, but exploiting the whole body' (Dennett 1991: 224). There is a prima facie case for suggesting that processes which deliberately suppress the dominance of the intellect may, in fact, be helpful to a broader-based kind of learning – what management and organisation development people call 'affective' learning. The less 'in touch' managers are with their intellects, the more chance the other functions have of working in harmony to generate deeper learning experiences.

Many managers are quite likely to resist such attacks on the hegemony of their intellects; there is often an uncomfortable loss of control, loss of status, loss of immediate understanding of what is going on when pressure goes up so far that they 'cannot think straight'. What makes it worse is that, along with this loss of ability to think straight, there is also a frequent reduction in the effectiveness of short-term memory (Kleinsmith and Kaplan 1963: 190–3). The upside to this state of affairs, according to the same research, is an increase in retrieval in the long term. In other words, managers may be more confused by events at the time, but they remember better in the long run. Perhaps this is what outdoor development seeks to achieve?

The exploration we undertook in Chapter 7 clearly aligns with these findings. One of the reasons why many managers (especially British male managers) find it hard to 'get in touch with' their emotions is precisely that dominance of the intellect. Yet whether we are aware of it or not, the prefrontal/amygdala circuit is active at all times, having attitudes to what we are experiencing and tainting our memories of these attitudes with secretions of adrenaline and noradrenaline. Heightened arousal, stress of the kind which managers may feel in the outdoors is simply becoming more aware of the impact of the activities of the limbic system as it stores up value-laden memories for our later reflection and (limited) access. Pulling back the 'net curtain' of intellect simply makes it easier for our conscious minds to get in touch with the largely unconscious processes which largely develop and refine our attitudes and our values. As Jung puts it: 'the unconscious is heightened, thereby creating a gradient for the unconscious to flow towards the conscious. The conscious then comes under the influence of unconscious instinctual impulses and contents' (Jung 1952: para. 856).

It is in this kind of 'highly charged' environment that we are much more likely to be able to regain contact with 'deep down values, abilities, energies or passions' (Bank 1994: 78). Creating situations of perceived risk and threat may even trigger the kinds of mental responses reported in some 'near-death' experiences, in which perceived threat kicks off a massive 'associative search. Red alert. Open the emergency doors. Search all the stored data nets and search them in parallel and search them fast' (Kosko 1994: 213).

If we are trying to help managers change behaviour, and if behaviour is highly influenced by the inferences we draw about our environments, and those inferences are coloured by attitudes and values which are often unconsciously developed, then providing environments and situations in which stress can draw back the intellectual curtains seems to be a potentially positive element in outdoor development. It has potential for a great deal of damage as well. But this is the case with any management and organisation development activity which 'messes with managers' minds'.

This means that management and organisation development professionals have a significant duty to act responsibly with this increased vulnerability. Later in the chapter, I shall explore how my colleagues and I do this. But first, let us take a look at one of the images, or 'models' of outdoor development which has been used by some people to exploit the opportunities offered by this more 'emotional' kind of managerial learning.

OUTDOOR DEVELOPMENT AS RITE OF PASSAGE

We don't have many opportunities, in our rational, western organisations, to create situations which deliberately disorientate people for the sake of helping them to develop. The uncertainties which such a situation throws up have led some writers to seek models and concepts from other cultures to enlighten us on what is going on. Many such writers have been attracted to the idea of the outdoor development event as a 'rite of passage', usually citing van Gennep (1960) as their primary source of information on these phenomena.

Rites of passage are common in almost all cultures; some persist in our own, such as christenings, weddings and funerals. Most cultures have a much richer complement of such events; this may be one reason why some writers are tempted to believe that we in our culture are now busy reinventing our own. Apart from the outdoor development event, such writers may be tempted to ascribe 'rite-of-passage' status to stag and hen parties, initiation rites which some organisations retain, driving tests, and so on (see, for example, Morris 1967).

As a piece of 'pop' anthropology, such associations are harmless fun; when they are taken seriously, as when outdoor development is said to be a rite of passage, then we may need to clarify what this means, and whether it is a helpful or dangerous connection. What I am concerned about in this section is not the writers who use rites of passage in other cultures as a source of understanding psychological or sociological processes, in order to learn from them, but those who, willy-nilly see a superficial link between initiation among people of other cultures and managers in our society building rope bridges across gorges in the Lakes, and develop from there some kind of idea that outdoor development activities are some kind of rite of passage, just like the 'real' ones.

Do Rites of Passage Tell us Anything about Outdoor Development?

One of the essential points about rites of passage is that they tend to mark clearly defined transitions from one social state to another. They frequently enact 'rebirth' activities, pointing up the highly 'social' nature of the concept of the self in many other cultures (often at the expense of the more private concept of self which our culture has fostered). They are often (but not always) public events, since these social transitions are only validated by the witness of the society at large; and they can involve extraordinary numbers of levels of meaning. They are frequently intimately associated with the mythology of a culture.

Many writers on management and organisation development point to the variously perceived 'functions' of such rituals: Campbell (1972) talks of 'the function of ritual'; Burnett (1995) says of the 'altered reality' which comes about through a rite, that it 'serves several purposes'; Feinstein and Krippner (1988) suggest that rites of passage provided a relatively unambiguous direction for regulating people's lives; and so on. The problem with such readings is that the anthropologists who themselves study and examine such rites of passage no longer talk about the 'function' of any such phenomena in society. Functionalist interpretation in social anthropology was shown to be unhelpful over thirty years ago. I suspect that if rites of passage are to enlighten us in our search for enhancement to outdoor development, they will not do so if we focus on their supposed 'functions'.

Functionalism in social anthropology died out alongside functionalism in other disciplines at around the same period. It did so because it failed to provide anything like satisfactory answers to at least two kinds of key questions:

❑ Why, if such phenomena are so functionally useful, do so many of them contain so many potentially dysfunctional elements?
❑ Why do these people use this and not that or another kind of ritual to perform the same function, since we can imagine hosts of economically less-expensive ways of achieving the same goals?

These and many other associated kinds of questions made anthropologists realise that a ritual's being functionally useful was not a sufficient condition for its explanation: indeed, it became increasingly clear that it was not even a necessary condition.

Social anthropologists replaced functional interpretations with more culturally-specific ones. In so doing, they deliberately turned their back on generalisations (see Chapter 5, p. 152). What we lost in this eschewal of general principles which can be applied to all or most cultures, we gained in a much deeper understanding of symbolism, meaning, and so on. So far as rites of passage (and their associated myths) are concerned, we gained insights into the seemingly infinite resources of the human mind to perceive, talk about, classify, group, associate and play with our concrete and abstract ways of dealing with the world, ourselves, each other, and the problems and challenges of being happy and human. My favourite example of the fruits of this period of cultural research is Alfred Gell's *Metamorphosis of the Cassowaries* (Gell 1975), which, in its several hundred pages, is an attempt to understand one ritual performed among the Umeda people of new Guinea. As a piece of theatre, the ritual is exemplary, since it combines aesthetics, ethics, exercise, social structure, story-telling, and a host of other facets all at the same time.

What writers such as Gell have been able to point out to us is how deeply ingrained such rituals are within a culture. The reason it took so much work to explain the ritual to us is largely that there are so many layers of meaning, so many connections, that the ritual seems almost to replicate the neuronal maps within the mind. There are literally hundreds, probably thousands of cross-references being made at any moment within the preparation and enactment of the ritual. It takes the Umeda people years to learn to become competent to prepare and enact the ritual. And this learning is made so much easier for them than it is for us because so much of their language, social structure, geography, architecture, and so on, act as reminders – physical and semantic 'motivators' of the multiple meanings within the culture.

The richness of the Umeda ritual is not unique. One reason why so few monographs fail to match this book in its depth of understanding is that many anthropologists do not have Gell's gift of patient understanding of another culture's riches. But there are still sufficient numbers of ethnographies from different parts of the world which attest to the frequency with which rituals are deeply and irrevocably embedded within a rich cultural heritage. When cultures become diverse, rituals lose their meaning, as we have witnessed in our own culture.

Creating new rituals which have anything like the same significance as the rites of passage written about by van Gennep and others is a tall order. Clearly, by focusing on just a few features of rites of passage, we may miss the point altogether. Take, for example, the idea (based upon van Gennep's observation that rites of passage typically have three stages: separation, transition and incorporation) that a management and organisation development course satisfies the 'separation' requirement (Holman and Hall 1996: 198); and that, during the second phase, 'participants are shown, or can discover – the breakthrough – the proper way – a new language of managerial practice' (ibid.).

It is this kind of simplistic association between one world (an MCI course for NHS managers) and another (rites of passage such as the Umeda ritual) which trivialises any potential learning one discipline can gain from another. If we are to borrow any ideas and learning from another discipline, we have to treat what that discipline tells us with respect. An MCI course for NHS managers remains a largely cerebral, intellectual, culturally spare experience. In a rite of passage, 'the communication of cultural symbols does not occur chiefly as abstract communication detached from contexts of involvement of feeling and emotion, intention and action. It occurs through personal engagement in day to day transactions with a social and symbolic environment, especially other persons who are not only the propagators but also the living embodiments and exemplars of cultural symbols' (Much 1995: 104).

There are two vital points to bring out from this observation. The first is that, despite the enormous cultural richness embodied in most rites of passage, ritual remains essentially a *mundane* phenomenon to the people of the respective culture. They are mundane simply because they are so deeply and irrevocably embedded in the everyday network of symbolic meanings – the very fabric of the culture and society. The more they become detached from that mundane word, the more ludicrous (or sinister, depending upon your perception) they can become; we only have to think of attitudes to the rituals of Freemasons or members of other Friendly Societies so recognise this.

The second point is that people actually going through a rite of passage may have experiences which are far from mundane; many of the elements of many such rites quite clearly contribute to the extraordinary nature of personal experience during a rite. But these are pretences: participants and perpetrators know this. There are varying levels of suspension of disbelief, perhaps enhanced if the elders' masks are really scary, or if the initiates are deprived of sleep or other comforts. The 'rebirth' may be an enormously complex, emotional, highly charged experience for the initiate; but it is almost always done within a more-or-less familiar context. The ritual leaders will be the initiates mothers' brothers in many societies; the initiates will personally know brothers, cousins, friends who have gone through the same process. Whatever the personal experiences may be, there is a familiar and mundane context within which all this takes place.

That there is a spiritual element to many rites of passage in many cultures does not refute the point concerning the mundane. What we mean by 'spiritual' and what people from other cultures mean by 'spiritual' can be very different things. Early anthropologists, such as Frazer (1890) and Tylor (1964; see also Evans-Pritchard 1933) created for us an expectation that 'your average native' is a fearful chap frightened of the spirits in the forest. This is nonsense. What is quite reasonable, however, is that, in the absence of the particular history which we in the west have experienced, people from many cultures are far more comfortable with accessing and working with those parts of the minds which we have to work harder to access. The myths of many cultures are puzzling jumbles to us – rather like our dreams. But to people far more comfortable with the positive power of the unconscious, the metaphorical, the emotional, the archetypal, myths have a richness and meaning which enables them to be told and retold over and over without boredom setting in. Each time there is the possibility of seeing a new meaning, a new lesson to be learnt.

There is a difference of enormous magnitude between the cultural richness of a traditional culture or society in which rites of passage have evolved and sit amidst semantic networks of almost endless complexity, and the 'strongest organisational culture'. No matter how well vaunted an organisation's culture may be by such cultural advocates as Tom Peters (Peters and Austin 1985) there is no point is expecting anyone to be able to recreate for managers of that organisation, through any kind of ritual, anything even vaguely approaching the kind of experience which a genuine rite of passage can offer. Even a small department comprising people who have worked, played, laughed and cried together for twenty or more years will have generated the tiniest fraction of semantic richness which the hundreds of generations have created for cultures in other societies than the west. In other words, looking to the rites of passage of other cultures for spiritual guidance is madness. Whatever 'spirituality' they may entail is no more than the 'spirituality' which is available to us if we can harness our own minds effectively.

Rites of Passage and Cargo Cults

A final word on rites of passage: when I studied social anthropology in the 1970s, I took a particular interest in a collection of social phenomena in Melanesia which anthropologists collectively called 'cargo cults'. These manifested themselves in native Melanesians building 'dummy' airstrips, making 'false' two-way radios, and setting up 'shrines' to such bizarre gods as Prince Philip. The overt aim of these activities was to gain access to the 'cargo' (radios, steel axes, jeeps, and so on) which the European and Australian people they came across seemed to be able to conjure out of the sky at will. Mistakes had been made by both the Melanesians and the Europeans as each tried to explain how each other's world worked. The cargo cults were pathetic mistakes, crudely fashioned artefacts which lacked the capacity to do what they were intended to do simply because it was not the look or feel of the radios and air strips which were efficacious: it was the enormously complex contexts in which transistors, aeroplanes, electricity, and so on interact to make radios work and planes land.

When we borrow from other cultures such ideas and activities as rites of passage, taking only the empty framework of 'separation, transition and reincorporation', and omitting the enormously rich cultural heritage which makes them work, we are making exactly the same kind of mistake as those who followed the cargo cults, with the simple difference that they expected material wealth to drop from the sky with no effort; we expect spiritual wealth to drop from our rites of passage with similar ease.

WHAT MIGHT WE BE ABLE TO LEARN FROM RITES OF PASSAGE?

There is a difference between learning from the study of rituals in other cultures and assuming that we are doing the same things as people in other cultures. Therefore, it is worth noticing one or two aspects of the rite of passage which might inform what we are trying to do in outdoor development. One such aspect is that, in their very different ways, both a rite of passage and an outdoor development programme are, for their respective participants, both out of the ordinary (from their own personal point of view, often strange and potentially stressful), and overtly given a 'learning' rationale.

One of the findings we have already referred to in Chapter 7 is that 'Some experiences simply pack more developmental wallop' (McCall *et al.* 1988: 5). We suggested then that such experiences may be those which we are innately programmed as humans to 'pay attention to'. From an evolutionary point of view, such archetypal responses are more likely to be effective if they are automatically stimulated by the strange, the stressful, those situations in which the rational part of our minds is more likely to 'underperform', requiring us to fall back more on those more ancient parts of our learning and survival equipment which is driven by the 'quick and dirty' limbic system. Rites of passage which put significant pressure on initiates are therefore more likely to create a 'learning readiness' in those initiates.

It would make sense in evolutionary terms if the mind were able not only to 'pay attention' to these special kinds of experience, but also have a limited set of ready-fashioned templates from which the limbic system could rapidly select in order to know what to do next: 'The changes that may befall a man are not infinitely variable; they are variations of certain typical occurrences which are limited in number. When, therefore, a distressing situation arises, the corresponding archetype will be constellated in the unconscious' (Jung 1968, Vol. 8, para. 450). From the four most 'primitive' archetypal responses (fight, feast on, fornicate with, flee from), Jung suggests that humans may have developed a more sophisticated, but nevertheless still archetypal, set of responses, based upon relationships.

Some Key Relationships for Learning

It is not uncommon for one of the key learning points of a rite of passage to shift the focus of an initiate's attention from one relationship to another – from one with father to one with mother's brother is not uncommon. In doing so, part of the drama is often the ritual 'killing' of the father – the death of the archetypal relationship to allow for loyalties and allegiances to be shifted.

Once again, if individuals are consciously to explore and review their actual relationships (as manifested through their personal unconscious and their complexes of 'father' and 'mother's brother') it helps if they can be brought to a state of mind which enables such reflection to surface; where such questions can be directly addressed. The fact that so many rites of passage involve such archetypal characters represented through masks, costumes, ritualised speeches, music and so on, merely serves to make it easier for initiates to bring to mind those very complexes which they are charged with exploring and changing their approach to.

Outdoor development is not about such clear-cut shifts of allegiance and social status, and it would be dangerous to suggest using it for such ends – this would be to make the 'cargo cult' mistake. But we can suspect that the similarity in personal experience of strangeness and stress may unconsciously bring into focus some of the basic archetypes, ready to be called into action as guides of behaviour. Participants may be more alert to some basic relationship issues simply through the aroused state in which they find themselves.

Disorientation may well lead to a search for authority – certainty, often manifested in the person of an authority figure. Frustratingly for this 'primeval' search, it is common practice in today's management and organisation development for facilitators deliberately to back away from such positions of authority. If, for many people, such authority figures are constellated from the father or mother archetypes, for example, the absolute authority which may be vested in these archetypes (but not in most people's complexes of mother and father, in our society), is not exercised, is positively denied by most management and organisation development facilitators.

In low-impact, non-risk, development situations, it is difficult for participants to identify anyone from the facilitator teams on whom to project their potential need for an absolute authority figure. But in high-impact programmes, this may be different.

Tutors and Authority Figures on High Impact Programmes

The difference between low-impact and high-impact outdoor development, for the purposes of this debate, is that between situations of low physical risk and those where the degree of risk has to be managed by professionals in outdoor activities. Low-impact outdoors development involves nothing more outlandish than walking or running in 'safe' countryside, or the potential for falling from heights of no more than about a metre onto grass. In low-impact outdoor development, physical risk is the same as it is in everyday activities, and is largely managed by the participants themselves.

High impact outdoor development, in our terms, involves such activities as abseiling, canoeing, rock-climbing, and so on. They involve a degree of physical risk. Writers such as Irvine and Wilson (1994: 28–30) assure us that there is never any 'real' physical risk on such events, since providers manage the risk away through all the protective equipment and rules they use. They argue that any physical risk is in the minds of the participants, as they peer over the cliff at the descent they are about to make in complete safety.

In exploring the circumstances of such a high-impact outdoor development event, let me set a typical scene from our experience: there are two distinct groups of facilitators. One, from Cranfield, for example, is responsible for the overall learning design and activities of the programme as a whole. For these facilitators, the outdoors may be just a part of an overall learning experience. Their job is to help in the overall learning process. Typically, on such an event, they will take a low profile during any physical tasks, moving significantly more into view during the review processes about which I shall write later in this chapter.

The other group I shall refer to as 'tutors' rather than facilitators, simply to differentiate them within the text. By using the terms 'facilitator' and 'tutor' I imply nothing about the quality or intent of the respective roles in learning. The tutors are more likely to be based at or near the outdoor centre. They may be full-time employees or associates of an organisation like Outward Bound. They are the professionals in outdoor activities, and are expert at all the physical activities which may be involved in a programme. They know the terrain, the equipment, and, most importantly, the potential risks. Their roles are primarily to attend to the physical tasks and the safety of the participants.

In achieving such high levels of safety, the tutors insist upon complete and unquestioned authority on matters of such safety. Whatever scheme participants may come up with in their complete freedom to be innovative and creative in problem-solving, must receive approval from the tutor acting as safety officer, whose decision is final. This makes practical sense; it also 'sticks out like a sore thumb'; in the midst of empowerment, uncertainty, disorientation, where facilitators are positively stepping back from any kind of involvement, guidance, interference, there is an immovable, absolute figure of authority. If the psychological concept of projection has any validity, this, surely, is where such projection is likely to take place.

I suspect that it does. I have met quite a few tutors from Outward Bound and other providers. They are good people; likeable, dedicated, peaceful, and splendid company. Despite the fact that they devote themselves to relatively poorly paid work with long hours, often in cold, wet weather, does not mean that they are gods or heroes. But for some participants, they come pretty close. As one 'purchaser' of outdoor development, David Chambers, Director of the London executive programme at the London Business School, where outdoor development has been in use for a decade wrote of them to John Bank at Cranfield (Bank 1994: 47–8), 'These dedicated, hard-working and rather saintly figures do hold up a mirror to us and this is quite a disturbing experience for both the managers and the academics, and at quite deep levels.'

In aligning the responses participants may have to tutors with the notion of the projection of archetypes and complexes, I do not wish to give the impression of denigrating these responses in any way. The responses are genuine: they are the very stuff of the emotional life which I have consistently argued is of benefit to managers. Knowing a bit more about how and why we have emotional responses should not, I hope, make them less significant or important. The fact that some of the affection managers may feel for tutors could be the result of those tutors satisfying an archetypal need for authority in times of disorientation renders the affection no less 'real'; just as our love for our mothers is no less 'real' just because we are innately inclined to respond in such a way to our archetypal mothers.

The Notion of the Guide

Relationships have at least two nodes, and in any relationship constellated upon authority, the valency of the opposite pole must be subordination. In evolutionary terms, we see such authority-subordination relationships every-where; in sociological and anthropological terms, we can also identify such universality of relationships. Not all relationships are equal. If within each of us we have an 'authority' archetype, which each of us develops up into our personal complex of authority figures (often but not necessarily based upon a father-figure), so we have a 'subordinate' archetype. But, for the benefit of self-esteem, our 'subordinate' archetype is not based upon such negative images as cowering and giving in. For males, it is built around freedom from responsibility, adventure, rule-breaking, and dreams of conquest. Jung calls this archetype *puer aeternus*, the 'eternal boy' (see von Franz 1970); for females, the relevant archetype is Hetaira.

The eternal boy in males is that element which manifests itself in the search for identity and fulfilment. In doing so, he does his own thing, and seeks his own way, always off on new adventures. Many outdoor development tasks provide precisely the kind of adventure which the eternal boy revels in. The eternal boy is energetic and active; fun is important, permanence is unwel-come. It is the eternal boy who, in those rites of passage which signal the arrival of manhood, must be ritually killed. In such rites, the idea of the archetype appears to some westerners to be taken 'literally'; it is, clearly, a symbolic, metaphorical killing which takes place. In our culture, we no longer have a rite of passage to 'kill' the eternal boy in men.

For women, the corresponding archetype is Hetaira, from the Greek word for female companion. Companionship is characterised by 'lateral' relation-ships, and based upon equality. In other words, the archetypal male response to authority is based upon moving on, biding one's time, finding new adventures, thankfully being absolved of the responsibilities of authority, individual and self-centred; perhaps waiting for the moment when authority can be wrested from the grasp of the elders. The archetypal female response is to focus on the one to one rather than the one away from one. Hetaira finds herself through other people, but in so doing, gives back a great deal, conveying to those whom she associates with a sense of personal value. When she befriends a man, she can be enormously influential helping to put him in touch with his unconscious (Guzie and Guzie 1984: 4).

Archetypes and the Manager's 'Life Story'

Some writers (see, for example, Guzie and Guzie 1984) have suggested that each of us is likely to be 'living our lives through' one or two of the primary archetypes. For men, these are 'father', 'warrior', 'sage' and 'eternal boy'. For a woman, they are 'mother', 'Amazon', 'mediatrix' and 'Hetaira'. In other words, there are those men who, despite the specific circumstances in which they find themselves, rarely settle, are constantly engaged in that search which others are far less engaged in. Some women, similarly, seem to move from relationship to relationship, never really feeling comfortable with the responsibilities and attachments of wifehood or motherhood. The various stories of the archetypes are one way of explaining why some men, even at an early age, 'seem grown up', and why some women seem to have 'deep intuition into others' thoughts and feelings.

The 'basic', 'life story' archetypes supplement our understanding about ourselves. Those whose 'life archetypes' are conflicting, 'Amazon' and 'sage', for example, are less likely to be happy in a relationship since our 'life archetypes' seem to provide a great deal of the focus for those goals and ambitions which are so important to us. Those who are driven by outward achievements and success in the world are probably living the Amazon or warrior archetype; those for whom inner understanding is the most important goal are living the mediatrix or sage archetypes.

How our 'dominant' archetype will be constellated by attending an outdoor development event will vary from manager to manager. It is quite likely that the 'Amazons' and 'warriors' will be the most active drivers for success in the tasks; the 'mothers' and 'fathers' may be more concerned with the welfare of their team colleagues, helping and encouraging more than driving and achieving. And those who are primarily 'living the eternal boy story' may be more prone to project the 'opposite' archetype onto the tutors than those who are, themselves, 'living the father story'.

If the absolute authority of the safety officer constellates the eternal boy and Hetaira archetypes in participants, what does the behaviour and role of the facilitators tend to constellate?

In rites of passage from other cultures, there is a highly 'experiential' element to learning. But there is often a 'guiding' element, one which is also noticeable from corresponding myths. The overriding notion seems to be that initiates must 'learn for themselves', but that this is not about just having an experience – it is about making sense of that experience within the relevant cultural norms. The elders (often the mother's brothers) take the role of guides, performing 'several key activities' (Burnett 1995: 104), such as helping to reframe perceptions of current reality, and evoking inner qualities and skills within initiates to overcome the challenges and puzzles they are confronting.

If the *adventure* of the tasks helps constellate the eternal boy in male managers, the *challenges* of the tasks themselves help constellate in partici-pants the 'warrior' archetype. Guzie and Guzie do not specifically refer to the 'guide' archetype; but it has a significant number of features in common with what they describe as the 'sage' in a man and the 'mediatrix' in a woman.

It is, among other things, this kind of parallel between the guide in a rite of passage and the facilitator in an outdoor experiential programme which many writers find so attractive. We certainly can learn from the study of rites of passage (if we were not to learn it some other way) that providing such guidance to reflection is a key part of the learning experience for participants. It would be impractical and irresponsible, having created arousal and preparedness for learning, having constellated personal complexes associated with authority, adventure and relationships, not to help channel the psychic energies which such preparation represent in ways which 'make sense' – in other words, help the learning process rather than simply confuse and anger participants.

MAKING SENSE – BUILDING LINKS

Task and Process

All reputable providers of, and writers on, outdoor development agree that the activities alone cannot help managers develop. By raising the emotional stakes and getting managers to pull back those intellectual curtains, we achieve nothing but confusion; what managers may learn from the experience is left very much to chance unless we supplement the tasks we get them to perform with a review process.

The specific tasks which are built into an outdoor experience can some-times be seen as irrelevant – they are simply generators of behavioural data. In so far as one is using such unusual activities as canoeing, abseiling and rock-climbing, this may be the case: managers do not, during their managerial activities, get into canoes, abseil down things, or climb sheer rock faces, so becoming successful at activities within which these are critical success factors cannot be the source of any direct learning about managerial skills.

I want to leave discussion of task design, and whether by designing different kinds of tasks we can enhance the quality of learning gained from them, to Chapter 10. For the moment, it is simply important to recognise that, by undertaking a number of activities which involve problem-solving, some (apparent) risk, and so on, managers have been able to achieve a readiness to be guided through the learning implications of the activities; they have some data with which to work.

Reviewing Process

In Chapter 7 (building upon ideas from earlier chapters) we concluded that it was misleading to talk of people having 'pure' experiences. People approach experiences with a 'full set' of attitudes, values, expectations, and so on. They draw from what they see different kinds of inferences. In many respects, one could say that it is rare for two people to go through 'the same' experience, even where they stand shoulder to shoulder working on a task together. The task may be 'the same' from the point of view of the brief they are working to, but the experience, even the desired outcome (finishing, winning, finding out the best way, having fun, not falling off, being seen to be a good team player, being the leader, hiding my fear, making that chap fall over . . .) will look very different, depending upon where each manager is 'coming from'.

For the 'guide' in a rite of passage, there will be an enormous amount of 'motivating' material available – the myths, architecture and art, the social structure, language itself – which will help ensure that initiates can be guided along prescribed channels. Making sense within this kind of semantically rich and highly motivated cultural environment means most people being drawn, inexorably, to very similar conclusions. But doing the 'same' in a process review after an outdoor exercise is significantly more uncertain in terms of outcome. While the experience, the myths and so on of another culture will inevitably mean that initiates of a particular rite will all come to similar conclusions – 'I now have to take my responsible, adult place in society, find a wife, and plant my garden'- building rafts with half a dozen other managers does not point quite so clearly to what a manager should learn or do as a result of this experience.

Facilitators are also plagued by the uncertainties of our own culture. In other cultures, the lessons are clearly mapped out in the laws, the morality, the prescribed behaviours. But, whatever we may believe about good and bad management, facilitators as guides are not encouraged to review process with statements like 'So now you have learnt that you should always consult others before taking decisions,' pointing to, as 'proof', the relevant myths which tell that truth. Our role is built upon the relativism which Chapter 1 introduced.

This is not to say that any conclusions are as good as any others. The review process is about airing and sharing perceptions; an opportunity for managers to surface their assumptions, and to check them against the assumptions of others. This enables the 'shared' data to be used to explore and consider the key lessons which the experience will teach. There are no 'right' answers in behaviour, and there are no accuracies – we cannot 'prove' the validity of exactly this amount of time is right for planning before exactly that amount of time for execution. But we can become more adept at exploring every situation on its merits, how our personalities and complexes influence how we see things, what other people say and do in 'similar' situations, and so on. The review process is a social learning process where managers explore their subjective perceptions, views, conclusions, attitudes and values against the many other subjectivities of their colleagues and (to some extent) those of the facilitators.

The role of the outdoor activity itself in all this is complex. Theoretically, one 'ought to be able' to group managers together to explore their mutual subjectivities without getting them first of all to undertake some 'irrelevant' physical activity. Most practitioners would agree that, without the data generated by the outdoor activity, such explorations are significantly attenuated. The exercises provide data, a 'sense of mastery' (Conger 1993: 27–8) (but less so if the tasks are unsuccessful), an aroused state, and a greater activity within the kinds of archetype which can more or less consciously influence quite significantly managers' overarching values, drives and life stories.

This enables managers to be more receptive to 'making sense', to allowing links to be made, through metaphor and metonymy, between hitherto unconnected neuronal maps. It is at the review process that 'metaphorical connections' (Irvine and Wilson: 1994: 31) are made between the anxiety of hanging off a cliff face and facing organizational uncertainty, or that the risk taking of the task is seen as a metaphor for risk-taking in other areas of life (Conger 1993: 25–6). For some managers, the links will be made relatively easily; for others, the links may need to be 'motivated', for until the connections are made, the two will remain isolated from each other until the links are made overt.

By making the links, managers are more able to recognise (often with more than just their rational, conscious minds) the inner resources which they called upon in a task, and which will still be available to them in times of crisis in the office. What may have made these inner resources less accessible in the office than they were in the outdoors could be that very rationality which the arousal of the outdoor experience was able to push aside.

CONCLUSIONS – OUTDOOR DEVELOPMENT AS A VEHICLE FOR LEARNING

In this chapter I have attempted to explore outdoor development from the point of view of principle, not of practice. What I wanted to find out was what kind of things may be going on during such an event, and the degree to which they could comprise an effective vehicle for learning.

On balance, I believe that the exercise has demonstrated that, in principle, this kind of activity can provide an excellent vehicle for learning to take place. This is not to say that using the outdoors will produce effective learning. Sceptics may, for example, see the review process as the opportunity to brainwash sensitised managers. Having taken them through a rough experience and broken down their defences (the very intellects which heightened stress make less accessible), trainers can now make managers believe any old rubbish they choose. And some providers of outdoor development may create havoc with people's minds and self-esteem with no visible return on the investment in terms of learning which can be used to good effect.

This chapter has not been about good or bad development; it has been an investigation into the kinds of ways in which the learning processes described in Chapter 7 may manifest themselves in outdoor development. From it I conclude that outdoor development provides a powerful vehicle for learning. But like any vehicle, it is dangerous; those who would drive it need to be well trained and experienced.

In our experience, one of the most crucial factors in making outdoor development effective and successful is the quality of the facilitators and tutors. The other critical factor is good learning design which is explored in Chapter 10.

9 Personality Types

INTRODUCTION

One of the key learning points for us over the years has been the influence of personality on learning. In the next chapter, we shall explore how we incorporate personality factors into learning design. In this chapter, we introduce a language for talking about personality. There are many such languages; this is one which many of my colleagues find most useful.

Managerial learning is not simply about the intellect. Moreover, the intellect cannot function effectively without input from those other parts of our minds which we have written about in Chapter 7. The more that organisations challenge the paradigms of the past, the more they create cultural climates in which broader kinds of learning can take place, the more management and organisation development will be able to make positive and lasting contributions. This is because management and organisation development, properly delivered, is about more than rationality and the intellect; it is about helping integrate the various aspects of brain and behaviour for effective learning and change to take place.

An Organiser for our Ideas

The major thrust of Chapter 7 was about exploring a number of the key factors I have taken to be influential in how managers learn, factors which management and organisation development professionals need to be conscious of if they are to do their jobs properly. But what has been missing so far has been any way of organising these disparate ideas into a framework with which we can hold on to them. It would be quite easy to create such a framework from scratch; fortunately, I do not have to, since much of what we have written about in this chapter was so well anticipated by Jung that we can, once again, borrow from his fertile output.

I shall use the Jungian-based Myers-Briggs Type Indicator (MBTI)® as an organising framework, not because it is the only model which is available, but because of its clear links to the findings of recent years into brain, mind and behaviour, and because it is accessible and makes sense to managers. It also has significant parallels in the works of non-Jungian writers. For example, Donaldson (1992) has developed a model of the 'unfolding' of human minds whose component parts are a very close match to the MBTI® model, although at no point in her book does she cite Jung or any other writer on the MBTI®.

Her conclusions seem to be so close not because she has been influenced by this other school of thought, but because she has come, independently, to very similar conclusions. This, in itself, lends further validity to the framework.

Based upon the earlier writings of Jung, the MBTI® was first developed by Katharine Briggs and Isobel Myers in the 1940s as a means of helping people find out more about themselves. They used Jung's notion of 'psychological type' (Jung 1968, Vol. 6) as the organiser of their own search for different 'types' of people. They stuck closely to Jung's theory, although they did add a few ideas of their own, especially in the area of how people plan and organise themselves, which Jung did not explore in depth. Since their initial work, the MBTI® has been extensively studied and used in the past 20 or 30 years by an increasing number of people. I shall not attempt to delve deeply into what has been researched within this framework; others have written very accessible and helpful books on the subject, including some highly practical works on the MBTI® and management (see especially Myers 1980; Keirsey and Bates 1978; Isachsen and Berens 1988). I suggest that readers unfamiliar with the MBTI® refer to one or more of these texts for deeper insights into the ways in which the terminology and approaches are used among managers, as I intend to put a management and organisation development 'spin' on the Jungian roots to the MBTI® which will not serve well as a 'primer' in the subject.

The 'Judging' Functions

Jung introduced us to the idea of mental functions. These came in two pairs, of which one pair, which he called 'thinking' and 'feeling' are the 'judging' functions. This is because, says Jung, they are used to make judgements, and to take decisions. 'Thinking' and 'Feeling' are often abbreviated to T and F respectively in the MBTI® literature, and I shall follow this convention.

There are very strong parallels between Jung's 'thinking' and the 'agonic' mode, the 'rational', the intellectual, the logical. For those who like the (largely spurious but still basically useful) idea that different functions reside in different parts of the brain, 'thinking' (T) 'resides' in the left hemisphere of the brain. There are similarly strong parallels between Jung's 'feeling' and the 'hedonic' mode. As Jung agreed, 'feeling' is not logical; when we use this function, we can be very comfortable with implicit contradiction. Where Jung did use a different approach was in his insistence that 'feeling' is 'rational'. He did so in defence of a function which, otherwise, may have been seen as less important. Jung at no time wanted to give the impression that any one of any pair of functions was 'better' than the other. Despite his good intentions, however, it is easy for people to fall into such evaluative traps.

In Chapter 7 we discussed the ways in which we acquire attitudes, mostly unconsciously, which colour and influence how we perceive things. Jung argued that one of the factors which may influence our attitude-forming itself may be an innate 'preference' for the use of one function over the other.

Preferences

For Jung, the notion 'preference' was analogous to handedness. Just as some of us are 'right-handed' and some 'left-handed', so some of us prefer 'thinking', while others prefer 'feeling'. Just as right-handers do not choose to be right-handers, so 'thinkers' do not chose to be so. Just as right-handers remain right-handers throughout their lives, so do 'thinkers'. Just as right- and left-handers learn to use both hands in harmony, so most of us learn to use both 'thinking' and 'feeling' in harmony. But just as right-handers trust and favour their right hands as the 'senior partner' of the pair, so, more or less consciously, each of us trusts and favours our preferred judging function.

Most of us go through life unaware of this internal bias. We do so because our preference seems so natural to us that we assume that everyone feels the same. We get bewildered by the differences between people, but we tend to dismiss these differences as 'failings' either on our part or on the part of others. It is not uncommon, for example, for 'thinkers' to suspect (more or less consciously) that those people they meet and interact with who are 'feelers' are 'less intelligent' – stupid, even. Similarly, it is not uncommon for 'feelers' to see thinkers as insensitive and callous. It is only when we delve more deeply into the notion of function and preference that we are able to uncover these (often unconsciously formed) biases and to manage them through learning. It will not surprise the reader to find that the vast majority of managers have a preference for thinking (Myers and McAuley 1985: 90). People with a preference for feeling tend more often to find other ways of satisfying their personal needs than management. With the current mood swings in organisational behaviour, this may be changing.

It may be important for such a change to take place. It is the 'feeling' function which is used to appreciate. With most organisations becoming increasingly aware of the need to appreciate and then to meet the needs of key stakeholders in their businesses, managers need to be able to harness their feeling functions. All managers can do this, even those with a preference for thinking. But there are psychological, cultural and motivational reasons why many 'thinking' managers will continue to struggle with making such appreciation a reality. Intellectually, any well-educated, experienced manager can understand stakeholder needs; but turning such understanding into effective behaviours may be very difficult, especially for managers with a clear preference for thinking, and who have, for reasons of motivation, help, or even recognition that there is a job to be done, failed to develop their feeling function.

Developing

We can learn how to develop our judging functions, both the function we prefer and that which we don't. Just as right-handers can learn to use their left hands effectively (as in playing the piano or typing, for example), so both 'feelers' and 'thinkers' can learn to become better both at thinking and feeling. The fact is that thinkers may have a harder time developing their feeling function than their thinking function (especially as education provides a great deal more help in developing thinking than it does with feeling), while feelers may have a harder time developing their thinking function (especially as they may feel disadvantaged by their undervalued strengths – appreciating people gets fewer brownie points at school than getting sums right; and boys with a preference for feeling soon learn how hard it is to get their thinking peers to value those skills as feelers are naturally better at developing).

We constantly continue to develop the use of our judging functions, although we may not always take an organised or deliberate approach to this. In Chapter 11, I shall return to the idea of self-development in more depth. For now, it is worth noting that managers are constantly expected to use both of their judging functions in harmony when taking decisions.

Deciding – with the Head or the Heart?

It is fairly common in the MBTI® writings to come across this idea of deciding with the head or with the heart. It is used as a means of illustrating the key difference between the ways in which we use our thinking and feeling functions: the thinking function drives us to decisions based upon our heads – logical, rational (in our sense, if not Jung's), intellectual, cool, objective, detached, uninvolved, impartial, and so on; the feeling function drives us to decisions based upon our hearts – value-based, emotional, appreciative of others, warm, subjective, involved, and very partial. The left brain is moving us to the 'logical' decision which is fair and reasonable; the right brain moving us to the decision which others will appreciate, which creates harmony, and which 'fits in with' what people want, or what we believe they want. To the thinker, 'feeling' decisions may appear biased, politically influenced, weak; to the feeler, 'thinking' decisions may appear harsh, insensitive and politically naive.

As we have argued earlier in the chapter, it is unlikely that the brain works in this divided way. There is a great deal of communication going on between the right and left brains, through the corpus callosum. When a manager is asked to judge whether an employee has been 'too liberal' with company resources, 'too revealing' in what he or she has said to the competition, 'too ambitious' in his or her career plans, and so on, neither of the judging functions alone can provide anything like a satisfactory answer. Logic alone cannot determine how much is 'too much' in any of these instances, unless each has been so completely circumscribed by rules and regulations that there is no 'decision' to take; merely matching one measure against another. But most managerial decision-making situations are not like this; that's why we need managers. But on the other hand, managers who simply say what they feel, with no regard for 'the rules' are unlikely to last long in management.

Our preferences (as well as our complexes, our experience, what we have learnt, and so on) will influence our decisions, in so far as it is most likely that thinking managers will place greater emphasis on the apparently logical elements of a decision. This will seem 'natural' to do. But it will not just be our preference for thinking or feeling which will provide such potential bias. Jung identified other aspects of our personalities in which innate preferences may influence how we approach managerial tasks such as decisions.

Sensing and Intuition

Jung identified another pair of functions as 'sensing' and 'intuition'. Like thinking and feeling, these are 'opposites' – a pair like left and right. They share many other aspects of the judging functions, especially in how our preference for one over another manifests itself, often unconsciously, and in the ways in which, in managerial life, we make use of both. Jung called 'sensing' and 'intuition' the 'perceiving functions', since he saw them as primarily concerned with what we pay attention to about the world; information which is the raw material of the decisions which the thinking and feeling functions help us to make. The abbreviations for these are S and N respectively, where N stands for intuition, rather than I, since, as we shall see below, I stands for introversion in Jung's scheme of things.

'Sensing' concerns itself with 'real data'. It is what gives us awareness of what is going on around us through our five senses. 'Intuition' provides us with the capabilities of the imagination (primarily metaphor and metonymy) which enable us to understand abstract concepts such as 'profit'. What Jung and those who use MBTI® call sensing and intuition, other writers call, for example, 'particularization' and 'categorization' (Sillince 1995), 'field-dependency' and 'field-independency' (Witkin 1976: 27), 'surface' and 'deep' processing and learning (Gibbs 1981), and so on.

It is simply another pair of concepts which we recognise in everyday life and in the worlds of management and academia. Profit and Loss accounts are more about sensing than they are about intuition: they are about reality, here and now, observable things (numbers on paper), and so on; twenty-year strategies are more about intuition than they are about sensing: they are about futures and possibilities, imagined rather than real situations, 'leaps of faith'. Some people have a preference for sensing: they tend to be practical people; others have preference for intuition: these tend to be imaginative people.

How we see the world is through a blend of the sensing and intuition functions. We see the evidence of our senses, and we 'jump to conclusions' about what we are seeing, both things and events (Tversky and Hemenway 1984). The less evidence we have upon which to base our inferences, the more we depend upon intuition to 'fill in the gaps'. Almost all learning demands a marriage between sensing and intuition. Effective learning capitalises upon the ways in which the 'facts', the data, are handled by the intuition – given 'meaning', even if that 'meaning' seems unrelated. Early mnemonic systems of the Greeks and mediaeval scholars capitalised upon this harmony, using multiple media to enrich their memorising; for example, they would imagine a walk through a familiar cloister, associating each familiar image with the next item on the list of things to be remembered, thereby linking the visual with the verbal (Yates 1969). Countless performance artists, such as Sherevski, 'the memory man' who used to make deliberate metaphorical connections between his senses (differently pitched sounds for different colours, for example) in order to enrich the remembered data (Luria 1968) have exploited the same multiple media reinforcement for learning lists, facts and other data.

Understanding, as well as memory, depends upon harmony between sensing and intuition: studies of children's comprehension of stories by Luria (1973) and Donaldson (1992) and others illustrate how much more children understand about parts of a story (sentences) when they are embedded in an ongoing story; while Bransford and Johnson (1972) have demonstrated how much more effective people are in understanding and following instructions if they know what the instructions are about. Our sensing function gives us the data, the sentences, the instructions; our intuition function deals with the 'about-ness', contextualising and enhancing the ways in which we can make use of those data.

Where people like Sherevski use their intuition primarily as a support function of their sensing to collect and remember vast amounts of data, others, such as chess grandmasters use their sensing as a support function to their preferred intuition. After only a five-second glance at any new configuration of pieces on a chessboard, grandmasters can remember every piece and every position (de Groot 1966). This is because what they primarily 'see' is a chess board as an organised whole; for them, the primary elements they remember are lines of strength and weakness, potential strategies for progressing, and not 32 individual pieces.

Researchers use sensing and intuition to develop their theories of the world, too. They may start by observing data (sensing) and wondering about patterns (intuition). They may develop a hypothesis (intuition) and then collect data to test the hypothesis (sensing). From the data they will draw conclusions – often in the form of a model or set of categories. Managers do much the same. When a company sets up a 'model' of the core competences it wants its managers to develop, they use sensing to identify all the possible ways of describing competences; they make the 'intuitive leap' – now there are 6, or 7 or 3, or 72. When managers pore over the production figures from several regions, and decide on a three-point marketing strategy, they, too, are making the 'intuitive leap'.

The 'intuitive leap' is commonplace. It is that shift from consideration of what is presented to us in hard data (sensing) to what it all means. It is often a 'eureka' moment (Stevens 1995: 132). It creates a new 'reality'; it is what, from now on (until the next intuitive leap in the same area) will 'make sense' of what we are doing. Until this moment there were just behaviours at random (Lewis 1993), sales returns; from this moment there are five core competences, three parts of a marketing strategy. It depends upon metaphor and imagination. It can create a high sense of 'reality' from very little. When it does so, it is not because it reflects 'reality' (that's what sensing does), but because it 'makes sense' of things. An intuitive leap is a piece of learning.

THE FOUR FUNCTIONS WORKING TOGETHER

The earlier parts of Chapter 7 set out to show how rare it is for us to be engaged in 'pure' thought; the 'street market' in our heads is a confusing blur of sensing, intuition, thinking and feeling. Clearly, we do occasionally 'go for it' in the sense that we try to focus all our mental energies on one function – usually thinking, if we are managers. Yet most of us 'cannot easily or ordinarily maintain uninterrupted attention on a single problem for more than a few tens of seconds. Yet we work on problems that require vastly more time' (Dennett 1991: 224–5). One reason for this is the 'limit on the number of factors that can be considered simultaneously in working memory' (Greene 1987: 146). Thinking is hard work, although some people have developed their thinking function so much that they seem to enjoy this kind of thing. The same can be done for the other functions.

In the normal run of events, in management, for example, we more or less consciously engage in wandering about from sensing to thinking, from feeling to sensing, and so on as we try to get to grips with the tasks of the day. Much of this wandering about is, as we have established earlier in the chapter, done unconsciously. And one of those things we do unconsciously (unless we train ourselves to focus and manage this phenomenon) is to 'favour' sensing over intuition (or vice versa), thinking over feeling (or vice versa), depending upon our innate preferences. This gives us four combinations of function preferences: sensing and thinking (ST); sensing and feeling (SF); intuition and feeling (NF); intuition and thinking (NT). These *pairs* of preferences will tend to influence the *individual* preferences; in other words, sensing and thinking together, for example, are prone to produce different kinds of behaviours and ways of thinking than sensing and feeling together.

The following 'caricatures' are not meant to be accurate representations of 'all' people who share these preference pairs. They are simple illustrations of a point – one which can have a powerful impact on how we and they approach management and organisation development. I shall briefly point to some managerial characteristics most closely associated with each function pair.

In each case of the function pairs, managers will tend to trust one pair more than the others, although they use all four functions in their working lives.

ST – Sensing and Thinking

Managers with this combination of preferences tend to trust their sensing and thinking more than their intuition and feeling. Their preferences for sensing and thinking tend to make them practical, down-to-earth managers.

Their response to the kinds of thinking and behaving which are characterised by the intuition and feeling functions is often of the kind: 'Of course you have to have a vision, but, in the end, business is about making profit, and this means getting the details right'; or 'Of course you have to avoid hurting people, you have to get them to 'buy in', but letting everyone have their own way would be just chaos.' In other words, they are fully conscious of the importance of these kinds of factors and approaches, but they trust them far less than the factors and approaches which align with their preferences.

SF – Sensing and Feeling

Managers with this combination of preferences tend to trust their sensing and feeling more than their intuition and thinking.

Their response to the kinds of thinking and behaving which are characterised by the intuition and thinking functions is often of the kind: 'Of course you have to have a vision, but, in the end, business is about people and what makes them tick. Visions only make sense if they can be lived on a day-to-day basis by everyone in the organisation'; or 'Of course some people may get hurt when hard decisions are taken, but you have to recognise that everyone needs to be brought along in their own individual ways.' In other words, they are fully conscious of the importance of these kinds of factors and approaches, but they trust them far less than the factors and approaches which align with their preferences.

NF – Intuition and Feeling

Managers with this combination of preferences tend to trust their intuition and feeling more than their sensing and thinking.

Their response to the kinds of thinking and behaving which are characterised by the sensing and thinking functions is often of the kind: 'Of course you have to make a profit, but you'll only stay in business if you care about all the key stakeholders, and not just the shareholder'; or 'Of course you have to compete to survive, but this does not mean there is no room for a collaborative style with our partners and customers – even with our competitors in some cases.' In other words, they are fully conscious of the importance of these kinds of factors and approaches, but they trust them far less than the factors and approaches which align with their preferences.

NT – Intuition and Thinking

Managers with this combination of preferences tend to trust their intuition and thinking more than their sensing and feeling.

Their response to the kinds of thinking and behaving which are characterised by the sensing and feeling functions is often of the kind: 'Of course you have to be able to implement new ideas and strategies, but this should not be used to constrain your thinking about the future'; or 'Of course you have to ensure 'buy in', but this should not mean dragging our feet, waiting for everyone to understand, while the competition wipes the floor with us.' In other words, they are fully conscious of the importance of these kinds of factors and approaches, but they trust them far less than the factors and approaches which align with their preferences.

In the chapter on learning design, I shall revisit this set of four preference pairs as a key factor in designing for learning; and later in this chapter (pp. 261–6), I shall provide a case study which illustrates the potential power of preferences to influence the course of events in a multibillion dollar international organisation. Before coming to that case, however, it is important to finish the job of introducing the other key elements in Jung's theory of psychological type.

Extraversion and Introversion (E & I)

The popular uses of the terms extraversion and introversion tend to focus upon a limited aspect of these two 'attitudes', as Jung referred to them. Like the function pairs, each of us has an extraverted and an introverted aspect to our personalities. The extraverted aspect or attitude is manifested when we are dealing with the outside world of other people and of things 'out there'.

Language, for example, is an extraverted phenomenon; even though we 'talk to ourselves', we do so both 'as though' there were someone else there, and using a socially constructed vehicle – a language. As Wittgenstein taught us, there can be no such thing as a 'private language'.

The introverted attitude is taken when we 'switch off' our focus on the outside world, and reflect, ruminate, meditate, 'think to ourselves'. The fact that many of us in our western culture use language to do much of this should not deflect us from recognising the potential for non-linguistic reflection. Introverting allows us to take a greater degree of interest in what's going on in the 'street market' in our heads. Sometimes we introvert through our thinking function: here we are trying to work things out in our heads, find answers, and so on; sometimes we introvert through our feeling function: here we may be 'getting in touch with our feelings' about something (a process which many 'thinking' people – especially male managers – find excruciatingly hard; in consequence they often dismiss it as pointless); we can introvert through our intuition function: here we may be 'letting our imagination wander'; and we can introvert through our sensing function: here we may luxuriate in recalling events which have given us a great deal of aesthetic, sensuous or sensual pleasure, and so on.

Similarly, when we extravert, we may do so 'through' one of our functions: we may enjoy the moment (sensing); share a dream or vision of the future (intuition); explain why something has to be (thinking); or share our commitment to a deeply held belief or value (feeling). Which of these things we feel most at home with depends to some extent upon our preference for extraversion or introversion. Like the functions, we are 'extravert-handed' or 'introvert-handed'; in other words, we feel more at ease in one attitude than the other, even though, clearly, and on a daily basis, we use both attitudes.

In MBTI terms, therefore, we can broaden the number of potential combinations of preferences by distinguishing between an extraverted ST (EST) and an introverted ST (IST). Clearly, these will produce quite different kinds of behaviours.

J and P

Jung suggested that these three pairs S&N, T&F, and E&I provide the available set of 'psychological types'. However, he did add that, of the four functions, each of us has a 'dominant'; that, for example, some ST people would find that their sensing is the most significant, powerful driver; others that their thinking takes that role. Katharine Briggs and Isobel Myers elaborated this idea into a fourth pair. Based upon whether our 'dominant' function is one of the 'perceiving' pair or one of the 'judging' pair, this influences us in our preference for J or P. (How this works differs for extraverts and introverts.)

J and P are 'orientations'. Briefly, the J orientation is associated with planning, organisation, order, decisiveness, deliberation, consistency, and so on. It is that part of us which enables us to take control. The P orientation is associated with curiosity, openness, exploration, letting go, seeing what happens. Clearly, as with the other pairs, it is hard to be in both orientations at the same time: if you are planning you are not waiting to see; if you are controlling, you are not letting go. But in daily life there are some circumstances where we use our J and some where we use our P. Preferences manifest themselves in how 'natural' and comfortable we feel about these behaviours. Many J managers, for example, are so overworked that they cannot plan, be in control, and have a tidy desk; but if they had more time they would love to take control of the chaos they have to live under; managers with a preference for P would normally find other ways of using any spare time than tidying, sorting, and regaining control.

Home Base

The four pairs of MBTI®, in combination, give us 16 'Home Bases'. By Home Base, I mean the unique combination of letters, such as ESTJ, INFP, and so on which map an individual's preferences. Because MBTI® is about preferences and not traits, Home Base is not a pigeon-hole. Traits are more like skills or attributes, having more or less of which can be construed as good or bad. Preferences are neutral: neither good nor bad; neither strong nor weak.

The fact that someone may have preferences for ENFP does not mean that he or she cannot or does not use his or her I, S, T and J relatively regularly and frequently in daily life. What it does say, however, is that, at such times, he or she is 'using his or her psychological wrong hands'. I am right-handed; when I use my left hand to do something I am conscious that I am performing less well than I would be if I used my right hand. Similarly, when I am using parts of my personality which are not preferences I am similarly conscious that I am in danger of underperforming – especially when compared to people who prefer these respective parts of their personalities.

Home Base feels natural. When we are using all four of our preferences in harmony, we feel at home. This leads most of us, more or less consciously, to assume (until we learn differently) that this is the natural way, rather than that this is what feels natural to us as individuals. Genuine personal growth and development has a lot to do with coming to terms with the benefits and potential pitfalls of working both within and outside one's Home Base.

Different 'Ideal' Managers

Borrowing from the notion of the 'ideal' (see above, p. 194), it is possible to identify the different ways in which people with different Home Bases may draw up different pictures of the 'ideal' manager. Some will stress the outgoing decisiveness, toughness, objective, down-to-earth qualities of the ESTJ 'ideal'. Others may focus more on the calm reflectiveness, caring and openness of the INFP 'ideal'. Clearly, it will not always be the case that the 'ideal' will be a direct reflection of that individual's 'type'. The influences of archetypes, of personal experience, of teaching, and so on will have a role to play. But one of the major influences of one's preferences is that behaviours which call upon the operation of one's preferred set (one's Home Base) will somehow 'feel' right. This 'feel' will act as a significant filter to experience, and is likely to produce the kinds of 'editing' of experience which we explored in Chapter 7.

'IDEALS' GET EMBEDDED IN ORGANISATIONAL CULTURES

One of the most powerful ways in which this 'feeling' that a particular approach is 'right' can be reinforced is within an organisational culture. Where organisations take on the kinds of rules, roles, habits, styles and behaviours which align closely with an individual's Home Base, that individual is more likely to feel at home within that organisation. The more the organisation attracts 'like minded' people, the more it will be believed that what individuals and the organisation are doing are not just a matter of choice, but are somehow 'the right or only way' to run an organisation.

In Chapter 1 I talked of social construction being somehow a matter of choice, or arbitrary. Clearly, few people feel this arbitrariness about the ways in which things are done in business. Most feel much more comfortable with the idea that, of the available choices, one is clearly better than another. One of the influences on this, we suggest, is psychological type. It makes radical organisational change that much harder to implement.

The best way to illustrate this point is by reference to a case which happened in one of our client's organisations, Global Technologies, who we have written about in earlier chapters.

THE FRUSTRATED VISIONARY

Introduction

In spring 1993, Global Technologies appointed a new CEO, who appeared to be intent on making sweeping and radical changes within the company worldwide. At Christmas 1994 the new CEO issued a statement tendering his resignation from the company. The intervening period had been turbulent and challenging for many people within the organisation. The CEO had tried to change the culture. Most people agree that he failed to do so, and left from sheer frustration. After he left, it was back to 'business as usual', except that they had to work twice as hard as before to 'repair the damage'.

Psychological type in Global Technologies

Global Technologies had been sending sufficient numbers of their managers to us over the years for us to be able to start developing a 'company profile'. In other words, we were able to check out the Home Base of every participant on our programmes. We were also able, through our increasing familiarity with Global Technologies, to draw some conclusions about the 'organisational culture', using MBTI as a cultural framework. In other words, we could ascribe to the organisation as a whole a 'Home Base'.

Ascribing a Home Base to an organisation may appear to be sloppy science. Clearly it is, in one sense, 'sloppy science'. If an organisation does not exist, as we have argued, then it is strange to ascribe to it some kind of 'personality'. So why do it?

Like most tools we use, we see MBTI as having far more value as a heuristic device than as an attempt to 'explain reality'. Managers from Global Technologies, like everyone else in daily life, are bombarded with huge amounts of data: people say things to them, they read things on paper and screens, and so on. They want to make sense of all these data. They do so through their intuition. Intuition works with models, with metaphor and metonymy. Rather than having to make new intuitive leaps every day, people share metaphors and models. Profits do not 'go up or down' in 'reality'; but by talking as if they do, people feel they know what to do with the data they receive about 'profits'. Organisations do not have psychological types; but by talking as though they do, we may help people make sense of what is going on around them. In this case, we believe that the heuristic device of MBTI, acting as a metaphor, a model, helps us and others explain what happened during a few extraordinary months in Global Technologies.

The indigenous 'culture' of Global Technologies was, we believe, ISTJ. At the very least, we could gain high levels of agreement that, of the function pairs, S and T were traditionally 'preferred'. It was, therefore, an ST organisation. Here's one brief summary of what that might look like (Hirsh 1991):

Emphasise	❏ Specific, factual details
	❏ Micro issues
	❏ Physical features of the work environment
	❏ Control, certainty, job specificity
	❏ Work and work roles first, then the worker
	❏ Organizational goals and hierarchy
Value	❏ People who responsibly complete their work on schedule
Set goals that are:	❏ Realistic
	❏ Down-to-earth
	❏ Financial

As a broad picture of what was seen to be important in the company, this seemed to make sense to most people we talked to.

The New CEO and his Vision

The new CEO wanted to change all this. He argued that, in the late 1990s, competitive edge would no longer come from technology, but that relationships were going to be the key: relationships with customers, partners, suppliers, and so on. In much of what he was saying about the business imperatives, he was repeating the driving forces for the programmes we were delivering to the Europeans within the company (see Chapter 5, pp. 162–5). However, what he wanted to add to the change process was a set of cultural changes which would turn fine words into appropriate behaviours, a point we echo in Chapter 10.

For the new CEO, a culture which was 'too focused' on details, 'too concerned' with micro issues, 'too much into' control, certainty and job specificity, 'too obsessed' with its own goals and hierarchy would never nurture the kinds of empathetic, exploratory, innovative behaviours which effective relationship management depends upon. For him, sales people who were rewarded for selling technology (not genuine solutions), managers who were punished for not accounting for every dollar of expenditure on travel, and executives who were more concerned with their own careers than with establishing lasting relationships with customers, and collaborative partners, would never bring about the kinds of environment in which the espoused strategy of customer focus would materialise. He introduced radical structural and programme changes.

At a structural level, he introduced the notion of a customer focused business model. Out went the functional hierarchy, in came integrated customer focused teams which were to be given the financial (they had their own P&L), technical and human resources to deliver integrated solutions to customers, without being dependent upon any other department or function within the company. Out went the Quarterly Review, in which Directors, region by region were traditionally 'ritually humiliated' by HQ bosses over their numbers. (I was told early in the relationship with Global Technologies not to bother trying to arrange an appointment with a Director during the month leading up to Quarterly Review, since this entire time was devoted exclusively to preparing their presentations for the review). Out went Directors and Managers, in came Coaches. Out went employees, in came Associates. Out went job descriptions, in came a set of values which were taught and explored in depth through a series of workshops world-wide over the next few months.

The direction of the change can be neatly summarised in the following contrasting set of notes on the NF organisation (Hirsh 1991):

Emphasise
- ❏ Growth
- ❏ Macro issues
- ❏ Personal and human goals of the organization
- ❏ Products/processes that serve society's needs
- ❏ Flexibility
- ❏ Change

Value
- ❏ People who work together for the good of all

Set goals that are: ❏ Humanistic
                       ❏ Innovative
                       ❏ Insightful

The new CEO never used the language of MBTI, nor came up with these comparative lists. Our comfort with using them to characterise the shifts in emphasis comes from sharing them with hundreds of employees of the company, who largely agreed that they paint as true a picture as they have seen of the situation.

Reactions to the CEO's Vision

Reactions to the new CEO and his vision and style were mixed, as you would expect. But, after the initial euphoria of fresh ideas had worn off, the vision came up against the 'party line'. We believe that this party line was to some extent a feature of the distribution of preferences among the population within the company.

Whether our database of people's preferences reflected the distribution across the company as a whole we cannot say. As a sample, it suffered from the same kinds of shortcomings of most samples. But what it did suggest has some face validity.

Of those whose type we had records of (sample size of 396 at the time), there were:

ST   49.5%
SF   3.8%
NF   7.6%
NT   39.2%

In other words, virtually half the population both had their Home Base in the kind of organisation Global had traditionally been; and had no preference in common with the NF approach of the new CEO. Only 7.6% of the population shared the preferences which aligned with the CEO's approach. In itself, this does not necessarily cause a problem. People can live happily within an organisational culture which is different from their personal preferences; we are capable of learning and adjusting. But to do so, we have to be able to believe in what we are learning about the future. This demands learning about the future in ways which make sense to us within our Home Base. In other words, the new CEO had to convince not the 7.6% of people with NF preferences, but, most importantly, the significant majority of ST people who may have had a problem or two with the past, but who needed to be sure about the future before burning their boats. Apart from anything else, ST people tend to be relatively sceptical about radical change anyway. They learn from experience, not from grand visions.

Therefore, when we talked to the ST people in the company at the time, most of them said that they were waiting for the evidence to prove that the new CEO's vision had substance. They wanted examples of organizations which had successfully trodden this particular visionary path. They wanted clear guidelines on what, precisely, they were expected to do, not broad homilies such as 'Be role models for teamwork', 'Let conversation grow', and 'Treat all our Associates with dignity'. When the ST manager was told 'Embrace and execute change – with a sense of urgency,' and to have 'total trust in everything we say and do', he wanted to know what this meant in terms of how he was to change the way he went about clearing his in-tray on a cold, wet Monday morning; how he was to alter the way in which he was to deal with an irate customer who was refusing to pay his maintenance charges this quarter; and how he should now go about explaining to staff that, although he is no longer a 'manager', he is nevertheless 'empowered' to 'downsize' by three heads within the next three months.

The new CEO failed to provide any specific answers to these kinds of questions. Perhaps he felt that to do so would be to replicate the culture of the past. He certainly seemed bent on changing the perceived infallibility of the CEO, as one of his earliest pronouncements on change, issued within weeks of taking office ended with the line 'How this will all work I haven't the foggiest idea,' which was certainly a radical departure from previous CEO styles based upon certainty and strength. Whatever his motivation, the majority of the ST managers we spoke to throughout his term of office expressed deep (and, as time went on, growing) scepticism. What was happening was that the new CEO, rather than answer the doubts, seemed to grow yet more vociferous. Like a foreigner in a strange land who does not speak the language, he began to shout; he did not learn the ST language.

Towards the end of his tenure, the new CEO started to issue veiled threats, interpreted by some managers as 'You will be empowered or else.' Other statements suggested that people who were not in tune with the new way were very welcome to find employment elsewhere. Some left; most waited for what they saw as the inevitable. You cannot run a business like this, they argued. In the USA, this became painfully true, as the newly empowered customer-focused teams haemorrhaged money, spent unwisely, built long-term strategies and failed to bring in revenue. Just as the new CEO did not understand the local language, so the new team members misunderstood the NF language. To them it meant throwing away the rule book, doing whatever felt good, and being nice to everyone. To managers whose Home Base is NF, this is a gross caricature of their approach to business, as it was to the new CEO. But to the ST manager, these extremes of new behaviour were a reasonable interpretation of the messages he was giving.

After he Went . . .

Soon after the new CEO left, the guardians of the old order reasserted their dominance. Events had proven them right. The new CEO had some nice ideas, but he completely missed the realities of running a business. Now they had damage to repair. They had lost a great deal of money. Cost cutting, control, and paying attention to the details were once again the order of the day; but now, they were even more rigorously enforced. They had a crisis on their hands. As the next CEO to take over said, 'Let's not talk about strategy. Let's get on with the business and create a sense of urgency around here.'

> As we argued in Chapter 1, there is no one 'right way'. But is does appear that people's psychological preferences tend to make some ways seem more right to them than others. When most people in an organisation tend to view the 'right way' in one direction, while the CEO looks in another, that CEO has to recognise that convincing employees to embrace change has to be done in their language, not his. I suspect that the CEO of Global Technologies had closed his mind to the language of ST. Whether he was 'right' to do so is not the issue; what happened did so because he failed to speak ST: to communicate effectively with people with preferences dissimilar to his own.

APPLYING THE LEARNING TO MANAGEMENT AND ORGANISATION DEVELOPMENT INTERVENTIONS

The case study not only illustrates a challenge for practising managers. It also sends messages to management and organisation development specialists. This is because, just like the CEO in the case, we are in the business of communicating and leading through change. Ironically, there are many in the management and organisation development business who appear to have no greater insights into the implications for learning of these kinds of lessons than the CEO in the case did.

Our own experience has been enhanced by reflections on situations in which we may have overlooked some of the key messages ourselves. In one instance, Tech-Test (see Appendix), we may have missed an important point, although, to be fair, they did not have access to the profiles of the participants until the final module. This may, in hindsight, have been a flaw in the programme design.

Unexpectedly, the modal type of the participants was ISFJ. More than half the management team had preferences for Sensing and Feeling. Interestingly, the Chief Executive, Michael Pope reported as an ESTJ – a dominant extraverted thinker. This may help to explain his frustration with, and possible lack of understanding of, the indigenous corporate culture of Tech-Test, which was heavily influenced by this overwhelming 'SF' approach to life. For the SF majority, the downsizing exercises, for example, created enormous stress and concern. SF organisations tend to be stable, people-oriented, caring, and highly personal. They avoid change and are not renowned for long-term strategic thinking.

By contrast every member of the tutorial team had preferences for iNtuition and Thinking. For them, models, strategies, broad, impersonal generalisations come easily. To the majority of the Tech-Test managers the novelty of what they were taught by these NT 'intellectuals' represented a vastly different way of thinking about business and organisations. It was exciting, it made sense, and it had to be the answer to their problems – or so it seemed at the time.

But bringing this kind of thinking to bear, long-term, in a culture steeped in SF ways may have been far too tall an order. It would have been difficult enough had it been recognised, and built into the learning design and activities. It appears, however, that it was only during the follow-up research activities that the point was raised – there was a major contrast in styles between the tutors and the participants; and this was bound to have an impact on the long-term effectiveness of the programme.

The euphoria of the programme itself, sustained by the clarity of presentation of the tutors, needed significantly more nurturing than was provided. Left to their own devices, and trying to adopt NT ways of thinking and acting, the largely SF managers lost their way. Among the things which people said in our small group discussions were, 'It is almost as though the programme never happened. Was it a dream?' and 'I don't see any changes that have occurred here. I'm not sure what we expected to occur, but nothing much has changed. It's difficult because I can't remember a lot of what we did because we didn't actually implement much'.

As a final observation on the role of type in the Tech-Test story, the 2 most active managers in their search for some meaning from the experience – the 2 managers who came to us to ask for help in exploring why things did not work out the way they had hoped, both had preferences for N and F.

In Chapter 10, I explore some of the design implications which we have drawn from the lessons not only of the MBTI, but also from the research described in Chapter 7, and from thoroughly reviewing the learning implications of outdoors development, as described in Chapter 8.

10 Designing for Learning

INTRODUCTION

As with almost any endeavour, managerial learning is susceptible to being attempted in an almost infinite number of ways. We can send managers off to the Lakes to build rope bridges over gorges; we can sit them in a darkened lecture theatre and lecture to them; we can give them case studies to dissect and analyse; we can get them to do mind-body exercises on the front lawn; the list is almost endless. It is also growing, as more and more management and organisation development providers try to establish their own Unique Selling Propositions, introducing the all-new wonder management development solution.

In the past, I believe a great deal of the 'justification' for the kinds of management and organisation development providers have provided has been post hoc. Methods have evolved, been enhanced and added to, modified in the light of experience and new ideas brought in by new members of staff, and so on. When I ask management and organisation development people from various organisations why they do management and organisation development the way they do, the most common answer I get is of the 'We have tried lots of ways, and have found that this is the most effective' kind, usually followed quickly by something like 'and we get very good feedback from our managers'.

This is not to be wondered at; few organisations throw away their entire product range and start again from scratch, including those in the management and organisation development business. But it is important, I believe, not to get carried away with the 'paradigm effect' on one's own organisation and product set. This is one reason why I am writing this book: to ensure that we keep reminding ourselves of the principles upon which we operate, and to try to avoid sticking to a formula because it worked in the past.

This exploration of learning design is, therefore, both a historical record of things we have done, interventions we have designed; and a review of how what we know about learning informs the decisions we take about the designs we offer to out clients.

WHERE DOES LEARNING TAKE PLACE?

If we take the broad set of meanings of 'learning' which associate with internal processes, learning takes place wherever a manager happens to be. That learning will be the more intense and conscious, the more 'aroused' to learning he or she is at any one time. Given how busy most managers are today, the chances of such arousal for learning are relatively low, unless something radical is done to interrupt the flow of everyday activities, and the manager can have time and space (along with help from a facilitator, such as a coach for example) to reflect and consolidate the learning.

On the other hand, if we take the broad set of meanings of 'learning' which associate with behaviour, then learning cannot be said to have taken place until the manager changes behaviour at work.

In the context of the first set of meanings, it is reasonable to see the value of managers taking time out to pay attention to learning; in the context of the second set of meanings, it is plausible that attempting to learn 'off the job' is a waste of effort, since it will only make sense on the job.

On-the-Job or Away from Work?

There are writers who are increasingly arguing for management and organisation development to be located almost exclusively within the workplace, that all good management and organisation development takes place on the job. Citing his and Honey's 'own' version of Kolb's learning cycle as evidence, for example, Mumford (1993: 35) claims that there are three kinds of management development:

1. informal managerial accidental
2. integrated managerial opportunistic
3. formal management development planned

and that only one of these 'goes round the whole cycle'.

Informal Managerial Accidental

The first kind, informal managerial accidental, refers to those unplanned, chance situations which happen all the time at work. They correspond to a 'continuous, but largely unconscious' kind of learning. Mumford suggests that these are not normally effective since they rarely incorporate the reflecting and theorising elements of the learning cycle; it's all 'trial and error', with little consolidated learning coming out of it. Chapter 7 agreed with this principle. In practice, it helps good learning if 'learning reviews' can be established. For an overt management and organisation development intervention, reviews may be designed in. To generate good learning from on-the-job experiences, it may help to set up 'Learning Workshops' which seek to redress this imbalance, as the following case illustrates.

LEARNING FROM EXPERIENCE – A LEARNING WORKSHOP

The Background

I had been working intermittently with a client in local government housing, helping them to prepare for Compulsory Competitive Tendering (CCT). They recognised that, to compete successfully with commercial organisations for the various housing management contracts that their Borough was required to put out to tender may require some management and organisation development on their part. I ran some events for them, and they 'got on with the job'.

The housing stock was to be tendered in a number of discrete contracts, put out in several phases. Phase 1 was a 'pilot'. By chance, no outside organisation actually put in a bid for Phase 1, so, with a great sense of relief, they started to prepare for Phase 2. I was still in contact with the managers of the organisations, so I asked them, severally, what they thought they had learnt from the experiences of Phase 1.

Phase 1 – the Pilot

Phase 1 had been fraught. The Borough had voluntarily gone for the pilot scheme, in advance of the government's formal timetable – in effect they had gone for 'VCT' (Voluntary Competitive Tendering). There may have been outside bidders, and those bidders may have won the contracts. Staff, in general, were furious with management for 'playing into the hands of government'. What made things worse for staff was the 'strategy' which management had adopted.

There was no way of knowing whether any other organisation was planning to bid. On the day the bids were submitted, the appointed manager from the Borough had two bids to submit: one was 'very competitive', the other was more or less 'carry on as usual'. The 'competitive' bid was based upon reducing costs by a small number of selected redundancies; the 'carry on as usual' was based upon a higher cost to the Client, but retained all current posts and grades. Clearly, staff and the Unions would favour the second bid.

As part of the strategy, management kept almost every item of pertinent information to themselves. They felt that information on staffing levels, costs, and so on of their own bid could be used against them by their prospective competitors. Therefore, it was only after the event that staff and the unions were aware that there had been two bids prepared. It was also after the event that they learnt that the 'competitive' bid had been submitted, despite there being no bid from another organisation. This 'must have been', according to

---

staff and the unions, either incompetence by management, or a conspiracy to use VCT, in the shabby disguise of CCT, to attack staffing levels, and thereby reduce costs.

The manager responsible for physically submitting the bid was on his own for the last, crucial, minutes. The deadline for bids was 12 noon, and when he turned up the plan was to wait until 11.59 to see if there was to be a bid from anyone else. If no bid had gone in by 11.59, he would submit the 'carry on as usual' bid; but if a stranger turned up with what looked like a bid package, he should submit the competitive bid. There was a fair amount of activity at the relevant office; a stranger did, indeed, appear with a package, which, to the Borough's appointed manager did look suspiciously like a rival bid. He hesitated, deliberated, became anxious and stressed. He submitted the competitive bid, just to be safe. He calculated that, if that stranger had submitted a bid, and that this bid would beat the internal 'carry on as usual' bid, then he would be out of a job, as would a number of his managerial colleagues. No-one would thank him. On the other hand, if there were no other bid, nearly everyone within the Department would keep their jobs. It seemed to him the best thing to do at the time.

Once the dust had settled, each and every manager I talked to had a different spin on what had happened. They had talked, of course. But this talking had been unstructured, impassioned at times (nothing wrong with this in principle), unrecorded, and often slanted so that it was the narrator who usually 'comes off best' (Bruner 1990: 95–6). It became clear to me that the managers were preparing to go into Phase 2 without any 'formalised' learning from the pilot; that they had not shared the reflection and theorising stages of Kolb's cycle. They accepted the idea that a 'Learning Workshop' would be a good idea.

The Learning Workshop

I ran the workshop on lines which have proven successful in the past. The aim was simple: to bring to the surface and agree what had been learnt from the pilot; then to ensure that this learning was taken on board for the preparation for Phase 2 of CCT. We set aside two days for the event: the first was the workshop itself. The workshop was attended by those managers who had been intimately involved with preparing for the pilot. There were eight in number.

The second phase was a 'conference' during which the agreed lessons were shared with a large cross-section of the managers within the department. The general conclusions were that the workshop and conference had been a huge learning experience, from which the department subsequently drew when faced with later phases of CCT.

Conclusions

In so far as the phrase 'learning organisation' means anything, this local authority housing department has become 'more of a learning organisation' than it was previously. Managers have recognised that there is more to learning from experience than just having an experience and 'learning' from it. The problem with a great deal of 'learning' which is not questioned and challenged is that it is can simply be another way of describing the inferences we have drawn, and which we have not properly checked. Managers in this organisation are now more inclined to go through this kind of checking process. This, in itself, has not 'transformed' the organisation; managers here still have a long way to go before they can confidently take on competition from the commercial sector; but they have moved forward significantly by adopting the 'it isn't learnt until it's questioned, challenged and agreed' approach.

'Political' Learning

One of the most significant arenas in which 'unchecked' learning (in other words, open, public, constructive debate about the inferences we draw) takes place is what is often called the 'political' arena. Organisational politics is a wonderful place for this to take place because it satisfies a number of the requirements for such 'unchecked' learning. Many of the bases upon which 'politics' are built are necessarily inferential: we believe that manager X is after manager Y's job; but he will not say so, since this would make Y aware of the threat; manager A openly supports manager B in meetings, but is 'actually' preparing a coup; there is no point in pursuing this or that kind of strategy – it would be politically unsound. Naive managers who ask for evidence in support of these political inferences are warned not to ask too many questions.

'Politics' have a great deal to do with values and attitudes, those elements of our minds which are so often inaccessible to our consciousness. Having a particular 'political' stance is a good illustration of the influence of such attitudes upon inferences. (Politicians are potentially excellent role models for this kind of 'skewed' interpretation, although the predictability of today's politicians' responses upon partisan lines makes them less believable; too often they seem to be 'trying to have an attitude', rather than allowing the 'genuine article' to surface. Hence, for many people, the apparent 'hypocrisy' of modern politicians.)

But it is this very inaccessibility and robustness of many of our driving values which seems to make it possible for otherwise rational people to be credulous of 'organisational politics' on the basis of very little evidence. 'Politics' thrives on unchecked and uncheckable inferences, creating, in the most extreme cases, an almost 'mystical' or religious aura: you must believe what you are told by those in the know; you must not (for 'political reasons') seek evidence to validate what you are told; and you must have faith in one side or the other. Cynics may suspect that if you wrap up almost any old rubbish in a 'political' context, then you can get away with it.

I first came to suspect this many years ago when I was employed as a salesman for a finance company. Our products were money; therefore, gains and losses of business had very little to do with relative product quality; we had to compete on service. Listening to and learning from my more experienced colleagues introduced me to the 'political decision'; sales were often lost 'for political reasons'. I learnt that this meant that there was nothing wrong with the product or service, nothing wrong with the offer, but that someone of importance in the customer's organisation favoured a competitor. There was nothing we mere salesmen could do about this, apart from nodding sagely when we heard the reason, and sipping together, in consolation, from our beer glasses. In my experience, no-one of this close-knit group of companions (some of whom worked for rival organisations, and who were prepared to 'trade' customers to cut down on wasted competitive effort) ever broke into this sombre moment, smiled broadly and broke the conspiracy by saying, 'That's a load of garbage isn't it; and don't we all know it?'

It may have been that they did this, but not in front of me. For that reason, I cannot be sure to what extent they believed themselves in their excuses. However, what I learnt stood me in good stead for a while, as I was not a very good salesman, and lost more deals than I should have done. I played the 'political decision' card quite a few times before I left. It was cynical, probably inexcusable, even in one so young.

What I learnt from this experience is that 'politics' is often used as a euphemism. A good example of this kind of use can be found in Currie (1994), where he concludes of a case of management development evaluation, 'the evaluation strategy outlined presented a practical, even opportunistic, response to a situation which was political' (op. cit. 25). By the term 'political' he summarises the differences in perceptions and authority of several of the stakeholders in the management and organisation development intervention he is setting out to provide and evaluate. My reading of the case is simply that it was necessary to adjust various aspects of the intervention, including the post-event evaluation, to meet the various needs of those stakeholders. This is commonplace in the provision of any product or service; I do not think that his conclusion, that 'the research emphasises that political considerations represent a constraint on rigorous evaluation strategies' (ibid.) tells us anything more than that it is dangerous to learning to use 'politics' as a cop-out.

For 'cop-out' it often is; simply another, highly available, form of reductionism. Reductionism is that kind of explanation, sometimes, and inexcusably used by academics, which takes the form 'What it is all about is . . .' followed by a simplistic rendering of a complex situation. Examples abound: learning 'is all about memory'; business 'is all about profit'; neuroses are 'all about sex'; evolution is 'all about genes'; and so on. Organisations, people, relationships, and so on are complex. We do not enhance our understanding by this kind of reductionism. We make matters worse when the reductionist approach leads us down pathways in which seeking evidence, checking inferences, and so on, are said to be inadvisable.

From a learning perspective, therefore, I would argue that explanations which set off down the cul-de-sac of 'politics' are going in the wrong direction. This is not to deny that there are factors which may influence 'politics'. But as in the case of Currie's management and organisation development intervention, I believe that re-presenting these factors in other terms, which are more open and available for inference checking and validation will help us avoid the often shabby, whispered, unfounded, prejudices which often comprise what goes for 'political astuteness'. One of the most constructive re-presentations of organisational politics is to be found in James and Baddeley (1987).

Experiencing is not Necessarily Learning

If 'learning' is to mean anything significant, it is not something which simply happens by chance. Even if 'people know when to speak and when to keep quiet, [and they] . . . understand how the communication and other social systems operate' (Jones and Hendry 1994: 157), they are likely to know these things considerably better if they have explored what they have 'learnt' with other people, and through a number of different perspectives. Managers are students of social science; like any social scientists, they would be well advised not to stay wedded to their first, and highly individual, probably unique, impressions. Their attitudes, their complexes, their unique neuronal maps are personal. For their learning to be practical and useful, these personal inferences need to be checked.

Towards the end of Chapter 7 we came across the possibility that a manager could say that, from a workshop designed to enhance collaborative behaviours, he or she had learnt never to trust anyone. Good learning design and facilitation would make such outcomes unlikely. But unplanned experience, especially where there is a 'political climate' which appears to encourage the development of attitudes which cannot be expressed openly can and often does produce 'learning' such as

❑ women are too emotional to be good managers
❑ Germans are all bullies at heart
❑ all my staff think I'm a great manager
❑ my boss doesn't understand the business
❑ people will only work harder if they are paid more
❑ there's no need to prove my point, because I know I'm right

Until such attitudes are surfaced and challenged, they are just 'opinions'. If they are voiced, they may become 'prejudices'. Rarely will be they graced with the epithet 'learning'. But this has nothing to do with 'learning cycles'. People who say such things may very well have had many experiences involving women, Germans, their staff, their boss, and so on. On those experiences they may have reflected and reviewed, and do seem to have drawn some theoretical conclusions. They may also have 'tested' their theories, and found them to be validated every time. As Chapter 8 explored, it is all too easy for our inferences – how we see and would characterise situations – to be a direct product of our underlying beliefs and values, about ourselves and others, as Peter Walpole (see the case study on pp. 221–2, Chapter 7) found out the hard way.

The learning cycle can therefore be replayed as the self-fulfilling prophecy cycle. If we accept the meaning of learning that it is any perception, attitude, prejudice, and so on, which someone can say they have developed from experience, thought about, drawn conclusions about and 'tested against' the further evidence of their senses, then, in that sense, it remains a learning cycle. On the other hand, if we want to narrow the meaning of 'learning' to eliminate the kind of prejudices we listed above, then we have to add the social element: effective learning has to be 'socially constructed'.

This means that it only becomes good learning when it has been thoroughly reviewed, debated, thrashed out, openly aired. None of these will guarantee a 'right' answer. Social constructions can never be proven 'absolutely'; but the better the debate, the more the 'learning' is challenged by alternative views and holds its own, the more it makes sense to people who are deemed to have the right to judge on such matters, then the more it becomes 'learning' rather than 'opinion' or 'prejudice'. This raises challenges for those who would seek to introduce 'new' learning, new ideas, new opinions, and so on, which is often the role of the management and organisation development provider. This is a point I shall pick up shortly.

Integrated Managerial Opportunistic

Mumford's preference is clearly for this, second, option, a preference he shares with colleagues at the International Management Centres (see, for example, Wills 1993; Mumford 1980; Margerison 1980). It comprises facilitated learning on the job, and is, he argues, the only kind of management development which takes managers completely round the learning cycle.

There is clearly a great deal to be said for learning on the job. The Japanese organisational 'miracle' happened without much help from management schools; and there are large and increasing numbers of instances of organisations creating 'learning cultures' in which managers can develop without recourse to the classroom.

This makes a great deal of sense. If it is on the job that managers add value, it should also be on the job that they learn. One of the obvious benefits from this is that managers remain within the 'learning context', thereby being able to better remember what they have learnt. Organisations provide rich environments for 'extended memories' of the kind which are often used by those with poor internal memories and old people (Baddeley 1992: 21). So dependent for their memories can some old people become upon their familiar environment, that 'taking them out of their homes is literally separating them from large parts of their minds – potentially just as devastating a development as undergoing brain surgery' (Dennett 1996: 139).

It is quite probable that managers do take quite a few of their cues from the 'organisational memory' (Walsh and Ungson 1991) which is embodied within the very fabric of the workplace. No matter how good off the job learning may be, there is always the extra challenge of integrating such learning into the 'real world'.

Designing 'Reality' into Learning

It is often this concept of 'the real world' or 'reality' which is held up as the yardstick against which to measure the value of any management and organisation development activity. The more one moves away from reality, the less value there can be in any supposed 'learning' event, since, no matter how well managers do in the 'sparring ring' of a School of Management, if it isn't real, it won't help. This has often been one of the biggest barriers to the acceptability of outdoor development (Wagner and Campbell 1994).

The argument is that the closer to 'reality' the learning experience, the better that learning experience. The 'best' learning experience is, therefore, that which takes place there and then, on the job, as it happens, in the real world. The learning from that experience is enhanced if it is anticipated (the opportunity for learning is planned), and is consolidated by review and theorising after the event. This enables managers clearly to articulate an answer to the question, what have I learnt from this experience? The more 'natural' we can make a learning experience, the better it will be for the managerial learner (French 1981; Lippitt 1983; Stuart 1983).

Reality and Imagination

It is very tempting to get carried away with the idea of 'reality' as though it were a given. But 'reality' is not a simple given. The 'realities' within which managers work are socially constructed, complex and manifold. Getting alongside managers in their work environment and encouraging them to learn from what they are experiencing is to participate in 're-creations' of the 'realities' in which they work, not just to help them to see better the one reality which all can see (but which is better seen by better developed people, presumably).

Every step away from perceived 'reality' is one which calls upon the learner to make a greater effort to 'see the links', in his or her terms. In Chapter 7, I referred to the notion of metaphor as providing such links – that, through the review process, metaphorical connections are made between, for example, the anxiety of hanging off a cliff face and facing organizational uncertainty. In Chapter 7, we suggested that metaphor and metonymy imbue virtually every aspect of the 'realities' which are socially constructed by managers within organisations. In Chapter 9, we also talked of the 'intuitive leap' a process which enables us to generalise from specific instances, often from limited data. Even if we were to follow the strictest of regimes to provide managers with on-the-job, 'real' learning, we should find ourselves using metaphor and/ or metonymy in our review process, and asking the learner to make intuitive leaps.

This is because managerial learning (as opposed to learning lists, motor skills, and so on) involves generalising from the particular. Setting a manager a task at work, and then asking the question, 'What have you learnt from this?' is asking for the kind of answer, 'That I should be more assertive; that I should be prepared to make my point and stick to it'; 'That I should listen to people carefully before moving on'; 'That product launches are best done after a controlled pilot'; and so on. In these answers, 'make my point and stick to it' stands, metonymically, for the intention to be more assertive in the future; 'that I should listen' is an intuitive leap which will often have been built upon (inferred from) no more than one or two pieces of evidence; and 'controlled pilot' is a metaphor for a variety of actual processes.

It is misleading to assume that in management and organisation development there is 'reality' to which we must at all times aspire to approximate to or to replicate in some way. There may be degrees of *perceived* proximity; but what consitutes such proximity is not a matter of any 'objective' reality, but how easy each individual manager finds it to make such a metaphorical link; to reconstruct the metaphors and models within his or her mental maps. The proximity is not between 'reality' and 'non-reality' but between two different metaphorical perceptions.

For some managers, the metaphor that can be provided by, for example, hanging from a cliff, can be so 'real' that that manager feels comfortable with saying, 'I've learnt more about man management in the past three days than I have for the past ten years at work' (testimonial cited in Bank 1994: 51, from a manager who has been through an outdoor development experience). This manager may have been 'kidding himself' about how much he had learnt (see Chapter 7, p. 180), and he may have had real challenges in turning this euphoria into practical action. But there can be little doubt that the 'unreality' had done something to him which he felt inclined to put down to learning, and which he did not feel he had got from learning on the job.

Indeed, we may be actively harming potential learning by attempting to eliminate the imaginative processes (metaphor, metonymy, and intuitive leaps) which build bridges between different neuronal maps, and different ways of seeing the world. Learning by doing on-site and in close proximity to 'daily life' may be highly effective from the point of view of consolidating and applying behaviours, but it may, by its very proximity to 'mundane' reality, get in the way of the kinds of learning which are about 'breaking free' from habits and paradigms. The more we remove the hard work which goes with actively seeking new connections, the more we may be discouraging managers from learning anything new.

'Reality' and Kinds of Interventions

When exploring the factors which may help decide how much 'reality' needs to be built into an intervention, we may be helped by referring back to the Management Development Grid from Chapters 3 and 4. It also helps if the complex concept of 'reality' can be looked at from at least a few different perspectives.

This is something Binstead and Stuart did in 1979. They suggested that such 'reality' could be viewed from three dimensions: *content, process* and *environment.* Any learning event could be seen as 'high or low on each of these independent dimensions of reality' (Binstead and Stuart 1979).

Content could be more or less 'real' by being more or less based upon the day-to-day business of the learner – about his or her job or company rather than about another job, company, or industry; in this case, building a bridge over a ravine may have low *content* reality for an accountant, but would have high *content* reality for a civil engineeer.

Process reality could be more or less 'real' by calling more or less upon the processes which a manager may call upon in his or her job; here, having to work in a team to solve a problem may have low *process* reality for a sales manager who spends most of his or her time alone, having simply to bring together customers and products or services, but high process reality for a project manager working in an uncertain environment where 'firefighting' with a group of colleagues is a daily routine.

Environment could be more or less real by being either at work, or more or less like the workplace. In addition, *environment* reality is measured by 'ambience': how much does this experience 'feel like' the ambiance at work.

A learning environment which an individual manager found confrontational and challenging to his or her personal integrity would have low environment reality for managers who see their own working environment as highly supportive or unchallenging. It would have high *environment* reality for a manager who felt constantly surrounded by confrontation and challenge.

This reinforces the role of perceptions in assessing degrees of 'reality', since the 'same' learning event can be seen as highly confrontational and challenging by one participating manager, 'natural and normal' to another. This would mean that the level of perceived *environment* 'reality' is low for one, high for the other; as with so many factors in management and organisation development, what we mean by 'reality' has to be measured from the learner's point of view. Where there are different learners, there will be different points of view.

Both learning and the organisational world of management rely upon metaphor, metonymy, inuitive leaps, and so on to 'make sense'; the ways in which these mental links are made will differ from person to person, following the unique neuronal paths which make up their mental maps. Each of us will 'get the point' of a piece of learning at different times. One of the roles of a facilitator of learning is to help each learner to 'get the point' as quickly and efficiently as possible. (And in this, I mean by 'getting the point' not only the intellectual idea, but also the 'getting the point' in terms of a readiness to apply that learning.)

For example, it may be a learning aim that a group of managers should be able to think more strategically about the changing competitive environment in which they work, so that they can consider the impact of their decisions, deliberations and so on on the competitive outcome. The underlying 'reality' of this situation is likely to be some kind of competitive threat, perhaps manifesting itself in falling sales or lost potential business. There are few 'physical' realities in this situation, so it will often be the case that a 'teacher' of strategic management will use a metaphor – the organisation as a ship, the competitive environment as a compass, the market place as a battlefield, and so on. The purpose of these metaphors will be to enable managers to 'picture' (in other words, to bring to mind in a simple and 'complete' form) what is a complex set of circumstances, and to use that picture as a reminder of what to do. The 'intuitive leap' of 'getting' the picture is a key part (but not the whole) of the learning process. It is a leap from what is not 'real' to something which has sufficient appearance of reality to the learner to be capable of doing its job.

When we 'get' an idea, when the 'penny drops', or when something 'makes sense' to us, we are taking a crucial step in the learning process – that of making a semantic connection in our minds. That connection represents for the learner a shift from 'relative unreality' to 'relative reality'. When managers cannot see the point of an activity, it could be said to be 'unreal' in that sense; when they do see the point, it becomes 'real' for them. For some managers the very act of sitting in a darkened room watching an expert (or a Chief Executive Officer) point to a graph projected onto a screen is sufficiently unlike being at their desk or face to face with a customer to make it hard for them to 'see the point' or to 'learn' from the process. For other managers, the 'point' of being blindfolded and guided by sound alone across a car park is abundantly clear from the start. For this latter manager, the learning is 'very real'.

'Very real' is a phrase which makes no sense unless 'reality' is acknowledged to be a matter of perception. In the context of management and organisation development, at least, reality is a matter of degree rather than absolutes. 'Real' leadership is not a 'reality' in the same sense as 'real desk'. Many aspects of managerial learning become 'real' for learners at that moment when, often as an intuitive leap, but sometimes as a growing sense of confidence, a feeling of familiarity is experienced as a metaphorical construct begins to make sense. 'Now I understand,' means roughly the same as 'Now this is real for me'. Realising something about an organisation means just that.

'Reality' is a useful concept in management and organisation development, but it is most useful when it is seen as both individually determined and changing. All managerial learning is hoped to make a difference; to do so, what is learnt has to be applicable to the 'real' world; in other words, managers have not only to 'get the point' but also to change what they do at work. One dimension of the learning process could, therefore, be seen as 'turning unreality into reality'. One aim of the design process is to enable managers to take a situation of 'low' content, process or *environment* reality, to use it to 'get the point' and then find ways of making the point part of their portfolio of behaviours at work. The following case illustrates how this might work.

CHALLENGING 'REALITIES': HOW PERCEPTIONS OF REALITY MAY CHANGE DURING AN INTERVENTION

A client wanted some middle to senior managers to become more comfortable with ambiguity and uncertainty, the better to deal with the increasing rate of change within what had been a relatively stable and steady organisational climate. This was a *Generic* intervention: for the managers themselves, some of the learning would be about change; but there was nothing radical in the kinds of behaviours which were defined as the 'desired state'. They just needed, like many other managers today, to be ready, willing and able to deal with broader perspectives and with the uncertainties and ambiguities which characterise the situations of middle to senior management today.

The client was sure that the achievement of the desired state was more about doing than understanding; the managers in question knew, intellectually, what needed to be done. They just weren't changing their own behaviours very much. Current-state analysis suggested that the managers may have been 'too close to' their working situations to be able clearly to picture, appreciate, experience and fully get to grips with the implications of change.

We designed a three-module programme. The first was largely intellectual, and explored the business environment, the strategic options being pursued by the company, and the ways in which traditional systems, processes and behaviours were being replaced to meet the strategic challenges of the future. The second module helped the managers learn about themselves as people: their individual preferences and styles, and how their skills and behaviours manifested themselves and were interpreted by others. The third module was the opportunity for them to bring the two sides together: to use their own individual skills and strengths, in collaboration with others, to 'create' the organisational processes and behaviours for the future. We designed for this third module an extended management simulation.

Within this simulation was included a physical production process, as well as customers, financial stakeholders such as the bank and shareholders, group Headquarters, and so on. The products within the simulated business were different from the products which the managers' company actually produce. The managers were grouped into four 'subsidiaries', becoming involved in the kind of subtle mix of collaboration and competition which often characterises group organisations. As the simulation progressed, the requirements of the customers changed, their levels of credit fluctuated, and Group HQ modified its strategy in line with broad shifts in the markets. In other words, within an actual week, the 'businesses' of the managers went through life-cycle shifts which were a mix of market and other external forces, and the results of their own managerial and physical endeavours.

At the start of the week, there were potentially low levels of reality for most of the participants in all three areas: from a content point of view, they were, for example, making things which their company does not make; from a process point of view, they were working in 'companies' of only seven or eight people; and from an environment point of view, they were not only away from their offices, but also experiencing novelty rather than familiarity. I believe that the success of the previous two modules contributed significantly to the managers' accepting, at least at the outset, that there could be some valuable learning about to happen, despite the disorientation which these low levels of 'reality' may have been creating in their minds.

The 'willing suspension of disbelief' became strained by the middle of the second afternoon. We faced a potential mutiny. This was apparently the result of our insistence that the groups actually produce further batches of the products (even though they had 'proved' the process), as well as continuing to work on marketing strategies, business plans, and other obviously 'managerial' tasks. They felt that having to go through such mechanical activities as making things was a waste of their time, and failing to contribute to their learning. The implicit model of learning they were using was a model of 'once you've done it, you've learnt it'.

The situation came to a head in what started as a role play meeting between the 'Managing Directors' and the 'Board'. It was here that the first overt use of metaphor was called into play: the production process which was occupying so much of their time, and getting in the way of their 'managerial' work was, first, a metaphor for those 'million and one' interruptions which, in 'real life' prevented them from setting aside time and space to 'think strategically'. Secondly, it represented the need to turn 'theory into practice'; they had to deliver, and not just promise to deliver. This need to deliver something physical was meta-phorically related to the 'product' of their changed behaviours. It was not enough to agree to embrace change and ambiguity, and to live with uncer-tainty; they had to deliver. The message which they took away from the meeting was that, if they could manage to deliver product to the required and agreed specification, and not allow that process to become an excuse for failing to deal, at the same time, with strategic planning, then they would have proven to themselves that they could (as they would have had an experience of doing just that) succeed on the various and often conflicting levels which they had accepted (intellectually) they needed to.

Not all the managers at that meeting made a significant 'intuitive leap' there and then. Those who did not attend had to rely upon the messages being brought back to them by their respective 'Managing Directors'. But thereafter, in a series of small and large leaps, the managers recognised a greater number of connections with their daily lives, and how this experience provided an 'increasingly real' set of messages for them. As the 'businesses' evolved, and once the message had delivered its value, the production process was withdrawn from the exercise. Thereafter, the managers had time to devote exclusively to the more strategic planning and development aspects of their 'businesses'; the *content* part of the exercise assumed greater perceived 'reality'.

Process 'reality' was felt to increase as the challenges and problems they were addressing became more familiar, and as they learnt about their colleagues as fellow members of their 'businesses'. And as the metaphorical links became stronger, the managers started to think more and more about how to apply what they were learning back at work. This brought a lot of the 'ambience' of the company into the scenarios, increasing the perceived *environment* 'reality'.

Clearly, these perceptions of increasing 'reality' varied from manager to manager. Setbacks, especially in the early stages of the week, and even more especially if these were related to the physical production process, would have created downturns in the individual managers' imaginary graphs of 'perceived *content*, *process* and *environment* reality'. But the overall trend was upwards, and that was fuelled by 'trudging back and forth over [new mental] paths, making mind-ruts for yourself – really digging in and making yourself at home' (Dennett 1991: 300).

Some of the cases cited, and some of the learning I allude to in this book have been on-site interventions. But the lion's share of this book is devoted to management and organisation development interventions away from the office for the reasons cited above: that there are significant learning advantages to be had from this kind of management and organisation development activity. In Mumford's terms (1993), these are known as 'formal management development planned' activities.

Formal Management Development Planned

Mumford's criticism of these kinds of activities is that, in terms of the learning cycle, managers only go through stages 2 and 3: that they do not have 'real' data or experiences, only contrived ones; and they cannot, until the event has passed, test out the theories which they have worked on. What make data 'real', and what consitutes an effective 'test' are not absolutes. However, the challenges which Mumford throws down at this point cannot be ignored. Those of us involved in 'off-site' management and organisation development interventions have a duty to demonstrate the benefits of taking managers away from their 'real' environments in order to enhance their learning. I shall do so by working through the principles and practice of learning design which we bring to management and organisation development interventions to show how and why we believe that, within these learning interventions, managers do indeed go through genuine and applicable learning.

LEARNING DESIGN – SOME BASIC PRINCIPLES

After hundreds of years of being the cornerstone of highly respected teaching, the lecture is under vicious attack, as in 'The grotesque ineffectiveness of the lecture process, and the vociferous feedback of many managers bored with being its victims' (Mumford 1993: 27). If the lecture can only be justified in terms of the implicit model of management which previous chapters have questioned, then its days may truly be numbered. On the other hand, if our revised model can accommodate the lecture as a more or less valid tool within the learning toolkit, then it would seem profligate to throw it away altogether.

Clearly there has been a great deal of ineptitude in management and organisation development over the years; and it is crucial for those who seek to remain effective in management and organisation development interventions to learn, themselves, about the very activities which they undertake. But I am not convinced that everything which is being ditched in the name of progress is necessarily and always bad; nor that everything which is being adopted provides more than an additional tool for the toolkit.

There are many such tools, methods, approaches, styles, and so on available to management and organisation development these days. None provides everything managers need for learning; few have no contribution to make at all. This section is about sorting out the toolkit and showing the kinds of ways in which my colleagues and I bring together the features and functions of the various tools, and the specific learning aims of different kinds and components of an overall management and organisation development intervention.

Teaching versus Experience – a Fundamental Learning Distinction?

Cranfield School of Management is a University School, proud of its research tradition. Among the large number of full time academics we have recognised leaders in several fields, who, along with the support of research teams, continue to push back the boundaries of knowledge about what is going on in the world of marketing, corporate strategy, logistics, retailing, information systems management, business economics, and so on. One of the reasons why managers come to Cranfield to learn is to gain access to this research-based information. Managers are not going to find out what these researchers have discovered by abseiling down a rock face. There is, and will remain for the foreseeable future, a role for information-based, input-driven, management and organisation development.

A problem arises, however, when this insight provides managers or management and organisation development people with a one-dimensional model of what is going on when managers learn, such as will be manifested in situations where 'teachers' assume that managers come with 'open minds' like empty vessels to be filled. This kind of unidimensional model has, in the past made learning design simply a matter of deciding which order to give the lectures in – lectures on strategy on Monday, lectures on People Management on Friday' with the rationalisation that, 'until we have imparted to managers all we know about People Management, there's precious little point in getting them to do any "experiential" learning, since they'll not have any information on which to base their experiential work'.

Using Management Exercises to Stimulate Experiential Learning

I have often, in the case studies of interventions, referred to 'exercises' we ask managers to undertake. We have used exercises to help managers from organisations such as Scandabank (pp. 211–13), and Spaceco (pp. 201–3), learn 'experientially'. As with each of those cases we cited, we designed specific management exercises.

We design each exercise specifically to meet a particular learning aim or set of aims. For that reason, many of the exercises are used solely for the managers of one client organisation. Where different organisations have similar learning aims, and where the 'current states' of those client organisations are not too dissimilar, we do sometimes use similar exercises in those circumstances. The benefit of this is that we can gather information on how managers from different organisations differ in their approaches to the exercises.

This rarely produces 'scientific' data. This is largely because we are dealing with managerial behaviour, which is hard to measure meaningfully. But it does produce some broad, intuitive patterns which can be informative. For example:

WE CAN LEARN FROM EXERCISES, TOO

I had the opportunity to run in Sweden a very short event for a group of 35 managers I had never met. I was allowed 24 hours for the event itself, and only a few days to design it. Although I designed one brand-new exercise for the event (which went so well that I remember that day as one of the most fulfilling of my career in management and organisation development, but that's another story), I also decided to 'borrow' an exercise which a colleague had designed, and which we had used on a series of workshops for sales people. This borrowed exercise had been undertaken in roughly the same manner by about 15 separate groups of sales people, which suggested to us that this was the 'normal' way to solve the problem. On this very short event, which was for insurance managers, none of whom were sales people, all the teams approached the problem in a much more customer-oriented way than the UK-based sales people had.

This contrast proved nothing, since it could have been explained in many different ways. But it gave me some learning about a very different approach to the task which, I believe has enabled me to facilitate the use of that exercise (when it has been used subsequently) far more constructively and effectively.

The principles of exercise design which we use are based upon our understanding of the learning process. None of the exercises is 'real' in the sense Mumford means by his type-two management development, and none of them have high 'content' or 'environment' reality; most don't even have high 'process' reality. But they all have a great deal of potential metaphorical and metonymic richness. The Spaceco case illustrates the kind of learning which emerges from the imaginative review of experienced behaviours; while the Global Technologies case shows how, by re-presentation of the basis of a customer relationship, the underlying assumptions and concepts upon which sales people's customer-oriented behaviours are built can be exposed as flimsy at best. From these kinds of experience, managers recognise the depth of the foundations upon which they base their (more or less conscious) behaviours.

Drawing conclusions of this level of significance from 'games' (as some managers are initially tempted to call them) takes hard work and intellectual as well as emotional and imaginative endeavour. Some managers just don't get it – fortunately, these are a very small minority. But some managers (not necessarily the same ones) just won't get it whatever approach we take. There is nothing which 'proves' the supreme efficacy of the management exercise as a vehicle for experiential learning; and badly designed exercises can go horribly wrong. But, at the time of writing, we still find them enormously helpful in generating the data we and managers need for constructive, imaginative and honest dialogue about what they may have learnt, and what they still need to learn to achieve their targets for managerial effectiveness and personal growth.

Can Exercises Guarantee that Managers Learn 'the Right Stuff'?

This brings us back to a theme which has been hovering, unresolved, since the latter part of Chapter 7. There, and earlier in this chapter, I suggested that most of us would feel better if we differentiated between 'prejudice', on the one hand, and 'learning' on the other, where the former is ascribed to what individuals may say they have learnt, but since we strongly disagree with their conclusions, we do not want to call those conclusions 'learnt'. I suggested that one means of consolidating that conclusion rested upon a kind of consensus – open, honest, constructive debate ought to weed out the 'fringe' opinions. But I also suggested that this poses a problem for the introduction of 'new' ideas.

Suppose we wanted to convince a group of managers from a traditional, hierarchical organisation, in which the word of the boss was law, and so on, to change their behaviours to accommodate empowerment for all staff. Suppose also that in our current-state research it had become clear that the vast majority of these managers firmly believe that authority should be vested in the boss, that staff are not skilled and experienced enough to be allowed to do what they like, and that empowerment is just one of those management fads which will go away so long as it is resisted firmly by people who can see through these silly ideas which come from business schools.

We could teach these managers until we were blue in the face, and they would probably nod sagely (accepting the implicit authority of the teacher in the classroom) and could even 'agree' intellectually with the case being put. But the chances are that they would go back after the event and carry on exactly as they had before, muttering things like 'That's all very well in theory, but it won't work in practice,' and 'It may be fine for those other organisations, but we're different, and it won't work here.'

But if we were to take the opposite line, and get them to go through a series of experiences designed to help them come to conclusions for themselves, we run the risk that the conclusions they come to will be the very opposite from those we set out to get them to learn. I have heard (fortunately on only very rare occasions) managers say at the conclusion of an experiential learning activity designed to foster collaborative and egalitarian teamwork, 'I always knew that all a good team needs is a strong leader; the rest is immaterial.' Surely, one could argue, the more we rely upon experiential learning to get a message across, the more we run into the 'self-fulfilling prophecy'. If managers do have all those attitudes, complexes, mental maps and personal styles influencing how they see and interpret a situation, then allowing them to go through an experience is 'playing into their hands'. Doesn't experience simply reinforce prejudice rather than create new ways of thinking?

Introducing a 'new idea' such as 'empowerment' to our sample managers, means setting up a competition in those managers' minds between what they believe now, and what it is intended that they should learn. The neural paths which lead to the 'bosses are right to do the thinking' conclusions are well trudged and familiar. The maps which represent 'staff' and 'freedom to learn and grow through empowerment' are joined, if at all, by paths which are hardly traceable. In many cases, the idea that there could be a meaningful link between them is a false trail.

The trouble with this case is that illumination of this trail will not do on its own. For many experienced managers the path between the maps which represent 'staff' and 'freedom to learn and grow through empowerment' are well-enough lit by the literature and teaching which has been going on around the subject for some time; and this is another way of saying that 'teaching', in this instance, is unlikely to achieve effective change. They can see the path; they just don't want to go down it.

Well-designed and well-facilitated experiential learning enables managers to come at a managerial 'problem' through many different facets of their humanity. Whereas teaching relies on a 'cognitive' focus (although the experience of 'being taught' is far from exclusively cognitive – something which 'good teachers' take into account in what they do), experiential learning is overtly about the emotions as much as it is about the intellect, being put into potentially 'stressful' situations to heighten awareness and stimulate the archetypal 'pay attention' response, a mix of images, sounds, smells and feelings far richer than the images on a projection screen, being called upon to act and not just receive, and so on. In other words, experiential learning engages many aspects of the mind and body: emotions, complexes, mental maps, as well as the functions of Sensing and Intuition, Thinking and Feeling.

The outcome of all this is a significantly enhanced probability that the various 'engines' of learning will be engaged by the experience, including the many 'unconscious' ones, such as the limbic system. The consequence of this is that whatever is 'learnt' by managers through this mutually reinforcing set of experiential stimuli is likely to stick; it could be very difficult to 'unlearn' what comes out of a powerful experience such as this. This is one reason why, as I suggested in Chapter 8, outdoor development tends to be said by those who have gone through it to have provided them with something which they will remember for a very long time.

None of this, however, deals with the problem of ensuring that managers 'get the right message'; all it does is to suggest that the 'message they get' will stick. Therefore experiential learning needs very careful handling; it is a much more volatile mixture than teaching seems to be.

Good facilitation is required to handle the volatility of experiential learning. This is not just about skills; it is also about values.

Some people would say that 'good' teachers can teach anything, whether they believe it or not. Because of the essentially cognitive focus of the teaching process, a great deal of it is potentially neutral. Science tries to free itself from the 'scourge' of partiality, and relentlessly pursues objectivity; logic is, strictly, meaningless (both in the semantic and the 'values' sense of the word). Much of what teaching is about concerns the rational and intellectual; one can try to 'teach' values, but there is a strong sense in which this is misguided. One of the things which we can learn from the study of rites of passage, as I suggested in Chapter 8, is that most cultures recognise that, in order to instil good quality, lasting, behavioural, value-focused learning, you do well to supplement the myths and teachings of the elders with a good dose of experiential learning.

But if you want to facilitate learning which is more than cognitive, it is unlikely that you will be successful unless you, personally, believe in what you are trying to help others to learn. Believing, for an experienced facilitator, will be the result of a combination of 'innate' values, deep introspection (often accompanied by serious doubts), hundreds or even thousands of conversations and debates with authoritative figures, and so on. A 'good' facilitator will believe what he or she believes because of these many different experiences, instances, perspectives, and so on. He or she will therefore be likely to have personally experienced the kinds of emotional, cognitive, metaphorical and archetypal experiences which will be constellated by a well-designed experiential learning activity. This will enable him or her at any moment during or after that experiential activity to 'walk with' each and every manager down the kinds of path they will be walking down and exploring.

In the case of our 'traditional' managers 'learning about' empowerment, it will require facilitators who see the empowerment of staff as a positive, affirming and beneficial step for both the organisation in general and the managers doing the learning in particular. Those facilitators will be sufficiently in touch with the ways in which those managers may be experiencing the situation to know at what point, and in what style to 'confront' or to 'encourage' each manager individually, bearing in mind not only the similarities among the managers, but also their individual differences, and how these may influence their perceptions and receptivity to the learning.

Such facilitators will know when and how to ask such questions as 'how would you describe what happened between you and manager X?' 'what conclusions do you draw from the difficulties your group got into?', 'how else could you explain manager Y's behaviour, apart from 'a struggle for the leadership'?' and 'how did it make you feel when manager Z discounted your proposal for a solution?' Good facilitators are able, through their own personal history of facilitated learning experiences to re-present situations from such multiple perspectives, helping managers to build their own mental maps round these alternative but mutually supporting images.

In so doing, facilitators take the role of the archetypal guide (see, for example Chapter 8, pp. 244–5), not having the answers, but having the kinds of questions which enable managers to see the possibilities for reinterpreting such concepts as 'empowerment', and giving them the personal space to explore the implications for their own positions and behaviour of treating these alternative interpretations as, if not 'right', then, at least, feasible. The next step is to ask about how managers could, without taking more risks than they would feel comfortable with, try out behaviours which would be in line with new and alternative perspectives.

How this next step is undertaken will be influenced by many more factors than such issues and facilitator and learner style, since what constitutes acceptable risk, and so on, will depend partly on the nature of the intervention. For an Exploratory intervention, it will be important for the facilitator to help the manager prepare for radical change; in this case, plans for implementation will need to be more robust and adventurous than an intention to 'put a toe in the empowerment water'; whereas for a Core Capabilities intervention (assuming that the intervention is supported by those strategies, systems, and so on which are in tune and compatible with the learning aims) plans for implementation should align closely with extant projects and processes which will encourage and reward 'fitting in'.

Customer Focus – a Suitable Case for Teaching or for Learning?

Many organisations are encouraging their managers and staff to become more customer focused. Some managers may respond that they know nothing about what being customer focused means, and ask for a management development programme to help. Should we try to teach customer focus, or should managers learn how to become customer focused?

The case for teaching is that there may be evidence, rigorously researched, which will tell managers how many organisations have introduced customer focus, and what they have learnt about the pitfalls. More research may have been undertaken on some of the personality characteristics of managers who take on customer focus more willingly and with better effect than others. There is no foreseeable limit to the amount of well-researched data managers could acquire through such teaching. The question is, would this make them more customer focused in practice?

Let me explore this with a case study.

BECOMING CUSTOMER FOCUSED AT GLOBAL TECHNOLOGIES

The Strategy

We have met Global Technologies on a number of occasions throughout the book so far. These are the people whose senior sales staff were regrouped into Customer Focused Teams, with the aim of gaining strategic advantage over their competitors through 'customer delight' rather than the more traditional, and stodgy, customer satisfaction. This meant all staff, and especially those who actually interfaced with customers, being intensely customer focused.

By 'customer' they meant someone different from the traditional customer the sales people had sold to. In the past, they had sold technology to Information Technology managers at customer sites. In the future, they were to sell business solutions to the most senior business managers of the customer organisation. The goal was to work with customers to develop business-focused, integrated means of gaining competitive advantage through innovative applications of their technology. Prices would be high, but so would be the rewards. The people who would benefit most would be senior management at the customer organisation; the only people who would appreciate the enterprise-wide implications of such solutions would be the senior management at the customer organisation; and the only people with big enough budgets would be the senior management at the customer organisation. Becoming customer focused meant getting close to some very senior business managers whose knowledge of and interest in information technology was likely to be zero, but whose appreciation of the business and industry they were competing in, and of people who spoke their language was likely to be high.

The Intervention

It was for these senior sales and support people from the European part of Global that we designed and ran our first intervention for the company. Our 'current state' research was described in Chapter 5. Based upon that research we developed a three-week residential programme which contained, at its core, an experiential, team-based module which would help the managers explore their own approaches to working with each other and with customers in a Customer Focused Team environment.

Following the MUSIC model of Chapter 4, we started the programme with some input-oriented elements. This was to enable the participants to appreciate the kinds of issues and language which the senior managers in their customer organisations are grappling with. These elements also ratified the need for the kinds of customer focus which the strategy depended upon. The managers nodded wisely, agreeing that it was fortunate that the company had such experienced and customer-focused people as they were to implement the strategy. They all knew intellectually about being customer focused.

The Learning

During the experiential part of the programme, managers undertook a number of low impact tasks; this was not an outdoor development module. The tasks were aimed at bringing out their 'habitual' behaviours, including bringing out how they were to balance the needs of a customer against the development of product to a certain set of specifications. In almost every case, the customer's needs were poorly appreciated; in most cases, the managers assumed that the needs of the customer were completely circumscribed by the 'product specification', in many cases the customer was never consulted; in many cases, when he was, he was argued with, or told he was wrong. It was only on rare occasions that the customer was made to feel valuable, important, welcome, and human.

The base data upon which these observations about customer focus are based is 27 iterations of the programme, in which between two and four teams were given the chance through similar kinds of exercises to develop relationships with the customer. Between 70 and 80 teams went through the process; no more than one or two could be said to have *appeared* to the customer to be customer focused. This was important, since our reading of the strategy was that it should be the customer who would be the arbiter of customer focus, not the teams themselves.

Reviewing these dismal results was hard work at times. Some of the managers became angry, and accused the facilitators of tricking them. Some argued with the customer, saying that the customer did not appreciate how customer focused they were. Some said that they were customer focused in real life, but this was 'just a game'. But most recognised fairly quickly (with all but a very small handful following suit within the next few hours or days) that what they were calling upon in these tasks were their everyday behaviours; they made the same kinds of judgements about the relative importance of the variables (strategy, customer, process, product, quality, time, cost, and so on) as they would tend to in 'real life'; that, indeed, the fact that they did so 'off the job' where the boss, the environment, the habits of being there could not be blamed for what they did was recognised to be very revealing of the depth of the assumptions and habits which drove them during the exercises.

The review processes were an opportunity for the managers, one by one, to come to terms with what, if they were honest with each other, they had to agree were their key learning points:

- that knowing intellectually about being customer focused was not the same as being so in practice
- that most of them had known what they should do to appear customer focused, but that they had not done so
- that among the reasons why they had not done so is that they had not acquired or developed the skills to do so
- that one of the reasons why they had not so developed is that they did not realise the need, in other words, that they did not already have these skills
- that most of them had a preference for Thinking which focused them to develop solutions while suppressing their Feeling function's call to get alongside and appreciate the customer as a human being rather than a potential source of revenue and profit (most never heard this call from within themselves)
- that the solution to these problems did not lie in acquiring more knowledge, or being taught anything new, but in their personally developing the self-awareness and skills to put into practice what they knew they had to do to succeed

Conclusions

There was a wide range of difference between the managers and their approach to customer focus. As I said, on rare occasions one of the team members would demonstrate highly effective customer-focused behaviours. These felt, to the customer, hugely different from the scarcely disguised adversarial approach of most. What is interesting is that those who demonstrated these behaviours were not better taught; they had not been given more information than the others. They were just significantly more in touch with what it takes within us to work collaboratively, warmly and on a human-to-human basis with another person, whether he is a customer with your future bonus in his bank balance, or the person who comes to empty the bins in the office.

This kind of behaviour comes from our Feeling function. Most managers in Global Technologies (88%) report a preference for Thinking; of the handful who exhibited genuine customer-focused behaviours, over half had a preference for Feeling. This is not to say that people with a preference for Thinking cannot become customer focused; but in order to start to learn to do so, they (we) have to have the grace to admit that they (we) have to start so to learn. And for many Thinking managers, this is the hurdle they can't see, let alone jump over.

For these managers, then, more value was seen to be gained from a learning perspective than from a teaching one. But had they been unable, intellectually, to see the point of being 'customer focused' in the first place, we may have had to have provided more 'motivational' information about the benefits of such an approach before attempting to help them to learn the kinds of behaviour which 'lives' customer focus. The broadened model of the manager demands that we accommodate a wider set of learning perspectives than simply focusing upon lectures, on the one hand, or experiential exercises, on the other.

Designing so that 'Teaching' and 'Learning' are Mutually Supportive

For many managers, and for many learning aims, it is possible to use both 'teaching' and 'learning' in mutually supporting ways. The 'customer-focus' programme for Global Technologies is just one such example. In the first module we made the intellectual case for a customer-oriented strategy through processes which could be described primarily as 'teaching' oriented; and in the second module explored managers' own customer-focused behaviours through experiential learning.

But the distinction between 'teaching' and 'learning', useful though it has been as a means of opening some of the key issues in learning design, is too blunt an instrument to do justice to the subtleties and complexities of managerial learning.

'Teaching' versus 'Learning' is not Enough

The world of management and organisation development is complex – 'organisations' are socially constructed ways of hanging on to the complexities which, without this level of construct, would render management impossible. Learning is similarly complex. We cannot hang onto every facet of learning all the time, yet we have to avoid the reductionist trap of reducing the complexity to a simplistic cliché. Our search for organisers of our thoughts on learning has led us to bring together two sets of ideas which seem, together, to explain a fair amount of this confusion. In the following section, I shall explore how these two ideas – of psychological types, and the broad differences between teaching and experiential learning help us in our learning design.

THE DESIGN DIAMOND – A MODEL FOR LEARNING

One of the driving forces for the development of this model was to explain to colleagues new to learning design, and to managers who wanted to be involved in the design process, the rationale for locating different kinds of topics within an overall learning framework. Another was the recognition that the psychological preferences of both learners and teachers or facilitators can have a profound effect on the perceptions of everyone involved in a learning event.

As a result, we have worked up this simple tool.

The Two Key Dimensions

The model approaches learning through two orthogonal dimensions: that of discovery, and that of convergence. These are based upon the Jungian 'functions'.

The *discovery* dimension maps the Jungian perceiving functions, Sensing and Intuition. At the Sensing end, we are focused on discovering the here and now, realities, facts, data and specifics. At the Intuitive end we are focused upon discovering ideas, the there and then, possibilities, models and generalisations. We may start at the data end of the dimension, gathering facts; at some point, we will find ourselves making the 'intuitive' leap, as our Intuition kicks in, and gives us the 'grand conclusion' – the big picture. It is one of the features of our preferences for Sensing or Intuition that this 'intuitive leap' will be made by different people at different times, and with different degrees of confidence and certainty.

To caricature: people with a preference for Sensing are likely to dwell longer at the 'factual' end of the spectrum, to gather more data, and to be more tentative or even clumsy with their 'intuitive leap'. People with a preference for Intuition are likely to make the 'intuitive leap' far sooner, often 'too soon', having gathered considerably less data, but they will be far more confident of the big picture they draw.

The *convergence* dimension maps the judging functions, where all the information, values, rules and ideas we take into account before deciding on some action converge at that point of judgement. At the Thinking end we are focused upon the cognitive, the objective, the intellectual, and the logical; and we are using the left hemisphere of our brain. At the Feeling end we are focused on the affective, the subjective, the value-centred and significant; we are using the right hemisphere of our brain.

Broadly speaking, although not exclusively, most of our cognitive learning will engage our Thinking function – people with a preference for Thinking may feel relatively comfortable when engaged in learning in this way; they may feel challenged, but will be more ready to accept and rise to that challenge. Most of our affective, experiential learning will come through our Feeling function, although many people (especially Thinkers) will not feel comfortable with this kind of learning until it has been 'validated' by the intellect, through rationalisation, or through (in some cases) denial or excuses.

Bringing the two dimensions together provides us with the map in Figure 10.1.

It is a diamond and not a square for three reasons. The first is purely pragmatic: to avoid confusion with, or any attempt at integration with, the Management Development Grid: there is no correlation between these two models, focusing as they do on very different territories. The second is more

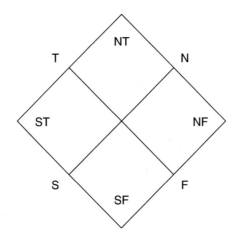

Figure 10.1 *The learning diamond*

imaginative: the apex of the diamond represents the 'up in the air', carefree, often careless, world of the NT; the base of the diamond represents the intensely practical, down to earth, and caring world of the SF. Finally, there is a very loose association between the shape and the 'geography' of the brain, with the ST, logical, factual segment on the left (to reflect the left brain's strong links with this kind of thinking); and the often largely unconscious SF lying at the base of the model, approximating to the location of the limbic system's location in the human brain.

The four internal diamonds are comprised of pairs of different functions (ST, SF, NF, NT), each pair being one perceiving function and one judging function. These represent quite different 'mindsets', none of which is better than another, and all of which are used at various times by all people. However, the research and our own experiences tell us that each of these four represents a broad approach to issues, ideas, situations, challenges and to learning in general, with which different people have different levels of comfort. Some approaches will feel more 'natural', more important to each individual than the others. This will influence some of the often unspoken approaches which learners and facilitators will bring to learning.

It is not only in the realms of managerial learning that we can experience the different 'pull' from each of the four approaches. They are likely to permeate a broader base of our attitudes and responses to life in general. To illustrate, consider the example in Figure 10.2, which explores briefly a social and/or political issue – that of 'the poor' in society.

Four quite different reactions to the issue of 'the poor' are characterised here. They may reflect the four different kinds of the neuronal groups or mental maps we discussed in Chapter 7. In practice, however, they deliver

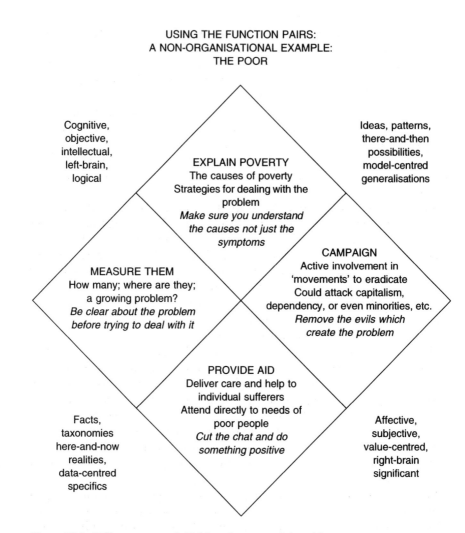

USING THE FUNCTION PAIRS:
A NON-ORGANISATIONAL EXAMPLE:
THE POOR

Cognitive,
objective,
intellectual,
left-brain,
logical

Ideas, patterns,
there-and-then
possibilities,
model-centred
generalisations

EXPLAIN POVERTY
The causes of poverty
Strategies for dealing with the
problem
*Make sure you understand
the causes not just the
symptoms*

MEASURE THEM
How many; where are they;
a growing problem?
*Be clear about the problem
before trying to deal with it*

CAMPAIGN
Active involvement in
'movements' to eradicate
Could attack capitalism,
dependency, or even minorities, etc.
*Remove the evils which
create the problem*

PROVIDE AID
Deliver care and help to
individual sufferers
Attend directly to needs of
poor people
*Cut the chat and do
something positive*

Facts,
taxonomies
here-and-now
realities,
data-centred
specifics

Affective,
subjective,
value-centred,
right-brain
significant

Figure 10.2 *Different ways of thinking about a social problem*

quite different approaches. In so doing, they frequently form the basis for
heated debates about social and political issues.

In this example, the 'ST' part of the personality pulls us toward a data-
focused and logical approach. In this approach, problems need to be fully
appreciated and mapped out before plans can be drawn up to address them. It
is an approach which suggests the need for clarity, certainty, facts, and so on
before resources are wasted on rushing after what may be inappropriate
solutions. It is the part of the personality which helps us to ensure that we can

and do focus what are often limited resources upon the 'right' problem. It is the part of the personality which wants us to define problems and solutions. People who have preferences for S and T may find themselves more comfortable with this down-to-earth, planned and considered approach than they do with some of the other approaches.

The 'NT' part of the personality wants to *explain* the causes of things. Just as the ST part of the personality wants to avoid wasting resources on the 'wrong' problem, so the NT part wants to avoid wasting resources upon symptoms – it wants to get at and deal with causes. It may use models and diagrams to help in this task, seeking understanding through matching metaphors.

On the right of the diamond lies the part of the personality which wants to 'wage war' on the problem. Like the 'NT' approach, this approach focuses not upon the specific instances of poverty, nor upon the ways in which those instances can be added up and otherwise measured. It wants to remove the moral evils which lie at the heart of the problem, be they capitalism, greed, or even the activities of a particular minority (for some these may be the rich, for others, a racially-based conspiracy: the values implicit in these approaches do not always lead to harmony for all). The underlying NF driver is the *campaign*: it is action- and values-oriented.

The 'SF' approach is essentially practical and immediate. It is the part of the personality which simply goes to the nearest sufferer and provides practical aid – food, shelter, money. The underlying driver in this approach is to *help*. By focusing upon empathy rather than data, models or grand schemes, it generates action. It does not care whether there may be too many to care for right now with our limited resources; it does not care that providing assistance may take away the motivation for self-help; it does not care that the 'evils' remain unaddressed while soup is being provided. It just deals with the problem as it presents itself.

As we reflect upon these four different approaches, we are calling upon those different aspects of our personality which we have heuristically mapped onto the 'diamond' model. Most people will respond differently to each approach. In some cases, people will be irritated by some aspects of some of the approaches. For some, the ST approach will be pedantic and bureaucratic; the NT approach will, for some, seem ridiculously intellectual – an excuse to avoid dealing with reality in the raw; for others, the zealous approach of the NF will appear dangerous and potentially divisive; while others will despair at the ways in which the SF approach simply perpetuates the problem rather than solving it.

I have used this example to show how deeply rooted some of our responses may be. The more deeply rooted our approaches, the more we may tend to overlook their influence upon our thinking and behaviour. When it comes to managerial learning (the 'myth of the empty vessel' having been set aside), it seems important for us to recognise that these kinds of underlying approaches may significantly affect how managers approach learning in general.

Managers with different 'mindset' preferences may approach learning from very different points of view. Should a manager approach a learning event from the ST perspective, for example, and be 'taught' from an NF perspective, he or she is likely to feel more or less dissatisfied by the experience, having 'learnt' very little. Learning expectations, therefore, can be very significantly influenced by underlying assumptions about learning which may frequently not be surfaced. Unless they are discussed, there may be (at least) four very different experiences taking place in any managerial learning intervention.

How Mindsets May Influence Attention (and Learning)

The four different 'mindsets' are likely to deal with the concept of 'learning' in very different, but often unspoken ways.

The 'ST' approach is likely to be based more upon the *acquisition* of new knowledge; here learning 'means' gaining such new knowledge. It may be that people with preferences for S and T may not say that they have learnt anything from a learning event unless they could write down or otherwise express the 'things' which they had acquired from the event. Rediscovering what they knew already may not feel like learning to them. Proof will be another important element in learning.

The 'NT' approach is more likely to see learning as *understanding*. People with N and T preferences may be more likely to say they have learnt something if they can reproduce new ways of modelling the 'realities' they have to deal with. They may not feel the need to acquire new facts, so long as the models, metaphors or new organising principles they have been acquainted with are tools which help them understand complexities and puzzles which had previously concerned them.

The 'NF' approach may tend to equate learning with a more value-centred change. Statements such as 'I have learnt the power of teams,' or 'I now see the value of active listening in establishing good client relations,' are descriptions of an approach to learning which is much more to do with *motivation* than with new facts or understanding theories. The 'NF' kind of learning does not depend upon proof or conceptual understanding; it relates to what the learner now wants to do differently. It is measured not in volume of new facts, nor in the quality of new models, but in the passion with which the learning is taken forward into action.

The 'SF' approach to learning is often highly *personal*, and frequently *emotional* (in the sense we explore in Chapter 7) in a much more conscious way. It rarely takes place within a classroom or lecture theatre. It most frequently takes place through introspection or working with one or two trusted colleagues. Externally, it is exemplified in learning to love someone, for all their faults. Internally, it is about confronting the hitherto unconscious aspects of oneself which may be powerful influencers on one's life and attitudes to life. For reasons we touched upon in Chapter 7, this kind of learning is often the least attractive to many male western managers; it may not be coincidental that of the four function pairs (ST, SF, NT, NF), the SF combination is hugely under-represented in the reported preferences of managers in western organisations.

Different Approaches to Learning within Management Development

These different approaches to learning may have a great deal to do with how managers respond to the different activities and themes with which many management and organisation development interventions are populated. See Figure 10.3.

On the left of the diagram are the management and organisation development activities and themes which concern the logical understanding of facts and 'realities'; the rules and processes for how we do things properly. When we are picking apart a balance sheet, or calculating workflow through a process diagram, or summing the weighted customer critical success factors from a competitor analysis, the Sensing and Thinking functions are working together. People with ST preferences are more likely to be engaged at these stages, often getting to the answers before anyone else; less often considering the human implications, or the customer's feelings, or whether this calculation actually tells us anything about where we are going to be in five years from now.

At the top of the diamond are the management and organisation development activities and themes which concern the use and exploration of objective ideas, models, and strategic generalities. When Porter's 5 Forces model (Porter 1980), or the McKinsey 7S model (Waterman *et al.* 1980), or a 20-year strategy for beating the competition are on the agenda, the Intuition and Thinking functions are working together. People with NT preferences are more likely to be engaged at these stages, often wanting to chip in with refinements to the models; less often considering the human implications, or the customer's feelings, or the practical issues of implementation.

On the right are the management and organisation development activities and themes which are about our 'ideals' concerning organisational behaviours and values. When we are exploring the relative merits of empowerment and authority, or questioning whether profit comes before the needs of society, the Intuition and Feeling functions are working together. People with NF preferences are more likely to be engaged at these stages, often

LEARNING BY . . .

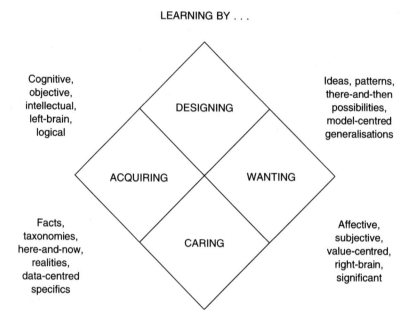

Cognitive,
objective,
intellectual,
left-brain,
logical

DESIGNING

Ideas, patterns,
there-and-then
possibilities,
model-centred
generalisations

ACQUIRING   WANTING

Facts,
taxonomies,
here-and-now,
realities,
data-centred
specifics

CARING

Affective,
subjective,
value-centred,
right-brain,
significant

Figure 10.3 *Key themes and approaches in management and organisation development*

becoming unexpectedly impassioned in their advocacy; less often worrying about the practical implications of empowering staff tomorrow, or whether valuing society's needs above profit might give the competition a field day at our expense, in the short term.

At the bottom of the model are the management and organisation development activities and themes which are about solving the individual problems brought to the table by the people in the group. When we are talking one to one with each of the managers about the things which are bugging them right now at work, or building a six-point plan to help this or that manager get through his or her next appraisal with a difficult boss, the Sensing and Feeling functions are working together. People with SF preferences are more likely to be engaged at these stages, often becoming deeply involved with the problems of the individual manager in question, and asking many questions to ferret out the key facts which could provide the clues to success for this person; less often worrying about whether dealing with this problem will move the agenda along its scheduled path, or the theories which may be offered to 'explain' how this manager got into difficulties in the first place.

Themes and topics are often what represent the 'product' in a management and organisation development intervention. 'Becoming customer focused' is the kind of topic which is often found on the agenda of such an intervention;

the fruits of the design process so far. But 'becoming customer focused' can mean a number of different things. If we see the 'same' topic through the framework of the diamond, we can readily recognise how differently this topic can be represented.

As an example, let us imagine two different kinds of 'becoming customer focused' modules in a management and organisation development intervention. One is positioned at the ST point of the diamond (version A), the other at the NF point (version B):

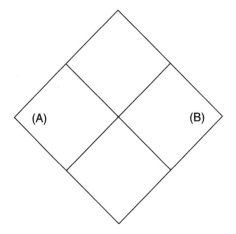

The kinds of output we may get from the (A) version would be the following:

❑ History of customer focus, and organisations that have tried it
❑ Check lists – ten steps to becoming more customer focused
❑ Bullet points – four key advantages to being customer focused
❑ Prescriptions – do these things and you will become customer focused
❑ Things which being customer focused will lead to.

If we move the intervention or module to position (B) on the diamond, we move from fact-based input to experiential activities, allowing participants to find their own styles, test these out, and monitor how they and others feel about the various approaches. We should expect very different kinds of outcome:

❑ Empathetic responses to customers
❑ An appreciation of the value to customers of being customer focused
❑ A sense of empowerment to go and be customer focused
❑ Enhanced customer-oriented skills
❑ Learning behaviours rather than facts, theories or models.

We have taken this example, and run it through two of the extreme 'points' of the diamond simply as an illustration of how, in so doing, we can think about the options available to us in planning to meet a specific learning aim, and what the possible implications of each of those options may be. It seems to me that neither of these, alone, is likely to 'guarantee' that the desired learning takes place.

Implications for Learning Theory

The simplest implication of the idea that there are four distinctly different approaches to learning is that good learning design should cater, in turn, perhaps, for the different needs of learners by adding to the recipe a good dose of all four kinds of ingredient (or, in many cases only three, since there are many instances of interventions where there are no SF managers reported). This is, I suspect, oversimplistic.

How one goes about designing an activity to achieve a learning aim depends upon where managers are coming from. Good 'current state' research is important in this. This is because I am suggesting that lasting learning, which leads to sustained behavioural change, is dependent for success upon the engagement of all parts of the manager's personality. In other words, successful managerial learning comprises the use of all four of the approaches we have been describing. This will lead to the kinds of criteria for successful learning shown in Figure 10.4.

A manager has gone through successful learning if he or she

❑ knows what to do when a relevant situation arises; knows why it makes sense to undertake this kind of response; and can articulate evidence to 'prove' the efficacy of this way of working (ST)
❑ can 'model' situations where the learning is needed, and adapt the acquired rules to meet the unexpected; knows how this model or theory fits with other tools and concepts into a holistic framework or overarching 'theory' (NT)
❑ has internalised the learnt behaviours into 'belief systems' and values; wants to make it work for self and for others; has the determination to push aside barriers to the implementation of the new approaches and behaviours (NF)
❑ has explored and challenged any unconscious assumptions and habits which may have prevented learning; can empathise with and care about those who will be impacted by any consequent change (s); has embedded into their unconscious the 'new' habits, and will (unconsciously) do it every time (SF)

LEARNING: FOUR ELEMENTS

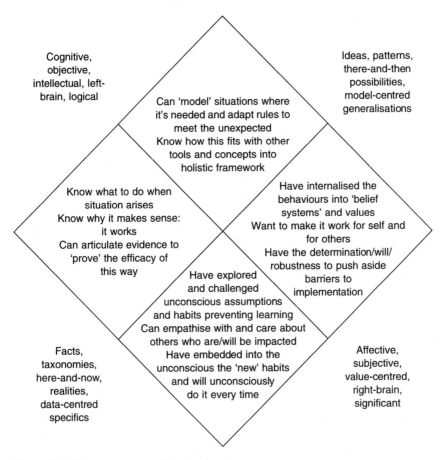

Figure 10.4 *Key components of lasting learning*

These four conditions depend, respectively, upon the collaborative engagement in the learning process of the manager's four sets of function pairs. The absence of the engagement of any of these leaves a 'hole' through which the putative learning can escape:

❏ Without engaging the ST pair, the manager may fail to 'test' out new ideas and behaviours against the 'realities' of the situation, thereby adopting models, beliefs and responses which will be inappropriate or 'wrong'. An example of this would be the untested adoption of practices which work in the private sector into the public sector. Probably because of both the prevalence of managers with preferences for S and T, and the historical focus of management training upon facts and logic, this kind of potential error is easily spotted before it is carried too far. It is often referred to as 'healthy scepticism'. It can, however, spill over into an unwillingness to adopt any idea or practice which cannot be proven there and then to be efficacious.

❏ Without engaging the NT pair, a manager may fail to understand the significance of a new theory; in many cases this stems from a failure to understand the theory at all. This kind of lack of engagement often manifests itself in an accusation of new ideas being 'too theoretical', a charge which we explored in Chapter 1.

❏ Without engaging the NF pair, a manager may understand the ideas and their application as an idea, but lack the willingness or commitment to do anything with them. This can be disguised during a management and organisation development intervention by the 'flow' (Csikszentmihalyi 1990) which can be generated during such events. Fully engaging the NF pair means accessing managers' deeper value sets, helping managers to assess more than their cognitive responses to learning, and exploring how the new ideas, behaviours and approaches will fit within the concepts of self, career and future which make each manager what he or she is as a person, as well as a manager. This issue is more fully explored in Chapter 11.

❏ Without engaging the SF pair, a manager may fail to explore his or her emotional and deeper metaphorical responses to the learning. Most of our emotional responses remain, unless we actively seek to get in touch with them, within the unconscious. It is not a habitual response to any managerial situation, including 'traditional' learning, for managers to confront how they feel about it. Work has to be done; rules have to be followed; profits have to be achieved; and staff have to be disciplined. Emotions get in the way. From the beginning of Chapter 7 we have been touching upon this issue. And in Chapter 9 it was noted that there are few managers with preferences for S and F combined. There is a prima facie case for arguing, therefore, that it is here that the most common holes will be found in holistic learning

The SF part of our personality is that which deals with the emotional here and now – emotions of our own, and those of people close to us. In Chapter 7 we explored the (often unconscious) influences of emotions on perceptions, judgements, decisions and actions – all key activities of managers. It is clear that far too many management and organisation development interventions produce little in the way of deep or lasting impact (Coleman 1998: 245–8). It is also clear that, traditionally, a significant number of management and organisation development interventions have shied away from engaging the SF parts of the participants' personalities.

Ideas, models, new approaches have been 'validated' by 'proof' (ST) that they work elsewhere; by 'making sense' (NT) within an overall cognitive framework; by 'being in line with where we want to be as an organisation' (NF); but rarely are they 'validated' by appeal to how managers feel about them. Indeed, it is often the case that such emotional responses are 'dealt with' as barriers to understanding, or resistance to learning which needs to be got out of the way, rather than as part of the learning process itself. ('You're bound to feel like that at first, but just go and try it, and you'll see that it works/makes sense.')

This is not an argument in favour of rejecting new ideas and approaches simply because some managers may not like them at first. It is, however, an argument in favour of taking as serious an approach to the SF aspects of learning as we do to the others. It can be time consuming, and it does demand different skills on the part of many management and organisation development providers and facilitators. But it may have the longer-term advantage of eliminating a great deal of the 'wasted' effort on management and organisation development which manifests itself in a large proportion of what is 'learnt' not being implemented.

My argument is that, without engaging, involving and aligning all four parts of the personality in learning, then learning has not, fully, taken place.

Engaging all four aspects of the personality as we have 'mapped' them in the diamond model depends upon a number of factors. Among these will be how the intervention is put together, both in terms of the activities and tools incorporated within the intervention, and the overall 'story' which the intervention seeks to unfold. Another concerns the degree of awareness of these influences on the part of facilitators of learning, who may carry their own unconscious assumptions about what constitutes learning. Yet another relates to the 'learning maturity' of participants – how prepared they are to engage different aspects of their personality within a learning experience. It is these factors which we deal with next.

Using the Diamond to Plot Associated 'Learning Technologies'

In the examples I have used of plotting topics and themes on the diamond, I clearly involved some 'learning technologies'. By learning technologies, I simply mean all those teaching and learning methods which have evolved over the years, and which we can call upon as required, to help achieve a learning aim. For a handy list of such 'learning technologies' see, for example, Burgoyne and Stuart (1978).

It is reasonable and helpful, therefore, even if not scientific, to use the diamond to 'plot' learning 'technologies'. It is often the process of doing such plotting, more than the outcome which is most helpful. By this I mean that, although one may expect a 'technology' such as 'role play' to appear roughly in the same zone each time we decided to consider its position on this map, role plays may be used for a variety of different learning aims. It is in the very discussion we have among ourselves and with our clients that we uncover hitherto hidden assumptions we may have made but not shared about one or other aspect of the learning aims (in this, the diamond serves a similar purpose as the management development grid).

Because of the potential for shifting, albeit subtly, around the diamond by the various 'technologies' I have not included such a plot here.

'Tutor' and Learner Styles – the Third Dimension

In my introduction to the diamond I also made brief reference to some examples of individual learner preferences.

The notion that different people have different learning styles has been recognised since people first studied learning. However, doing something with this information demands some kind of organised thinking about those differences. Both Kolb, with his Learning Styles Inventory (Kolb *et al.* 1974) and Honey and Mumford, with their Learning Styles Questionnaire (Honey and Mumford 1992) use their respective versions of the learning cycle model as a basis for questionnaires which seek to identify individuals' preferences for or dislike of each of the four stages of learning as they describe them, producing, respectively 'concrete experience', 'reflective observation', 'abstract conceptualisation', and 'active experimentation' (Kolb 1984); and 'activators', 'reflectors', 'theorists' and 'pragmatists'.

It is argued that taking the learning styles of learners, as ascertained by these questionnaires, into account, and designing interventions in line with their preferred learning styles, produced better learning for managers. And in so far as anecdotal evidence is concerned, this seems to be good advice. However, when subjected to 'rigorous' research, it is hard to find a great deal of evidence which gives us confidence that these kinds of questionnaires can do more than provide us with another kind of mental reminders to be more sensitive to individual needs (Hayes and Allinson 1996). Nothing in the research confirms conclusively anything about learner styles, trainer styles, whether it is better to match these or not, whether learners can change their styles, or whether tutors can do the same.

One of the problems with this research base, as Hayes and Allinson acknowledge, is that, in order to generate the kinds of statistically valid data required to generate 'valid' results, a limited range of variables have been worked on, and these have explored only cognitive learning. This seems to me to be far too narrow a field of research to be able to offer a great deal of 'scientific' support to our ideas of learning styles.

Personal Styles Used in Learning, Rather than Learning Styles

Throughout the book, and through the experiences of working with managers and my colleagues, I have treated learning not as a 'different' kind of activity from everyday life, but as an integral part thereof. This is in line with the observations of such writers as Burgoyne, Stuart, Mumford, French, and so on, so there is nothing radical in this idea. But it does explain why my colleagues and I choose not to use either the Kolb or the Honey and Mumford learning styles questionnaires in our own learning design. It is because the MBTI® offers us what we believe to be a much deeper and more pertinent picture on the managers we work with, and on ourselves as facilitators of learning.

Because learning is part of living, how we learn will be affected by how we live our lives; this, in turn, will be influenced (in very subtle ways) by our preferences for Extraversion or Introversion, Sensing or Intuition, Thinking of Feeling, J or P. From the point of view of active learning, we take the functions as primary; although, clearly, we do then follow through, in micro design, with the other two pairs. In this, we are in line with, for example, Fairhurst and Fairhurst, who describe the output from the four functions as 'learning skills', and the output from the other preferences as 'living skills' (Fairhurst and Fairhurst 1995: 26–9).

I have also argued that learning is about change. How we go about managing change is also significantly influenced by our personality types (Barger and Kirby 1995). It seems, therefore, that approaching managers as different kinds of learners is simply another way of approaching them as different kinds of people, and not as groups of 'activists' or 'pragmatists'.

Of course, one could argue that, in practice, the caricatures of 'ST' people, 'NF' people, and so on, are no different from the simple four categories of Kolb or Honey and Mumford. Indeed, this could well be the outcome of using MBTI® solely in this way. However, here is the key reason for our using what, at this level, provides no better nor no worse set of four classes of learners. It is that we do not stop there. The guidelines we can obtain from the diamond, and the respective locations of the four function pairs, ST, SF, NF and NT, are the *beginning* of a journey which involves some of the enormous subtleties of the MBTI®. Sharing information with managers about their preferences may start with thinking about the impact on their learning styles (and of our facilitator styles), but it can then develop into almost as many different aspects of them as people and as managers as is appropriate for the particular intervention. The dialogue can be pursued into such areas as the impact of personality on their managerial styles, their approaches to coaching, their attitudes to strategic planning, and so on. It can also help in explorations of the interfaces between individuals, and between home and work, and so on.

Because we see MBTI® as a 'way into' the broader areas of managerial and personal behaviours and learning, therefore, we tend to use the function pairs as the key to guiding our thoughts on learner styles in our interventions.

The Implication of 'Learner Styles'

Most groups of managers with whom we work tend to be a fair mix of psychological types. Although we can accommodate individual differences in some of the micro design work, such as in one-to-one coaching or counselling, from a macro design point of view, it would be misleading to suggest that learner styles play a major part. There are two key ways in which they can help.

The first is simply in reminding us (although we should need no such reminders) that although at any one time groups are likely to contain Extraverts and Introverts, Sensing people and Intuitives, Thinkers and Feelers, J and P preferences, and that therefore whatever we happen to be doing at that moment is likely to be better for some than for others, even in group work we can provide the kind of variety which will variously engage different kinds of people. Where individual work is being done, of course, managers can satisfy their own needs.

The second point is often more telling. Some organisations attract a disproportionate number of people with one kind of preference rather than another; some organisations evolve 'cultures' which seem to value and reward some kinds of behaviours over others. In some cases, these two phenomena coexist, and reinforce each other, as we (and the new CEO) found to be the case at Global Technologies. In situations such as these, which good 'current state' research ought to expose, we may have some clear pointers to macro design considerations.

The first thing we may feel the need to do is draw attention to what is, from our point of view, a potentially dangerous bias, as the following case study may illustrate:

THE GM TEAM – A CASE OF THE BLACK HOLE

Background

In this case, our client was the UK operation of an international, American-headquartered high-tech organisation of long standing. The whole company had adopted a team-based model for its sales and marketing activities, and undertook a series of team initiation activities to try to establish the teams as quickly and effectively as possible.

We ran about 20 team initiation sessions for teams in the UK. Some of the teams were brand new; others had, for a variety of reasons, been in existence for some time. The team we shall be describing, let us call them the GM Team, was one of those which had been together for quite some time, having been formed from the core of a successful but smaller independent company which had been acquired by the large multinational about two years previously.

The team retained a number of the cultural elements from its former independent existence, and team members often freely described their new parent organisation in less than complimentary terms; to them it was bureaucratic and slow, and posed something of a threat to their way of working. It is fair to say that at the time we started to work with the GM Team, they had not been fully assimilated into the parent company's culture, and were proud of it.

Team Initiation

The blueprint for the team initiation sessions we ran for the UK teams was not perfect. Time and financial constraints meant that each team was available for only 48 hours. In that time we had to try to bring the team members to an awareness of themselves as a team and as individuals, and start the process of enhancing their interworking skills. We decided to use MBTI within the sessions, partly because of its inherent value in the process, and partly because we had already been using it within the European operations of the company in a wider developmental context.

The sessions normally took place at the weekends (from 4 p.m. on Friday to 4 p.m. on Sunday), as most teams considered that they could not spare two days out of the working week to work together on team development issues. They were dynamic sessions with limited time devoted to input of models and concepts, and most time allocated to team development exercises and reviewing learning from those exercises. Information and insights into MBTI were interspersed among those more experiential activities.

Each weekend was different from the others. This was partly due to our own learning as we progressed with the teams; fortunately we recognise that every intervention we make into an organisation is as much an opportunity for us to continue to learn as it is for the managers who attend. The differences were more a result, however, of the dynamics of the teams, each of which was a unique blend of people and preferences.

The GM Team weekend was among the most memorable; as a team, the members impacted us more than any other team from the UK organisation had done or would do during the whole team initiation programme.

The GM Team Weekend

It was clear to us from the outset that the GM Team had some very strong characteristics. Not untypically for a sales-oriented team, they did not all arrive on time for the 4 o'clock start. By the time we did gather them all together to start the weekend with a review of goals and ground rules, it was getting a little late in the evening. This being Friday, we stood between the team and drinks at a bar, a dangerous position, we learnt very quickly, as the team assured us that they did not need any team development since they were as near perfect as any team could get: 'So let's all go and get bladdered' (which we correctly interpreted to mean 'drunk'!)

Among the frameworks we shared with the team during the weekend were two related ideas: the idea that a team could exhibit a 'type' (building on the concept of 'group type' explored by Sandra Hirsh (1991); and the notion of adaptive and negative forms of preference behaviours as described by Naomi Quenk (1993). These were to prove important to our understanding of the team as we went through the weekend and beyond.

Individual Preferences

The reported types of the team members came out as the following:

ISTJ	ISFJ	INFJ	INTJ
		Paul	Ron
ISTP	ISFP	INFP	INTP
ESTP	ESFP	ENFP	ENTP
Terry			Kevin
			Doug
			Joe
ESTJ	ESFJ	ENFJ	ENTJ
Martin	Gary	Steve	Patrick

During the weekend, as we had the chance to talk to the individual team members, few of whom had any previous knowledge of MBTI®, some of the individuals modified their perceptions of their 'best fit' from the reported type.

The 'best fit' we ended up with after the weekend was:

ISTJ Doug	ISFJ Gary	INFJ Paul	INTJ Ron
ISTP	ISFP	INFP	INTP
ESTP Patrick Terry	ESFP	ENFP Joe	ENTP Kevin
ESTJ Martin	ESFJ	ENFJ Steve	ENTJ

A few words of explanation for some of the 'moves'.

Patrick had attended a much longer programme at Cranfield at which we had explored his preferences. On this programme, he had become very comfortable with ESTP, and agreed that this was his best fit type, even though his scores for the retake of the indicator for this weekend had given ESTJ, with the S/N scores being 14 each, and with a small margin for J rather than P. Given his behaviour, we were all puzzled at the reported 'preference' for J; he really did seem more comfortable with P.

Gary had reported a preference for E, but quickly, and with full support from his colleagues within the team, considered his best fit type to be ISFJ (both in terms of a preference for Introversions, and in terms of a greater comfort with the type description of an ISFJ than of ESFJ).

Joe 'discovered' his preference for Feeling only late in the weekend, and it was only after the event that we had any chance to explore with him the implications of this late realisation. As the Team Leader, there were wider implications for the team as well as for himself as an individual.

Doug never fully confirmed his 'best fit' as ISTJ, although agreed during the weekend that it was quite likely that, if any set of preferences reflected the way he was, this set was closest. However, even after the event, as we talked further, he remained the most sceptical of the entire issue of preferences and type.

Team 'Type'

During the weekend, and in order to enable people to work on the exercises and reviews in small enough groups to participate fully, the team of ten split into two teams of five, except for the 'plenary' sessions where we discussed such broader issues as type and team dynamics in principle. The two 'subteams' which formed themselves (before they had received any feedback on MBTI® and their own types) were as follows:

	BEST-FIT TYPE (REPORTED)		BEST-FIT TYPE (REPORTED)
Joe	ENFP (ENTP)	Patrick	ESTP (ENTJ)
Terry	ESTP	Martin	ESTJ
Paul	INFJ	Gary	ISFJ (ESFJ)
Ron	INTJ	Steve	ENFJ
Kevin	ENTP	Doug	ISTJ (ENTP)

We decided, on the morning of the second day, to get the two teams to undertake an exercise which included a 'Team Health Check'. The reason we could get away with this idea by this stage was that, as the first day and a half progressed, team members were able to recognise that, despite their previous arrogance, the team as a whole had significant imperfections.

In addressing this task, the team of Joe, Terry, Paul, Ron and Kevin made what for them was an interesting discovery – that the GM Team as a whole could be characterised as an ENTP team. However, they also recognised that, in Naomi Quenk's terms, they were not a well-adapted ENTP. Through the process of selecting descriptive words which characterised for them their key interfaces with their customers; with people within their company but outside their immediate team; with each other; and with people who were outside their team, but who shared the second floor of their building with them, they repeatedly chose words which related to Extraversion, iNtuition, Thinking and Perceiving, both in their adaptive and negative forms. And while their list of words which related to their interfaces with their customers contained more 'adaptive' than 'negative' words (they believed their relationships with their customers were very good), the other lists contained an uncomfortable number of 'negative' words.

They concluded, and reported back to the other five GM Team members (who concurred with their findings), that it was useful to think of their Team as having a 'type', that the Team type was ENTP, and that it was a poorly adjusted ENTP team. For the first time they were prepared to accept both that they may have some weaknesses as a team, and that those weaknesses may have unfortunate consequences for them in their business and for them as individuals. They were able to start the process of seeing themselves as others see them, and accept that from the outside they may not present a pleasant aspect.

Reflecting Upon Some of the Team Members

Clearly, we have been referring to 'the team' and what 'they' admitted and accepted; and in so doing, generalising. It may not have been the case that each individual went through the 'same' revelations and processes of accepting. What stimulated the follow-up we undertook with the Team was primarily the response of Joe, the Team Leader, the team member who reassessed his preferences from ENTP (the same as the 'team type') to ENFP.

We spoke at some length about some of the individuals in the team. Gary had concerned the Cranfield facilitators. His reported type was ESFJ, but he and his colleagues agreed a 'best fit' type of ISFJ. And yet Gary, within 48 hours, found three separate opportunities to make gratuitously hurtful remarks to me or my Cranfield colleague; remarks which may have been attempts to replicate the 'humour' of the 'classic' ENTP, but which were crude, clumsy and hurtful. He made no attempt at apology. These were not the behaviours we would expect from someone confirmed as having ISFJ preferences.

Patrick had reported and accepted ESTP on his previous programme with us; indeed he had proudly adopted the role of 'exemplar' of the 'classic' traits of the ESTP, one which received further support when he arrived at this weekend, very late, and driving at speed in a thinly disguised racing car right up to the front door of the country house we were working in, braking only at the last moment, and sending gravel flying in all directions. Here was Extraverted Sensing in action. Yet in the environment of the team, iNtuition was the favoured preference – Sensing was considered 'dull', 'fussy', 'boring' 'detailed', 'unimaginative', short-term', and so on. A dominant Sensor, wanting to be accepted, may have (albeit unconsciously) adjusted his behaviour more closely to match the team culture. Where the reported preference for J came from, nobody was able to explain!

Doug, the reported ENTP who seemed to be heading inexorably towards ISTJ, was among the least comfortable members of the team. A technical specialist by training and choosing, he seemed out of place and stressed by the loud, lively, crude, 'pally', flexible, imaginative environment of the team. No-one, not even he, could explain how his reported type was ENTP, as very little in his behaviour or his style came even close to what we would associate with ENTP. Was Doug simply trying, through the way he completed the instrument, to become 'one of the lads'?

Terry was one of the lads. The Team culture was tough, macho, 'laddish'. The pub was more of a home to them than the office. Drinking was mandatory – preferably heavy drinking. Women were there to be leered at, chased, patronised, conquered and then abandoned. Terry is a woman, the only one on the team, and a secretary. She is a very attractive woman, named Theresa; but to fit into the team culture, she had to accept a masculine version of her name. She did not complain. Few people did. Complaining was not an acceptable part of the Team culture.

It was through his reflecting upon these individuals, and what the Team culture may be doing to them; and through his recognition that others from outside the Team may see him, as Team Leader, as an unpleasant, sexist bully that Joe began to worry. He realised that he cared a great deal about people liking him as a person; and he knew, but had not wanted to admit it, that he wanted people to be happy and comfortable in their work. He had assumed that, by fostering the, for him, exciting, innovative, fast-moving, tough culture of the Team, he was maintaining for others an ideal working environment. Discovering that people such as Gary, Doug, Patrick and Terry may be suffering, daily, within this environment hurt Joe.

In less extreme cases, however, we may simply need to recognise that the bias we detect ought to tell us something about the style, structure, approach, and even the aims of a management and organisation development intervention. Should we fail to do so, it can have the effect of seriously minimising the value of the intervention. As Chapter 9 shows, this was one of the key learning points for us from our research into the Tech-Test case. That case also highlighted for us that our own organisation is not immune from the kinds of bias which we have found in Global, in the GM Team, in Tech-Test, and many many other organisations.

We encourage all members of faculty involved on our interventions to take into account in planning their contributions, not only the learning styles of the learners, but the degree of match and mismatch between the four elements: learners' styles (if there is a pattern within the group); the tutor's own preferences; the topic or theme the tutor is responsible for; and the 'technologies' or learning methods they may be thinking of using. We do not insist that these should all match; the research (Hayes & Allinson 1996: 70–71) is inconclusive on the relative values of matching or of mismatch (where mismatches may provide the kind of challenge which wakes up the 'pay attention' part of our minds). However, in the light of the non-rigorous research which comprises the many years of our own experience, we do ask that tutors recognise the potential impact of such matches and mismatches on how the event may unfold.

In conclusion, the diamond model enables us to bring together a whole range of learning design factors:

❑ learner style
❑ tutor style
❑ learning method
❑ learning topic or theme

It does not tell us how to design an intervention; but it does raise the kinds of questions which a good design process needs to address and to answer.

DESIGNING IN LINEAR TIME

One of the greatest problems with management and organisation development interventions is that time is unilinear: some things have to precede others. Anyone who has attempted to write about a set of intimately interrelated set of ideas will feel the same about writing – it has to end up as one word in front of another, all, effectively, in one dimension. So we have to make a virtue out of necessity in learning design, and call it 'building', so that, once managers understand one thing, they can build on this and understand the next. Since the human mind works with millions of neurones all talking to each other at the same time, this seems criminally inefficient. But despite the imaginative efforts of the likes of Buzan (1981; 1983; 1988) and de Bono (1971; 1984) to help us shake off this temporal shackle, I believe we are unlikely to lose this design constraint in the foreseeable future.

This does, however, provide us with a design clue, which is based upon the notion that, whatever goes on during a management and organisation development intervention, managers are likely to go through an 'acclimatisation' process; to get more and more used to the situation. This clue was picked up by Stuart and Holmes (1982) who married the notion to that of Hersey and Blanchard's (1977) 'situational leadership'.

The ensuing basic model looks like this:

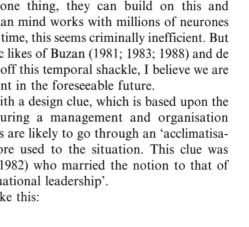

Figure 10.5 *Successful tutor styles*

The three key behavioural 'variables' described by Stuart and Holmes are as follows:

❑ *Tutor directive behaviour*: which is about the amount and quality of direction provided by the tutor. Direction, in this sense implies relative responsibility and authority on such matters as the what, how and where of the learning activities: goals, content, process, structure, balance, and so on.

❑ *Tutor relationship behaviour*: which is about the amount and quality of the social and emotional support given by the tutor, through warmth, friendliness, respect, encouragement, to the learner.

❑ *Learner situational maturity*: which is 'situation-specific'; in other words, it is not about how mature or how good at being a learner a manager may be in the general sense; but is about reactions to and involvement in a specific learning event. It involves the learner's relative capacity to set appropriate learning goals and his or her willingness and ability to take responsibility for their own learning, as well as any previous experience with management development or education.

In their paper, Stuart and Holmes provide brief elaborations of the terms they use within their model. Much of the justification Stuart and Holmes provide for this model is based upon its 'making sense', or having 'face validity'. It is not based upon rigorous research; but I wonder how helpful such rigorous research, should it be undertaken, would be. The model, as well as management and organisation development interventions themselves, are so 'riddled with' socially constructed concepts that I suspect any attempt at 'proving' the model through such means would provide little more than years of work and internecine debate for droves of academics.

Clearly, the guidelines provided in their approach are meant as such, and not as absolutely hard and fast rules. We have already explored, for example, the influence of personality type on such matters as the perceptions people may have of what is 'appropriate'; the 'boundaries' between the different behaviours will be seen differently by different 'types'. People with a preference for Feeling, for example, will tend to be ready for tutors to move up the 'relationship scale' earlier than those with a preference for Thinking, who will want tutors to 'earn respect' through demonstrating rigour and competence before moving on. This latter perspective will be even more likely from Thinkers with a J preference, who value the structure and order of well-directed activities. And so on.

None of these perspectives is guaranteed, no matter how clear an individual manager's preferences may be. Other factors will come into play as well, among which will be each manager's immediate impression of the tutor.

Chapter 7 explored the notions of instant emotional response and archetypes. These are likely to be brought into play as soon as a manager meets a tutor. The limbic system's emotionally charged memory banks and 'library' of archetypal templates will be working away within milliseconds (often quite undetected within the subconscious) to 'project' onto the tutor an impression which will stand as the yardstick against which to measure subsequent tutor behaviours.

In many instances, what will be projected will be some kind of 'authority' complex. Anyone who has worked in management and organisation development will recognise the first moment of contact with a group, a moment which is the more highly charged the earlier in an intervention that meeting takes place. Those ultimately responsible for the entire learning event, the Management Development Consultant in our terms (see Chapter 2), often receive the most powerful of such projections. At this moment the tutor is often seen to have all the knowledge, even, unfortunately at times, to the extent of being the only one in the room who knows what the event is about! So yet another, largely unconscious, factor in increasing learner maturity and the concomitant tutor behaviours will be the metaphor of parenthood and childhood, authority being gradually relinquished as the 'child' grows confident and competent enough to become an 'adult' side by side with the 'parent'.

Still further, the tutor's role at the early stages may be to help provide a 'neutral' or 'standard' set of mental maps for managers to explore and incorporate. Given the enormous variety of the mental maps of a group of managers (especially those who may be coming together for the first time) and the (in principle) equal validity of each of these manager's maps, high direction may be required at the outset to avoid the Tower of Babel which may result from a 'free-for-all' of undirected exploration.

These considerations are simply some of the ways in which to 'make sense' of Stuart and Holmes's approach to the 'evolution' of the directive and relationship behaviours of tutors as learners mature. None of them 'prove' that their approach is right; but all suggest that, as a guiding principle, it is compatible with the various aspects of learning which Chapter 7 explored.

Bringing the 'Maturity Model' and the Diamond Together

Earlier in the chapter I suggested that different themes or topics, along with different learning 'technologies' lend themselves differently to different broad approaches to managerial learning. This was illustrated by the diamond model. What that model could not do by itself was to tell us anything about how to move around the diamond, from topic to topic, module to module, in linear time. But since it is feasible to map onto the same diamond model the various 'tutor directive' and 'tutor relationship' styles, and since these are said to be variously applicable over time, we have the beginnings of 'programme generator' mechanism.

By 'beginnings' I mean just that. Just as management and organisation development is not a mechanical process, so design for learning cannot be mechanical. And just as identifying one's Home Base in MBTI terms is the start of a journey of self-discovery and development and not the end, so the output from the process of feeding learning aims, learner and tutor styles, themes and topics, and learning technologies into the diamond is where we start to talk about learning design, and not where we end with a 'proven' agenda.

What it helps us to do is to say why, if we deviate from what the mechanical process tells us about what we should be doing, with whom, how and why at each step of the learning design, we are choosing so to deviate. In other words, we are forced to consider, carefully, and against a significant amount of 'evidence' that the process has produced a design which 'makes sense', the reasons for and possible consequences of, doing something else.

DESIGN, LIKE LEARNING, IS A CONTINUING PROCESS

The 'quality' movement of the 1980s (Crosby 1984; Deming 1988; Macdonald and Piggott 1990) left us with the impression that it was sloppy management not to get it 'right, first time, on time, every time'; in other words, by the time you deliver, the 'product' should have 'zero defects'. There is a sense in which this principle ought to apply to management and organisation development as much as making cars, and the aim of good design is to get as close as possible to 'zero defects'.

But working with people is not the same as working with machines and inorganic raw materials. People are unpredictable, even when they have been interviewed, psychometrically tested, and have 'come with an open mind'. Involving managers actively in the learning process, especially through experiential learning, means that 'things may not go exactly as planned'. Every management and organisation development intervention is different, even when the agenda and facilitator team stay the same.

This means that the job of developing managerial learning entails a deep understanding of the learning and design processes.

CONCLUSIONS

The complexities which we have been exploring in this book demand a sophisticated response from management and organisation development providers. Managerial learning cannot be reduced to a simple model; and it is therefore legitimate to continue to seek different perspectives on the learning processes, and different means of tapping into those processes. Some of these means will appear highly 'naturalistic', as where two managers sit together to explore their understanding of a situation; others will seem 'strange', as with some of the activities which accompany outdoor development, for example. Some will be effective, others will hinder learning. But there is nothing inherent in any learning approach or technique which makes it a better or worse tool. Like all tools, those of management and organisation development need expert handling.

This is why it seems to me unhelpful when writers deliberately narrow the field, as, for example, when Mumford says, 'Organisations get overwhelmed by the latest approach to appraisal, or decide to send all their top people to Harvard, or send everyone on an outdoor training course. My argument would be that such fads . . . arise when management development is not driven by business needs but by someone's idea of clever processes and when development activities are not appropriate to need or to individuals' (Mumford 1993: 43). In Chapter 3 I also suggested that it was easy for organisations to be swayed by such attractive 'technologies'; but using the outdoors can, indeed, be a highly positive and appropriate response to business needs. In some circumstances, it may be the best response we can find.

Throughout the earlier chapters of the book, I argued for the centrality of linking management development directly to business needs. In this chapter, I have suggested that making such links, and ensuring that learning is most effectively designed to meet those organisational, business needs is not about fads, but about taking a sophisticated and mature approach to all the possibilities we have available as learning tools, techniques and approaches. Designing for learning is no longer about doing what feels right for the designer; it is about treating learning design as seriously and professionally as engineering design.

11 Managers as People

INTRODUCTION

This book is written from the perspective of providing management and organisation development interventions to client organisations. Our customer is the person or persons within our client organisation who pays the bill – the sponsor for the intervention, or our key partner in the management and organisation development venture. But the 'raw material' upon which we operate (I use a mechanistic analogy deliberately to bring out the hidden assumptions the better) are people – the managers whom we actually work with. Their needs may not always be completely in line with the learning needs of the organisation, needs which we will have explored through our current- and desired-state analyses (see Chapter 5).

This can pose a dilemma. If the managers with whom we work need something which appears to be contradictory to what we have been charged to 'deliver', what should we do? Should we accede to the demands of the fee-paying customer, ignoring the problems of the managers as 'not our problem'? Or should we cleave to the managers, and form a caucus of resistance to the manipulation being attempted by the organisation, thereby abandoning our 'collusion'?

Clearly, such dilemmas are rarely so stark. Effective work in the current-state and desired-state analyses tends to highlight such potential clashes well in advance, and we are able to confront them before they become a problem. But this is a naive position to take. To assume that one can, through the vehicles available to us in our current-state work, eliminate all potential mismatches of need between the organisation and the managers is to ignore the essential subtlety of the management and organisation development process.

The dilemma is normally resolved by ignoring one of the two manifestations of the self: the inner self. There is, in a great deal of the assumptions about management and organisation development the belief that its focus is exclusively the social self. Like many assumptions, this is rarely spoken; like many assumptions, people who make it may not even be aware they are making it.

Most of the earlier chapters of this book were written with this assumption unspoken. It made sense, and, for a great deal of the work we do with our customers and the managers from those client organisations, the assumption does not appear to interfere significantly with the apparent effectiveness of the interventions.

The language of management and organisation development focused on the social self exclusively contains such words and phrases as 'behaviour change', knowledge, skills, attitudes, competences, and so on. These words, like most words in English, have multiple meanings. But when we explore their use in dialogues with our customers and the managers, their primary use is in an impersonal arena. It is as though these behaviours, skills and so on were independent, impersonal entities which are susceptible of mechanistic manipulation through teaching. In this conceptual space, managers bring their behaviours, skills, and so on with them; these are then exposed to 'development'; they are then packed back into the managers' proverbial briefcases and taken back to work to be applied to the managerial tasks they perform.

With this as a dominant image for management and organisation development it is not surprising that writers such as Mumford see no value in outdoor development or in almost any off-the-job activities. If these 'tools' of behaviour, knowledge, skills and competences are designed to be used on the job, then why not hone them there and then?

Chapter 7 showed that, although there is clearly a very powerful social element in managerial learning, there is also a very powerful element which relates to the other side of the pairing – the inner self. The influence on learning of the largely unconscious elements of our minds makes it clear that any model for management and organisation development which ignores the inner self is likely to be constrained in its usefulness. Learning takes place at the interfaces of inner and social self.

Given the amount of physical time in a waking day which managers will spend at work, and given the influence that organisational life has upon most managers, many of those managers' interactions between inner and social self will be grounded in the emotional, metaphorical, archetypal as well as intellectual relationships the managers have with their organisations. It will be within the very organisations who are sponsoring their participation in a management and organisation development intervention that many managers will seek a significant part of their meaning, significance, self-esteem, personal values and growth. Any management and organisation development has the potential to influence those meanings, significance, self-esteem, values and growth.

As providers of management and organisation development we can choose to ignore this, or we can embrace the opportunity to work with managers as people, rather than managers-as-competences. As we suggested at the beginning of Chapter 7, managers may not want us to do this; they may feel more comfortable with the 'conspiracy' which keeps them protected from personal change and growth. Given the ineptitude of many management and organisation development interventions in the past (and, unfortunately, in the present in some cases), this is not surprising. For managers genuinely to open themselves to the full range of learning opportunities which a management and organisation development intervention can provide, they need to be convinced that the exercise will be handled professionally, sensitively and with understanding of the processes which may be taking place. Not all management and organisation development providers deliver this.

PERSONAL GROWTH – THE MANAGER AS DEVELOPING PERSON

Our inner and social selves can sometimes seem to be working towards 'opposing aims' (Modell 1993: 42). Some managers find themselves in situations in their working lives which are not necessarily what they would have chosen, in an 'ideal' world. If we ask managers to step back and ask themselves the question 'Is this really what you want to do with your life?' (Stein 1992: 12), many are likely to answer 'No (but this is the best I can do with the cards I have been dealt).' Organisations provide us with the wherewithal to survive; they can, to a greater or lesser extent, provide for other needs (Maslow 1954). But they can also provide for individuals severe challenges which can manifest themselves in a split between the aims of the social self – to fit in, to survive, to succeed – and those of the inner self.

In order to appreciate the kinds of 'frustration' which organisations can place in the path of personal growth and development, it may be helpful briefly to explore the kinds of personal growth and development which organisations may frustrate. What, in other words, does the inner self want?

Personal Growth – the Intellectual Approach

One of the features of being involved in management and organisation development today is that there are an increasing number of managers who, once they feel comfortable with us, are prepared to share with us that they have adopted a route to self improvement of some kind. Increasing pressures and rapid change throw up a great deal of demand for ways of coping with, and transcending those pressures, and riding the crest of the waves of change. Paths to such transcendence may be primarily cognitive (see, for example, Engleman 1966; Hill 1966; Buzan 1974 and 1977; Russell 1979), focusing upon the power of the intellect to produce better performance.

There is clearly a great deal to be said for this kind of cognitive work. A significant proportion of the 'product' of many management and organisation development interventions is cognitively based. And Chapter 1 argued that the ways in which the 'world' of organisations and management are 'constructed' has a lot to do with the ways in which managers' cognitive maps are created and modified through experience. From Kelly (1955) to Fournier (1996), exploration of the role of the cognitive in how managers deal with the world, and cope with change is a well-established and respectable part of what we do.

Chapter 7 includes a concern in western culture with an overdependence upon intellect – the 'dictatorship of the left hemisphere' – and it is clear to most that personal development is more than simply getting our left brains to take greater executive control. Yet that is what a great deal of the kinds of 'self-development' approaches seem to lead to. Even works purporting to explore the less cognitive, less intellectual side of ourselves are often thinly disguised means of broadening the hegemony of the left brain. Simply providing names for emotions (Modell 1993: 173) brings them into consciousness and gives a sense of control; but far from broadening our personal capacities, it simply increases the dominance of the intellect over those emotions. Telling oneself that one is calm, or counting our blessings can have powerful short-term effects which can be highly beneficial (Donaldson 1992: 206). And it may be helpful for Thinking dominant male managers to undertake a number of exercises to 'nurture the feeling component' (Martin 1993: 40–3). Such approaches are highly valuable ways of helping managers on a practical plane. But they clearly approach self-development through the cognitive, conscious intellect.

In so doing they work, they appeal, and are practically useful; but in so doing, they may make it even more difficult for managers to see the point of accessing other parts of themselves, including parts of their unconscious which may be 'driving' them towards or away from self-development. 'The conscious mind allows itself to be trained like a parrot, but the unconscious does not' (Jung 1968, Vol. 14, para 51; see also Olsen 1992: 157 on the same theme).

Personal Mastery – Compensating for Shortcomings

Clearly, there is more to personal development than intellectual growth. The notion of 'personal mastery' seems to offer a broader base. It can manifest itself in a number of ways: in 'emotional intelligence' (Goleman 1995), in 'joy' (Modell 1993: 52), in 'flow' (Csikszentmihalyi 1991), in 'love, traditional values and spiritual growth' (Peck 1990), in 'characterological transformation' (Johnson 1985), or as part of a set of disciplines (Senge 1990), and in an almost limitless number of other ways.

Few such formulae will cut much ice with today's rational managers if they are based upon what they see as 'mysticism' (although there are one or two managers I have met who have more or less jumped upon a 'mystical' bandwagon). They do not need to be. Embracing mysticism would be the kind of overcompensation which bedevils, unfortunately, a number of these 'personal mastery' approaches.

This is not the place to engage in a thorough exploration of the many texts which offer themselves up as the path to self-development. It is, however, simply worth noting that some of those which I have explored do seem to build upon a fairly simple formula: identify an aspect of personality which some people may be underperforming in, and show how you can enhance your performance in that area of life. This formula is easy to spot when presented overtly, as in the 'brain' books of Buzan, de Bono, or in the language of IQ (Eysenck). It is less easy to identify when more or less consciously 'disguised' by the authors.

One of the fascinating games to play with these texts is 'spot the preferences'. Some years ago I started to play this game at the unwitting suggestion of a presenter at a conference. The conference was for people who worked with Jungian type theory; the presenter announced herself as an INTJ. She presented a wonderful set of ideas and thoughts, many of which I have been able to use myself. I make no criticism of what she provided for the audience. The point is that she seems to have simply focused upon what she could do well through being a very well developed INTJ. Not being one of these myself, I could clearly learn from her, and I did. What I learnt was how to enhance those parts of my personality which she 'did' better than me. But because I had started to play the game I realised that, to develop personal mastery, I did not, despite what she was teaching, need to 'become' an INTJ.

It is now helpful to me to play the same game with personal mastery texts. The game is to spot which one or more of the eight aspects of personality (Extraversion, Introversion, Sensing, iNtuition, Thinking, Feeling, Judging and Perceiving) the author is building his or her programme upon the improvement of. As I read them I am struck by how often I am exhorted to be more outgoing (E), reflect more (I), be more aware of what is happening around me (S), use my imagination more (N), improve my ability to think (T), be more empathetic and in touch with my emotions (F), become more determined and self-willed (J), or rediscover the playful child in me (P). Inevitably, because I am not perfect, and because even my preferred functions can often do with a bit of a brush up, I find myself reading these books with a sense of 'must try harder'. The really tough books to handle are those which, chapter by chapter, touch on different parts of the personality, thereby ensuring that, for anyone less than a saint, a raw nerve will be hit somewhere along the line.

There is clearly nothing wrong with such an approach. Compensating for underdeveloped parts of our personality is a valuable element in personal development. There are some elements which are crying out for dealing with. Goleman (1995), Peck (1990) and Csikszentmihalyi (1991), for example, are together addressing some very important shortcomings which are clearly prevalent in our broader cultural heritage. The concept of 'emotional intelligence', in a culture dominated by rationality is wonderfully helpful.

Each of us has his or her shortcomings which we must deal with and overcome. This is a necessary but not sufficient condition for personal development. In other words, genuine personal development does not comprise swinging like a pendulum from one extreme to the other, from energetic engagement to reflective withdrawal, for example. The risk managers run by focusing upon personal development through compensation is that, rather than moving forward, they may find themselves moving sideways, substituting one 'narrow' band of behavioural traits with another.

None of the texts I have referred to above have been written, I believe, with this 'sideways' shift in mind. All their authors, I am sure, would support the idea that, to develop, one needs not simply to compensate, not only to build certain aspects of the personality, but to address oneself on 'all fronts'. This kind of approach is too challenging for younger people, who are likely to be busy developing themselves as unique individuals, finding their paths to identity, and creating careers for themselves. In later years, however, maturity and experience allows managers to take stock, and to know that the answer to the question 'Is this really what you want to do with your life?' (Stein 1992: 12), can no longer be, 'No, but I have plenty of time to get there.'

The Notion of 'Individuation'

One of the concepts which Jung gave us was 'individuation', the notion that the 'system' of body, mind, individual and collective which makes up ourselves (Lepper 1992: 74), has a purpose, and that purpose is to nurture differentiation in the first half of life (through personality preferences, and so on), and to enable, in the second half of life, those differences to become reconciled into a sense of wholeness or completeness. This means, for example, that as one matures one's psychological preferences (for Extraversion or Introversion, for Sensing or iNtuition, and so on) become less influential as one explores those parts of the personality which have received less focus earlier in life. For some, this provides a strong sense of inner peace and contentment in their declining years, as I saw in my father during the years of his retirement. Others, however, resist this maturing process; they can often become caricatures of themselves – even more extreme versions of the personalities which they developed in their youth. For these latter people, individuation does not happen.

In our earlier years we still have to pay attention to the needs of all aspects of our personality. There is no excuse for total withdrawal from the world, even for Introverts; no value in ignoring reality even for iNtuitives. But in those earlier years, struggling to be 'all things to all people' is to ignore the value of good 'type development'. For maturity to take place at its appropriate time, firm, individual foundations need to be built upon personal preferences. Earlier type development is about building upon strengths while not ignoring the call of less preferred parts of the self. Dreams can often tell us a great deal about the parts of the personality which are being ignored. Stevens (1995: 108), for example, illustrates how an unconscious need for greater assertion to deal with a difficult situation (the repressed Extraversion of an Introvert) can be symbolically represented as a fierce dog in the mind of a woman failing to cope with a challenge largely because she is unwilling to engage this less preferred side of her personality.

There is a subtle 'balancing act' being undertaken, then, in our maturing years, between becoming different from other people and avoiding the risk of becoming parodies of ourselves through failing to develop the less preferred parts of our personality in support of our preferences. But there is also the 'pull' of the archetypes, which exert their pressures as we grow older. Just as our genes take us through a relatively predictable set of somatic changes as we mature through childhood, puberty, adolescence, maturity and old age; so they throw into the frame a number of 'archetypal' demands. We learn to become independent from our parents, to associate with peers, to respond to our hormones by pair bonding, to parent, and to do those things which people in virtually all cultures tend to do, and at approximately the same stage of their lives.

The fact that we live in a complex, changing, technologically dominated, populous, multicultural society is of no interest to our genes. Rationality and science do not protect us from our genetic destiny (yet). In so far as that genetic destiny includes propensities to do things at various stages of our lives, it may be helpful if we associate our thoughts about personal development with such propensities. We may resist the 'call of the wild'; that is our choice. But it is, I believe, naive, to ignore it altogether; to pretend it does not exist. The evidence from psychotherapy is just too vast to ignore. And for those who know how to listen, the evidence from our unconscious is just as impelling.

Jung's famous dream of murdering Siegfried (Stevens 1995: 117) was as powerful a signal from his unconscious for him to 'kill the inner hero' as was his dream of the Swiss Austrian border guard (op. cit.) a signal for him to shake off the guilt he felt about his break with Freud. The 'private myths' which comprise our dreams are often the sole access many people in our culture have to the meanings of the archetypal messages which characterise the human experience. Other cultures have their myths and rituals, the characters of which clearly tell the stories of various parts of the personality, how they war with each other for supremacy; and how to grow and develop, we sometimes have to 'kill' those characters.

In the absence of such culturally accessible guides as myths and rituals, managers have to rely upon other sources to find out at what point he must 'kill' puer aeternus, the 'eternal boy' (see Chapter 8, p. 244), or where he must shake off the 'hero' and become the 'sage'; at what point she must destroy Hetaira and adopt Mediatrix (Guzie and Guzie 1964). In the 'rational' world of management, however, such archetypes are wrapped not in rich symbolic layers of meaning, but in checklists, guidelines, and the 'lessons of experience' (McCall *et al.* 1988). These are the language of everyday management, to be sure; and management and organisational life are replete with the kinds of metaphor which abound in myths and dreams. But because we don't associate management (even the personal development of managers) with overtly metaphorical language, it is often hard for managers to align their practical experience of being a manager, of becoming more and more senior, of taking greater responsibility, with the kind of 'stuff' which is going on inside, which is emanating from the archetypal inheritance, and which is often saying with greater or lesser clarity and audibility, 'No, this is not what I want to do with my life.'

'In private space the self is fuelled from within by creative apperception, passionate interests, and moral values' (Modell 1993: 177). The problem is that a great deal of this is not consciously explored, but remains under-developed within the unconscious, still highly influential on how we see things, believe in things; but not really open to scrutiny. Sometimes it takes managers a long time to get in touch with their true feelings, their full creativity and their ultimate values. One reason for this is that much of what we need to get in touch with, in order to know even our inner selves is repressed – deliberately hidden from consciousness by projection, intellectua-lisation, displacement, reaction-formation, repression and denial. The collec-tivity of those repressed parts of our personality is sometimes referred to as the 'shadow', not an easy aspect of ourselves to deal with, since, it represents that part of our mind which 'lulls us into believing that we know all about ourselves and then relished suddenly bringing us up short to expose our arrogance and ignorance' (Mitroff 1989: 93).

For those who are uncomfortable with the implicit anthropomorphism in such a term as 'shadow', think of it as 'unfinished business'. The process of individuation is the process of confronting and dealing with this unfinished business (Colman 1992: 95). Individuation means achieving the kind of wholeness which we cannot deal with in our youth: time is too short, there are careers to be carved out, we have an identity to establish, money to earn and a family to bring into the world. As we go, we leave bits of unfinished business, parts of ourselves which we don't like or want to admit to, experiences which are too painful to confront. Personal development may be something to do with taking stock of this totality of repressions, our individual 'shadow' and (at last) dealing with them.

The inner self, then, 'wants' completeness, time and space to deal with the individuation process, which involves getting to grips with the shadow. Does organisational life help or hinder in this pursuit? And what are the implications of this for management and organisation development providers?

ORGANISATIONS AND THE PURSUIT OF INDIVIDUATION

Organisational life, especially during times of change, can have a devastating impact upon people. Each of us is likely to be able to point to cases in which individuals have 'come off the rails' largely due to what happened to them within an organisational context. The following brief case is fairly typical:

A SENSE OF PURPOSELESSNESS

Richard Ness was, when I first met him, a successful AVP in a large multinational organisation. He was second in command of the Europe Group. His organisation went through a number of changes, taking him first of all to the Unites States, in a Headquarters job, and then back to Amsterdam, as head of Northern Europe.

Like many of his colleagues, he had sent a good proportion of his senior managers and sales managers to a programme we had run for them in Cranfield. It was during one of our follow-up visits to the Northern European HQ that I had a chance to meet him again.

Before talking to him, my colleague and I visited many of our friends from the sales teams, with whom we had worked over the past few years. During that time, the organisation had introduced a number of structural and other changes designed to enable customers' needs to be met more efficiently and effectively. One of these was the reorganisation into 'customer-focused teams', groups of sales, support, marketing, and finance people, each of which was meant to operate almost like a business in its own right. This was a major change of direction for an organisation which had traditionally been hierarchical, functional and internally focused. It was during those earlier days that Richard had established his credentials as an effective manager.

The other key change was the introduction of the notion of a 'Coach'. Managers would now be called coaches, and were to facilitate their Area teams, rather than 'manage' them in the traditional sense. That sense had meant high levels of hands-on measurement of financial and planning aspects of people's work. Senior managers had been very powerful, and often feared for the rigorous, often aggressive ways in which they reviewed their staff.

Most of the members of the sales teams were much younger than Richard. Many had embraced their newly found 'freedom' and were energetically pursuing long-term partnerships with their customers. It became clear as we talked to them that they had little to do with Richard these days. The regular reviews had been abandoned in favour of what was meant to be a more 'collaborative' relationship between senior people such as Richard and their staff. The teams were busy; they could not see a great deal of value in involving Richard in what were new approaches, and exciting times. Some said to us that they felt Richard to be bureaucratic, pedantic, adding little value when he did get involved.

Towards the end of our visit, we spent a few hours with Richard in his large office on the top floor of the Northern European Headquarters building. He was not happy with the teams' progress. He felt that they were spending 'too much time on relationships' and failing to do proper account planning. He said that the teams rarely involved him these days, because 'they are afraid that I'll find out how badly they are doing'. He did not impose himself upon them, trying in his own way to follow the 'hands-off' approach which the organisation had introduced.

In the rapid changes which had been introduced to the organisation, Richard had lost a great deal of what had given him his sense of purpose, his self-esteem, and his identity. He was an intelligent and experienced manager. But he could not reorient himself to what he inferred was his new role in the organisation.

A few months after our visit, Richard resigned from the organisation. Clearly, it could no longer provide the kind of things his inner self wanted from organisational life. He felt that the new 'culture' was not an environment in which what he needed from organisational life, could readily be provided.

Lepper (1992) contains a related case which is more thoroughly worked through.

Organisational Culture

The significant literature on organisational culture (Schein 1985, Daft and Weick 1984, Deal and Kennedy 1982) cautions us against making sweeping generalisations concerning the impact of organisational life on individual managers. Clearly, some organisational cultures suit some individuals, and thereby provide richer and more rewarding environments.

Organisational culture is not a 'thing' to be studied in isolation from the perceptions of the individuals who comprise the organisation. To 'create' an organisational culture is to manage its participants' perceptions: 'organisations will be shaped, in part, by the unconscious concerns of their members' (Fineman 1993: 25). Those who try to do so from the top will, to some degree, be influencing others' perceptions through their own emotional attitudes to that organisation (Kets de Vries and Miller 1984). But as Richard Ness discovered, those attempts at influence may not be effective. And the influence senior people have may not be what they intend.

DIFFERENT PERCEPTIONS OF PERSONAL CHANGE

We recently ran a programme for the most senior managers and consultants of a financial services organisation; the Managing Director participated through-out to share the learning with his colleagues. The programme comprised a number of modules, and was primarily focused upon strategic and service issues. The organisation was broadening its range of services to enable it to grow its revenues and profitability through providing more for its existing and largely loyal customers.

On the final day of the fourth module. I worked alongside the Management Development Consultant to explore with the participants some of the issues in implementation for them as individuals. It was towards the end of the day that one of the participants took me aside and told me that he and many of his colleagues felt that the whole process was doomed because of the personality of the Managing Director. He could not be trusted.

The Managing Director had, according to the Management Development Consultant, attempted to be a model of openness, honesty and disclosure. He had invited feedback throughout the event, and had not been seen to blame others, rationalise, make excuses, attack those providing the feedback, nor deny what he heard. He had shared with the group many insights he had received about his own behaviour, and had resolved to develop himself to improve his weaknesses. Yet for some of his colleagues, this was 'play acting'; for them, the Managing Director had no intention to change, and was simply using this 'openness' as a means of getting the other managers to lower their guard.

Despite his efforts to change a culture of individualism, mistrust, and self-seeking through role-modelling open behaviours, this Managing Director was soon to realise that managing the concerns of the members of his organisation and changing their perceptions concerning the 'culture' of the organisation, could not be achieved solely by participating in a largely cognitive review of the future strategy and structure, aligned with his own role-modelling of 'desired' behaviours.

Changing organisational culture means changing people's minds. It means changing their perceptions, many of which are mutually reinforcing attitudes to what they see. Because our organisations, though socially constructed, are constructed by individuals whose mental maps are so different from each other, an organisation's 'culture' is rarely 'the same' for all its members. What some people will see as a friendly, open, honest environment, others will perceive as threatening, secretive and dishonest. Because managers are people, organisational culture is no more than the sum of the many inferences and perceptions of the very different kinds of people who live within it. And because so many of those inferences and perceptions will be largely unconsciously held, describing an organisational culture is difficult. Changing it is even more difficult, even for the person at its head.

Despite the apparent 'richness' of some organisational cultures, and despite the attempts by some senior people to create rewarding cultural climates for their people, there is no way in which a business organisation can replicate the enormous richness and consistency of perception of the societal cultures in which the history of humanity has been based. For the most part, organisations are not families (Colman 1992: 101); and they do not provide the kind of community which 'other' cultures provide (Stein 1992: 17; see also Chapter 8, pp. 237–8, on cultural richness). In some senses, it is thoroughly misleading to talk of organisational 'cultures', since the distance between traditional cultures and what organisations deliver is so great as to render the two phenomena fundamentally different.

Yet for many people, it is the organisation which provides the place in which they live a great deal of their waking lives. Managers often work long hours; this means that they spend more time 'at work' than they do anywhere else. The unconscious is not discriminating; the demands for fulfilment do not switch off at work. Despite the best efforts of some organisations, managers cannot and do not leave their brains, their egos, their personalities, their archetypes or their needs for development at the front door as they enter work. It is often within the workplace that our unconscious mind seeks access to the kinds of meanings, community, sense of purpose, values, and so on which were traditionally provided by society. Because it is beyond the power of organisations to provide for such needs that many managers feel that they are not, while at work, 'psychically alive' (Modell 1993: 160).

Managers and Organisations – Doing a Deal

Organisations, whether this is recognised consciously or not by their senior managers, have a great deal of responsibility for the psychic well-being of their staff. Not only does a great deal of the psychologically significant need for an individual's self-esteem come from how they perform at work (as William James said, 'self esteem equals success divided by pretensions' – James 1890: 310), but how managers fit into the hierarchy can have powerful effects: 'Promotion comes to mean self-esteem and life; demotion, abandonment and death' (Stein 1992: 4). One could argue that the author is exaggerating; after all, demotion 'only' means these things metaphorically. But this would be, once again, to raise the question where, in organisational and managerial life metaphor leaves off and 'reality' begins.

Managers are more or less conscious of the powerful influences on their lives which organisations represent. The organisation has something to offer, but at a price: 'In return for collective power and action, the individual gives certain critical parts of his or her psyche to the organisation' (Mitroff 1989: 154). This trade-off, partly because it is often done largely unconsciously, can lead to 'alienation from the private self' (Modell 1993: 67), an alienation which has been extensively explored by many 'political' writers (Burrell and Morgan 1979: 323–349), but which has not received a great deal of attention from elsewhere. For example, 'American approaches [to these issues] have stressed bottom line utility analyses which attempt to subject psyche to cost-accounting principles' (Hollwitz 1992: 21).

Many organisations have contracts with their managers, which attempt to clarify the terms and conditions of employment. Few such contracts cover these kind of psychic issues. It would be hard to imagine how they could do so. Paper contracts are drawn up between organisations and managers; the implicit contracts between people in organisations are 'fuzzy contracts' (Kosko 1994: 265), invisible, but nevertheless of major significance to the people who happen to be managers, in terms of what they feel they should and should not do for and within the organisation.

Archetypal Responses to Organisational Life

It is part of the archetypal inheritance of humans (especially males) that when their environment cannot meet their psychological needs, this 'constellates' the warrior or hero archetype. In other words, they are unconsciously encouraged to improve the situation by engaging in aggressive behaviour in the external world. In traditional cultures, the constellation of the warrior or hero archetype in young, fit males was functionally valuable, and would have been more or less consciously managed through ritual processes designed to turn the aggression outwards, to hunting or defence. In chronology in most such cultures, this archetype would soon have been replaced by the 'father' archetype in males, directing energy to the nurturing and guidance of the next generation; the short, sharp, often explosive period of warrior behaviour, the extension of which for too long would tend to be dysfunctional, would give way to an extended period of relative calm and stability.

The parallel constellations in male managers in our own society often meet their 'crossroads' between 'warrior' and 'father' when the manager gets staff to look after. However, in most organisational hierarchies, this managerial post does not carry with it the kinds of symbolic messages of stability and superiority or authority which our archetypes may be 'expecting'. There are layers within the hierarchy, each of which, in so far as the manager constellates 'father', acts like another generation. There are few positions within most modern organisations in which the 'father' archetype can emerge without considerable challenge and confusion.

One of the possible responses to this potentially confusing situation is a more or less unconscious 'cognitive dissonance'. For example, executives whose deeper emotions were explored through a battery of psychological tests showed considerable inner problems: 'The Rorschach responses of executives suggested that one of their most repressed feelings is humiliation at having to perform for others . . . to be vulnerable and judged by [others] no matter how much the corporate policy emphasises "respect for the individual" ' (Maccoby 1976: 117). The author goes on to suggest that these repressed feelings lead to 'compensatory toughness', a reinforcement of some aspects of the 'warrior' archetype.

Repressed feelings, by their very nature, have to be inferred from behaviours. However, most informed managers today will be prepared to accept the socially constructed notions of repression and the effects of the unconscious on behaviour. Those 'shadow' parts of our personality which we more or less consciously repress do seem to have a habit of surfacing one way or another (Goleman 1995; Quenk 1993).

Repression happens when our conscious mind refuses to acknowledge messages from our unconscious. In neurophysiological terms this is often manifested by the suppression of information passing across the corpus callosum from the right brain to the left. Different people are likely to accept or inhibit this information in differing degrees. Some people suggest that those people most likely to inhibit such information passing are 'extraverts and convergent thinkers' (Stevens 1982: 266), in other words, those with preferences for Extraversion and Thinking. These two preferences are combined in people with a dominant preference for Thinking, people with preferences for ESTJ and ENTJ. As it happens, the most common sets of preferences for managers are ESTJ and ENTJ (Myers and McAuley 1985: 90). This kind of finding is in line with, for example, the observation that 'Some senior managers . . . are particularly skilled at blocking out personal feedback,' (Bank 1994: 86), since much of that feedback will probably be the same kind of message as is being inhibited internally.

Just as managerial learning does not comprise the filling of an 'empty vessel', so a manager's response to organisational life is not 'all rationality'. People respond to the circumstances which organisations put them in, and those responses are, like responses to learning opportunities, largely unconscious, but nevertheless significant. Identification and projection take place: 'When we enter an organisation and our unconscious becomes activated by our relationship to its other members and structures, we typically enter a state of unconscious identity with some part of it, with a role, a function, or a position' (Stein 1992: 9); we can become 'wedded' to a job through a process Freud's translators call 'cathexis'. Cathexis is what makes us 'fall in love with' habits, hobbies, possessions, and roles. It acts as a powerful, but often invisible, bonding agent: something like psychic 'superglue'.

A fair amount of managerial work is done in groups – meetings, project teams and so on. The 'rational' approach to meetings management or team building is built upon the simplistic assumption that managers come into such groups, fully conscious, rational and, except for the obviously devious, politically motivated individuals, committed to the overt goals of the group as laid out more or less clearly in the terms of reference for the group. Such assumptions seem ill-founded; groups of managers do not always form efficient and effective, fully functioning units.

'Although the hidden and unconscious aspects shape how the leader and group members struggle for control or drive the group's commitment to its norms or structure, the unconscious factors are generally ignored by both managers and consultants. As a result, group processes become blocked or deadlocked, splits in the group develop, sides are chosen, and persons despair that the conflict or impasse will never be resolved' (Olsen 1992: 156).

At several points I have suggested the image of a street market inside our heads to conjure up the chaotic yet functioning and effective activities of the brain. Conscious thought is restricted to a very small part of the market at any time, as we 'pay attention' to one or a group of interrelated stalls in the market. When managers meet and work together, the need for everyone to 'pay attention' to the same thing ('one meeting, please, not several', is sometimes the cry when fragmentation is threatened) signifies an exponentially greater restriction on the attention being paid to the activities in each manager's brain. While the meeting discussed the agenda, unconsciousnesses are constellating archetypes, forming attitudes, projecting aspects of the shadow, and forging metonymic links between individuals and archetypal leaders, fools, warriors and amazons. Yet people persist in attempting to 'teambuild' by providing clearer terms of reference, allocating roles, and in hundreds of other ways engage only the rational, cognitive, and intellectual parts of team members' personalities.

The alternative may be difficult, it may cause embarrassment, but it would start to confront the problem instead of the symptoms.

THE ORGANISATION AS OPPORTUNITY FOR PERSONAL GROWTH

The Challenge for Management and Organisation Development

The bleak picture of the previous section does not imply that it is inevitable that organisations must be 'psychic deserts'. The purpose of the review was not to complain, so much as to identify the size and nature of the challenge.

My argument goes like this. My colleagues and I have a role in the provision of management and organisation development interventions. To do this effectively means that we have to recognise the paradoxical nature of the 'raw materials' we work with. These 'raw materials' are both managers and people; they have inner as well as social selves. Our brief is to impact their social selves – to help change behaviours, through the development of the managers' competences, skills, knowledge, and so on. However, we have learnt that superficial changes to behaviour are not what managerial learning is all about. If we are to fulfil our part of the bargain, we have to make the learning stick. This means acknowledging and positively impacting managers' inner selves as well as their social selves. However, although all management and organisation development activities will have an impact on the inner selves of managers, that impact is unpredictable. The less we acknowledge the unconscious elements of managers (where a significant proportion of their inner selves 'reside'), the more unpredictable will be that impact.

The challenge is to find ways in which, in principle, organisations can provide nourishment to managers' psyches, and to build upon those ways. In this way we can fulfil our commitments to the organisation, while at the same time operating with managers as though they are people, and not just bundles of competences and skills. To do this, we need a mandate not only from the organisational sponsor, but also from the managers themselves. In Chapter 7 I talked about the way in which some managers distance themselves from the learning process deliberately, thereby trying to avoid being 'changed'. Taking an objective view of the 'material', they can then decide what to accept and what to reject. They remain, apparently, in control. These are kinds of managers who are least likely to plunge into an experiential activity without a great deal of trepidation.

Some may even refuse to take part. Most of us in the management and organisation development business have come across managers who actively refuse to engage in anything but the most obviously objective and intellectual of activities. Many feel affronted by experiential activities. When I ask them why, I find that many of them feel that anything which goes beyond rational consciousness is a kind of invasion of their privacy. In the sense that we are addressing their inner selves, they are absolutely right. But what constitutes an unacceptable invasion of privacy may itself be worth exploring with managers.

It is worth engaging in exploratory dialogue with reluctant managers who, for example, seem to find it acceptable (in the sense that they do it, albeit, they say, reluctantly) to sacrifice 50, 60, or more hours of their private time to the organisation every week, jeopardising family life and personal health in some cases, but unacceptable to be asked to work with colleagues on building a solution involving Lego or bricks and planks, or to draw a picture of the organisation as they see it. Finding that being asked to perform such tasks is a greater invasion of their privacy than the demands made week in and week out by the organisation, suggests to me that some kind of repression is going on. Managers may repress their feelings of humiliation at having to perform for the organisation, but some of them are certainly not willing to repress for the sake of a bunch of management and organisation development providers. Here we have the basis for a dialogue about the organisation, the manager, and the social and inner selves of the manager.

This dialogue may start the process for such a manager of genuinely taking stock, for the first time for a while, of the costs and benefits of the role he or she has adopted within the organisation. This does not mean that I want managers to leave their jobs in droves. It does mean, however, that, in order to engage in any kind of genuine process of development, of change, and of getting a good return on the investment in management and organisation development, it may be necessary at times to go below the surface of the pond, and to deal with more personal issues than raw competences and skills.

In Chapter 1 I argued that managers are students of social science. Our job is, partly, to help them become better students, so that they can be more confident and assured of the decisions they take. Part of this process has to be frequent questioning of the assumptions, the givens, the paradigm. Unless we do so, our interventions will remain on the surface. If this is what all parties – sponsors, managers and providers – agree is what is needed, then we back off from such deep questions. A short course in financial analysis may not require more than a superficial examination of the 'meaning of managerial life'. But the efforts stressed in Chapter 5 to get to grips with the current state, and the efforts stressed in Chapter 7 to get to the bottom of the motivation of the sponsors both point to my concern that we do our best genuinely to align the aims of ourselves, our sponsors and the managers with whom we work. And this, as I have argued throughout this book, means considerably more than coming up with a set of inspirational words and phrases, called the 'aims of the programme', but meaning very little.

The organisation is where the inner self and the social self of managers have the opportunity to come together, to be closely aligned and mutually supporting. Management and organisation development interventions overtly address the social selves – the overt behaviours – of managers, while, through the complex processes of 'learning', having significant impact on their inner selves. As such, those interventions are very similar to the daily round for managers. Sometimes how a manager feels he or she is doing is closely paralleled with how others would evaluate how he or she is doing. Sometimes a manager is conscious of 'putting on an act' – fully aware that what is being seen by others, the social self, looks very different from what he or she is conscious of 'inside'. Sometimes a manager is unaware of how he or she is coming across, being so fully engrossed in the inner self that he or she fails to notice that the social self is very different from what he or she would expect. And sometimes even the inner self becomes hard to read, as when repression, projection or denial creates a screen between consciousness and unconsciousness.

The many ways in which the social and inner selves can become disconnected are simply a reflection of the complexity and volatility of human
experience in social settings. Bearing in mind that most organisations in
which managers spend the majority of their working lives have not been set
up for the benefit of those managers, but to serve other stakeholders, such as
customers and shareholders, it is not surprising that few organisational
settings successfully provide environments for personal growth.

Social settings, however, can and do provide precisely that. Personal
development can be fostered in a social context – some would argue that it
is only in a social context that the concept of personal growth makes sense.
There is historical evidence that until the end of the seventeenth century in
western Europe, the idea of 'being alone' was considered bizarre (Bruner
1990: 170; Ariès 1962: 398); in many other cultures, being alone is an unusual
state, and one which is often transitory, signalling a move from one social
state to another. In most of human history, people have developed themselves
in a social context. Students of some kinds of eastern mysticism may argue
that, to achieve a higher spiritual plane demands separation from others. But
this book is not about spiritual nirvana; it is about helping managers do their
jobs better. I believe that this aim is enhanced by the personal development of
managers – a happy coincidence of benefit for both manager and organisation.

The Socially Constructed Manager

How we see ourselves, whether we are managers or not, depends a great deal
on how others see us. Our self-esteem, self-image, and so on are not solely
constructed out of the immediate impressions which we accumulate from
introspection. We find out about our inner self partly by helping to construct
the social selves of others. The more I think about other people, the more I
can take an 'objective' stance about myself (Fournier 1996: 89). We thereby
construct self caricatures, based upon more or less firmly held beliefs about
how brave we are, or how cowardly, how clever or stupid, how loved or
loveable (Donaldson 1992: 82). These constructs, however, are more than
simply descriptive; they are explanatory and predictive: 'When somebody
says, as if summing up a childhood, 'I was always a pretty rebellious kid,' it
can usually be taken as a prophecy as much as a summary' (Bruner 1990:
121).

There is already an internal dialogue or dialectic going on in most of us, in
which our inner self is being modified by feedback we get from observations
on our social selves. In some cases, this feedback is highly inferential ('You've
never loved me!'); in many cases, the dialectic is confused by repression and
denial ('I don't have a problem, it's he who is immoral, not me!'); the

situation is exacerbated by the realisation that, since these selves are constructions, they are not more or less accurate representations of some kind of objective 'reality', but are, collectively, that complex and shifting reality itself.

One of the reasons why organisational life (as contrasted with traditional social life) is a difficult environment for personal growth is that these kinds of social constructs – of the organisation, of managers, and of ourselves – are anathema to the orthodoxy of management.

Management Orthodoxy and Consciousness

Many of our organisations are built around an orthodoxy of certainty, of objectivity, of 'things' and of logical rationality. They are physical manifestations of, projections of, the left hemisphere: male, cool, authoritarian, hierarchical, agonic, thrusting, aggressive and achievement oriented. They provide environments which, inevitably, constellate archetypes which associate with such experiences; they do not appear to constellate archetypes associated with love, nurture, play, and so on. This may be true at the conscious level, but our minds do not simply switch these archetypes off. The other parts of our minds get their 'exercise' through the unconscious activities of myths and stories, dreams and repressions.

We may ascribe such mental activities to 'purely rational' reasons. The lessons of experience are, for the rational mind, simply that – what has been learnt because of the circumstances in which we find ourselves, not because of some predetermined propensity to take notice of a limited number of 'charged' events. The stories we tell within our organisations are just that – reflections of what has happened; the fact that organisation after organisation tells virtually the same limited range of stories (Mitroff 1989: 138) is put down to coincidence rather than to unconscious archetypal intent. The rational mind is almost endlessly skilful in rationalising away the 'undiscussable', and in ensuring that its authority remains unchallenged by 'woolly thinking' or 'sloppy emotions'.

Learning from Women – Breaking the Paradigm

If we think of an organisation as 'mother', we engage in metaphorical or metonymic language. The language of archetypes is a language in which things 'stand for' other things, in which meanings are symbolic, and where the goal is 'making sense' rather than scientific or logical proof. It is the kind of language which works best when there is free interplay between different parts of the brain, when information is allowed freely across the corpus callosum.

Emotions are, in this mode, not an unwelcome intrusion, but a signal of the essentially value-laden nature of human thought and interactions. When we think of an organisation as 'mother' we increase the chance that we will 'hear' the messages of the unconscious (which will, whether we like it or not, influence our thoughts, feelings and behaviour).

Years of research by Bion (1961; 1977; 1984) and other group relations theorists have demonstrated that as individuals enter groups, what goes on at the surface level – the rational discussion, the logical argumentation – is underpinned by significant emotional, archetypal, unconscious activity which we tend, in most organisations, to ignore (see above, p. 334). And yet groups have the potential to be enriching, positive, rewarding, and successful meetings of minds. Intellectually we know this; in practice, we often find it hard to unleash the creative potential of group situations. One possible reason for this is the very paradigm of group and organisational life with which we operate.

To liberate the potential of groups 'requires a shift from the patriarchal perspective, to which we are so accustomed, to one that values chaos and disorder as harbingers of a new order. Jungian psychology tells us that for an individual to develop increasing consciousness, to integrate material which has been hitherto unconscious, it is necessary to break down old psychic structures to let in the new material arising from the unconscious. The process is never neat and linear; on the contrary, it is painful and disruptive, and the ego experiences that process as a defeat' (Perlman 1992: 189).

In Chapter 4 I talked about the need for 'unlearning' as a key element of management and organisation development intervention design. This is 'unlearning' on a major scale, but one which has the potential to create significantly greater progress as a consequence.

The key to this kind of unlearning is in letting go of the 'absolute' dominance of the intellect. Perhaps because of the different ways in which archetypes are constellated in men and women, men have often found it harder to embrace the 'non-rational' parts of themselves: 'Women have carried men's basic needs for belonging, for affiliation, those needs too dangerous to carry in consciousness for a male in the patriarchy,' (op. cit. 183). Learning from women is not about being just a bit more caring, just a bit more customer focused. It entails recognising how many of the basic assumptions upon which our approaches to organisational life are 'patriarchal', and questioning the absolute efficacy of those assumptions. It entails coping with the feelings of 'ego defeat' which accompany fully embracing group processes as interactions between people as much as they are interactions between managers, between minds as much as between intellects.

'If the creative possibilities in groups are to be realized, patriarchal assumptions about the necessity for order and for strong leadership centred in one person need to be examined. The creative potential in a group cannot be released unless group members are equally empowered in a collaborative way, until the process is recognized, even embraced, as necessarily chaotic, messy, and painful, and unless the group members take responsibility for maintaining, to the greatest extent possible, the containing presence of the good mother' (op.cit. 191).

Groups which achieve high levels of creative potential are often hard pressed to explain or describe the 'buzz' which accompanies their collaborative work. Among the features which I have found repeated to me by people who have been through this kind of experience are the following:

- ❑ an 'uncanny' ability to know what other group members are thinking
- ❑ as a result, 'instant' responsiveness to each other's needs
- ❑ a sense of belonging
- ❑ feelings of absolute safety and trust within the group
- ❑ unquestioning commitment to each other
- ❑ highly charged emotions – sometimes described as 'love for each other'

These are the kinds of things which Perlman identifies as the presence of the good mother. Successful groups, more or less consciously, recognise the ways in which groups constellate 'mother-child' archetypes, producing responses from our individual complexes which orbit around senses of belonging and trust, or around being smothered and held back. Many of the kinds of frustrations which group members describe concerning their relationships with 'committees' are uncannily like the kinds of frustrations which adolescents ascribe to their relationships with mothers who will not let go. This, in Perlman's terms, is the 'bad mother' archetype.

Groups have it within their capacity to help constellate for group members positive archetypal responses or negative ones. I have argued above that personal development is predicated upon broadening one's capacities on all fronts – intellectual and emotional, conscious and unconscious, inner and social, and so on – rather than a narrow focus upon one, albeit vital, aspect of ourselves. I believe that groups and organisations, being no more than collectivities of individuals, can gain similarly from embracing a broader set of ways of thinking, feeling and acting. The intellect is a wonderful gift, and its exercise through consciousness provides us with valuable gifts. But it is not the only child in our mental family.

DEVELOPING PEOPLE WITHIN ORGANISATIONS

The argument so far has been that development is likely to be the more effective, the more it can work with a broader set of mental attributes than are encompassed by the rational intellect. Our unconscious minds are going to influence how we learn, work in groups, and plan our lives anyway; it seems far better to admit to, and to work with this knowledge than to pretend that the unconscious has no place in the rational world of management and organisation development.

This is the principle. How would such an approach look in practice?

Learning How to Coach

When Global Technologies (see pp. 112–14) introduced the notion of managers as coaches, one of the complaints which I heard from many of the managers in the company was that they did not have any experience in, or training for, being a coach rather than being a manager. The inference I drew from this was that these managers felt somehow exposed, incompetent, unsure, uncertain, and so on. The new CEO had clearly stated what was his vision; the problem was that he had not painted a clear enough picture for most managers. He had not communicated in 'their language'. What they needed was a clearer idea of what would constitute 'coaching' – what behaviours would legitimately be called coaching behaviours, as contrasted with managing behaviours.

Had he done so, he would have helped these managers know what was expected of them. But, as I argued in the case of 'becoming customer focused' in Chapter 10, he would not, thereby, have turned them into coaches. They were all aware that there is another step to be taken – from intellectual understanding to behavioural change.

One way of looking at this behavioural change is to describe it in terms such as 'acquiring the skills of coaching'. This would be the traditional model. It conjures up images of an external 'territory', known as 'coaching' from which the 'skills' have to be 'imported' into the behaviour set of the manager who would be coach. This is a rational, intellectual, impersonal, and non-threatening model. Managers who cannot coach are not to be 'blamed', since they have not yet had the chance to 'visit' the territory called coaching to acquire the skills which are to be found there.

There is another model. I am not suggesting that this alternative model is 'better'; I am suggesting that it may be a useful additional way of approaching the challenge. In this model the 'territory' is not 'out there' in the 'real world', but is 'in here', in the archetypal world of the unconscious. The model suggests that managers already know how to coach, already have the skills, have the innate ability to coach within them, and do not, therefore, have to 'acquire' the skills; they have to 'give birth to' them. This model recognises that the vast majority of activities which would be characterised as coaching are not special skills of management, but are what all people are capable of doing for others, namely helping them to discover through various means their own inner strengths, resources and capabilities. And although many of us will do a fair amount of our coaching through the medium of language, many of the skills of coaching are clearly proto-linguistic: most mammalian mothers coach their young in the basic skill sets they need in life.

The traditional model of skills *acquisition* is masculine, acquisitive, adventurous, and exploitative. The alternative model of skills *emerging* is feminine, creative, affirming, and personal. Should a manager approach coaching through the first model, he or she would appear to be learning something new; should he or she approach it through the second model, this would be more like a rediscovery.

The first model attracts because of its proximity to the discoveries of science. Science works on the basis that there are 'out there', things to be discovered which people cannot know about through any other means than active experimentation. Science makes progress; it provides the foundations for technology which gives us material wealth and benefits. Because it works so well, we find ourselves lured into believing that answers to all the important questions must be found out there; by association, if we already know the answer, then it will not help us to make progress.

But Chapter 1 argued that there is no such territory 'out there' as 'coaching'. This chapter adds to that, and argues that, therefore, we should be prepared to think about learning how to coach from within. Management and organisation development providers, according to this model, are more like midwives than leaders.

Whatever a manager may be 'taught' about coaching, how he or she actually works with those who would be coached will be fundamentally influenced by that manager's feelings and values; by his or her unique complexes, built around the vastly complex neuronal networks which inform his or her world-views; by his or her personality, as manifested through such frameworks as the Jungian preferences; by the relationship he or she has with the coachee – the conscious and unconscious interplay of feedback and signals which will pass between them – and by the manager's own stage of personal development and self awareness. Checklists, rules, guidelines, prescriptions or any other externally acquired source of influence will more or less alter the course of the coaching which the manager will steer. But the broad direction will be set, more or less consciously, from within.

Helping a manager become a good coach is about helping that manager bring into consciousness those unconscious influences which will, in practice, drive his or her coaching behaviours. This can only work if both parties – manager and facilitator – are agreed about the model of learning to which they are working. The facilitator will make a hopeless midwife if the manager is expecting a waiter.

Behavioural Blindsight

Coaching is not a unique theme in management and organisation development. One of my most memorable moments was at a conference of management development people, when I overheard the phrase 'teach them to work in groups'. This set off a train of thought which rapidly covered the kinds of team development activities I have both facilitated and participated in over the years. The intellectual part of me had its antennae tuned to 'the answer' – it was looking for what would constitute the epitome of good teaching of group working; 'epitome' quickly linked to 'archetypal' and I realised what I was doing. I was being, once again, seduced by the masculine model. I wanted to be the provider of the ultimate answer; far better to turn to the person who uttered the phrase and explore whether a more appropriate model would be 'help them to remember how to work in groups', delving into the various ways in which people are encouraged by early schooling to suppress their innate collaborative skills . . . But the moment had passed. It was for me a learning experience. I am only sorry I couldn't thank the midwife of that piece of personal learning.

Blindsight is a psychological disorder in which people claim to be blind, yet have absolutely no damage to their eyes, optic nerves or brain. Moreover people with this condition are significantly more adept at manipulating things they cannot 'see' than people who are medically blind. One way of putting the condition is that they can see, but they are not conscious of being able to see (Dennett 1991: 327; Modell 1993: 152). It is an apt metaphor for a great deal of managerial learning, since, I believe, many managers are looking for things which they can already see; they are just not conscious of being able to see the answers.

The Midwife Facilitator

In so far as one of the key strands to management and organisation development seems to be helping managers access what may otherwise remain in their unconscious, I may be accused of dabbling in dangerous waters. Managers reading this may decide that they would prefer a professional on hand if their minds are going to be 'messed' with. Clearly, they would not welcome brain surgery being performed upon them by amateur brain surgeons. Similarly, managers may be chary of letting any old management and organisation development provider get inside their heads – you want a professional psychologist for that kind of stuff, don't you?

The unconscious has been with us for far longer than consciousness has; archetypes have been part of our inheritance since natural selection started to favour hard-wired responses. Freud and Jung did not create the personal unconscious nor the collective unconscious. People have been helping each other understand their inner selves throughout history. Myths, stories, literature, art, drama, ritual, and plain, old-fashioned talk are all perfectly well-formed tools for this kind of process. You do not need psychiatric expertise to help people to learn and grow.

Clearly, there are ways in which this process can be done well, and ways in which it can become a horrible mess. I am not advocating the idea that just anyone is as good a facilitator of learning as anyone else. I like to think that my colleagues and I have developed skills which are not commonplace. But we have not developed these through the narrow medium of psychotherapy. Our field is broader. It is true that the unconscious falls within this broad field. But it is an unconscious modelled upon health and growth, rather than upon mental illness and instability. Psychology informs this, but so do anthropology, sociology, political theory, philosophy, neuroscience, as well as the various arts which fall beneath the umbrella of management theory. The unconscious is part of everyday life, and not something which should only be 'exposed' in clinical circumstances.

Part of our role, then, is to help managers refamiliarise themselves with their inner selves, the better to call upon their inner resources to confront the challenges both of organisational life and of their own process of individuation. Within each of us lies the potential to do things and to be selves which are far wider than the relatively narrow paths we tend to pursue. For the sake of both the individual manager and the organisation, it is often helpful to create the environment in which managers can start to get to know their various selves.

These will include the social self or selves (those outer manifestations of themselves which are the sum of the images created about them by those with whom they work), as well as the inner self. But there are other selves which managers may wish to get to know through guided introspection: the self he or she might become; the self he or she would like to become; the self he or she is afraid of becoming (Markus and Nurius 1986: 954), and so on. Each of these 'selves' is not a 'real person', but an archetype, coloured by the individual's attitudes. By meeting and evaluating how he or she feels about them, managers are learning more about the decisions and options which they need to pursue in order to become or avoid becoming these selves.

This kind of activity often seems more like play than serious managerial work. But managers are people, and the more they are aware of the unconscious drivers which colour their judgements, the more 'in control' they will actually become. We have all come across managers whose very lack of insight into themselves causes them to fall far short of their own and their organisation's goals. It often seems to be the unfortunate case that, the more 'serious' they get, the less competent they become. The tighter their grip on the steering wheel, the less freedom of movement they have to steer.

Some of the 'fringe' activities which take place under the guise of management and organisation development at Cranfield are definitely more like play than they are like being a manager. We have managers doing exercises every morning as part of the 'mind-body' development known as Bioenergetics; we have managers crossing car parks without touching the ground; we have managers jogging round lecture rooms; and we have managers sitting silently in darkened rooms. These and many other non-standard activities are potentially embarrassing; taken out of context they can appear to be 'clever gimmicks'. Evaluated through the lens of the traditional model of skills acquisition, they are way off track. But considered in the context of the manager as person, they start to make sense.

Of course, there is nothing guaranteed in any of this. Such activities can be pointless and of no help whatsoever. But this is not a function of the kind of activity itself; more traditional activities can be just as poorly designed, developed, performed or provided. Lectures can be mind-bogglingly boring; books can be a waste of paper; case studies can be devoid of significance; discussions can be rambling and frustrating; mentoring can be the blind leading the blind. What makes effective learning is not only the method but also the quality of learner and facilitator. I am not, therefore, advocating a free-for-all in management and organisation development, where any old activity is fair game; I am, however, suggesting that good quality managerial learning can take many forms, and that some of those forms will fall well outside the boundaries which the more traditional model of learning by acquisition has set.

Making the Unconscious More Accessible

Activating the relevant parts of the unconscious which will help managers capitalise upon their inner resources can be done, it seems, in many different ways. Some may be hard to justify, even though they may contain more than a few seeds of 'truth'. For example, one may argue that, given the role of archetypal expectations in what we tend to learn, and given the very long history of western culture, during which this will have been more or less known to people, some of the key lessons of management may be more effectively learnt by managers becoming familiar with the 22 cards of the Tarot (Nichols 1980) than by listening to lectures given by successful businessmen. The Tarot will teach at least 22 lessons, and those lessons will most probably activate managers' archetypes more directly than will the life story of someone else. The Tarot will speak directly to the managers' unconscious; the life story of the businessman will have to go through a transformation from specific facts to generalisable learning before it can be used.

I could continue the argument at length, bringing more and more evidence to show the relative efficacy of this alternative way of learning. But my point is not to 'prove' one means or another; it is simply to encourage as broad and creative an approach to managerial learning as possible. So long as it helps managers get closer to their inner resources, methods could include talking to themselves (Dennett 1991: 301–2), discussing dreams (Stevens 1982), writing, drawing, fantasising, exercising, reading and discussing literature and art. None of these are particularly arcane or mystical; they are the stuff of everyday life. The purpose of the activities will be to complement rather than replace the more overtly positivist, rational processes which have become commensurate with a great deal of what we call 'management'.

The complementarity of these 'irrational' parts of the learning process are positively enhanced when managers are away from the environment in which their paradigm is daily reinforced. When Mumford argues 'separation of learning experiences from work experiences is illogical, unreal, unhelpful, unnecessary' (Mumford 1989: 22), I would agree that it is illogical and unreal, and so much the better for being so; I would not agree that it is unhelpful or unnecessary. But I can see how the *acquisition* model of learning could be seen to support Mumford's argument. I hope that, by adding to this model the additional model of learning by rediscovery, I have reinforced our belief in the validity of learning off the job.

Do We Have a Mandate for All This?

Finally, I want to return briefly to the question of our right to become involved in the personal development of managers. I suggested that some managers expect management and organisation development providers to provide answers, and not to 'duck the issue'.

There are some elements in management and organisation development which seem to lend themselves to the acquisition model far more readily than they do to the rediscovery model. It may be hard for a lecturer in financial accounting, or a researcher in logistics studies to associate strongly with the latter version. But my brief has been broader. I have not written about any of the 'subjects' traditionally taught to managers. My colleagues and I are tasked with designing and developing management and organisation development interventions which are predicated upon 'learning aims' or behavioural outcomes, and not academic subjects. For us and our clients, the issue is not whether managers 'know about' or even 'understand', but what they do. It may be necessary, as part of achieving the learning aims – the behaviours, to provide some knowledge, some facts, some data, some models, and so on. But these are not the end in themselves – they are means to an end.

Our experience is that, in many instances, these means are far from sufficient to achieve the kinds of aims which we discussed in Chapter 6.

Managers are people. Learning is not just about adding another function to a machine. It is a process which changes people. And because managers invest so much of themselves in the organisations who sponsor the management and organisation development interventions, they have the right to expect those changes to be pointing in the same direction as their own personal growth and development. Indeed, the more they are, the better for both managers and the organisation.

I have argued that a great deal of such personal development is about self-discovery rather than acquisition. Self-awareness is not a fringe benefit, but something to be pursued as an objective in its own right (Dainty and Lucas 1992). The more self-aware managers are, the better able they will become to capitalise upon the limited amount of 'new' information we can provide for them. Managers are people – complex systems of mind and body, brain and behaviour, inner and social selves.

'If it is to address the system as a whole, the task of management development, in addition to providing the technical and fiscal tools to assess and make use of information about the operations of an organisation, must also enable and empower managers to comprehend and manage the information inherent in the psychic system of the organisation, to move between levels of knowledge and comprehension, to transform information into meaning and effective communication' (Lepper 1992: 89–90).

OPIT – PUTTING THE THEORY INTO PRACTICE

Introduction

One of the projects I have been involved with more recently is a public course, called 'Organisational Politics and IT Management' (OPIT). Although not part of my core brief for Cranfield, I was attracted to the idea for a number of reasons. One of those was that it provided an arena in which many of these theoretical notions could be put into practice.

The course is designed for senior IT managers. It is a characteristic of many IT managers that they are down to earth and practical. They are not the kinds of people who would gladly submit themselves to 'airy-fairy', 'touchy-feely' nonsense such as may be the most obvious product of the kinds of idea which this chapter has been pursuing. Yet if the theories I have postulated are to have any validity, they must apply to the management challenges facing people like senior IT managers.

The course's purpose is to help senior IT managers help themselves and their organisations by giving those managers a higher level of credibility and political awareness. Research has shown that one of the key barriers to the adoption of many of the potential benefits to be had from IT lies in the attitudes other senior managers have to their IT colleagues. IT managers need, we believe, political and interpersonal skills to influence at the highest level. OPIT helps provide these.

Designing the Course

The overall structure of OPIT was built upon the principles of the design diamond (Chapter 10). Starting with the knowledge acquisition segment (ST), we gradually draw participants round the diamond, and away from the acquisition approach towards the discovery approach.

To help in this journey, we used a variety of learning tools and techniques. Early in the programme we introduced humour, through extracts from TV comedy shows, and cartoon strips many of which we drew ourselves to ensure direct pertinence. We also used a management exercise to help participants 'discover' that in organisational politics they are not innocent victims, but full players; the problem is as much within them as without.

Later we introduced role plays, to help the experiential aspects of learning, and introspective exercises to help participants get in touch with their values and emotions. By the end of the week we were exploring with the participants a model based upon the Jungian archetypes, helping the participants to delve very deeply into themselves, their values, and their deepest aspirations.

The Learning

Most IT managers who have signed up for OPIT would not have done so if we overtly publicised the course's underlying philosophy of learning through discovery; most of them unconsciously bring with them the knowledge acquisition model of learning. For some, this is clearly illustrated in their stated aims, 'to acquire political skills with which to get my own way.'

A very small proportion of IT managers who have attended the course go away with the same model still firmly lodged in their minds. The great majority undergo a transformation during the course which enables them to recognise that almost all the answers they have been seeking lie within themselves. During OPIT, my colleague and I shift quickly from providers of knowledge to midwives of learning.

One of the key moments for many participants occurs when we finally explore with them the issues of this final chapter, especially the issue of role and person. Although superficially concerned with learning about organisational politics, the course is, at this moment, an opportunity for participants to take stock of themselves as people as well as managers. Several participants have made full use of this opportunity, and have made significant turns in their personal lives as a direct result of confronting who they really are, and how they are using their careers to fulfil their life wants and needs.

It is this kind of experience with real live people as managers that makes sense for me of the deep questions which this book, and especially this chapter, have been asking. The approach of the book may be philosophical, but the practical application of the ideas through such events as OPIT suggests that, to understand managerial learning to the full, we need to be prepared to go further than simply providing ideas and models.

Some of the learning experiences from OPIT have been among the most satisfying of my career to date. Overall, the course has proved to be one of the most valuable for most participants, as measured both by their responses during and at the end of the event, and by the positive strides they have been able to take in their personal careers back at work.

For me, OPIT has helped validate the ideas of this chapter. It is a practical learning experience for down-to-earth people, but which breaks the mould of traditional teaching methods, and provides an integrated learning experience which taps into virtually every aspect of learning which this book introduces.

CONCLUSIONS

I am conscious of many of the shortcomings of this chapter and of this book. I have not provided many answers, although I have asked significantly more questions. I may have irritated some readers by seeming to move towards solutions, only to veer away from committing to such solutions. Readers who have had the patience to get this far through the book will know that it does not contain, for example, anything which could be taken out and used to teach coaching, or teambuilding, or any other hot topic of the day. There is no lecture on leadership in here.

The book has been written far more from the point of view of the rediscovery model than the acquisition model. Its purpose has not been to say 'this is how it is', but to say 'let's see how we can reframe some of the challenges of management and organisation development in order to help stimulate our own learning'. The many real examples embedded within the text go some way to illustrating how we have put to practical use many of the ideas of the book. Clearly, there are many more such applications than can usefully be described here. The examples are guides, not 'how to' sets of rules.

I hope that the overall approach of the book will enable readers to give birth to answers of their own; answers which are likely to be far more meaningful for them than any I may have tried to foist upon them. Like a coach, I have taken the stance that each of us has far better answers inside us, waiting to be raised into consciousness and articulated by the 'right' question, than those which we can acquire from 'experts'.

Appendix: Tech-Test – A Case Study

A PHILOSOPHICAL DIVERSION

One of the arguments of this book is that it is unlikely that we can do much effective work in management and organisation development unless we know a great deal about the organisation and people involved. We have argued in the introduction that it is misleading to search for a set of 'laws' or rules by which we can draw up the 'perfect' formula for management development, or for a 'management development methodology'. Therefore, in one sense, we recognise that every situation is unique, and has to be dealt with afresh.

We believe, however, that the uniqueness of an organisation does not preclude us from learning from our experiences with that organisation. What we have found is that it is this very uniqueness of each organisation which demands of us that we rethink each opportunity afresh, and assume nothing. The organisation we have chosen as our main case study is different in many respects from the other organisations we have worked with; we must devote space within the book describing as much as we can about them and their challenges if we are to be able to use the case effectively.

Before moving into the detail, it is worth reflecting briefly on the essence of this dilemma. As an anthropologist by background, I have become familiar with arguments concerning generalisability, and the pendulum swings of academic 'fashion' which accompany those arguments.

On the one hand we have those who say that there are some very basic patterns of behaviour which are common to all societies, such as having a language, incest taboos, arrangements for child-rearing, myths and rituals, and so on. One of the tasks of those who study other cultures is to draw out from comparative studies of those cultures some of the learning about the essential nature of being human and living in society. It may be that these studies will tell us something about what we are capable of, and what we should avoid as social beings. At best, they may highlight certain things about the ways our brains work, or how language is acquired, and so on.

In the context of management and organisation development, this stance is equivalent to one which seeks to draw out some basic principles of organisational life and management. It is the position which enables us to write and say such things as 'All organisations must . . .', 'Management is . . .', 'The five (or any other chosen number) basic functions of a manager are . . .' and 'Organisational life is characterised by . . .' It is an attractive way of providing help and advice for managers who want to learn about their organisational and managerial lives, since such statements appear to lay firm foundations upon which they can plan and build.

On the other hand, we have those who argue that every culture, every situation is so different from every other that any attempt to compare one with another is flawed from the start. As an example, let us explore the argument concerning a comparative study of 'marriage' in different cultures. In Chapter 1 we suggested that concepts such as 'marriage' are socially constructed – in this case, abstractions from different behaviours concerning cohabitation, sexual congress, child-bearing and rearing, and a whole host of other duties and obligations. We may be able physically to witness a 'wedding', but not a 'marriage'.

Given the essentially constructed nature of the concept, given the differences in culture, language, and so on between societies, and given the highly complex ways in which the idea or concept which we call 'marriage' is differently interwoven into the fabric of each culture, comparisons are said by those who take this stance to be highly spurious. They say that the process of reducing such social phenomena to the 'lowest common denominator' necessary to reach a level at which one could say all societies, at least, contain this within their 'marriage' concept and associated behaviours thereby omit so much of the meaning of what goes on in each culture as to render the exercise pointless.

In the context of management and organisation development, this stance is equivalent to one which rejects any 'simplistic' views on organisations and management, rejects universal panaceas for organisational health, and looks exclusively within each specific organisation and to its participating managers for answers. In its extreme form, it manifests itself in the 'We are unique, so you can tell us nothing' response to outside 'help'.

As with so many academic disputes, the 'generalisability' pendulum is likely to swing back and forth for some time. In our own approach to learning about management and organisation development from working with different organisations, we recognise that each argument has its attractions.

In our practical work with client organisations we take the unique aspects of each seriously; one of the most important things we have learnt over the years is to assume nothing about a client organisation, and to start from 'scratch' in thinking about how we may work with the people within it. At the same time, at a practical level, we do recognise that we can and do learn from each experience, and that the very ability to learn from these experiences is predicated upon some kind of generalisability.

In this appendix, I assume that, at least, the case provides some kind of data (it is largely focused on Stage 1 of our evaluation model from Chapter 1 – the 'facts'), and let the story speak for itself.

This appendix provides a relatively detailed case study of a management and organisation development intervention from the past. It is provided partly for readers who prefer to explore the ideas and concepts described in the book in a more concrete form, and partly as a sample against which we may be able to match some of the ideas expressed in the book.

We recognise that different managers approach matters in different ways. Therefore, this appendix will be seen by some as refreshingly concrete and accessible, as a helpful basis upon which to map the more abstract, 'theoretical' arguments of the book, and as a way of showing immediately how the ideas relate to a real situation. By other readers, it will be seen as a diversion from the main theme of the book, which is not about one organisation, but about most organisations and their potential approaches to management and organisation development. Readers who find detailed case studies frustrating and distracting, I suggest, may wish to omit this appendix altogether, and ignore, similarly, references to the case which occur in the body of the book.

INTRODUCTION TO THE STORY

People from Tech-Test approached us in the Management Development Unit at Cranfield School of Management in late 1991. They asked us to work with them to develop and run a management development programme for senior staff. A programme was designed and delivered during 1992, following our normal approach at the time. This comprised a number of preliminary meetings with the initiating sponsors in the company, interviews with a selection of the potential programme participants, outline programme design, briefing of relevant teaching staff at the School, and modularised programme delivery, with each module being 'reviewed' by participants via a feedback form.

I shall tell the story of this intervention is some detail, using the company and our programme with the company as a case study to illustrate some of our key learning points. I have chosen the company as a suitable case study largely because it is a relatively small organisation, who came to us for a relatively self-contained, and brief intervention. This makes it untypical in that most of our clients are large organisations who work with us for considerably longer periods. However, many of the key lessons we have learnt from working with other clients can be applied to our chosen case study. Its very compactness, in addition, enables us to examine many of the key interactions, such as those between strategy and personality, and between broad aims and perceived achievements, with a degree of rigour which would be difficult to sustain in a larger case without the case becoming extraordinarily unwieldy.

In this largely descriptive appendix, I shall start by painting a picture of Tech-Test (not its real name), and the people within it (whose names will also be changed to protect anonymity). I shall begin to explore the issues facing the organisation, and attempt to explain how they (or at least sufficient numbers of them to make it happen) came to the conclusion that some kind of intervention was appropriate for dealing with these issues. We shall then describe how they involved an external agency in helping them to provide such an intervention, and briefly outline what they did with them. Finally we shall look at some post-event research to find out what impact the management and organisation development activities had, and how closely these met the people's expectations.

The purpose of this is not to attempt to prove how 'good' or 'bad' the company's venture into management and organisation development has been; it is certainly not to promote any particular approach. It is to explore through this (and other examples) what we have learnt about in-company management and organisation development in recent years by contrasting what actually happened in this case with what we would recommend today.

The purpose of the case is to enable us to relate the more generalised learning, which we explore in the body of the text back to the case. In this way we hope to make the broader story of what we have learnt more accessible to readers who prefer a more concrete, applied approach.

TECH-TEST AND ITS BUSINESS

Tech-Test is a specialist, highly technical organisation with a very limited set of 'products' and customers. It was set up in the 1950s by one man, a specialist engineer, who was mandated and initially funded, by fourteen British companies. His brief was to establish a specialist test environment for the industry within the UK. He picked a group of high calibre young engineers who formed the company core, the last of whom retired in 1990, shortly before the 'management development story' began.

The 1950s and 1960s saw a period of growth during which time the core test department remained dominant. Even as, during the 1960s, the company developed other departments, providing ancillary services, the Head of the Test Department remained second in command, and heir apparent to the Chief Executive. The original ethos of promotion on the grounds of technical competence still pervades to this day.

Tech-Test was established as a independent, self-supporting organisation. Since the original injection of capital it has received no loans or other borrowings from any external or internal source, and has financed its operations and the refurbishment, updating and expansion of its facilities entirely from earned revenues. By early 1990, its turnover was a little over £8.7 million, and it had just over 300 staff. Most sales were to UK customers, although 17% of turnover went in exports to Europe.

The paternalistic/family feel of the organisation was reflected in the autocratic and charismatic direction of the original Chief Executive, and in the retention of a great deal of 'confidential' information in the hands of the few most senior managers at the top of the organisation. Staff were said to be highly motivated and, although there were few opportunities for promotion due to the flat structure, much personal development took place via informal mentoring processes. Responsibility, achievement and the challenge of the work itself, demanding technical excellence, were further motivators. Good pay and holiday entitlement seemed to enhance low staff turnover and long service.

At the end of the 1970s, the founder retired and was replaced by the Head of the Test Department, who led the organisation through increased technical specialisation. This made the company more complex in both the work it took on and its organisational structure. Levels of management were created, thereby enhancing a bureaucratic culture.

In 1985 the main Test Department was split into divisions with middle managers as division heads; each position reflected an extension of the individual's technical supervisory responsibility. All aspects considered to relate to 'management', such as customer liaison and financial responsibility were taken away from specific projects, and vested in these divisional heads. For some people, this meant the removal from them of 'time wasting administration', allowing them to get on with their technical jobs. However, as a result, the hitherto close connection between the workforce and top management was cut. This, apparently, impacted on the morale of the professional staff.

At the end of the 1980s a new Chief Executive was appointed from outside the organisation, thus breaking the pattern which had been established within the 'family tradition'. Relatively quickly two consultancy assignments brought in other, albeit temporary, outsiders. The first group were brought in to improve working methods and increase productivity in one of the newer departments. Their recommendations were, apparently, resented by the majority of staff in the workshop.

In 1989 in response to an increasingly critical business situation another major consultancy carried out work and produced a strategy document which, by the spring of 1992 had not been made available beyond the top management team of five people. The recommended organisation structure did not meet the approval of the CEO, and an alternative was devised by his office (although most people we talked to say that it was devised by the CEO in complete isolation) and implemented during the latter part of 1991. This included a significant downsizing exercise, reducing the work force by a quarter through what the company called 'Special Early Release'. With these changes, a great deal of experience was lost and many staff found themselves in new jobs, either jobs vacated by retirees or jobs which did not exist before the restructuring.

There were appreciable changes in management structure and working arrangements in some departments and a start was made on the introduction of procedures to improve project management and cost control. This put many people into 'management' jobs for the first time. There was a call for 'management training' to help individuals effectively to fulfil these posts. Most of the traditional mentors had left, and managers we talked to gave the impression that they saw 'management' as no different from staff supervision. Many of the individuals expressed at the time a lack of certainty about their capabilities and suitability, since promotion was based on their technical rather than their managerial ability. This significantly affected the ways in which the managers themselves thought about the 'management development' activities which they eventually went through, and what they thought they might get out of the experience.

SOME OF THE SENIOR PEOPLE WITHIN THE COMPANY

This section introduces some of the senior people within Tech-Test, although the story affects them all in different ways. It would be inappropriate to our argument, however, to attempt to give the personal stories of all 300. Clearly, some subjectivity is inevitable in our selection of the people to describe and to involve in the story. For this we have no excuse other than the prerogative of all anthropologists to edit the raw data for the purposes of clarifying the central themes.

Michael Pope, Chief Executive

Structurally and symbolically the most important person to our story is the CEO, Michael Pope. Although he was well known in the industry, his arrival from outside the company in the late 1980s seems to have signalled significant change. He was the first non Tech-Test senior manager, and has brought with him some very different behaviours.

Recognised by all we spoke to as having a brilliant intellect, Michael Pope came to Tech-Test from a largely technical background. He gained first class honours and a doctorate from Cambridge, and spent some time in government-related posts as well as in the industry.

He often gives the impression that he is irritated by people within Tech-Test. He seems to find it hard not to make occasional remarks which disclose his attitudes, despite the potential impact such remarks may have. In a 'strategy' document, prepared shortly before the start of the management development programme, he wrote of Tech-Test, 'It has provided a stable, *possibly too comfortable*, environment for most staff' (emphasis added). According to one story, he was reluctant to emerge from his office to praise a team for outstanding achievement against all odds; when he did, although most of his speech was well crafted and very welcome to the team, he destroyed all the good work by adding at the end his view that, since he did not know how they could have achieved so much in so little time, they must be over-staffed. This, coming relatively soon after the first downsizing exercise, and not long before the second, was seen by many as gross insensitivity.

It is hardly surprising that Michael Pope is seen as a focal point for many of the grievances which have more recently beset the company. As we shall see as the story unfolds, he represents a significantly negative symbol for quite a few of the managers.

Bill Gillies, Head of Research and Business Development

Also a relatively recent recruit into the company, Bill Gillies was, and still is, a member of the top management team. However, he is very different from Michael Pope. Bill

Gillies describes himself as 'not a leader; a very able second lieutenant.' It was he who has been the prime mover in getting the management development initiatives going.

He was brought into the company with the remit of 'bringing awareness to management.' His previous role had been fairly senior within one of Tech-Test's major and largest customers; an organisation which has and does invest in management development as a matter of course. He is very aware of the significant cultural differences between Tech-Test and his previous employer, and has acted as our major 'informant' (in the ethnographic sense of the word).

Roger Wales, Chief Engineer

Roger Wales is a central character in our story. In 1991 he had been with Tech-Test for 31 years, making him definitely one of the 'old school'. As a very senior member of the top management team, he had a high level of influence. He is described as interpersonally very able. He is eloquent, bright and commercially minded. He was not bothered about the politics of the company, and was 'old and wise enough' to feel comfortable in challenging Pope.

His division was originally split in two but since the 1991 reorganisation (which accompanied the downsizing exercise), it came back together again, making him responsible for 100 people. His division provided a service to internal and external customers.

Wales left the Company after the management development programme. One interpretation of the situation we were given was that Pope found the combination of Wales and Gillies too much for him. Gillies says that he believes that Wales sacrificed himself by resigning in order to save Gillies' position.

Norman Castle, Chief Tester

Norman Castle has been at Tech-Test for over 20 years, although he is a very different character from Roger Wales. For example, whereas Roger Wales referred to the Critical Success Factors of the company as 'involvement and vision', Norman Castle saw only one, 'cheapness'. Although his position as Chief Tester traditionally puts him second in command at the company, he saw his job as having an estimated 70% technical component, and only 30% management. Before the programme, Norman Castle described his situation as 'a phasing out of hands-on technical chasing, but it is still currently necessary due to the downsizing.' In other words, like some others we have talked to, he expresses the opinion that one of the more lasting implications of downsizing activities is experienced in a need to continue to deal with jobs which, otherwise, could have been delegated. But with fewer people to delegate to, he says there is no choice but to carry on ensuring that the jobs get done, even if it means doing them himself.

He is responsible for projects, the choice of people for each being 'usually obvious'. It is a very intense process with, he says, more pressure than the other operations. Castle is a very different personality from Wales, his predecessor. Wales used to challenge; Castle does not appear to, giving the impression to those we talked to as being a 'yes' man, in awe of Pope because of Pope's status as CEO as much as of him as a person.

Derek Stubbs, Company Secretary

The final member of the five man top management team as it stood before the programme, Derek Stubbs became Company secretary designate during the 1991 reorganisation and downsizing. Previously he had been deputy Chief Tester; he has lost the technical aspects of his job, although he retained computing.

It was never his ideal to move into this position, but as someone who came over as 'softer', more people-oriented, and less technically 'hard-nosed', he was the 'obvious' choice. He was given very little help or training for his new role, and apparently received no support for becoming part of the top management team.

Victor Parrot, Head of Systems

Victor Parrot, unlike most of colleagues who grew up steeped in engineering and technical qualifications, has a theology degree. He had been at Tech-Test for over 20 years, and made slow progress to his post as head of department. His position within systems gives him one third technical responsibility, and 'the remaining two thirds is for giving technical advice.' He says he feels a little out of his depth with the 'establishment' ethos perpetrated by Pope, and stays out of the way when he can.

Don Goler, Head of Research Group

Reporting to Bill Gillies, Don supported the management development initiatives, and was present at one of the preparatory meetings with representatives from the business school they used for the programme. He helped push Gillies to get it through. He is seen as a 'loud agitator' who has taken the initiative on several occasions (along with Sally Freeman, a Business Development Manager, also reporting to Bill Gillies) to agitate upwards.

THE ISSUES AS THEY SAW THEM

In mid 1991 the management (which, in Tech-Test's context, means the top management team of, by then, five people) had been approached by a group of staff concerning areas of staff dissatisfaction and concern for the future of Tech-Test. A management meeting had been called, which had aimed to address some of the issues raised. Change was required, it was agreed by many. It was time for action.

There seems to have been a broad agreement about the nature of the changes facing the company: it had been a competent, technically focused organisation with relatively low competition. It was not highly commercialised, and there had been few drivers in the past for significantly adding to the core competences. Now there was increasing competition, customers were looking for keener pricing, and there was a recognised need to go out and seek business, rather than wait for it to come to them. Pricing was no longer cost-plus based, demanding very different styles and systems for managing projects. There were increasing market pressures; and a globalisation of those markets, leading to global competition against countries with very different cost structures.

There were serious questions about the company's ability to be successful in this new arena without strategic change.

As such, issues such as these are not uncommon for many organisations we work with. Increased global competition; a need for external, customer focus; demands for managerial and commercial competences; and so on are themes which recur frequently. It may be because of the implicit generalisability of the nature of the challenges facing Tech-Test that these issues could be couched in terms which already hinted at a management development element in the 'solution'. One of the differences between Tech-Test and other organisations we work with is the fact that this company's ethos was so firmly rooted in the 1970s that the transition they faced was greater than for most.

So there were a number of business and management issues which were broadly agreed upon by people we spoke to. However, there were also key differences in what they saw as the key issues to address, which had an influence on the lead up to and the implementation of the programme. By this stage, however, we had no clear idea of these differences, and started to learn about the company through the normal channels of background research, and through a meeting with two of the Tech-Test managers.

The Preliminary Meeting

In November 1991, Bill Gillies and Don Goler visited Cranfield to talk about management development initiatives. Most of the meeting focused upon how management development was seen to have a role in the changes felt to be necessary, which we deal with in the next section. There was, however, a number of observations made concerning the issues confronting the organisation.

The picture they painted was one of change, but the picture was not as clear as it might have been. Although Michael Pope had brought with him a number of intentions regarding changes, not all of these intentions had been carried out, or have been perceived in the same ways.

They told us, for example, of very different ways in which managers of the company perceived the changes from the historically more 'relaxed' approach to the business. In the 'cost-plus' days, it was agreed, there was little perceived need to control budgets, so there were no formal budget-holders; any number of people could be involved in all sorts of ways in any projects. With the abolition of cost-plus came the allocation of budgets, for which people asked for recognition, and thus, 'self-ascribed' titles. For some people, the 'reality' was that there was not strict observance of the hierarchy or job titles. As one of the middle managers said at a later stage, of the same issue, 'The organisation needs more structure: people have just given themselves names and titles.' But from another point of view, the hierarchy within the business was clear; the management of projects was not.

During the 'issues' meeting which had preceded the initiative, apparently, the search for a precise definition of the personnel constituting 'management' had provided some discussion. Clearly, there was a recognition that, although some of the superficial elements of 'management' were in place, such as job titles, for many people these were having no impact on what actually happened within the company. For others, 'management' seemed to be equivalent to any form of staff supervision. These differences of view led to the constituency of the proposed management development programme being anything from the top management team of five, to a very large number of people: anyone with direct reports. (The actual number of attendees was 19.)

Staff and middle management dissatisfaction with the confused role of 'management' within the organisation had become increasingly obvious as time went on. There were strong suspicions that the top management team was divided.

Meanwhile, a strategy document had been compiled by the second set of consultants. This strategy document had still only been available to the senior team plus one or two others; it was agreed that it would need to be widely available in order to form the basis for development. Bill Gillies said the document would need to be developed into a five year plan. (As it turned out, however, a new strategy document, which bore only a passing resemblance to the consultants' document, was compiled by Michael Pope shortly before the start of the management development programme itself; the consultants' document did not seem to make much of a contribution to the changes which some of the staff and managers expressed a desire to see.)

It is unclear the extent to which the consultants' strategy document was approved of by managers within the organisation. Few of them saw it, in any case. Those who did apparently read it in a clandestine fashion; it was not 'acceptable' to talk about it at all, let alone have an open forum for discussion. Many people did seem to suspect that there were divisions within the top management team itself. During the preparatory meeting, this was expressed in terms of the Board and senior management having 'territorial tendencies.' Differences of opinion and approach among the key players were seen to be both part of the problem, and also a potential threat to any management development programme.

Climate Setting

The preliminary meeting of November 1991 both focused upon programme aims and was used by Bill Gillies and Don Goler to 'set the climate'. We have already identified an important consideration in the various 'pictures' individual managers would bring to the programme about what the programme might achieve. Added to this there is the associated set of considerations concerning the perceived threats posed by programmes of this kind. It is not simply, 'I don't know what to expect.' It is often 'I don't want certain things to happen.' And this is not simply a matter of dignity; it imbues a great deal of what it means to be a manager in today's business culture. For many managers, the 'management development programme' is an opportunity to let loose much of what remains well under control within our organisational cultures. Keeping them under control is not just a matter of status; it is a matter of identity. In Chapter 11, I look more deeply at what implications this has for management development; for the present, I shall explore how these issues were woven into the fabric of the Tech-Test story.

At the preliminary meeting, we were told that the three senior team members (Bill Gillies was the other top management team member, and he did not include himself in this assessment) plus the CEO were likely to feel threatened and exposed by the prospect of a management development 'course'. Derek Stubbs would be committed to the principle of the programme and would 'cement the group'. Roger Wales was described as operations oriented: practical, and would address the operationalisation issues. Norman Castle, said Bill Gillies, was a self declared 'agnostic' and, it appeared, wished to remain somewhat removed from the changes afoot.

It was clear, then, that not all the members of the top management team were fully committed to the idea of using management development as a means of making progress within the company. And yet, clearly, Bill Gillies and Don Goler, at least, had some kind of belief that running the programme would be beneficial. One of the early challenges was, then, to allay fears at least enough to get the people onto the programme; thereafter, it was felt, the dynamics of the programme, and the quality and impact of the intervention would be the vehicle for handling such fears.

For this reason, it was agreed at the meeting that members of the Cranfield team would interview the key players before going ahead with the programme. Pre-course interviews would be conducted with the CEO, the four senior managers plus three or four others in order to check their different perceptions regarding the issues and concerns. This would 'help engender the perception of a development programme, and not just a management course.' By this, we interpret that they felt such interviews would help potential participants to feel less personally threatened. As the Tech-Test people said of their colleagues, each has a technical rather than a management orientation and would need to be approached in a non-threatening manner. There was a further reason, which was to try to get buy-in to the programme from Castle and Stubbs, who were expected not to want to 'rock the boat'.

This notion of threat clearly played an important part in the preliminary meeting. Not only were interviews thought to be a necessary part of setting the climate for the programme (during the meeting the interviews were referred to significantly more in the context climate-setting than that of the needs of the organisation), but also it was stressed that management style issues would need to be addressed through a focus on the organisation's needs rather than individual needs.

Here we are presented with a 'get-out' clause in the notional learning contract. It allows individuals a spurious protection from the implicit threat, given that it is not those individuals who are the 'problem', but the organisation. A common 'displacement' behaviour we come across is this very notion that 'it's not me, it's the organisation which has to change.' By a subtle adjustment, which brings to a programme of activities, 'the organisation' rather than the key people who actually comprise that organisation, we entice into programmes those who would otherwise stay outside altogether.

Discussion of how far this is a sleight of hand, an obfuscation which has even a hint of dishonesty about it, is embedded within the body of in the book, especially Chapters 7, 9 and 11. In the case of Tech-Test, the 'trick' worked, in so far as it did get all the key people to attend the programme, despite the significant reservations of one or two of the most senior people.

The next 'trick' had to be to make a difference, given that there was a recognition that all this energy and political intrigue had a serious purpose. Bill Gillies and Don Goler were keen that the programme should go ahead as soon as practicable. Expectations had been raised; disbelief had been, apparently, willingly suspended by sufficient numbers to make the programme viable; now it was time to start to bridge the gap between the organisational and managerial issues and expectations of what a 'management development programme' could actually do for them.

The Interviews

Before the programme was put together, therefore, several of the participants were interviewed to gain their impressions of the nature of the business, the issues facing the organisation, and what a management development intervention might help them with. All five members of the top management team were interviewed, along with a 'random' sample of the other managers targeted for the programme. These interviews provide some of the insights we have into the people's perceptions.

Michael Pope, the CEO, clearly has the prime responsibility for the future success of the business, especially in terms of the company's Articles of Association, which specifically place that responsibility with the Chief Executive, and not with other senior managers of the business. He was therefore very detailed in his responses concerning the issues facing the company.

His view was focused on maintaining quality while looking for expansion in markets addressed, especially the USA (he had worked in the US for a few years before joining Tech-Test). However, he expressed a number of things which seemed to concern him regarding the ability of the organisation as a whole to respond to the business issues as he saw them. In the light of increasing competition, and with the competition having lower cost structures, and having a number of other advantages (in some cases, funding from their respective governments), Tech-Test had to 'get its act together' (a phrase which, in Tech-Test, is very closely associated with Michael Pope).

His observations of the internal capabilities of the organisation were not all complementary. Although expressing satisfaction with the technical competence of the people, he used such expressions as 'the company is controlled by home-grown specialists', and 'people have got used to having their thinking done for them,' which suggest a personal concern for how ready his colleagues seem to him to be to cope with the challenge of becoming 'a different organisation' as he called it.

He referred to the 1991 restructuring, and said that, at an organisational level, 'we have to be better at picking ourselves up off the floor.' He uses the phrase 'got to come of age', when describing the company. He also has a history of taking work away from his managers to do by himself, such as a job grading exercise, and a set of Quality guidelines. Although he did not say so in as many words, we feel reasonably comfortable in drawing an inference from the data so far; that Michael Pope saw one of the key issues facing the company being a dangerously and irritatingly low level of managerial and commercial competence among his colleagues.

Bill Gillies, Head of Research and Business Development saw the organisation as too big and bureaucratic, and anticipated another reduction in staff numbers to match the volume of business. He took on responsibility for a series of 'projects', which were internal activities aimed at helping the organisation, and enhancing communications. He reduced the current projects list from 33 to 9 in order to try to ensure that some of them were actually completed. He described the organisation as 'funny', explaining that he could never find the right person to make a decision.

Bill Gillies's perceptions of the issues are those of a man brought into the organisation within the previous two years, from a much larger organisation, and to head up a completely new part of the company, the Business Development Group. He is therefore doubly more likely than his peers on the top management team to look forward to change than backwards. But these factors did not bring him into league with Michael Pope; fairly early in the interview he referred to 'conflict between Michael Pope and myself.' This conflict had resulted in Bill Gillies being sacked from Tech-Test for three days before being reinstated.

Bill Gillies's perception was that there was a great deal of inertia, that 'the organisation does not want to change'. He said, 'we keep avoiding agreement.' One of the main distractions from reaching agreement on change was the culture in which it was seen (through what people do rather than what they say) to be more important to put fires out, to solve technical problems, than to get to grips with more strategic issues. He said that the lack of change was creating staff dissatisfaction.

Much of the staff dissatisfaction could also be explained by the significant downturn in the business at the time. Staff at all levels receive bonuses based upon profit; no profits had been received for some time.

Roger Wales, Chief Engineer, felt that the company was 'floundering as it is led by scientists and not managers'. Communication was not disciplined; there were too many meetings resulting in matters not being decided. 'The place is run by committee,' he said. 'We currently go about things in a long-winded fashion.' Of his colleagues, he felt that they ought to be aware of other methods of working and how to implement them. He gave the example that although they talk of flexible working, they are still stuck to rigid tea breaks.

He believed that, on the business front, diversification of some kind was possible within the core markets and areas of core competences. Originally, the company was not aware of the other competitors and their relative strengths, but they are now. The CSFs for the future are, he claimed, involvement and vision. He said he would like to share the vision with wider audience, that is to show the design team what and who they are designing for. He was trying to introduce again a project management scheme to encourage customer focus and individual responsibility.

Norman Castle, Chief Tester, said, 'There is a question of leadership,' which we suspect is as much a reflection on his own style as it is on Pope's. He said that his staff look to him to solve technical problems and undertake planning while they deal with the project detail. His stated view concerning potential differences of opinion regarding the running of the organisation was that if people don't like the culture they can get out. Regarding the business future, his view was that diversification was possible but it doesn't earn big money; it would be better to improve the technology base.

Derek Stubbs, Company Secretary, expressed the belief that there is a great need for training so that people in new jobs since reorganisation could feel more comfortable and do a better job. He felt that many individuals did not possess the right managerial training or skill to carry out their new responsibilities effectively. He expressed very personal concerns in what he said.

Victor Parrot, Head of Systems, said that a key issue was that people were unsure of their new roles following the 1991 reorganisation. It was unclear who had authority. 'Everyone has moved around; it was quite a dramatic change.' Looking at the business issues, he said that because Tech-Test has had a captive market for many years, they had left it late to be looking at themselves and discovering, for example, the need to cut costs.

The New Strategy Document

Immediately prior to the programme itself, Michael Pope took it upon himself to write a new strategy document. Although this document appears to have received little use since that time, it is instructive in that it sets out the CEO's perceptions of the strategic issues facing Tech-Test at the time; both his selection of issues, and the style with which he writes about those issues give us a great deal of information which is of use in understanding the dynamics and realities of the case study.

Within the document there are a number of references to broad aims, some of which we refer to in other sections of the book. To summarise, however, we quote: 'The primary objective of Tech-Test is to continue as a profitable independent organisation.' The 1991 downsizing crisis is assumed to have told everyone in no uncertain terms that the survival of the organisation is no longer guaranteed. Of that crisis, he continues, 'Much of the disruption is now past but a sustained effort is needed to rebuild morale and team spirit and it will be a long slow haul to achieve the standards of programme and cost control across the company that are needed to keep Tech-Test competitive.'

To reinforce this message, Michael Pope highlights the increasingly aggressive commercial approach by Tech-Test's traditional customers: 'We are having to compete for work which would previously have come to Tech-Test without question, we are facing greater pressures to reduce our prices and the commercial environment has changed from being 'more or less cost plus' to 'more or less fixed price'. This demands, he argues, a real improvement in company performance, which 'will only be achieved if the workforce is committed to that improvement.'

For Michael Pope, then, as he goes on to say in his strategy document, a key strategic objective is 'to increase the motivation and job satisfaction of every individual in the company, to provide the necessary training and to ensure that responsibilities are delegated in a way which makes use of the full potential of every member of staff.' He points out that, in his view, staff development and improvements in working practices are closely interrelated. He goes on specifically to link these with Total Quality Management (TQM).

Pressure from their customers has led Tech-Test to adopt a programme of TQM in order to achieve ISO9000 accreditation. Without it, it is questionable whether they will survive, basing, as they do, their perceived competitive edge on 'quality'. However, achieving accreditation is recognised by most of the managers we have spoken to as difficult, given Tech-Test's history and 'inertia'. There is more than simple encouragement, then, in Michael Pope's statement: 'Reshaping the working methods of Tech-Test to embrace the principles of TQM is a strategic aim for the company.' Clearly, for him, there is a very significant issue at stake, and it has, so far as the strategy document is concerned, very little to do with 'leadership'; it has to do with the willingness of everyone in the company to change how they operate.

Michael Pope's strategy concludes with references to his own views as to why this may prove difficult. As he writes, 'staff have developed good skills as specialists but have tended to be narrow in experience. There has been almost no management training of middle level and senior staff and historically there has been relatively limited delegation of authority.'

As a set of perceptions about what the key issues are for the company, this document provides clarity and consistency. It is fairly clear where Michael Pope saw development needs.

Summarising the Issues

Up to the point at which the management development intervention was to be designed, a number of key business and organisational issues had been identified. Not all of these issues were described or referred to by all of the people interviewed or met, nor were they all apparent from the strategy document. Some of the issues seemed somewhat contrary to others, and some perceptions were at odds with others.

As far as the external environment was concerned, those few who mentioned it were agreed that the globalisation of the markets and Tech-Test's resulting competition made life significantly more challenging for them. Although Michael Pope briefly explored the possible penetration of the American market as a means of achieving growth as opposed to slow death, few others used the opportunity of the interviews or meeting to explore such issues. Roger Wales was the only clear exception to this rule. He discussed the need for an external, customer focused approach, and was the only interviewee who could refer to initiatives he had put in place, at that time, which had this externalisation of vision as their goal.

So far as the business and its processes were concerned, the issues referred to were cost control, an improved technology base, quality, and the reshaping of working methods in line with the principles of TQM. Again, there was a relative scarcity of reference to the latter topic, it being apparently Michael Pope's view, but not one which was enthusiastically or voluntarily brought into the other interviews.

Organisational issues were clearly influenced by the continuing impact of the 1991 downsizing activity, and were not a major input to the interviews or meetings. Whereas one view was that the organisation needed more structure, another was that it was still to large and bureaucratic. We cannot be sure whether and to what extent these two views are opposed to each other.

Most people said that technically the organisation was competent. However, training was needed, it was agreed, which reflected several references to low levels of managerial skills. How interviewees responded to this latter point may, however, have been influenced by the fact that the interviewers were people from a school of management, and that 'managerial skills' were explicitly on the interview agenda. Some of the issues referring to management may have been less influenced by 'what I expect they'd like to hear', such as the issue of who, exactly, were managers within the organisation, the question which may have been a major contributor to this story actually taking place. The fact that one informant thought that the place was run by scientists not managers was reinforced by references to a preference for fire fighting over planning, and a reluctance to delegate, for whatever reason. Clearly, there were a lot of issues concerning just what management ought to look like for the company.

The issues coming out of the top management team seem consistently to point to significant differences in perceptions; for some people, these differences manifested themselves in divisions, meetings which led nowhere, and an 'avoidance' of agreement. If the organisation was to go through change, there were severe doubts whether the top management team would be in a position to lead it through that change.

Yet the need for change was one of the most regularly cited issues of all. The inertia of the present was contrasted with a whole set of more specific needs. There were quoted a need for: more resilience; more flexibility; involvement and vision; rebuilt morale and team spirit; increased motivation and job satisfaction; and more commitment to improvement.

In sum, there was a complexity and disparity of views concerning the issues facing Tech-Test as it moved towards the management development programme. From this complexity it was clear that at least one of the key issues for the company was that there was little or no consensus on what the problems facing the organisation actually were. Tech-Test had a lot of issues to deal with. How was 'management development' expected to help deal with those issues?

THE PERCEIVED ROLE OF MANAGEMENT DEVELOPMENT

'Design' Considerations

There were a number of design considerations which were introduced even before the interviews were undertaken. In the November meeting six design elements were agreed.

First, it was recommended that, given that the strategic document which had been drawn up by the second group of consultants would form the basis of the organisation's strategy, the programme focus would be implementation, rather than a reworking of the strategy itself. The strategy document in question had still only been available to the senior team plus one or two others; it was agreed that it would need to be widely available in order to form the basis for development. As it happens, the consultants' strategy document was superseded by Michael Pope's own strategy document immediately before the programme started, as we noted above (page 361). What was also interesting was that neither of the two documents actually played a part in the programme which did take place.

This raises one of the key questions which is explored in Chapter 5. That is the question concerning how far 'back' it is appropriate to go in in-company management development programmes. It is not uncommon for organisations to approach us with ground rules, such as clear instructions not to attempt to go over matters they have already covered; in this case, the formulation of strategy. In many cases, events during programmes unfold such that there is a demand from participants that these instructions now be countermanded. Chapters 5 and 11 explore, among other issues, who is the 'customer' for in-company management development programmes, and what that implies for how an honest relationship between providers, buyers and participants can be established and maintained as programmes impact the very perceptions which may have established those initial ground rules.

It was already anticipated at the meeting that the programme itself would effect changes in attitude as it developed. For example, Bill Gillies and Don Goler were happy that the required 'agenda for action' would emerge during the programme. This emergence, they suggested, would thereby increase the likelihood of buy-in and ownership from the participants. Similarly, the consensus necessary for the development of a 'mission' for Tech-Test, it was agreed, could be achieved through the use of a workshop approach which would enable managers to define the issues. Don Goler was keen for 'lasting solutions not just solving current problems' and agreed that the workshop would achieve this more effectively.

The participants at this preparatory meeting clearly were working with a set of assumptions or beliefs concerning the nature of the 'product' they were outlining. It may well be that these are well-grounded assumptions or beliefs. In designing any kind of activity, we base our design considerations on what we believe we know. At this meeting, the assumptions or beliefs were not challenged; they were discussed and agreed. They formed a common set of foundations upon which to build. Whether they are 'right' or 'wrong' is, again, not to be questioned here. They are simply recorded as important data in understanding how the case actually progressed.

One of the assumptions or beliefs was that the 'product' needed to be made as attractive as possible to doubters. A second was that it was likely to be 'volatile'; that is, it could not and should not be set in concrete. The word 'workshop' implied an unstructured approach, with a level of involvement by participants which would make the process and outcomes relatively unpredictable. Thirdly, there was an agreement that this approach would enhance 'buy-in and ownership'. Fourthly, that this approach would also be more effective in achieving 'lasting solutions and not just solving current problems'.

It was also agreed that any personal development issues would be faced after the organisational issues. Here, there were two possible interpretations: The first was that, until people were comfortably into the process, and convinced that it was 'the organisation' which had the problems, not themselves as individuals, they would not be willing to confront their own, personal needs. (This leads also to the assumption that this process will lead to a greater willingness 'after the organisational issues' to confront those needs.) The second possible interpretation is that people will only be prepared to identify and address the need for personal change if the changes need by the organisation as a whole can be identified first, leading to the 'cascaded' need for personal change within that overall change.

These assumptions were then combined with some broad decisions concerning the overall shape of the programme. Bill Gillies agreed that the first module would be three days, and that the programme would be residential. The initial module was to be followed by a six week gap. The second module was to consist of two days – probably both as weekdays. It was proposed that there should be four modules in total, with further potential for roll-out as necessary. It is unclear how crude the estimates were at this time concerning the ways in which the time allocated to the programme, and the inter-module gaps, would be best suited to meet the programme's aims, and the needs of the organisation and the individuals.

Clearly, some thought went into this process. For example, there was concern expressed by the Tech-Test people over the absence from site of the entire senior team and so Bill Gillies suggested the use of the weekend. In response, the business school representative preferred the composition of two workdays and one weekend day as, symbolically, it would represent the organisation's commitment to the programme. This was agreed.

There is clearly, then a mix of 'precision' and guesswork going on in these preparations; there is also a recognition that there are 'symbolic' aspects to the entire process. Another question which arises out of this concerns, therefore, how important or significant these preliminary activities are to the overall effectiveness of the interventions. Are they a vital part of the design process, in which mistakes made now could have devastating impact during implementation; or are they largely symbolic meetings, whose decisions are largely irrelevant, given that, no matter how much planning goes on here, the 'real' stuff only starts when the participants are gathered together and the programme 'proper' is under way?

These are the kinds of questions which the body of the book addresses in more depth.

Aims

It was clear by this time that a number of people had associated the prospective management development programme with the chance to make a difference, to address some of those issues which had emerged from the meetings, interviews and strategy document. It is unlikely that any individual manager at Tech-Test believed that one management development programme would resolve all these issues, but we suspect that many of them had a degree of confidence that the programme would provide an opportunity, which they had not had before, to tackle some of them in a fresh and effective manner. For some, the programme represented their last chance. Those involved with the programme speak of hope (and continued after the event to refer back to those feelings of hope) that their fears and perceived inability to take individual responsibility would finally be dealt with.

The preliminary meeting and the subsequent interviews included opportunities for participants to make their own views felt on what the programme should aim to achieve. Some interviewees were unable to articulate clearly and concisely what they wanted from the programme; others provided some relatively clear pointers.

Once again, Michael Pope provided significant input. He focused first on a 'contextual' aim, saying the programme needed to establish that Tech-Test is a good place to work; that the work is interesting; and there is comparative pay. Overall, he said, the aim of the programme was to create a better educated management team, with commonality of approach in the management team as well as commercial awareness and communication. They needed to learn, he said, the skills of how to do, how to get through an in-house project (such as the implementation of the first set of consultants' recommendations). As managers, they need to create a disciplined regime, that is to produce results to deadlines and targets. There is a tendency, he reminded the interviewers, to take on things and not to complete them.

From a 'training programme' Norman Castle said they 'would be looking for advice on: improving efficiency; delegation; how to relate to other people better (in this technological environment); personal organisation; how to run a business.' He also said that he would be looking for 'a tangible end product.'

Derek Stubbs said that they needed firstly to identify who exactly constitutes management. Other 'aims' related to his perception that there was a need to improve teamwork, and encourage people to come forward with new ideas. There is a need, he said, as he considered what management development might provide, 'to become harder nosed and more business wise.' Victor Parrot added that 'training' should address communication and man management and making use of management tools. It should aim to improve efficiency and morale. He also said that the programme should focus on the team and away from the individual; he was the only interviewee who raised this issue as such.

Interlude

One of the unusual factors in this case is that, of the senior managers who were actually running the organisation, virtually none had had any exposure to formal management development activities at all, despite many of them being well into their forties and fifties. One of the key implications of this is that it was very difficult for them to respond realistically or confidently to the questions concerning their aims from the programme. With no experience to speak of, they had little to go on, and were, in some cases, probably at a loss to know what kind of answer they should give to such questions.

There may also have been other, unspoken concerns. Evidence from the programme itself points to reluctance on the part of several of the participants to face interpersonal issues, including their own style of managing. By this time, relationships and the ways of doing things at Tech-Test were so entrenched that it would be easy to understand a fear of coming out of the trench to look into the future. It is also not an excuse for, but a fertile soil for such entrenched attitudes about each other as managers, which lead to an unspoken unwillingness to countenance the possibility that one (in this case 'I' as participating manager) may have misjudged, undervalued, or got the wrong idea about another.

At this early stage of the relationship between the business school members and the managers of Tech-Test, formality, seriousness, and the kinds of superficiality to be expected from people having so little experience of 'formal' management development imbued the interviews and meetings. Instead of responding to the questions concerning aims bluntly: 'I haven't the faintest idea of what is possible to aim for; I have no experience of these things; what, in your experience, is achievable . . .' most pointed to 'wishes'. If none of the interviewers fell of their chairs laughing in response to these 'wishes', the protocol of the interview told them that their 'wishes' had been noted, and would, with luck, be fulfilled.

That is what happened in this case. By adopting a 'data gathering' stance, the interviewers (both significantly younger than their interviewees, and both, therefore, less experienced in management development than the interviewees were in their own professions) did not 'negotiate' aims during the interviews. We do not wish to suggest at this stage that this was either 'right' or 'wrong'; merely to highlight that the participants, ingenuous in the matters of management development programmes, were able to come to the events with some very different images in their minds about what these events were going to achieve. It may well be that this is an inevitability which we need to build into each and every intervention.

THE INTERVENTION: A MANAGEMENT DEVELOPMENT PROGRAMME

Since this book is not primarily about techniques of management development, I shall describe what happened during the programme only very briefly. It is sufficient for the purpose simply to outline the kinds of activities the participants experienced, rather than go through the programme step by step in detail. My suspicion is that the specific contents of the programme were of less significance than the overall experience, with one or two exceptions which I shall refer to as they are relevant. My suspicion is largely supported by the research we have undertaken since the end of the programme. People, in general, do not remember the specifics, they appear to remember implications.

The programme took place between March and September 1992. The first module was designed on the basis of our understanding of the organisation, its people, and their expectations. The design and development of subsequent modules were influenced to some degree by feedback from participants. At the end of each module, and as the participants became more aware of the possibilities which 'formal' management development activities could provide, the participants were asked to identify topics or themes which they felt were important to explore in later modules.

The programme which actually took place was structured as follows:

Module 1: 29–31 March 1992

As planned, the first module started on a Sunday (whether the fact that this was Mothering Sunday has any symbolic significance remains uncertain!). The first day and a half were devoted to lecture and syndicate exercise-based work on 'strategy'. There were lectures on the strategic management process, how businesses compete, and the blockers and drivers to strategy implementation. Interspersed between the lecture sessions, which were themselves designed to be 'interactive' were exercises, undertaken in smaller groups, 'syndicates' which were designed to help consolidate the learning. Included within the sessions were some well known 'models' of strategic management, which, in almost all cases, were new to the participants. On the Sunday evening (29th March) the syndicates undertook a relatively light case study exercise upon which they reported back on Monday morning. The business school lecturer consolidated the report backs, and drew further conclusions from the case study they had been working on.

On Monday afternoon, the participants were given a very different experience, which involved getting out of doors and collecting data. The aim of the exercise was to involve them in group work, and to show through experience how working together, planning, communicating, and so on, are important to success. According to the feedback from the participants, this was a largely enjoyable and fruitful activity, despite its being very different from what they had been expecting from the first day and a half. The Monday evening was devoted to drawing out the learning from the exercise.

Tuesday saw a return to the 'classroom', with sessions devoted to organisational culture and perceptions of strategy. They received data from a questionnaire on 'strategic decision-making styles', which explored how they individually and severally perceived how strategic decisions are taken Tech-Test, and they discussed what they had learnt from this. In the afternoon, action planning and agenda setting for inter-module work was undertaken.

Module 2: 11–13 May 1992

The second module, which took place on a Tuesday and Wednesday (the group gathered on Monday evening for some preparatory work), dealt with the concepts of Mission statement; stakeholders; competitor analysis and competitive advantage; Return on Assets framework; factors which drive profitability; and the value chain. The plan for Tuesday was to run, as had been agreed, in 'workshop' mode, dealing with a Mission statement for Tech-Test itself.

The participants were also asked to make presentations to each other on the projects they had undertaken since the first module. As before, the first afternoon was devoted to planning further actions, and further projects. However, the projects spawned from this module were to be of a larger scale, and there was a plan that, irrespective of what happened subsequently on the formal programme, these projects would become part of the internal business of Tech-Test, and would outlive the programme; they were to continue until they reached a satisfactory conclusion. During Module 3, however, it was anticipated that each of the four project groups would make a presentation on progress so far.

Module 3: 16–18 July 1992

This module took in a Friday and Saturday, and was aimed at cementing some of the learning on putting strategy into action. The bulk of the time was devoted to a business simulation exercise which brought out both business and behavioural implications. Although a simulation, the exercise had as one of its aims to draw out some implications directly relevant to the experiences of being a manager at Tech-Test. Especially during the second day, effort was put into encouraging the belief that the learning from the exercise could be transferred back into the organisation, but that this requires creative and innovative thinking in order not to be constrained by what already exists.

Module 4: 9–11 September 1992

There was, as usual, a get-together on the evening of the Wednesday, 8th September, and this was used for the project groups to report back. Thursday was a 'busy day', during which a series of models and exercises were introduced which enabled participants to reflect upon teamworking, managerial behaviours and themselves as individuals. It was during this day that the participants were introduced, briefly, to the Myers Briggs Type Indicator, which I explore in some depth in Chapter 9.

Friday focused on project and contract management.

The Immediate Feedback from the Participants

On the whole, the programme was very well received. Each part of each module was appraised both in verbal form, and by a 'score'. Scores were generally very high, and a great deal of the written feedback was very positive. For example, one of he comments referred to the business school representatives' 'Patience shown in the face of our naiveté at times,' a self-deprecating comment which scarcely conceals some of the dynamics going in during these complex interactions. Other early comments, taken from the first module, when many of the participants were responding to their first 'formal' management development experience, show that the humour expressed by the people from the school was appreciated; the module helped Tech-Test's teamwork; it was valuable to have to work to strict times on exercises; and the 'very suitable' tutor styles matched the needs of the delegates, in, for example, sometimes letting the discussion run on rather than curtailing it.

However, as we argued in the book's introduction, the purpose of this kind of activity is not to achieve good feedback immediately after the event. It has to do with making a difference in the longer term. It is interesting to note, therefore, some of the key points brought out by delegates at the end of some of the modules, which refer specifically to what they say they 'learnt'. The reason for doing so is to check these against what happened later, and to use that as part of our broader exploration of what we mean by 'managerial learning'.

There was a great deal of data provided by the participants after each part of each module. Each session was followed by a facilitated discussion on what they had learnt, and there was a broader discussion on the same theme at the end of each module. They were also asked to complete feedback forms which asked of each session how valuable it had been, and how they might apply any learning to their own situation back in Tech-Test. In other words, there was a significant emphasis placed on asking participants to reflect upon and to discuss their learning.

At the end of the first module, for example, the final review produced a list of 'agenda items' for the later modules, ensuring that these focused upon what seemed important for them to learn more about. That list was:

❑ Teamwork including leadership and making the best out of other people's contributions are at the top of the list. Also teambuilding
❑ A strong call for understanding and increasing skills in releasing the human resource potential including delegation, improving communication leading to involvement and commitment.
❑ The management of quality and achieving professional status
❑ Time management
❑ How to reduce overhead costs; do we analyse the competition correctly?
❑ More commercial awareness
❑ Ethics

Clearly, some of these issues were directly addressed in those subsequent modules. Responding positively to the participants' stated development interests was felt to be a positive way of involving them in the learning process. The immediate impact of this approach was apparent in the high scores for the evaluation of Module 2, which, according to the feedback session at the end, 'increased focus on actually doing something, and not just talking about it.' From the module, there was a 'general raising of enthusiasm and confidence, along with improved morale.' Of significance, in the light of what happened later, was a quotation from one participant: 'The module provided a structure on which the difficult process of self examination could move forward without unnecessary recrimination.'

Feedback from the subsequent modules was less formally collected, for reasons I cannot be clear about. However, from talking to both participants and some of the tutors, the mood of the group seemed to remain fairly bouyant. On the surface, therefore, the programme seemed to have gone well. However, management and organisation development initiatives need to make a difference. The goal of this extended case study is to look closely at the extent to which this particular intervention did make a difference in the longer term. Therefore, the remainder of this appendix is devoted to exploring what actually happened at Tech-Test between September 1992 and the summer of 1996 when these notes were collated, and how this matches up to the expectations participants had as the programme ended.

SOME POST-EVENT RESEARCH ACTIVITIES

After September 1992 we undertook a number of 'research' activities with Tech-Test. Informal contact with Bill Gillies and one or two other managers was maintained, and this provided us with very valuable data. However, we recognised the dangers of single-informant based research, and supplemented what Gillies told us with two specific exercises.

The first exercise was a pair of 'Focus Group' meetings which we held with several of the participants on 25 May 1993, approximately six months after the programme ended. The second was a more complex set of activities which we undertook over four days in February and March 1995, gathering data from approximately two years after the start of the programme. Our aim was to find out as much as we could about what, if any, difference the programme had actually made to the organisation.

Focus Group meetings, 25 May 1993

A total of thirteen of the original nineteen managers who had attended the programme spent about half a day in a free-ranging review of the programme and its impacts on the organisation. The morning session comprised seven of the managers, while the afternoon session had six attendees. Of the top management team, only Michael Pope attended, and he was present at the afternoon session.

The morning session was very different from that of the afternoon; Michael Pope's presence may have been a contributory factor in this. However, the two sessions were able to provide two perspectives on 'the same' situation. The broad conclusions were that some progress had been made, but that some people saw this as superficial. There were still, especially as voiced during the morning session, significant views that the issues of the pre-programme era remained as pressing as they had been.

We had no particular hypothesis or research agenda as we planned and executed the Focus Group meetings. We went with as much of the naive curiosity of the ethnographer as we could muster. Our aim was primarily to gauge the degree to which the programme had had an effect; it was not, at this stage, to attempt to provide any explanatory frameworks. However, the data we gathered, and the reflecting we did subsequently began to generate some thoughts which we have been pursuing ever since. Some of these thoughts are to be found spread throughout this book.

As a research exercise in its own right, then, we feel that the Focus Group meetings were inconclusive. Given their essentially exploratory nature, this was not a significant cause for concern. However, we did make a note to ourselves to recognise some of what we had learnt about Tech-Test in particular and 'management development' in general in the next stage of our research activities with the company.

Further Research: February–March 1995

We approached the next round of 'research' with Tech-Test differently. During four days in February and March 1995 we spent time with 12 of the remaining senior managers, using small group discussion (with between two and four managers at a time), and two specially devised questionnaires to find out more about both the impact of the programme, and what had happened to Tech-Test during the intervening years.

The key piece of data is that, although the company does still exist, and is apparently now coming out of the effects of the recession, and soon to make its first profits for some years, several of the managers who attended the programme have gone, and some of those were victims of a second downsizing exercise, which, apparently, was even more painful that the first.

HOW THE PEOPLE'S EXPECTATIONS MATCHED THE 'REALITIES'

At the end of the programme there was a fair amount of euphoria and hope, and, during the review sessions, we started each discussion group by attempting to refocus the people's minds back on the mood of the moment as they left the programme. Typical quotes at this point were, 'I certainly left with a feeling that there was hope, hope at the end of the road.' 'I was on a high – euphoric. We'd identified the power of teamwork, and the importance of having rapport.'

However, from the data we gathered during the 'research' sessions, it would be more accurate to suggest that the programme had not been effective. Among the things which people said in our small group discussions were, 'It is almost as though the programme never happened. Was it a dream?' and 'I don't see any changes that have occurred here. I'm not sure what we expected to occur, but nothing much has changed. It's difficult because I can't remember a lot of what we did because we didn't actually implement much. Even the good news board didn't last very long, did it?' (The Good News Board was an idea which was fostered by participants during the programme as a means of celebrating the good things in life, and balance the 'negatives' which seemed to be ever-present. They agreed to set up a notice board at a prominent place in the main building, upon which any good news stories could be posted.)

One of the managers said during our discussions, 'A blunt analysis of what we learnt on the course is that we collectively learned very little; individually we learned a lot, collectively we learned very little . . .' and this seems to be a good summary of what many of the managers in the company feel about the after-effects of the programme. Patrick Standish, for example, who works in Finance and Administration, continues to be very positive about what he got from the programme. He spoke positively about a 'bond' which was established, which contrasted with his earlier feelings of isolation within the company. This 'bond', he says, remains as strong now as it was during the programme, and feels a part of a wider whole within the company.

However, this manager's positive attitude to his personal learning was stronger than most. It was even possible for a level of agreement to be reached in one of the discussion groups that, in some ways, the programme had an overall negative effect, rather than a positive one. People are said now to know more about what they should be doing for the company to be successful, but aren't doing. 'People have learnt to be more dissatisfied,' was one way of describing this phenomenon.

So the impacts seem to have been more attitudinal that behavioural. A fair amount of the discussions reinforced that most of the traditional behaviours remained as they were. People are still firefighting, and the focus remains primarily operational rather than strategic. We had a practical demonstration of this on the morning of the first of the discussion groups, when Don Goler rang from another part of the site to say he would not be attending this session as planned since he was working on a technical problem which had suddenly arisen. It was Don himself, at the later meeting he was able to attend, who made this link without prompting.

Even in behavioural terms, there are some areas where 'things' have seemed to get worse, despite good intentions. In one extract from the discussion groups, two of the managers commented: 'I think at the moment the level of communication between different departments is the worst it's ever been.' To which the other responded, 'In fact, you've got a feeling that there's been some instructions from various places to be difficult or less than helpful.'

Here is a more specific example. In this extract, the managers are discussing one of the main departments in the company, which we shall refer to as the S&C department: One manager says, 'The major thing was the method of operation in S&C. That's changed totally now.' To which the other responds, 'That's changed totally now to a team based structure. That's got a feel that it might work about it. Yes, something positive's happening. At last, something positive is happening in our neck of the woods.' The 'good' news, however, has a catch: 'But what has happened has actually meant that S&C has become even more isolated. It's been caused by the team. Because now people who in other parts of the establishment were involved with things happening in S&C are now very blatantly told, 'Don't touch it'.'

However, managers have not all been completely inactive in attempting to implement some of what they learnt during the programme. They have established a marketing function, although the manager responsible is apparently having a hard time working with divisive departments on what should be a company-wide set of activities. And they have pursued a number of initiatives, some of which were direct spin-offs from the programme. Among the initiatives were a 'mission statement' group; a communications task force; a 'stop press' system to broadcast information rapidly; a 'SWOT' analysis group, and several others. One of the most visible was a programme to go for Investors In People (IIP), but this has been abandoned, despite quite a lot of investment having been put into it. Apparently, communications standards were too low for the company to achieve certification.

One of the most energetic of the initiatives was the 'mission statement' group, which had among its earlier members Bill Gillies. It started as a project between modules 1 and 2, and a draft mission statement was available for comment shortly before the second module. After the input on mission statements during the management development programme, the project continued with energy. Its continuation, however, was not matched by that of other projects which had similarly been set running after the second module. By late June 1992, Bill Gillies was apparently concerned about getting the projects 'completed' for the third module. The whole group of nineteen participants were planning to get together before the third module to provide the projects with an injection of energy; but there were 'rumblings'; not everyone was happy about the exercises. Some people had a 'tendency to intellectualise the issues, and then not do anything about them.' By this stage, Bill Gillies was fairly sure that, of the four projects set up at the end of module 2, only the 'mission statement' would get done.

Two days before the third module, his predictions were confirmed. The communications task force was seen by the participants as 'still too much of an academic exercise,' and had ground to a halt. From the initial programme-generated projects, the only one which saw its way through to completion was the 'mission statement'. It was adopted by the company, and copies were placed prominently throughout the site.

Interestingly, and maybe symbolically, it was during our review discussions in March 1995 that Bill Gillies noticed that the copy of the mission statement which, since the management development programme, had hung on the wall of the meeting room we were occupying, was missing. As Bill Gillies said, 'it was the one tangible thing we brought away from' the programme; and now it had gone.

Most of the initiatives which the company was pursuing have ceased since the end of the programme, and this includes initiatives which were not brought about by the programme itself. As one of the managers remarked in 1995, they just 'fizzled away – died a death.'

The one initiative which does remain is the programme leading towards ISO9000 accreditation. Tech-Test's customers are insisting that they achieve this, so there is a degree of motivation driving this initiative which apparently was not present for the others. There is an immediacy of impact should this project fail.

Another initiative which started and then stopped was the resurrection of staff meetings, in which managers at the levels which included those who went on the programme got together to swap information. One reason given for their relapse was that people took it in turns to prepare the agenda; as time went by people left the agenda preparation later and later, until meetings were being held on agendas which had been hurriedly put together at the last minute, and therefore nobody came fully prepared. To fill the ensuing vacuum, Michael Pope used the opportunities to brief staff, which was not the intention of the meetings, which had been set up as informal opportunities to build on the progress in team spirit and openness which had been experienced on the programme, and which many of the managers referred to as the key aspect of the programme which they believed they could take away with them. As one of the managers said, 'The course allowed you to speak your mind without retribution, or fear.'

After the demise of the increasingly formalised staff meetings, the momentum of the programme found another outlet. This was through what came to be known as 'get-togethers' of the more junior members of the group who had been on the programme, that is, those not on the top management team. The group met at lunchtimes, as they stressed, 'out of working hours', The first meeting was held off-site, so concerned were several of them that a meeting of this kind smacked of 'mutiny'. These sessions achieved the level of informality which some wanted to resurrect from the programme; but they also had the problem that they raised questions which they themselves could not answer, since the information remained with the top management team members.

It was at the point in one of the discussion groups when this topic was raised that an interesting dialogue took place between one of the managers, Sally Freeman, and Norman Castle, a member of the top management team. Sally Freeman said, 'Senior management manage with a cloak of silence and secrecy.' To which Norman Castle responded, 'If you did lift the cloak, you'd be disappointed, because there's nothing there.' Even at this stage, after the nine intensive days away on the programme together, it took a 'research review day' to stimulate this feedback between two managers who had worked together at Tech-Test for many years.

The 'get-togethers' seem to have started to go the way of most other initiatives. Senior management were finally invited to the sessions to provide answers to those questions only they could provide. Thereafter, the dynamics of the sessions changed. Some people claim that Michael Pope 'ground them down.' Others said that the meetings 'turned into slogging match between two or three people.' According to one manager, the whole thing was 'topsy-turvy' – middle managers should not be trying to drive the business, and 'inviting' senior management to join in. The spectacle of the informal 'get-togethers' becoming what one manager says were 'griping sessions – that word has been used by the Chief Executive Officer' – finally, for Sally Freeman, 'took away my hope.'

Apart from that, there were other issues which were getting in the way of progress. According to Michael Pope, about one year after the course, relationships at the top of the company got very bad. Staff were clearly aware of the tension in senior management, but, 'I was unable to circumvent these tensions.' He went on to describe the period as 'a pretty desperate time', plagued by personality conflicts and by 'different perceptions of how we go about these things.' Unfortunately for him, he found 'nothing from the toolkit of the course to fix it.' It was clearly for Michael Pope a bad summer. For him, 'The whole course process was undermined by it.' Much of this centred on the build up to the acrimonious departure of Roger Wales from the company.

The final historical element which impacted the managers' perceptions of the ways in which they could or could not implement the learning from the programme was another downsizing exercise which took place in 1994. Some managers say that they had anticipated this further round of cuts, that, indeed, it had been predictable since the publication of the consultants' strategy document in 1991. Given the narrow readership of that document, few would have been aware of this. In this round, numbers were further reduced to below 200.

Comparisons with the 1991 downsizing were fairly consistent in viewing the earlier one as relatively painless. Both had been carried out on the basis of voluntary redundancies; but whereas during the 1991 event, most of the retirees were relatively elderly, and were in receipt of a very good financial package, the 'voluntary' nature of the 1994 event was less evident. The impression which managers carry with them of the 1994 redundancy programme was that those who were targeted had two chances: volunteer and get a reasonable package; or wait to be pushed and get considerably less. The problem was that no-one could know whether their name was on the list. Some people may have been scared into 'jumping' unnecessarily.

This second round of redundancies is blamed by some of the managers for a great deal of the lack of progress since the management development programme. It is said to have instilled a fear in people's minds which has removed the openness and honesty which was achieved during the programme. People are now, apparently, afraid to speak their minds. For some managers, this was the main reason for the ultimate failure of both the staff meetings and the 'get togethers', especially after senior management was invited. As Victor Parrot put it regarding the timing of the management development programme, 'it was not a good thing to have immediately before another load of trauma, because in that trauma you actually lose everything you've gained.'

Clearly a great deal had happened since the end of the programme which cannot have been factored into the programme itself. One could argue that successful programmes need to be able to provide resilience against the contingent circumstances which will beset any organisation which takes learning away and tries to implement it in the real world, and this argument certainly has a lot going for it. For that reason, the brief history of Tech-Test since the programme which we have provided here is not an apology, but simply a presentation of the circumstances which occurred, so that we can make occasional references to the case as a yardstick against which to measure the book's ideas.

The fact that life has been very hard for the company, and the fact that there is a strong feeling among many of the remaining managers that, on balance, the programme has had little or no impact, makes it a very challenging test case. And since we are unable to 'try out' on Tech-Test the ideas we have learnt from and with other organisations we have worked with, it shall remain a largely 'academic' exercise. We may almost be tempted to run a new programme for Tech-Test, applying everything we have learnt in recent years, to 'see' if it is more 'effective'. But such spurious scientism would prove nothing, and would, by the very nature of the 'experiment' fly in the face of the most important learning we have acquired.

THE CHALLENGE FOR MANAGEMENT AND ORGANISATION DEVELOPMENT PROVIDERS AND ENABLERS

Was it worth doing? Would they have been in the same situation if they had not gone through the programme? Is it not the case that the primary driver of this business is, indeed, the market, over which they have no control?

There are a host of questions such as these which are tempting to ask both for this case, and for many other instances. As managers become more sophisticated in their approach to 'courses' it is important for those of us who have any role in managerial learning to be able to recognise what lies behind such questions, and to be able to respond positively to the genuine concerns they articulate.

It will not surprise anyone to hear that we have a great deal of faith in the validity of 'management and organisation development' as a contributor to organisational and personal well-being. The challenge of this book, therefore, is to address these and other such questions, and to provide what we believe are the best answers we can, given our current state of understanding of the processes of managerial learning.

In so doing, we shall reflect on the Tech-Test case, and explore ways in which what we describe may be applicable to such a case. Several years have passed since that programme took place; during which we have learnt a great deal. We suspect that, faced with a similar challenge today as the business school faced in early 1992, we should go about it in different ways. We should retain some elements of the approach, such as the preparatory meetings, the interviews, the mix of input styles, the follow up activities, and so on, as they appeared to be helpful. But we should also be in a position to add a number of different perspectives which have arisen out of our own and others' research into the area, each of which, we believe, would make this different programme that much more effective.

The body of this book explores that learning we have gone through, and how we have applied the learning to actual management and organisation development interventions we have made with various organisations. As we do so, we shall refer now and again to the Tech-Test case, so that we can demonstrate the application of the learning as it would relate to an organisation we have been able to explore in some depth in the book.

Bibliography

Allport, G. W. (1937) *Personality: A Psychological Interpretation*, Henry Holt & Co, NY.

Analoui, F. (1993) *Training and Transfer of Learning*, Avebury, Aldershot.

Argyris, Chris (1982) *Reasoning, Learning, and Action: Individual and Organizational*, Jossey-Bass, San Francisco.

Argyris, Chris (1992) *On Organizational Learning*, Blackwell, Cambridge, Mass.

Argyris, Chris (1993) *Knowledge for Action: A Guide to Overcoming Barriers to Organizational Change*, Jossey-Bass, San Francisco.

Ariès, P. (1962) *Centuries of Childhood*, Knopf, New York.

Arroba, T. and James, K. (1992) *Pressure at Work: A Survival Guide for Managers*, London, McGraw-Hill.

Austin, J. (1975) *How to do Things with Words*, Harvard University Press.

Baddeley, A. (1992) *Your Memory: A User's Guide*, Penguin Books, London.

Bailey, K. (1987) *Human Paleopsychology: Applications to Aggression and Pathological Processes*, Lawrence Erlbaum Associates, Hillsdale NJ.

Bank, John (1994) *Outdoor Development for Managers*, 2nd edn, Gower, Hampshire UK.

Barger, Nancy and Kirby, Linda (1995) *The Challenge of Change in Organizations: Helping Employees Thrive in the New Frontier*, Davies Black Publishing, Palo Alto, California.

Barr, F., Stimpert, J. and Huff, A. (1993) 'Cognitive Change, Strategic Action, and Organisational Renewal, *Strategic Management Journal*, Vol. 13, 15–36.

Bartlett, F. C. (1932) *Remembering*, Cambridge University Press, Cambridge.

Becker, H. S. and Geer, B. (1970) 'Participant Observation and Interviewing: A Comparison', in Filstead (1970), 133–42.

Beddowes, R. L. (1994) 'Reinventing Management Development', *Journal of Management Development* Vol. 13, No. 7, 40–6.

Benson, D. and Hughes, J. (1983) *The Perspective of Ethnomethodology*, Longman, London.

Binstead, D. and Stuart, R. (1979) 'Designing Reality into Management Learning Events: Toward Some Working Models', *Personnel Review*, Vol. 8, No. 3.

Bion, W. (1961) *Experiences in Groups*, Basic Books, New York.

Bion, W. (1977) *Seven Servants*, Jason Aronson, New York.

Bion, W. (1984) *Elements of Psychoanalysis*, Heinemann, London.

Bono, E. de (1971) *Lateral Thinking: A Textbook of Creativity*, Penguin, London.

Bono, E. de (1984) *Six Thinking Hats*, Penguin, London.

Bowlby, J. (1969) *Attachment and Loss. Volume 1: Attachment*, Hogarth Press and Institute of Psycho-Analysis, London.

Bowles, M. L. (1993) 'The Gods and Goddesses: Personifying Social Life in the Age of Organisation', *Organization Studies*, Vol. 14, No. 3, 397.

Bowman, C. and Daniels, K. (1995) 'The Influence of Functional Experience on Perceptions of Strategic Priorities', *British Journal of Management*, Vol. 6, 157–67.

Boydell, T. and Leary, M. (1996) *Identifying Training Needs*, IPM, London.

Bransford, J. and Johnson, M. (1972) 'Contextual preprequisites for understanding: some investigations of comprehension and recall', *Journal of Verbal Learning and Verbal Behavior*, Vol. 11, 717–26.

Broadbent, D. (1981) 'Non-corporeal explanation in psychology', in Heath (1981).

Brown, R. (1965) *Social Psychology*, Free Press, New York.

Bruner, J. (1990) *Acts of Meaning*, Harvard University Press, Cambridge, Mass.

Bulmer, R. (1967) 'Why is the Cassowary not a Bird? A Problem of Zoological Taxonomy among the karam of the New Guinea Highlands', *Man* 2: 5–25.

Bulmer, R. and Tyler, M. J. (1968) 'Karam Classification of Frogs', *Journal of the Polynesian Society* 77: 333–85.

Burgoyne, J. and Stuart, R. (1976) 'The Nature, Use and Acquisition of Managerial Skills and Other Attributes', *Personnel Review*, Vol. 5, No. 4.

Burgoyne, J. and Stuart, R. (1978) 'Teaching and Learning Methods in Management Development', *Personnel Review*, Vol. 7, No. 1, Winter 1978.

Burnes, B. (1992) *Managing Change: A strategic approach to organisational development and renewal*, Pitman Publishing, London.

Burnett, D. (1995) 'The Heroic Journey: Viewing Manager Development from a Mythological Perspective', *New Perspectives in Management Education, Conference Proceedings*, Leeds University, Jan 1995.

Burrell, G. and Morgan, G. (1979) *Sociological Paradigms and Organizational Analysis*, Heinemann, London.

Buzan, Tony (1974) *Use Your Head*, BBC Publications, London.

Buzan, Tony (1977) *Speed Reading*, David and Charles, Newton Abbot, England.

Buzan, Tony (1981) *Making the Most of Your Mind*, Pan, London.

Buzan, Tony (1983) *The Brain User's Guide*, E. P. Dutton, New York.

Buzan, Tony (1988) *Harnessing the Parabrain*, Wyvern Business Books, London.

Campbell, Joseph (1972) *Myths to Live By*, Viking Press, New York.

Campbell, Joseph (1993) *The Hero With a Thousand Faces*, Fontana Press, London.

Carroll, C., Pandian, J. R. M. and Thomas, H. (1994) 'Assessing the Height of Mobility Barriers: A Methodology and an Empirical Test in the UK Retail Grocery Industry', *British Journal of Management*, Vol. 5, No. 1, March, 1–18.

Carroll, Lewis (1989) *Alice Through the Looking Glass*, Dragon's World, London.

Chance, M. (ed.) (1988) *Social Fabrics of the Mind*, Lawrence Erlbaum Associates, Hove and London.

Cicourel, A. V. (1973) *Theory and Method in a Study of Argentine Fertility*, Wiley, New York.

Clarke, Liz (1994) *The Essence of Change*, Prentice Hall International (UK) Ltd, Hemel Hempstead, UK.

Cole, G. A. (1986) *Personnel Management: Theory and Practice*, D. P. Publications Ltd, Eastleigh. Hants.

Colman, Arthur (1992) 'Depth Consultation', in Stein and Hollwitz (1992), pp. 92–117.

Conger, J. A. (1993) 'Personal Growth Training: Snake Oil or Pathway to Leadership?', *Organizational Dynamics*, Summer 1993, pp. 19–30.

Converse, J. M. and Schuman, H. (1974) *Conversations at Random*, Wiley, New York.

Crockett, W. H. (1965) 'Cognitive Complexity and Impression Formation', in B. A Maher (ed.).

Cronshaw, M., Davis, E. and Kay, J. (1994) 'On Being Stuck in the Middle or Good Food Costs Less at Sainsbury's' *British Journal of Management*, Vol.5, No. 1.

Crosby, P. (1984) *Quality Without Tears: The Art of Hassle-Free Management*, McGraw-Hill, London.

Csikszentmihalyi, Mihali (1991) *Flow: the psychology of optimal experience*, Harper & Row, New York.

Currie, G. (1994) 'Evaluation of Management Development: A Case Study', *Journal of Management Development*, Vol. 13, No. 3, 22–6.

Daft, R. and Weick, K. (1984) 'Toward a model of organizations as interpretation systems', *Academy of Management Review*, Vol. 9, 284–95.

Dainty, P. and Lucas, D. (1992) 'Clarifying the Confusion: A practical framework for evaluating outdoor development programmes for managers', *Management Education and Development*, Vol. 23, part 2, 106–22.

Damasio, Antonio (1994) *Descartes' Error: Emotion, Reason and the Human Brain*, Grosset/Putnam, New York.

Dawkins, Richard (1976) *The Selfish Gene*, Oxford University Press, Oxford.

Dawkins, Richard (1986) *The Blind Watchmaker*, Longman, Harlow.

Dawkins, Richard (1995) *River Out of Eden: A Darwinian View of Life*, Phoenix, London.

Dawkins, Richard (1996) *Climbing Mount Improbable*, Viking, London.

de Cock, C. and Rickards, T. (1996) 'Thinking about Organizational Change: Towards Two Kinds of Process Intervention', in *International Journal of Organizational Analysis*, Vol. 4, No. 3 (July), 233–51.

de Waal, Frans (1989) *Peacemaking among Primates*, Harvard University Press, Cambridge, Mass.

Deal, T. and Kennedy, A. (1982) *Corporate Cultures: The Rites and Rituals of Corporate Life*, Penguin Books, London.

Deming, W. (1988) *Out of the Crisis: Quality, Productivity and Competitive Position*, Cambridge University Press.

Dennett, Daniel (1987) *The Intentional Stance*, Bradford Books/MIT Press, Cambridge, Mass.

Dennett, Daniel (1991) *Consciousness Explained*, Back Bay Books, Little, Brown & Company, Boston, Mass.

Dennett, Daniel (1996) *Kinds of Minds: Towards an Understanding of Consciousness*, Weidenfield & Nicolson, London.

Descartes, Rene (1641) *Meditations on First Philosophy*, Michel Soly, Paris.

Donaldson, M. (1992) *Human Minds: An Exploration*, Penguin Books, London.

Douglas, Mary (1975) *Implicit Meanings: Essays in Anthropology*, Routledge & Kegan Paul, London.

Douglas, Mary (1986) *How Institutions Think*, Syracuse University Press, Syracuse, NY.

Douglas, Mary (1992) *Risk and Blame: Essays in Cultural Theory*, Routledge, London and New York.

Dworkin, R. M. (1968) 'Is Law a System of Rules?', in Summers (1968).

Edelman, G. (1989) *The Remembered Present: A Biological Theory of Consciousness*, Basic Books, New York.

Edelman, G. (1992) *Bright Air, Brilliant Fire: On the Matter of the Mind*, Penguin Books, London.

Edwards, Chris and Peppard, Joe (1994) 'Business Process Redesign: Hype, Hope or Hypocrisy', *Journal of Information Technology*, Vol. 9, 251–66.

Engleman, Therese (1966) *Give Your Child a Superior Mind*, Leslie Frewin, London.

Evans-Pritchard, E. (1933) 'The Intellectualist (English) Interpretation of Magic', *Bulletin of the Faculty of Arts (Cairo)*, Vol. 1, Part 2.

Eysenck, H. (1962) *Know Your Own IQ*, Penguin, London.

Fairhurst, Alice and Fairhurst, Lisa (1995) *Effective Teaching, Effective Learning: Making the Personality Connection in the Classroom*, Davies Black Publishing, Palo Alto, California.

Feinstein, David and Krippner, Stanley (1988) *Personal Mythology*, Jeremy Tarcher, Los Angeles.

Ferguson, A. (1989) 'The Feminist Aspect Theory of the Self', in Garry and Pearsall (eds).

Filstead, W. J. (ed.) (1970) *Qualitative Methodology*, Markham, Chicago.

Fineman, S. (ed.) (1993) *Emotion in Organizations*, Sage, London.

Fodor, Jerry (1975) *The Language of Thought*, Crowell, Scranton, PA.

Fournier, Valerie (1996) 'Cognitive Maps in the Analysis of Personal Change During Work Role Transition', *British Journal of Management*, Vol. 7, Issue 1, 87–106.

Frazer, J. (1890) *The Golden Bough: a Study in Magic and Religion*, London, Macmillan.

French, J. (1981) 'Natural Learning', *Journal of European Industrial Training*, Vol. 5, No. 4, 10–13.

Gadamer, H. G. (1965) *Wahrheit und Method*, J. C. B. Mohr, Tübingen.

Garfinkel, H. (1967) *Studies in Ethnomethodology*, Prentice Hall, Englewood Cliffs.

Garry, A. and M. Pearsall (eds) (1989) *Women, Knowledge and Reality: Explorations in Feminist Philosophy*, Unwin Hyman, Boston.

Gell, A. (1975) *Metamorphosis of the Cassowaries: Umeda Society, Language and Ritual*, The Athlone Press, London.

Gibbs, G. (1981) *Teaching Students to Learn: A Student-Centred Approach*, Open University Press, Milton Keynes UK.

Giddens, A. (1976) *New Rules of Sociological Method*, Hutchinson, London.

Gilbert, Paul (1989) *Human Nature and Suffering*, Lawrence Erlbaum Associates, Hove and London.

Goleman, Daniel (1995) *Emotional Intelligence*, Bantam Books, New York.

Goleman, Daniel (1998) *Working with Emotional Intelligence*, Bloomsbury Publishing, London.

Gould, C. C. (ed.) (1984) *Beyond Domination: New Perspectives on Women and Philosophy*, Rowan & Allanhead, Ottawa.

Gramsci, A. (1971) *Selections from the Prison Notebooks of Antonio Gramsci* (eds Quinten Hoare and Geoffrey Nowell-Smith), Lawrence & Wishart, London.

Greene, J. (1987) *Memory, Thinking and Language: Topics in cognitive psychology*, Methuen, London and New York.

Grimshaw, J. (1986) *Feminist Philosophers*, Harvester Wheatsheaf, London

Grossberg, S. (1982) *Studies of Mind and Brain*, Reidel, Boston.

Grint, K. (1995) *Management: A Sociological Introduction*, Polity Press, Cambridge, UK.

Groot, A. de (1966) 'Perception and memory versus thought: some old ideas and recent findings', in Kleinmontz (ed.) 1966.

Grundy, Tony (1993) *Implementing Strategic Change: A Practical Guide for Business*, Kogan Page, London.

Guzie, T. and Guzie, N. M. (1984) 'Masculine and Feminine Archetypes: A Complement to the Psychological Types', *Journal of Psychological Type*, Vol. 7, 3–11.

Haber, R. and Alpert, R. (1958) 'Test Anxiety', *Journal of Abnormal and Social Psychology*, Vol. 13.

Hammersley, Martyn (1990) *Reading Ethnographic Research: A Critical Guide*, Longman, London and New York.

Harding, S. (1984) 'Is Gender a Variable in Conceptions of Rationality?', in Gould (ed.).

Harre, R. (1972) *The Philosophies of Science*, Oxford University Press

Harre, R. (1995) 'Discursive Psychology', in Smith, Harre and van Langenhove (1995), pp. 143–59.

Hay, Julie (1990) 'Managerial Competences or Managerial Characteristics?', *MEAD*, Vol. 21, Part 5, 305–15.

Hayes, J. and Allinson, C. W. (1996) 'The Implications of Learning Styles for Training and Development: a Discussion of the Matching Hypothesis', *British Journal of Management*, Vol. 7, No. 1, March 1996, 63–74.

Heath, A. F. (ed.) (1981) *Scientific Explanation*, Clarendon Press, Oxford.

Hersey, P. and Blanchard, K. (1977) *Management of Organizational Behavior*, 3rd edn, Prentice-Hall, Englewood Cliffs.

Hershey, R. (1993) 'A Practitioner's View of 'Motivation', *Journal of Managerial Psychology*, Vol. 8, No. 3.

Hill, N. (1966) *Think and Grow Rich*, Wilshire Books, North Hollwood, California.

Hirsh, S. (1991) *Using the Myers-Briggs Type Indicator in Organizations*, Consulting Psychologists Press, Palo Alto, California.

Hollwitz, John (1992) 'Individuation at Work: Considerations for Prediction and Evaluation', in Stein and Hollwitz (eds) (1992), pp. 19–37.

Holman, D. and Hall, L. (1996) 'Competence in Management Development: Rites and Wrongs', *British Journal of Management*, Vol. 7, 191–202.

Honey, P. and Mumford, A. (1992) *Manual of Learning Styles*, 2nd edn, Peter Honey, Maidenhead.

Hope, Veronica and Hailey, John (1995) 'Corporate Cultural Change? Is it still relevant for the organisations of the 1990s?', *Human Resources Management Journal*, Vol. 5, No. 4.

Horowitz, D. (ed.) (1971) *Radical Sociology: An Introduction*, Harper & Row, New York.

Hume, David (1962) *A Treatise of Human Nature: Book 1, of the Understanding*, Collins, Fonata Library, London.

Humphrey, N. (1986) *The Inner Eye*, Faber & Faber, London.

Humphrey, N. (1992) *A History of the Mind*, Chatto & Windus, London.

Hunsley, John (1987) 'Internal Dialogue During Academic examinations', *Cognitive Therapy and Research*, December 1987.

Hunt, H. T. (1989) *The Multiplicity of Dreams: Memory, Imagination and Consciousness*, Yale University Press, New Haven and London.

Hyman, H. *et al.* (1954) *Interviewing in Social Research*, University of Chicago Press, Chicago.

Irvine, D. and Wilson, J. P. (1994) 'Outdoor Management Development – Reality or Illusion?', *Journal of Management Development*, Vol. 13, No. 5, 25–37.

Isachsen, Olaf and Berens, Linda (1988) *Working Together: A Personality-Centered Approach to Management*, Institute for Management Development, San Juan Capistrano, California.

James, Kim and Baddeley, S. (1987) 'Owl, Fox, Donkey, Sheep: Political Skills for Managers,'. *Management Education and Development*, Vol. 18, No. 1.

James, William (1890) *The Principles of Psychology*, Vol. 1, Dover, New York.

Jaynes, Julian (1990) *The Evolution of Consciousness in the Breakdown of the Bicameral Mind*, Penguin Books, London.

Johnson, G. and Scholes, K. (1988) *Exploring Corporate Strategy*, Prentice Hall, New York and London.

Johnson, Stephen M. (1985) *Characterological Transformation: The Hard Work Miracle*, W. W. Norton & Company, New York.

Jones, A. M. and Hendry, C. (1994) 'The Learning Organization: Adult Learning and Organizational Transformation', *British Journal of Management*, Vol. 5, 153–62.

Jones, S. (1993) *The Language of the Genes: Biology, History and the Evolutionary Future*, Harper Collins, London.

Jung, C. G. (1968) *Collected Works*, transl. R. F. C. Hull, Princeton University Press.

Kahn, R. L. and Cannell, C. F. (1952) *The Dynamics of Interviewing*, Wiley, New York.

Kakabadse, Andrew (1996) 'Boardroom Skills for Europe', *European Management Journal*, Vol. 14, No. 2, 189–200.

Kakar, S. (1970) *Frederick Taylor: A Study in Personality and Innovation*, MIT Press, Cambridge, Mass.

Keirsey, D. and Bates, M. (1978) *Please Understand Me*, Prometheus Nemesis Books, Del Mar, California.

Keohane N. O. (eds) *et al.* (1982) *Feminist Theory: A Critique of Ideology*, Harvester Press, Sussex.

Keller, E. F. (1982) 'Feminism in Science', in N. O. Keohane *et al.* (1982).

Kelly, G. (1955) *The Psychology of Personal Constructs*, Norton, New York.

Kets de Vries, M. and Miller, D. (1984) *The Neurotic Organization*, Jossey-Bass, San Francisco, California.

Kleinmontz, B. (ed.) (1966) *Problem Solving*, Wiley, New York.

Klein, L. and Eason, K. (1991) *Putting Social Science to Work: The Ground Between Theory and Use Explored Through Case Studies in Organisations*, Cambridge University Press, Cambridge.

Kleinsmith, L. J. and Kaplan, S. (1963) 'Paired association learning as a function of arousal and interpolated interval', *Journal of Experimental Psychology*, Vol. 65.

Knights, D. and Murray, F. (1994) *Managers Divided: Organisational Politics and Information Technology Management*, Wiley, Chichester.

Kolb, D. (1984) *Experiential Learning*. Prentice Hall Inc., London.

Kolb, D. *et al.* (1974) *Organisational Psychology: An Experiential Approach*, Prentice Hall, New Jersey.

Kosko, B. (1994) *Fuzzy Thinking: The New Science of Fuzzy Logic*, Flamingo, London.

Kuhn, Thomas (1970) *The Structure of Scientific Revolutions*, Chicago University Press, Chicago.

Lakoff, George (1987) *Women, Fire and Dangerous Things: What Categories Reveal About the Mind*, University of Chicago Press, Chicago.

Lepper, Georgia (1992) 'The Complex in Human Affairs', in Stein and Hollwitz (1992), pp. 72–91.

Lewis, C. and Mitchell P. (eds) (1994) *Children's Early Understanding of Mind: Origins and Development*, Erlbaum, Hillsdale NJ.

Lewis, R. (1993) 'A Jungian Guide to Competences', *Journal of Managerial Psychology*, Vol. 8, No. 1, 29–32.

Lippitt, Gordon (1983) 'Learning: Doing What Comes Naturally', *Training and Development Journal*, August 1983.

Long, J. W. (1987) 'The Wilderness Lab Comes of Age', *Training and Development Journal*, Vol. 41, No. 3, March 1987, 30–9.

Luria, A. (1968) *The Mind of a Mnemonist*, Basic Books, New York.

Luria, A. (1973) *The Working Brain*, Basic Books, New York.

Mabey, C. and Mayon-White, M. B. (eds) (1993) *Managing Change*, 2nd edn, Paul Chapman Publishing Ltd, London.

Maccoby, M. B. (1976) *The Gamesman*, Bantam, New York.

Macdonald, J. and Piggott, J. (1990) *Global Quality: The new management culture*, Mercury Books, London.

Maher, B. A. (ed.) (1965) *Progress in Experimental Personality Research*, Academic Press, New York.

Margerison, C. (1980) 'How Chief Executives succeed', *Journal of European Industrial Training Monograph*, Vol. 4, No. 5.

Markus, H. and Nurius, P. (1986) 'Possible Selves', *American Psychologist*, Vol. 41, 954–69.

Martin, C. L. (1993) 'Feelings, Emotional Empathy and Decision Making: Listening to the Voices of the Heart', *Journal of Management Development*, Vol. 12, No. 5, 33–45.

Maslow, A. (1954) *Motivation and Personality*, Harper, New York.

McCall, M. W., Lombardo, M. M. and Morrison, A. M. (1988) *The Lessons of Experience: How Successful Executives Develop on the Job*, The Free Press, New York.

Mehan, H. and Wood, H. (1975) *The Reality of Ethnomethodology*, Wiley, New York.

Messick, S. (ed.) (1976) *Individuality in Learning*, Jossey-Bass, San Francisco, California.

Mitroff, Ian I. (1989) *Stakeholders of the Organizational Mind: Toward a New View of Organizational Policy Making*, Jossey Bass, San Francisco.

Modell, Arnold H. (1993) *The Private Self*, Harvard University Press, Cambridge, Mass.

Morgan, G. (1986) *Images of Organization*, Sage Publications, Beverly Hills.

Morgan, G. (1993) *Imaginization: the art of creative management*, Sage Publications, London.

Morris, Brian (1984) 'The Pragmatics of Folk Classification', *Journal of Ethnobiology*, Vol. 4.

Morris, Brian (1994) *Anthropology of the Self: The Individual in Cultural Perspective*, Pluto Press, London.

Morris, Desmond (1967) *The Naked Ape: A Zoologist's Study of the Human Animal*, Cape, London.

Much, N. C (1995) 'Cultural Psychology', in Smith *et al.* (1995) pp. 97–121.

Mumford, A. (1980) *Making experience pay*, McGraw Hill, London.

Mumford, A. (1993) *Management Development: Strategies for Action*, 2nd edn, IPM.

Myers, I. (1980) *Gifts Differing*, Consulting Psychologists Press, Palo Alto, California.

Myers, Isobel and McAuley, Mary (1985) *Manual: A Guide to the Development and Use of the Myers-Briggs Type Indicator*, Consulting Psychologists Press, Palo Alto, California.

Nagel, Thomas (1986) *The View From Nowhere*, Oxford University Press.

Needham, Rodney (1972) *Belief, Language and Experience*, Basil Blackwell, Oxford

Nichols, S. (1980) *Jung and Tarot, An Archetypal Journey*, Samuel Weiser, New York.

Nisbett, R. E. and Ross, L. (1980) *Human Inference: Strategies and Shortcomings of Social Judgement*, Prentice Hall, New York.

Olsen, Edwin (1992) 'Opening to the Change Process: The Transcendent Function at Work', in Stein and Hollwitz (1992), pp. 156–73.

Ortner, S. B (1974) 'Is Female to Male as Nature is to Culture?', in Rosaldo and Lamphere (eds).

Parikh, Jagdish (1994) *Intuition: The New Frontier of Management*, Blackwell Business, Oxford.

Patching, K. and Chatham, R. (1998) 'Getting a life at work: developing people beyond role boundaries', *Journal of Management Development*, Vol. 17, No. 5, 316–37.

Peck, M. Scott (1990) *The Road Less Travelled: A New Psychology of Love, Traditional Values and Spiritual Growth*, Arrow, London.

Pedler, M. and Boydell, T. (1985) *Managing Yourself,* Fontana Books, London.

Perlman, M. S. (1992) 'Toward a Theory of the Self in the Group', in Stein and Hollwitz (1992), pp. 174–93.

Peters, T. and Austin, N. (1985) *A Passion for Excellence: The Leadership Difference,* Guild Publishing, London.

Phillips, D. L. (1971) *Knowledge From What?,* Rand McNally, Chicago.

Porter, M. (1980) *Competitive Strategy,* The Free Press, New York.

Putnam, L. and Mumby, D. (1993) 'Organizations, Emotion and the Myth of Rationality', in Fineman (1993).

Quenk, Naomi (1993) *Beside Ourselves: our hidden personality in everyday life,* Consulting Psychologists Press, Palo Alto, California.

Quinn, R. E. (1988) *Beyond Rational Management: mastering the Paradoxes and Competing Demands of High Performance,* Jossey Bass, San Francisco.

Ratui, I. (1983) 'Thinking Internationally: A Comparison of How International Executives Learn', *International Studies of Management and Organisation,* Vol. XIII, Nos 1–2, 139–50.

Rosaldo, M. Z. and Lamphere, L. (eds) (1974) *Women, Culture and Society,* Stanford University Press, San Francisco, California.

Russell, Peter (1979) *The Brain Book,* Penguin Books, New York.

Sahlins, Marshal (1995) *How 'Natives', Think: About Captain Cook, For Example,* The University of Chicago Press, Chicago and London.

Schein, E. (1985) *Organizational Culture and Leadership,* Jossey-Bass, San Francisco, California.

Schutz, A. (1969) *The Phenomenology of the Social World,* trans. G. Walsh and F. Lehnert, Northwestern University Press, Evanston.

Senge, Peter (1990) *The Fifth Discipline: The Art and Practice of The Learning Organization,* Century Business, London.

Shotter, J. (1995) 'Dialogical Psychology', in Smith *et al.* (1995).

Sillince, J. A. A (1995) 'Extending the Cognitive Approach to Strategic Change in Organisations: Some Theory', *British Journal of Management,* Vol. 6, No. 1, March, 59–76.

Smith, J. A., Harre, R. and van Langenhove, L. (eds) (1995) *Rethinking Psychology,* Sage, London.

Stein, Murray (1992) 'Organisational Life as Spiritual Practice', in Stein and Hollwitz (1992), pp. 1–18.

Stein, Murray and Hollwitz, John (eds) (1992) *Psyche at work,* Chiron Publications, Wilmette, Illinois.

Stern, Daniel (1985) *The Interpersonal World of the Infant,* Basic Books, New York.

Stevens, A. (1982) *Archetype: A Natural History of the Self,* Routledge & Kegan Paul, London.

Stevens, A. (1995) *Private Myths: Dreams and Dreaming,* Penguin Books, London.

Stuart, Roger (1983) 'Training and Development: a natural everyday activity', *Management Education and Development,* Vol. 14, Part 3.

Stuart, R. (1984) 'Using Others to Learn: Some Everyday Practice', *Personnel Review,* Vol. 13, No. 4.

Stuart, Roger and Holmes, L. (1982) 'Successful Trainer Styles', *Journal of European Industrial Training,* Vol. 6, No. 4.

Summers, S. (ed.) (1968) *Essays in Legal Philosophy,* Oxford University Press.

Temple, C. (1993) *The Brain: An Introduction to the Psychology of the Human Brain and Behaviour,* Penguin Books, London.

Thoreau, Henry (1910) *Thoreaus' Walden,* edited by Raymond Macdonald Alden, Longmans, Green & Co, New York.

Tversky, B. and Hemenway, K. (1984) 'Objects, Parts and Categories', *Journal of Experimental Psychology: General,* Vol. 113, 169–93.

Tylor, E. B. (1964) *Researches into the Early History of Mankind and the Development of Civilization,* (ed.) Paul Bohannan, Phoenix Books, University of Chicago Press.

van Gennep, A. (1960) *The Rites of Passage,* Routledge & Kegan Paul, London.

Volosinov, V. N. (1973) *Marxism and the Philosophy of Language,* trans. L. Mmatejka and I. R. Titunik, Harvard University Press, Cambridge, Mass.

von Franz, M-L. (1970) *The Problem of the Puer Aeternus,* Spring Publications, Zurich.

Wagner, R. J. and Campbell, J. (1994) 'Outdoor-based Experiential Training: Improving Transfer of Training Using Virtual Reality', *Journal of Management Development,* Vol. 13, No. 7, 4–11.

Walsh, J. and Ungson, G. (1991) 'Organizational Memory', *Academy of Management Review,* Vol. 16, No. 1, 57–91.

Waterman, R., Peters, T. and Phillips, J. (1980) 'Structure is Not Organization', *Business Horizons,* Vol. 23, No. 3, June.

Weber, Max (1949) *The Methodology of the Social Sciences,* Free Press, Glencoe, Ill.

Whiten, A. (1994) 'Grades of Mind Reading', in C. Lewis and P. Mitchell (eds).

Wilber, K. (1981) *Up From Eden, A Transpersonal View of Human Evolution,* Anchor, New York.

Wills, Gordon (1993) 'Your Enterprise School of Management', *The Journal of Management Development Special Issue,* Vol. 12, No. 2, 3–6.

Wills, S. (1994) '2001: A Research Odyssey. Teaching Different Types of Learning. *Journal of Management Development,* Vol. 13, No. 1, 60–72.

Witkin, H. (1976) 'Cognitive Styles in Academic Performance and in Teacher-student Relations', in Messick (ed.) (1976), 38–72.

Wittgenstein, L. (1953) *Philosophical Investigations,* Basil Blackwell, Oxford.

Yates, Frances (1969) *The Art of Memory,* Penguin Books, London.

Zadeh, L. A. (1987) *Fuzzy Sets and Applications: Selected Papers,* edited by Yager *et al.,* Wiley, New York.

Index

Note: As the whole book is concerned with *management and organisation development*, there are no specific entries for this in the index.